Modern French Pastry

The

Classic

and

Contemporary

Recipes

of

Yves Thuriès

MODERN FRENCH PASTRY

translated by
Rhona Poritzky Lauvand

JOHN WILEY & SONS, INC.

New York • Chichester • Weinheim • Brisbane • Singapore • Toronto

TX
773
.T513
1996

This book is printed on acid-free paper. ∞

Copyright © 1996 by Yves Thuriès. All rights reserved
Published by John Wiley & Sons, Inc.
Published simultaneously in Canada

No part of this publication may be reproduced, stored in a retrieval system or
transmitted in any form or by any means, electronic, mechanical, photocopying,
recording, scanning or otherwise, except as permitted under Sections 107 or 108 of the
1976 United States Copyright Act, without either the prior written permission of
the Publisher, or authorization through payment of the appropriate per-copy
fee to the Copyright Clearance Center, 222 Rosewood Drive, Danvers, MA 01923,
(978) 750-8400, fax (978) 750-4744. Requests to the Publisher for permission should be
addressed to the Permissions Department, John Wiley & Sons, Inc., 605 Third Avenue,
New York, NY 10158-0012, (212) 850-6011, fax (212) 850-6008,
E-Mail: PERMREQ@WILEY.COM.

This publication is designed to provide accurate and authoritative information in
regard to the subject matter covered. It is sold with the understanding that the
publisher is not engaged in rendering professional services. If professional advice
or other expert assistance is required, the services of a competent professional
person should be sought.

Library of Congress Cataloging-in-Publication Data:

Thuriès, Yves.
 (Livre de recettes d' un Compagnon du Tour de France. English)
 The classic and contemporary recipes of Yves Thuriès : Modern French
pastry / translated by Rhona Poritzky Lauvand.
   p.   cm.
 Translation of: Le livre de recettes d'un Compagnon de Tour de France.
 Includes index.
 ISBN 0-471-28599-4
 1. Pastry. 2. Cookery, French I. Title
 TX773.T513   1995   94-45675
     641.8'65'0944—dc20

Printed in Hong Kong

10 9 8 7 6 5 4 3 2

Yves Thuriès

Honors and Awards

Compagnon du Tour de France

Member of the French Culinary Academy

Best in the Field 1972

Grand Prize in Pastry 1973

First Prize for International Pastry Exposition 1973

Gold Medal from La Saint-Michel 1974

First Prize for Artistic Work 1975

Vase de Sèvres from the President of France 1975

First Prize for Chocolate Work 1973 and 1975

Vermeil Medal from the National Confederation of French Pastry and Candymaking of France 1976

Gold Medal from the National Confederation of Ice Cream Makers of France 1976

Meilleur Ouvrier de France for Ice Cream, Sorbets, and Frozen Desserts 1976

Meilleur Ouvrier de France for Pastry, Candymaking, and Catering 1976

Culinary Trophy 1979

Contents

Recipe Table of Contents ix

Foreword xv

Translator's Preface xvii

Translator's Notes xviii

The History of Pastry Making xxi

1 Cakes 1

2 Mousse and Cream Fillings for Cakes and Pastries 133

3 Biscuits and Génoises—Bases for Cakes and Pastries 157

4 Croquembouches 167

5 Tiered Cakes and Presentation Pieces 233

6 Sugar and Decoration Work 281

Glossary 389

Index 393

Recipe Table of Contents

1
Cakes 1

Brazilian 5
Special Milk Chocolate Coating No. 1 5
Special Milk Chocolate Coating No. 2 5
Brazilian Coffee Mousse 5
Charleston 6
Caramel Mousse 6
Dark Chocolate Biscuit 6
Dark Chocolate Ganache Cake 7
Butter Ganache 7
Special Praline Mousse 7
Praline Mazarin 9
Chocolate Mazarin 9
Special Milk Chocolate Coating 9
Spiral Cake Cream 9
Spiral Cake 11
Dacquoise 11
Dacquoise Base No. 1 11
TPT 12
Dacquoise Base No. 2 12
Praline Mousseline Cream No. 1 12
Praline Mousseline Cream No. 2 12
Caramelized Sliced Almonds 12
Almond Cognac Cake 13
Praline Mousse 13
Almond Meringue 13
Checkerboard Cake 15
Special Buttercream 15
Misérable 17
White Rose 17
Coffee Buttercream Cake 19
Coffee Buttercream Cake No. 1 19
Coffee Buttercream Cake No. 2 19
Coffee Buttercream Cake No. 3 20
Ingot 21
Strawberry Diablotin Cake 21
Diablotin Cake Cream 23
Chocolate Cream Cake 23
Coffee Almond Cake 25
Coffee Mousse 25
Sovereign 27
Sovereign Cream 27
Angels' Cake 27
Black Rose 29
Chocolate Mousse 29
Almond Buttercream 29
Cherry Almond Cake 29
Dacquoise Biscuit 31
Praline Dome 31
Special Pastry Cream 32
Praline Mousse 32
Angels' Hell Cake 32
Almond Paste 32
Special Almond Cream 33
Milanese Gratin or Macaroni 33
Gratin (Variation) 33
Banana Chocolate Cake 35
Special Génoise 35
Rum Mousseline Cream 35
Sprayed Chocolate 35
Coffee Rum Cake 37
Saint Hubert 37
Saint Hubert Coffee Mousse 38
Raspberry or Strawberry Saint Hubert 38
Special Cigarette Batter 38
Cherub 38
Almond Biscuit Flavored with Chocolate 39
Special Cognac Cream 39
Charlemagne 41
Hazelnut Progrès 41
Special Coating Chocolate 41
Chocolate Shavings 43
Gemini 43
Coffee Mousse 43
Chocodream 45
Chocolate Mousse No. 1 45
Chocolate Mousse No. 2 45
Majestic 46
Majestic Biscuit 46
Cognac Simple Syrup 46
Passion Fruit Supreme 47
Passion Fruit Mousse 47
Passion Fruit Simple Syrup 47

Lemon Supreme 47
Lemon Mousse 49
Lemon Simple Syrup 49
Blackcurrant Supreme 49
Blackcurrant Mousse No. 1 50
Blackcurrant Mousse No. 2 50
Blackcurrant Simple Syrup 50
Borsalino 50
White Wine Mousse 51
Orange Mousse Cake 51
Orange Mousse 53
Mandarin 53
Mandarin Orange Mousse 53
Orange Simple Syrup 55
Valencia 55
Special Orange Mousse 55
Gelée for the Valencia Cake 56
Banana Mousse 56
Creole Soufflé 56
Grapefruit Syrup 56
Grapefruit Mousse 57
Pineapple Willy 57
Pineapple Mousse 59
Strawberry or Raspberry Willy 59
Strawberry or Raspberry Mousse 59
Blackcurrant Willy 59
Blackcurrant Mousse 59
Banana Willy 61
Banana or Melon Mousse 61
Rum Indulgent 61
Indulgent Rum Mousse 61
Coffee Indulgent 63
Indulgent Coffee Mousse 63
Indulgent Liqueur Mousse 63
Strawberry Colisée 63
Strawberry Mousse 65
Lemon Mousse Cake 65
Special Lemon Mousse 67
Fromage Blanc Cheese Cake 67
Fromage Blanc Cream 67
Sultan 69
Chocolate Mousse 69
Banania 69

Strawberry-Cherry Mousse Cake 70
Maraschino Mousse 70
Apple-Cherry Mousse Cake 70
Little Duke 71
Kirsch Mousse 71
Cupid 73
Apricot Mousse 73
Maraschino/Apricot Simple Syrup 73
Cake Presentation Pedestal 75
Pear Caprice 75
Pear Brandy Mousse 77
Fruit Caprice 77
Kirsch Mousse No. 1 77
Kirsch Mousse No. 2 77
Blackcurrant Saint Ange 79
Blackcurrant Mousse 79
Blackcurrant Simple Syrup 79
Blackcurrant Gelée No. 1 79
Blackcurrant Gelée No. 2 80
Raspberry Saint Ange 80
Raspberry Mousse 80
Raspberry Simple Syrup 80
Raspberry Gelée 81
Strawberry Saint Ange 81
Strawberry Mousse 81
Strawberry Simple Syrup 81
Princess Meringue Cake 81
Special Buttercream 83
Princess Meringue 83
Sully 83
White Wine Mousse 84
Peteroff 84
Chestnut Mousse 84
Coffee Chestnut Mousse 84
Chestnut Paste 85
Poached Pears 85
Pear Charlotte 85
Pear Coulis 85
Pear Charlotte Cream No. 1 85
Pear Simple Syrup 87
Peach Charlotte 87
Peach Charlotte Cream 87

Gentleman's Whiskey 88
Mousseline Génoise 88
Whiskey Mousse 88
Whiskey Simple Syrup 89
Raspberry Saint Christopher 89
Raspberry Mousse 89
Passion Fruit Charlotte 89
Passion Fruit Charlotte Cream 92
Pear Charlotte 92
Pear Charlotte Cream No. 2 92
Pear Charlotte Cream No. 3 93
Strawberry Sublime Cake 93
Strawberry or Raspberry Mousse 95
Valencia 95
Special Almond Paste 95
Orange or Mandarine Mousse 95
Strawberry Charlotte 97
Strawberry Charlotte Cream 97
Strawberry Mirror 98
Strawberry Simple Syrup 98
Strawberry Mousse 98
Chocolate Chantilly 98
Belle Hélène Charlotte 99
Vanilla Bavarian Cream 99
Lemon Charlotte 101
Lemon Charlotte Cream 101
Raspberry Simple Syrup 101
Raspberry Charlotte Cream 101
Raspberry Mirror 103
Raspberry Charlotte 103
Raspberry Mousse 103
Pineapple Charlotte 104
Pineapple Charlotte Cream No. 1 104
Pineapple Charlotte Cream No. 2 105
Chestnut Charlotte 105
Chestnut Gelée 105
Chestnut Charlotte Cream No. 1 107
Chestnut Charlotte Cream No. 2 107
Rum or Cognac Simple Syrup 107

Strawberry Coulis   110
Sauces for Charlottes   110
Coffee Charlotte Cream   110
Praline Charlotte Cream   111
Chocolate Charlotte Cream   111
Vanilla Charlotte Cream   111
Blackcurrant Charlotte   111
Blackcurrant Charlotte Cream   113
Blackcurrant Gelée   113
Blackcurrant Simple Syrup No. 1   113
Blackcurrant Simple Syrup No. 2   113
Caramel Délice   114
Caramel Simple Syrup   114
Special Honey Almond Biscuit   114
Caramel Cream   115
Marigny   115
Coffee-Caramel Bavarian Cream   115
Gascony Prince   117
Bavarian Cream   117
Prune Mousse   117
Banana Cream Filling Flavored with Rum   119
Banana Rum Cake   119
Duchess Anne   121
Raspberry Syrup   121
Almond Mousseline Biscuit   121
Raspberry Gelée   121
Prince Albert   122
Almond Génoise   122
Brazilian Charlotte   123
Coffee Bavarian Cream   123
Coffee Simple Syrup for Miniature Babas   123
Coffee Gelée   123
Peach Brillat Savarin   125
Peach Mousse   125
Italian Meringue Reinforced with Gelatin   125
Vatel   127

Chocolate Mousse   127
Pineapple Cake   128
Pineapple Mousse   128
Seville   128
Lemon Syrup   129
Lemon Mousse   129
Imperial   129
Strawberry Simple Syrup   131
Strawberry Liqueur Mousse   131

2
Mousse and Cream Fillings for Cakes and Pastries   133

Very Light Chocolate Mousse   135
Chocolate Mousse No. 1   135
Chocolate Mousse No. 2   135
Chocolate Mousse No. 3   135
Coffee Mousse   135
Craquelin Mousse   136
Chocolate Craquelin Mousse   136
Blackcurrant Mousse   136
Chestnut Mousse   136
Pistachio Mousse No. 1   137
Pistachio Mousse No. 2   137
Walnut Mousse   137
Orange Mousse   137
Vanilla Milk Cream Filling   138
Almond Cream   138
Caramel Cream   138
Orange Buttercream No. 1   138
Orange Buttercream No. 2   138
Orange Buttercream No. 3   139
Lemon Cream for Tarts   139
Lemon Cream Filling No. 1   139
Lemon Cream Filling No. 2   139
Nougatine Cream   139
Nougatine Mousse   141
Buttercream (Quick Method) No. 1   141
Buttercream (Quick Method) No. 2   141
Yule Logs   141

Alhambra Yule Log   141
Coffee Yule Log   142
Whiskey or White Wine Mousse Yule Log   142
Domino Yule Log   142
White Wine Bavarian Cream   142
Chestnut Charlotte Cream   143
Caramel Charlotte   143
Charlotte Caramel Cream   143
Charlotte Coffee Cream   143
Italian Meringue   144
Chocolate Charlotte Cream   144
Mandarin Orange Mousse or Charlotte Cream   144
Liquor Mousse or Charlotte Cream   144
Chocolate Mousse for Fillings   145
Fruit Mousse No. 1—Blackcurrant, Strawberry, Raspberry   145
Fruit Mousse No. 2—Blackcurrant, Strawberry, Raspberry   146
Hazelnut Mousse for Fillings   146
Chocolate Suzanne Cream   146
Chantilly Cream   146
Whipped Cream   147
Orange Mousse   147
Lemon Mousse   147
Mogador   147
Almond Glaze   149
Almond Paste Filling   149
Coffee Extract   149
Coffee Simple Syrup No. 1   149
Coffee Simple Syrup No. 2   149
Strong Coffee for Flavoring   149
Simple Syrup for Moistening Cakes   150
Coating Cakes and Pastries with Liquid Couverture   150
Basic Ganache   151
Easter Nest Cakes   151
Praline Ganache   151
Pistachio Ganache   153
Bitter Ganache   153

3

Biscuits and Génoises— Bases for Cakes and Pastries 157

Génoise Mousseline 159
Special Butter Génoise 159
Chocolate Génoise 159
Coconut Génoise No. 1 159
Coconut Génoise No. 2 160
Hazelnut Génoise 160
Almond Biscuit No. 1 160
Almond Biscuit No. 2 160
Almond Biscuit No. 3 161
Chocolate Biscuit 161
Coffee Biscuit 161
Coffee Almond Biscuit 161
Almond Chocolate Biscuit 162
Orange Biscuit No. 1 162
Orange Biscuit No. 2 162
Cherry Biscuit 162
Pistachio Biscuit 163
Dobos Biscuit 163
Nougat Biscuit 163
Walnut Biscuit 164
Hazelnut Biscuit 164
Hazelnut Chocolate Biscuit 164
Sacher Biscuit 165
Orange Biscuit 165

4

Croquembouches 167

Conical Croquembouche 171
Decorating and Presenting Croquembouches 173
Chapel 175
Presentation Bases 175
Flower Basket 179
Choux Paste for Croquembouches 179
Choux Paste No. 1 179
Choux Paste No. 2 181
Grandmother's Basket 181
Jewelry Box 181
Drum 185
Pastry Cream for Croquembouches 185
Pastry Cream for Croquembouches No. 1 185
Pastry Cream for Croquembouches No. 2 187
Pastry Cream for Croquembouches No. 3 187
Flavoring for Pastry Cream 187
Grand Prize 187
Lovers' Windmill 189
Nougatine for Croquembouches 189
Nougatine for Croquembouches No. 1 189
Baby's Bassinet 191
Temple of Love 191
Baby Buggy 195
Caramel for Croquembouches 195
Special Caramel for Croquembouches 195
The Small Church 197
Podium 199
Pompadour 203
Special Nougatine 203
Prestige 205
Phoenix 207
Engagement Basket 207
Cooked Sugar or Caramel 211
Dawn Serenade 211
Reverence 213
Turtledoves' Cage 213
Floral Wheelbarrow 215
Dovecote 217
Basket of Flowers 217
Victory Ball 219
Mandolin 219
Modern Chapel 223
Mousseline Cream 223
Mousseline Cream No. 1 223
Mousseline Cream No. 2 225
Marie-Antoinette 225
Flower Vase 227
Trammel 227
Royal Icing 227
Wishing Well 229
Victory 229

5

Tiered Cakes and Presentation Pieces 233

Presentation Piece 237
La Mistinguet Tiered Cake 239
Open Book 243
Closed Book or Agenda 243
Star 245
Cake Presentation 247
Classic French Tiered Cake 249
Chocolate Icing No. 1 249
Chocolate Icing No. 2 249
Chocolate Icing No. 3 249
Nougatine Jewelry Box 251
Orange Bavarian 251
Spanish Tiered Cake 253
Cake Presentation 255
Poured Sugar Columns 255
Tiered Charlottes 257
Opera Presentation Piece 257
Tiered Wedding Cake 259
Cooked Sugar or Caramel 261
Classic French Tiered Cake 263
Preparing Cakes to be Glazed with Fondant 263
Nougatine Presentation Piece 265
Nougatine Roses 265
La Gaillacoise Tiered Cake 267
Poured Sugar Presentation Podium 269
Breton Cake 273
Special Almond Génoise No. 1 273
Special Almond Génoise No. 2 273

Classic French Tiered Cake 275
Glazing Cakes with Fondant 275
Presentation Piece 277
La Belle Epoque 279
Appliqué Sugar 279
Confectioners' Sugar Nougatine 280

6
Sugar and Decoration Work 281

Molded Sugar 287
Molded Sugar 291
Pulled Sugar 295
Pulled Sugar No. 1 295
Pulled Sugar No. 2 295
Pulled Sugar No. 3 296
When All Hope Is Revived 303
Park Corner 307
Rock Sugar 307

Galacté 313
Pastillage 313
Pastillage No. 1 314
Pastillage No. 2 314
Painting on Pastillage 321
Pulled Sugar Ribbons 323
Clown 329
Poured Sugar 329
Special Fondant for Creating Borders for Poured Sugar 330
Parcel from Nice 335
Woven Sugar 335
Blown Sugar 338
Blown Sugar No. 1 338
Blown Sugar No. 2 338
Blown Sugar Swan 341
Blown Sugar Animals 347
Blown Sugar Dog 347
Blown Sugar Elephant 347
Blown Sugar Carp 349
Blown Sugar Fish 349
Blown Sugar Squirrel 349
Blown Sugar Dog 349

Blown Sugar Vases 351
Blown Sugar Rabbit 351
Blown Sugar Still Life 353
Turned Sugar 354
Vase Filled with a Bouquet of Flowers 361
Assembling a Pulled Sugar Bouquet 361
Aged Cask 365
Earthenware Pitcher 365
Pastillage Candlesticks 365
Memoires of War 371
Sugar Candles 371
Poured Crystallized Sugar 372
Poured Crystallized Sugar No. 1 372
Poured Crystallized Sugar No. 2 373
Remnants of Time Passed 377
Spun Sugar 377
Pastillage Book 387
Presentation Piece: If History Were Mine to Tell 387

Foreword

In this volume, *Modern French Pastry*, I show how to modernize basic techniques and recipes. I've included the more recent innovations in pastry making that I refer to as "nouvelle pâtisserie."

In the *Cakes* chapter, you will find an assortment of pastries exhibiting contemporary presentations and flavors meant to inspire even the most critical professional. To help save time and make the work easier and more enjoyable, each recipe includes a procedure, detailed sketch, and is accompanied by a photograph of the finished dessert.

The *Croquembouches* and *Tiered Cakes and Presentation Pieces* chapters offer numerous presentations from the most simple and traditional to the most elaborate and modern. The *Sugar and Decoration Work* chapter offers a clear and precise manner of how to prepare pulled, blown, and other types of sugar work. I offer many personal recommendations that I have acquired over many years of experience. The step-by-step photographs are extremely helpful and aid to better understand how to apply the techniques. They will prove beneficial to those teaching this type of work.

This volume instructs the reader in the science of pastry making. Having a clear understanding of how and why things work makes it is easier to apply techniques appropriately. In compiling these elements of pastry making, I hope to inspire the student and novice by offering an explanation for the most minute and complex details of this profession. This knowledge allows individuals to develop their palette, personal taste, and creativity. Without this basic understanding of pastry making, it is difficult to truly appreciate the significance of the work.

I wish to contribute my own interpretation of pastry making to the continual evolution and modernization of methods adapted for today, ultimately to be enjoyed by the consumer. These ongoing developments and improvements in the craft of pastry making extend from France to the world over.

Always strive to work better,
Teach the metier,
Help and support those in the field.

Yves Thuriès

Translator's Preface

It is easy to remember meeting Yves Thuriès for the first time. Being in awe of his considerable knowledge and accomplishments, I was curious as to how seriously he would take me, an American pastry chef who had been trained in France. He graciously accepted an invitation to dine at Lespinasse, the restaurant of the Saint Regis Hotel in New York where I was pastry chef at the time. Afterwards, while awaiting his critique, he paid me the highest compliment when he asked for a recipe for one of the desserts. This pointed out that his brilliance as a chef was not only due to his talent but his ever enduring curiosity for, and love of, food.

Mr. Thuriès was born into a family of bakers in the Midi-Pyrénées (south central) region of France. His earliest memories are of food: going through the forest to hunt for mushrooms with his mother; visiting the farmers market; savoring a brioche from his favorite pastry shop, a taste he can still recall.

Mr. Thuriès left home at 14 to apprentice in pastry making and cuisine. It was immediately recognized that he was more than hard working but also extremely talented. He was mentored by some of the best chefs in France. Each night after work he wrote down the recipes learned that day. This was the beginning of his books as a Compagnon du Tour de France.

The title of Compagnon du Tour de France is one of the oldest recognitions a fine craftsperson in France can receive. In cooking, the Compagnon begins with an apprenticeship of several years. Afterwards, the apprentice is sent to other chefs throughout the country to continue learning and working in the best restaurants, often meeting with chefs who already hold the title of Compagnon. Only after considerable hard work, perseverance, and recognition is the person appointed Compagnon in a ceremony which includes receiving the traditional costume, walking staff, and sash. Today, few chefs are able to pursue their training in this manner making it all the more revered.

Mr Thuriès was awarded the Meilleur Ouvrier de France in two different categories in 1976. He holds the distinction of being the first person to have won two gold medals in one year. Mr. Thuriès has since received numerous awards in national and international competitions. He is a member of the association of Maîtres Pâtissiers de France (Master Pastry Chefs of France) and the Culinary Academy of France. He was voted chef of the year 1979.

In 1980, Mr. Thuriès opened his own restaurant and inn, the Grand-Ecuyer, in Cordes, a small village not far from his home town. Guests have included such dignitaries as the Queen of England, Elizabeth II, and former president of France, Francois Mitterand. Mr. Thuriès continues to teach, write, and cook all over the world, openly sharing his knowledge in classes and demonstrations. It is extremely important to him to partake in spreading the knowledge of pastry making and cooking as he continues to inspire a new generation of chefs.

Translator's Notes

The procedures in this series were prepared for professionals at all levels. The diagrams make it easy to quickly understand how a particular cake or dessert is assembled. Often, procedures are brief and succinct; this makes it extremely important to thoroughly read through the recipe before beginning. Occasionally, other preparations that are necessary for the recipe at hand are covered elsewhere in the book; these can often be found nearby or through the index. Garnishes are not always given since Mr. Thuriès leaves them up to the reader to encourage individual creativity.

Oven Temperatures

Rarely are exact oven temperatures given. Most often, low, medium, and high are indicated. Because no two ovens bake in exactly the same way, temperatures may vary, depending on the type of oven—convection, electric, gas, or otherwise. It is unusual for an oven to maintain perfect calibration at all times. A suggested guideline for oven temperatures: low, 300–325° F/ 150–160° C; medium, 350–400° F/175–200° C; high, 425–475° F/220–250° C.

Measurements

Professional pastry chefs customarily weigh ingredients rather than measure in volume. For this reason volume measurements are only used for liquids (fl. oz/ml). Liquids can be weighed as well and often are. All measurements in ounces refer to weight, unless indicated otherwise. Dry ingredients are difficult to measure accurately by volume; sifting before or after makes it more complicated. Sifting does not affect weight and can be done before or after an ingredient is weighed.

U. S. units of measure, the avoirdupois system, are given along with the metric system. It is recommended that those serious about pastry making and cuisine familiarize themselves with the metric system. Metric measurements are based on units of ten making it easier to reduce or increase a recipe. The metric system is also the most widely used system of measurement.

Most weight measurements in U.S. conversions have been rounded off to the nearest half unit of measure, except for smaller quantities when accuracy is important, such as with baking powder. Quantities of 20 g or less are given in tablespoons and teaspoons. Length measurements are rounded off to standard measures that are easier to apply such as the conversion of 1 centimeter into .5 of an inch rather than .4 of an inch.

Equipment

The equipment called for is based on standard sizes in France. For most equipment this presents little or no problem. It is perhaps the sheet pans that are most difficult. Standard French sheet pans are made of heavy steel with a low rim measure 16 × 24 in/40 × 60 cm. Some adjustment may be necessary when greatly increasing or decreasing a recipe.

Eggs

Typically, recipes indicate the number of eggs required. The number is based on medium, single-yolk eggs. If the egg size is in question, it is more accurate to go by weight.

Based on 1 medium egg:

Approximate Weight

1 whole egg	1.75 oz	50 g
1 egg white	1 oz	30 g
1 egg yolk	3/4 oz	20 g

Example:

8 eggs × 1.75 oz/50 g = 14 oz/400 g

Conversions of number of eggs by weight into volume:

Approximate Weight

20 eggs	34 fl. oz	1,000 ml
32 egg whites	34 fl. oz	1,000 ml
52 egg yolks	34 fl. oz	1,000 ml

Example:

8 egg whites = 8.5 fl. oz/250 ml

When working with large amounts, it is easier and more accurate to work with eggs by weight or volume rather than quantity. This is particularly helpful when the eggs are somewhat irregular in size, out of the shell, broken or frozen.

Flours

The type of flour should be determined by the recipe. In general, when preparing products that require lightness and little gluten, such as cake batters, pure cake flour (not self-rising) is used. When a dough requires more body, such as a tart or cookie dough, pastry flour is needed. Bread and yeast doughs require flour with a higher protein content, such as bread or patent flour. As flours can vary throughout a region or country, it is recommended to experiment a bit to find the best flour for a particular recipe. Combinations of flours are often used to raise or lower the gluten content in a given recipe.

Yeast

Compressed fresh yeast is most commonly used. The yeast can be dissolved first in a small amount of warm water (70°–100° F/20°–38° C). If a dry yeast is substituted, it needs to be activated with more water and at a slightly higher temperature than fresh yeast. Moisten the dry yeast with water heated to 110° F/43° C. A temperature higher than 140° F/60° C could kill the yeast in either case. Use approximately 2 tsp/8 g of dry yeast for every 2/3 oz or 5 tsp/20 g of fresh yeast specified.

Chocolate

The French government strictly controls the quality and appellations of chocolate. The percentage of cocoa butter, cocoa liquor, and sugar will determine the grade and sweetness. There are various qualities of chocolate, but it is the couverture chocolates that are recommended. Cocoa butter is the only fat used in couverture chocolate. It can be used in any preparation but must be tempered for molding and other decorative chocolate work.

Coating chocolate is sometimes called for, in which case no tempering is required. Coating chocolates are not as tasty as the couverture chocolates but are used when a thin layer is required to coat a cake or other pastry preparation, as it is more fluid than couverture chocolate when melted. To render coating chocolate more flavorful, it is recommended to combine it with equal amounts of bittersweet couverture chocolate. Mr. Thuriès calls this mixture "liquid couverture/coating chocolate". This combination eliminates the need for tempering, adds flavor to the coating chocolate, and maintains the thin coating quality needed for certain pastries.

Crème Fraîche

Crème fraîche is not always readily available, in which case an equal amount of heavy cream may be substituted.

Gelatin

In France, gelatin is marketed in 1/16 oz/2 g sheets. In the United States and other countries this weight may vary, making it important to weigh the sheets when they are used. Before they can be melted and incorporated into a dessert, gelatin sheets must be softened by covering them with very cold water for approximately 10 minutes. After they have softened, squeeze out the excess water. They are now ready to be melted. Never allow them to boil if melting them over a heat source or they will lose their bonding property.

Sugars

The recipes themselves generally call for granulated sugar, unless indicated otherwise. The decorating sugars will often vary. Pearl sugar is used in some of the recipes such as the Epiphany Cake. It is a white, opaque sugar with very large, often rounded granules that resist high temperatures. If this is unavailable, coarse sugar (sugar crystals) would be the best substitute.

Translator's Acknowledgments

Certainly my first thank you must go to Yves Thuriès for creating these books in the first place, and his continual love for, knowledge of, and devotion to extending his wisdom to those who share his passion for pastry. A sincere thank you to Pam Chirls, the original editor who started this project; her presence will be sorely missed. Thank you to all those at VNR who participated in this project, including Jacqueline Martin, Group Production Director, and Amy Shipper, Assistant Editor. Thank you to Jacques Torres for encouraging me to take on more than I would have dared. Thank you to Rémi Lauvand for his good will, lato sensu, and with the finer points of French. A profound thank you to my beloved cousins, Jean-Jacques, Beatrice, and France, who gave me the peace and warmth in which to work, along with wondrous food and drink for continual inspiration. I wish to dedicate my work on this project to the memory of Jean-Noël Béchamps, who brought this series to my attention; he will always be remembered.

The History of Pastry Making

Pastry making can be traced back to ancient times. The first pastry chef could have been a Neolithic man who first thought to cook a mixture of grain and water on a stone heated by the sun, therefore creating the first *galette* (pancake). These *galettes* were then improved upon. Barley, wheat, corn, poppy, fennel and anise seed *galettes* have been recorded throughout the centuries. They were sometimes flavored with coriander and sweetened with honey. There was originally very little difference between pastry making and baking. The *galettes* were lightly sweetened and flavored with spices, cheeses, and vegetables.

While pastry making dates back to ancient civilizations, the techniques and recipes do not even remotely resemble those used today. People were unfamiliar with many of today's ingredients. These ingredients were introduced into pastry making over time. The oldest ingredients are flour, which can be traced to 10,000 B.C. and honey, traced to 5000 B.C.

Sugar originated in Bengal or the West Indies. Sugarcane was given the name "honey plant" because of the sweet juice extracted from it. It was brought to Europe by Alexander the Great. Sugar at that time was called honey reed, Indian salt, or saccharon. The Persians invented the method for refining sugar. It then became known in the Mediteranean basin. Nonetheless, for the first fifteen centuries A.D., sugar was used for solely medicinal purposes and only apothecaries were authorized to sell it. It was not until the continental system in 1806 and the extraction of sugar from sugarbeets that sugar became popular.

Butter can be traced to the Greeks in 1100 B.C. Chickens and eggs were introduced to Europe around 700 B.C.

In Greece, Egypt, and Babylonia, the only known pastry served at banquets was a type of *galette* made of flour, honey and olive oil. The Greeks made a cake called the "*obélias*" or offering. It is possible this was the origin of the "*oublie*" or host.

In 400 B.C., a pastry chef corporation was established in Rome. At this time fruit was often added to the *galettes* (then called *pastillariorum*). The first pastry chef to have made a name for himself was Thearion who lived in Cappadocia in 457 B.C. The origin of the tarts made today is the tourte, which can be found in medieval recipes. A type of soufflé beignet, filled with apples was being made. However, it was not until the Middle Ages and the Crusades of Godfrey of Bouillon in 1099 that a distinctive evolution in pastry making began to occur.

Duing this time beignets were especially popular. They were made with egg, marrow, fish, figs, meat and cheese. Pastry chefs had less than respectable reputations. The meat they used for their patés was supposed to contain only high quality ingredients but sometimes it included the meat of cat or other small animals not intended for this purpose. One pastry shop on the *rue de marmouzets* was demolished and the chef was prohibited from rebuilding because he "made his patés from corpses that were hanging in the gallows."

Another pastry chef, well known for his meat pies, would not let anyone help prepare them so that he could protect his secret recipe. He was in a unsavory partnership with his neighbor, the barber, who offered a free shave to attract business. After luring clients into his shop for this free shave, he would cut their throats. He would then toss the corpses through a trap door into his neighbor's basement for the pastry chef to use in his fillings. This continued until one of the intended victims guessed his fate. He fought with the barber, threw him in the basement and escaped, revealing all. The pastry chef did not recognize his friend in the dark and began to dismember him. In this case, also, the shop was demolished and replaced with a memorial.

Pastry chefs were at one time called *obloiers* or *oblayehrs*. This name was derived from the word *oblée*, the original name for the host. Those who made the host were subjected to strict ecclesiastic regulations: they were not allowed to have women prepare the bread for church; they were not permitted to gamble; they had to be well respected by the community; they had to use fresh eggs and could sell only to Christians.

The *oblayeurs* did not only make the *oblées* that were used for the Church, but also the famous *oublies* (unleavened bread) that were served to the monks and canons. For holidays, special "waffles of forgiveness" were made. The batter was prepared with honey and spices and poured into waffle irons shaped like sacred figures. They also made *fouace*, a flat bread made with a special flour, which was baked under hot ashes.

The majority of the members were affiliated with the corporation on *rue des oublayeurs*, on *île de la Cité* which is now *rue de la Licorne*. According to the regulations at this time, stale cakes were not to be sold.

The difference between pastry chefs, bakers, roasters, and caterers was not clearly defined. It was recorded that in 1292, in Paris, there were 68 *patéiers* (pastry chefs), 2 *eschaudeurs* (those who made *échaudés*), 3 *fouaciers* (those who made *fouaces*), 7 *gasteliers* (those who sold cakes) and 29 *oubliers* (those who made *oublies*) in addition to those who sold waffles, *darioles*, beignets, and *nieules*. Pastry chefs also sold their wares as street vendors calling out to advertise their goods.

In the thirteenth century, these different branches of the same profession began to be strictly regulated. They gained exclusive rights to meat patés, fish, and cheese. They had to follow strict laws such as the ordinance passed by King Jean the Good, in 1351, that forbade the selling of stale paté. Vendors who held meat for more than one day were fined. When the meat used in a pastry was deemed "unfit for human consumption," it was burned in front of the pastry shop as a public reprimand. Precautions were taken in order to ensure profits. They obtained the right to sell beverages which caused friction with the bartenders' corporation.

During the thirteenth century, there were over 100 different métiers including the *oublayers*. Saint Louis gave them their statute. The first article stipulated that in order to become an oublayer in Paris, one had to: know the trade, have sufficient capital, and follow the customs and traditions of the trade. These statutes were recorded by Regnaut Barbon, Paris magistrate, in 1270. The guild, which was placed under the protection of Saint Michael, had its office on *rue de la Poterie*, next to the old market place.

It was not often that pastry chefs had even one day off. The feast of Saint Michael was one of the rare holidays they observed. On this day the pastry chefs followed a rather odd custom. They would parade into the chapel of their patron saint in the church of Saint Bartholomew. One half of the procession was dressed as the devil, the other as angels. In between was Saint Michael with a scale, pulling a group of men disguised as a dragon. In 1636, the archbishop of Paris forbade this event because it caused too many disturbances.

During the fourteenth century, pastry chefs were among the first to decorate their shop windows with bars and balusters in order to attract the attention of passers-by.

Under Philippe Auguste, a pastry chef from Albi, Garibous, created *échaudés* without ammonia or potassium carbonate.

Taillevent, Charles V's chef, wrote the first culinary manuscript in 1379 which was finally printed in Lyons in 1515. His surname was given to him because he handled puff pastry so lightly that he is said to have sliced it in the wind or "*taillait dans le vent.*"

Margaret of Flanders loved "*boichée*," a yeast bread with white honey which is thought to be the origin of spice bread.

On October 18, 1397 it was decreed that in order to set up shop, a pastry chef must be able to prepare 500 large *oublies*, 300 *supplications*, and 200 *esterels*, of high quality. The dough for these 1000 cakes was to be prepared in one day.

In 1406, a pastry chef was prohibited from taking an apprentice for less than five years because "any less than that would not allow him time to learn the trade and earn a good living."

The various pastries began to evolve at this time. Tourtes filled with ingredients such as quince, chestnut, gourd, oat flour, and elder flower as well as a variety of cakes: *darioles* or tarts decorated with strips of dough; *flanets*; *cassemuseaultx*; and *ratons* were now being seen in market stalls. Cakes were given assorted shapes and odd names such as "smallpox cakes;" even obscene names and shapes were used.

Around 1440 the profession divided into two groups: *oublayeurs* and pastry chefs, who began to incorporate fats and oils into their doughs. There were also the *gastelliers* who made cakes. However, not all of these masters were selling from market stalls. The more privileged ones worked for the king and even traveled with the court. All of the corporations that were useful to the court were represented. King Louis XII had 93 masters and in 1659, Louis XIV had 377; 26 roasters, 8 pastry chefs, 14 cooks, and 12 butchers, and 2 spice bread bakers.

Under King Louis XI, two types of cakes were particularly popular. One was the *talmouse*, the king's favorite dessert. It consisted of a tricorn of puff pastry with a filling of brie cheese, farmer's cheese, and eggs. His other favorite pastry was the *nieulle*, made with an échaudée anise-seed dough that was boiled the way bagels are today. This pastry was developed by the corporation of pastry chefs called the *nieuleurs* that disassembled when the Edict of Nantes was revoked. The term *nieuleur* is still used today in pastry making, in a pejorative sense, to refer to someone who does poor work.

Nieuilles were also used for certain religious services. *Nieulles* were attached to birds' feet and these birds were then released while the congregation sang Gloria in Excelcis.

The sale of *oublies* (also called "pleasures") was still flouishing despite the popularity of the *talmousse* and the *nieulle*. Lyons was renowned for making the best *oublies* at this time.

In 1506, Provenchère, a pastry chef in Pithiviers, created the almond cream or Pithivier cream. The preferred cake of Francois I was the *gohières*, a torte filled with one quarter liter of farmers' cheese, 2 eggs, 2 ounces of raw sugar or honey, 1 ounce of grated gruyère cheese, salt, and orange flower water. In Lyons in 1520, Cassati made ice cream for the first time in France. Marzipan and honey nougat were being prepared in Provence, a region in the south of France.

Under Charles IX, the number of different metiers increased and corporations were formed. In 1566, the king granted pastry chefs the title "Master of the Art of Pastry Making and Obloiers." Before this time, membership in these corporations was not mandatory. To achieve this status, the candidate was obligated to undergo an examination and prepare a masterpiece. Article 29 of the statute of 1566 allowed all masters the possibility of serving on the jury. Once the candidate was granted his title of "Master Pastry Chef Oblayeur of a Masterpiece," he swore to show loyalty to the trade and respect its ordinances.

It was very difficult to acquire the title in Paris for several reasons. First, the apprenticeship had to be fulfilled in Paris. Secondly, the master chefs wanted to keep their number to a minimum, so they separated themselves from the *compagnons* (those who traveled around the country to learn their trade), making it practically impossible for them to obtain the title of master pastry chef.

In 1566, there were many pastries, all as bland as their forms were varied. The "*ratons*", the "*gimblettes*", the "*craquelins*", the "*poupelins*" and the "*talmouses*" which were often covered with farmers' cheese, could all be added to the list of cakes previously cited. While pastry chefs from the Middle Ages were hardworking and resourceful, their pastries were still lacking. Their work barely exceeded bread baking.

The corporations required letters of recommendation to confirm their status each time a new king took the throne. The status in 1566 was confirmed by Henri II in 1576, in 1594 by Henri IV, in 1612 by Louis XIII, in 1653 by Louis XIV. Each confirmation required financing.

At the height of the Renaissance, with Catherine de'Medici's arrival into Henri II's court, French cuisine reached a peak, as did the sciences and arts under her influence. The Medicis were one of the wealthiest and most influential families of Florence, Italy. Queen Catherine brought the Medici tradition of elegance in dining to the French court through her entourage of qualified culinary personnel. This Italian contribution to French table arts shaped the future of the profession. She brought refined white sugar (among other things) with her from Italy to France where only raw sugar had been used until that time. She also brought ice cream which the Louvre chefs kept secret for more than one hundred years, after which it was sold in Paris by Procope in 1660. Procope was the owner of a famous café in Paris of the same name. He was awarded a patent by Louis XIV, the Sun King, for this product that he found to be "so pleasant and good tasting." This café later became the meeting place for intellectuals of the eighteenth century (principally writers such as Voltaire, Diderot, and Jean-Jacques Rousseau).

Catherine de'Medici's pastry chef, Popolin, knew of a recipe for a dough that was dried over a flame. This would come to be known as "popelin dough" and eventually evolved into what is now known as "*pâte à choux*" or choux paste. The dough was spread to about the thickness of two fingers over a buttered paper and partially cooked. It was then removed from the oven, cut in half, and the uncooked interior removed and replaced with fruit jelly. It was then decorated with a melted butter icing and sugar and returned to the oven until golden brown. At the end of the century, in 1596, we witness the birth of spice bread pastry chefs.

With the introduction of tea, coffee, and chocolate in the sevententh century, pastry chefs made great strides in creativity. Some of the new pastries developed were the brioche , macaroons from Nancy and ladyfingers. Ladyfingers are called *biscuits à la cuillère* in French, meaning spoon biscuits, as they were originally dropped onto a baking sheet with a spoon. Abraham du Pradel in his book *Livre Commode des Adresses,* published in 1690, maintains that pastry chefs made ragouts, layered cakes, marzipan tarts, and musk and amber tourtes.

Claude Gelée began as a pastry chef and some credit him with having invented puff pastry, although this is not certain. He went on to become a renowned painter under the name of Le Lorrain. Favart, another pastry chef at this time, contributed the "*croquignoles*" (a variety of *nieules*) and the *échaudées*. Vatel is credited with inventing chantilly cream, and Stanislas Leczinski created the *baba au rum,* that was served with this cream.

Then came Carême. His reputation as a chef masked his proud origins as a pastry chef. Pastries made great strides in Paris because of him. He brought us: "*nougat*", "meringues", "*popelins*", "*vol-au-vents*", and "*croquants*". He also perfected puff pastry.

Chocolate completely changed tastes and customs like no other new ingredient. Chocolate first came to Europe through Spain. A Spanish monk sent the first tablets of chocolate to Alphonse du Plessis, archbishop of Lyons and brother of Cardinal Richelieu who used it as a spleen medication.

Anne of Austria loved this innovation and along with Antonio Carletti, head pastry chef of the royal kitchen, can be credited with its popularity.

Chocolate was becoming accredited. In 1661, chocolate was recognized by the Faculty of Medicine. An edict of 1662 established a monopoly of the sale of cocoa. King Louis XIV granted David Chalon the rights to making chocolate for a period of 29 years.

The macaroons of Nancy, credited as being the first macaroons, had been prepared since 1553 for the French court, although the recipe was kept secret for many years. The recipe was somehow obtained by the nuns of Saint Sacrement of Nancy and are a specialty of this region even today.

As far as "*madeleines*" are concerned, it is difficult to know just which part of their history is fiction and which is fact as there are so many stories as to their origin.

Up until this time, pastry chefs were allowed to sell their pastries in the streets. This practice was abolished due to the "Cartouche," a band of thieves who disguised themselves as pastry chefs and robbed unsuspecting customers.

It is also at this time that the expression, "She had no shame; she walked through the doors of the pastry shop" originated. In order to fully understand this expression, it should be pointed out that clients did not only come to to these shops for cakes but for pleasure as well. The pastry chefs had back rooms for this purpose. "Honest" women would prefer, of course, to use a hidden door; however, a woman whose reputation was already tarnished would simply march through the front door.

By the eighteenth century, there were two hundred master pastry chefs including the guild whose patron saint was Saint Michael that met in the holy chapel. The "Great Pastry Chefs" were Raguenau, Favart, Flechmes, Mignot, and Carême. Shortly afterward came Rouget, of whom Grimod often spoke and whose specialty was a "*millefeuilles*", and the three Julien brothers whose shop was located at *place de la Bourse*. This dynasty would last until the Second Empire. These three brothers are credited with creating the savarin under the direction of or in honor of (it is not certain which) Brillat-Savarin. In either case, they were the first to imbibe biscuits in flavored syrups.

Favart was considered one of the most intelligent pastry chefs of the eighteenth century. He perfected Taillevent's *échaudés* by adding a type of chemical leavening composed of three parts ammonia and one part potassium hydroxide.

In 1720, the chef of Stanislas Leczinski, father-in-law of King Louis XV, created the famous "*baba*" in Lunéville. It was a type of "*kougelhof*" which was originally moistened only with rum.

In 1722, an ordinance banned pastry chefs from peddling their pastries in the street. One of the reason being that their pastries were said to be "unfit to enter the human body." In spite of this, the tradition had lasted 500 years.

Sugar finally experienced development due to the efforts of Margraff and Achard, two chemists, who devised a way of extracting sugar from the sugarbeet. This had already been noted in 1605 by Olivier de Serres, an agronomist whose discovery attracted little attention.

In 1776, Turot, minister to Louis XVI, disbanded the pastry chef corporations. For this reason, they lost their title of master pastry chef but were able to keep their title of master *oubliers* until the revolution.

In 1784, Carême was born. He would prove to be one of the most celebrated chefs of his time by publishing *The Royal Pastry Chef* in 1810. He developed the method for making *biscuit à la cuillère* (ladyfingers) without the spoon at the request of Talleyrand. During the French revolution, pastry development was limited. As there were many shortages during this period, potatoes were often used instead of flour. The *galette* was still quite popular even though the revolutionary commitee found bakers to have "intentions that were destructive of liberty." One deputy even asked the convention to rename the *galette* the "galette of equality;" this very unpopular measure did not survive long.

Upon entering the nineteenth century, we find ourselves in a century of innovators where a certain number of pastry chefs attained fame: In 1810, Gouffé created nougat presentation pieces; Lebeau knew everything about pastillage; the Julien brothers have already been cited for creating the *baba*. They were given the name "the pastry giants" by Alexander Dumas. Besides the savarin syrup (kept secret for fifty years), they created the "*pensée*" biscuit and the "three brothers."

Around 1823, Carême prompted the replacement of the traditional cotton bonnet worn by pastry chefs with the toque. He felt that this would promote good taste and cleanliness.

In 1830, ice cream was first prepared with a cooked base and fondant appeared. In 1835, candied chestnuts were first made, and in 1840, the first iced petits fours were prepared. Duchemin, a pastry chef in Tours, created the first génoise prepared with whipped egg whites.

All of these creations required new equipment. This is what Trottier set out to do in perfecting various types of molds and rings for tarts, which were originally called tourtes.

In 1840, Chiboust created the Saint Honoré pastry based on the Swiss flan. The Saint Honoré was originally given a hand-rolled brioche border as Aubriot did not invent the pastry bag nor Trottier pastry tips until 1847.

In 1845, Gazeau, a pastry chef from Bordeaux, prepared the first *tant pour tant* (equal weights) made up of ground almonds or hazelnuts and sugar.

In 1850, the Breton cake, not to be confused with the tiered cake we know today, arrived on the market. It was prepared with molds made by Trottier. In 1855, a pastry assistant from Genoa brought the recipe for génoise with him to Loison's pastry shop where he worked. From this recipe, Chiboust created a génoise with almonds, a variation of the Genoa cake.

The first coal oven was constructed in Paris at Chambrant's pastry shop. Whisks were now made with iron wires, rather than the heather, broom and wicker branches from which they were originally made. At Sergent's pastry shop on *rue de Bac*, napoleons were all the rage.

In 1865, the pastry chef Quillet invented the filling that eventually evolved into moka cream or buttercream. In 1879, Charabout's pastry shop prepared the first yule log. We should also mention Avice "the great" who created grilled choux, "ramekins", and "breads from Mecca" and finally, Seugnot who contributed the Breton cake fifty years earlier. He also created the "Genoa cake" in memory of inhabitants of Massena who ate only rice and almonds while under siege.

This is also the period when large presentation pieces came into vogue. Every detail was replicated and realized to make forms such as palaces, castles, cathedrals, and flowers. This type of ornate work that continued through the beginning of the twentieth century with pastry chefs Duval, Seurin, Léveillé, Mahieux, Michot, Jaquelin and Aubinot whose masterpieces are still displayed in recipe publications. Closer to our own era we should note the celebrated pastry chefs: Coquelin and Franchiolo who took many first place titles before World War II, and Paul Vigreux who received awards not only in Paris but in Brussels. Chanel, Deblieux, and Tholoniat are others who contributed much to their field.

We might ask ourselves what has happened to all these recipes. Few of them resemble what they were at their conceptions. They have been manipulated, tampered with, and simplified in order to lower costs and speed production. Materialism has made its mark in this field as it has in others. Today it has become impossible to continue to work in the same manner as before. Pastry making has grown to reflect the transformation in both living style and taste, although some of these changes are not necessarily for the better, as the quality of products suffers due to rising production costs and materialism. There are also some very positive changes due to better hygiene, modern equipment, and new product development.

In the second part of this century, pastry making has experienced an unprecedented development which will undoubtedly alter the course of pastry making history with a renewal and rejuvenation of methods and recipes. Finally a new style of pastry making, characterized by lightness and freshness, has emerged from all of this.

The tradition of quality craftsmanship must continue. It is encouraging to see younger members of our profession present such detailed and tasteful work at various culinary events. In fact, after the Second World War, this was not always the case, even at the highest levels of competition. Quality is no longer regulated as it once was. With the demise of the trade union regulations, and with all doing as they please, however they please, it is up to those who uphold the tradition of quality to play the significant role of preserving our trade in an ocean of mediocrity perpetuated by misleading publicity.

Modern French Pastry

CHAPTER

1

Cakes

La Nouvelle Pâtisserie

French pastry making did not change noteably during the first half of the twentieth century. It is only over the last thirty years that considerable growth occured. This is due largely to the advent of lighter fillings such as the creams and mousses that have become so popular. Until recently, certain fillings, such as the chiboust cream (also referred to as crème légère), were not encouraged or, in some instances, not allowed because of questionable sanitary conditions. Recipes, techniques, and equipment have evolved enormously and each of these areas has affected the others.

The classification of the creams is listed below. The lighter, newer fillings are generally referred to as mousses.

Mousses based on whipped egg whites
Mousses based on fruits
Mousses based on butter
Mousses based on meringue
Mousses based on whipped cream
Charlotte creams
Bavarian creams

This classification is not limited to the items listed; each of these is a category for many variations.

Mousses generally freeze well, which makes it possible to prepare cakes in quantity rather individually. "Nouvelle" pastries are based on methods using greater flexibility compared to some of the classic techniques.

The classic French style of preparing cakes consists of first setting up cakes on the work surface. A variety of biscuits are layered with an assortment of buttercreams using a palette knife. Buttercream is smoothed over the top and sides to finish the cakes.

The newer techniques given in this volume assure a very precise, even layering which is better suited to the lighter cream and mousse fillings. Faster techniques for assembling cakes are presented which use cake rings and cake frames, sheet pans, and other molds. In nouvelle pastry making, paper cone decoration is rarely used; this detailed work is reserved for presentation and ceremonial pieces.

The flavor, decoration, and styling of the cakes are essential to a modern look. Only natural decorations are used, such as fruit, fruit gelées, and chocolate. The cakes are lighter and more refreshing, making them more suitable for today's consumer.

It is important to understand that nouvelle pastry is not meant to replace traditional pastry, but to complement, rejuvenate, and augment all pastry making.

4 *Modern French Pastry*

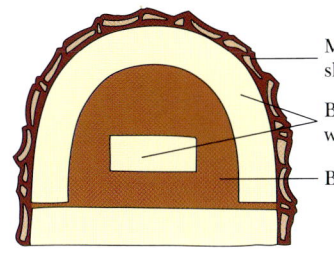

Milk chocolate coating with sliced almonds

Biscuit or mousseline génoise moistened with coffee simple syrup

Brazilian coffee mousse

Brazilian
Brésilien

This cake is constructed upside down in a semi-round mold called a gouttière. Line the mold with biscuit that has been baked on parchment paper, or mousseline génoise, and lightly moistened with coffee simple syrup. Fill half-full with Brazilian coffee mousse. Cover with a layer of biscuit, liberally moistened with coffee simple syrup. Smooth a second layer of mousse flush with the edge of the mold. Cover with a layer of biscuit. Freeze.

Unmold and cut into smaller cakes as needed. Smooth ganache over the two open ends. Coat the entire cake with either milk chocolate couverture with sliced almonds or special milk chocolate coating with sliced almonds (recipes follow).

Special Milk Chocolate Coating No. 1
Pâte à Glacer Spéciale au Lait

milk chocolate coating	35 oz	1,000 g
milk chocolate couverture	14 oz	400 g
oil	5.5 oz	150 g
sliced toasted almonds to taste		

Melt the milk chocolate coating, milk chocolate couverture, and oil (any neutral vegetable oil such as corn, safflower, or canola) to 98.5°F/37°C. Gently stir in the sliced almonds, adding enough to acquire the texture desired.

Facing Page: Brazilian, Charleston

Special Milk Chocolate Coating No. 2
Pâte à Glacer Spéciale au Lait

This recipe is easier than the first, yet still offers excellent results.

Cover the cake with special milk chocolate coating. Sprinkle sliced toasted almonds over the top and sides of the cake before the chocolate sets. After the chocolate has set, cover the cake with a second layer of the same milk chocolate coating.

Brazilian Coffee Mousse
Mousse Brésilienne au Café

butter, softened	35 oz	1,000 g
coffee extract	7 oz	200 g
sugar	35 oz	1,000 g
water	10.5 oz	300 g
egg whites	16	16
crème fraîche	10.5 oz	300 g

Combine the softened butter and the coffee extract. Prepare an Italian meringue by cooking the sugar and water to 250°F/121°C, while whipping the egg whites to soft peaks. Pour the cooked sugar in a fine stream, whipping it into the egg whites. Continue whipping until cool.

Whip the crème fraîche to soft peaks. Combine parts one and two, folding the meringue into the flavored butter. Fold in the whipped crème fraîche.

This mousse should be molded shortly after it has been prepared.

- Craquelin
- Biscuit moistened with caramel simple syrup
- Caramel mousse
- Progrès base

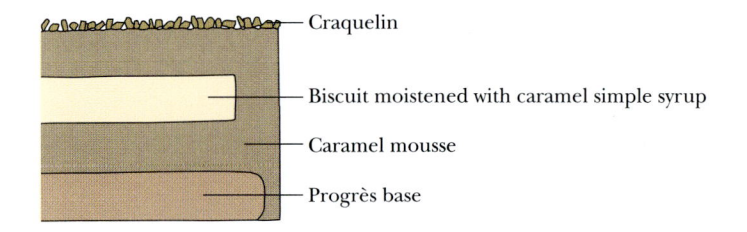

Charleston

Prepare the biscuit and progrès bases. This cake is assembled in a 1 in/3 cm high cake ring. Trim the biscuit and progrès bases so they are a bit smaller than the diameter of the ring; this will allow the mousse to cover the sides of the cake. After the cake is assembled and the ring is removed, only the mousse will be seen around the side of the cake.

Place the progrès base inside the ring. Fill the ring half-full with caramel mousse, spreading it against the inside of the ring. Cover with a layer of biscuit, moisten with caramel simple syrup. Smooth the caramel mousse flush to the top of the ring. Refrigerate.

Remove the cake ring by heating it with a propane torch. Cover the top of the cake with craquelin. Place a pastry shop label on top.

Caramel Mousse
Mousse au Caramel

sugar	17.5 oz	500 g
crème fraîche	14 oz	400 g
butter, softened	17.5 oz	500 g
Italian meringue	17.5 oz	500 g

Cook the sugar to a dark brown caramel. Deglaze the caramel by adding the crème fraîche. Set aside to cool.

After cooling, add the butter and whip to aerate the mixture. Gently fold in the Italian meringue.

Use this mousse shortly after it is prepared.

Dark Chocolate Biscuit

egg yolks	25	25
sugar	14 oz	400 g
flour	9 oz	250 g
cocoa powder	4.5 oz	125 g
butter, melted	9 oz	250 g
egg whites	18	18
sugar	3.5 oz	100 g

In the bowl of an electric mixer, whisk the egg yolks and sugar until light and aerated.

Sift the flour with the cocoa powder and fold into the whipped egg yolk/sugar mixture. Fold in the melted butter. Whip the egg whites with the sugar to medium peaks. Gently fold the whipped egg whites into the first batter.

Quickly fill the previously buttered and floured molds three fourths full.

Bake in a moderate oven. Unmold immediately after baking.

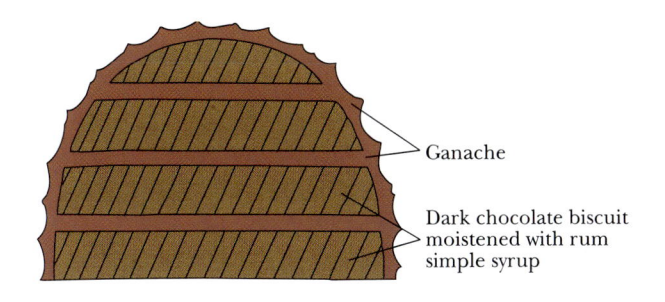

Dark Chocolate Ganache Cake

Bake a dark chocolate biscuit in a dome-shaped mold.
  Prepare the butter ganache (recipe follows).
  After the biscuit has cooled, attach it to a cake cardboard with a dollop of ganache. Cut the biscuit into four layers using a serrated knife. Set the top three layers aside. Moisten the bottom layer with rum simple syrup, then spread a layer of ganache. Repeat the procedure of biscuit, syrup, ganache until the four layers of biscuit are assembled, reconstructing the dome shape. Spread and smooth a layer of ganache over the top and sides of the cake. Refrigerate.
  After the ganache has set, spread a second, thicker layer of ganache around the cake. With a palette knife, pull on the ganache to create points all around the cake. Place a pastry shop label on top.

Butter Ganache
Ganache Beurrée

chocolate couverture	35 oz	1,000 g
crème fraîche	17.5 oz	500 g
butter, softened	17.5 oz	500 g

  Chop the chocolate couverture and place it in a bowl. Bring the crème fraîche to a simmer and pour it over the chocolate. Stir until smooth and set aside to cool to room temperature. Use a whisk to stir in the softened butter.

Special Praline Mousse
Mousse Pralinée Spéciale

praline paste	28 oz	800 g
butter, softened	35 oz	1,000 g
Italian meringue	2 lbs 10 oz	1,200 g

  Soften the praline paste by working it in an electric mixer with the paddle attachment. Whip in the butter. Gently fold in the Italian meringue. It is important to mold this type of Italian meringue-based mousse shortly after it is prepared, as it quickly breaks down.
  Any leftover mousse which has lost its lightness can be whipped until smooth, then used as a buttercream.

Modern French Pastry

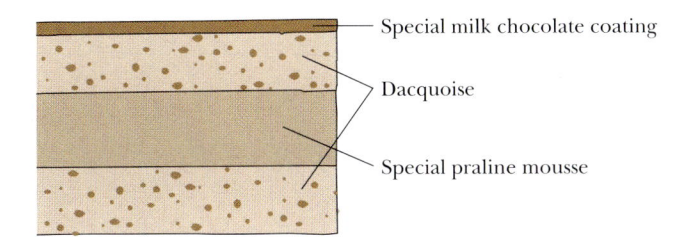

Special milk chocolate coating

Dacquoise

Special praline mousse

Praline Mazarin
Mazarin Praliné

This cake is assembled on standard sheet pans. Prepare two layers of dacquoise (see page 11). Bake the batter on a sheet pan covered with buttered parchment paper. The batter can be piped out of a pastry bag with a tip 1/2 in/12 mm in diameter. Dust with confectioners' sugar.

Bake at 350°F/180°C for 45 minutes. After cooling, remove the parchment paper.

On one dacquoise, spread a 1/3 in/8 mm layer of special praline mousse. Cover with the second layer of dacquoise, this time turning it over so the bottom side (that which was touching the parchment paper) is facing up. To even out the cake, gently press on it with a sheet pan. Spread a thin layer of mousse over the top of the cake. Glaze with special milk chocolate coating.

Heat a serrated knife with hot water and then cut rectangular, square, large, or individual cakes. Dust the top of the cake with cocoa powder, using a cardboard cutout or stencil.

Chocolate Mazarin
Mazarin au Chocolat

This cake is prepared following the same procedure given for the praline mazarin above, with the appropriate substitutions. The praline mousse is replaced with chocolate mousse. The milk chocolate coating is replaced with special dark chocolate coating as used for the opera cake.

Special Milk Chocolate Coating
Pâte à Glacer Spéciale au Lait

coffee coating chocolate	35 oz	1,000 g
milk chocolate couverture	9 oz	250 g
peanut oil	5.5 oz	150 g

Use a hot water bath to melt the coating and milk chocolates. Add the oil. The mixture should be used at approximately 100.5°F/38°C. It is best to strain the coating through a fine mesh strainer before using.

Spiral Cake Cream
Crème à Pie Neuf

mousseline cream	35 oz	1,000 g
rum	3 oz	80 g
chantilly	10.5 oz	300 g

Combine the mousseline cream with the rum. Gently fold in the chantilly.

Chef's Note: *The cream can be flavored with another liqueur or coffee, praline, or chocolate. The recipe and procedure remains the same.*

Facing Page: Dark Chocolate Ganache Cake, Praline Mazarin

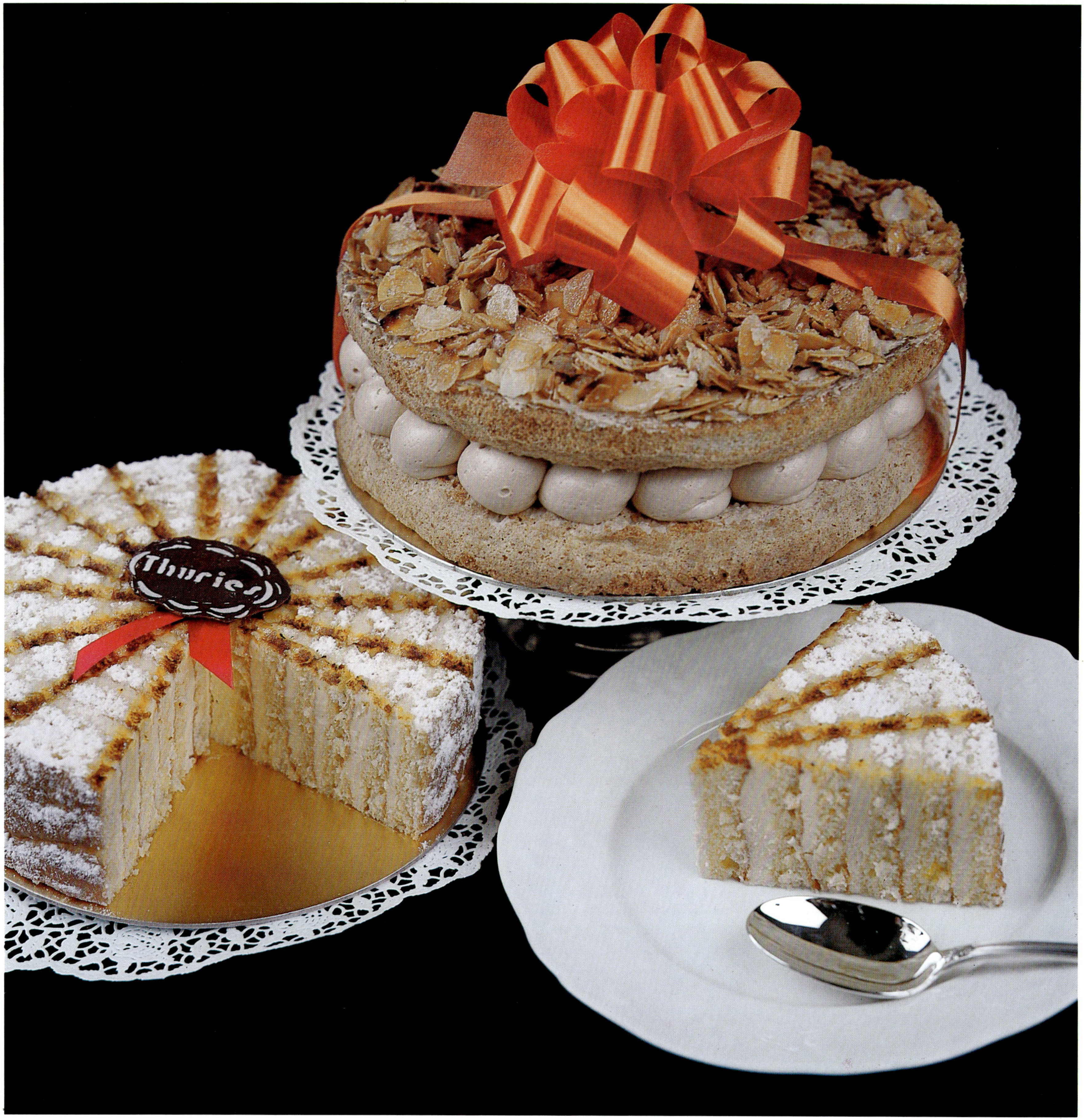
Thuries

Spiral Cake
Pie Neuf

This cake is assembled using the technique for preparing a large rolled yule log or jelly roll. The roll is cut into slices, the thickness of which will determine the height of the cake. Each slice is laid flat on its side with the spiral upright, then decorated.

Prepare two, three, or four sheets of biscuit, depending on the size of the cake desired. Remove the parchment paper from the first biscuit sheet and lightly moisten the back (side touching the paper) with rum simple syrup. Spread a layer of pie neuf cream. Roll the biscuit as for a jelly roll, but starting with the narrow end, rolling the length of the rectangle. Place in the freezer.

While the first rolled sheet is chilling, prepare a second sheet of biscuit. Moisten with rum simple syrup and spread a layer of pie neuf cream. Place the chilled log on top of one end (narrow) of the second biscuit sheet and roll it so the log is now twice as thick. Place in the freezer once again.

Repeat this step, continuing to roll the biscuit until the desired diameter is obtained. It is essential to place the log in the freezer after adding each layer to prevent it from unrolling or losing its shape.

Once the finished cake is completely chilled, dip a serrated knife in hot water and cut slices to the thickness desired. Eight cakes, each 2 in/5 cm thick or high, will be obtained from a roll 15.5 in/40 cm long. Four cakes can be made from a log rolled from an 8 in/20 cm sheet of biscuit.

It is possible to make a single cake at a time. Cut strips of biscuit 2 in/5 cm wide, moisten with simple syrup, and spread a layer of pie neuf cream. Roll the strips around each other, adding the next strip where the last one left off. Place the cake flat side down (spiral upright) and finish rolling the biscuit strips around the cake until the desired size is obtained.

With the spiral upright, dust the top of the cake with confectioners' sugar. Decorate using a hot iron to caramelize a design into the sugar. Wrap a ribbon around the cake and place a pastry shop label on top.

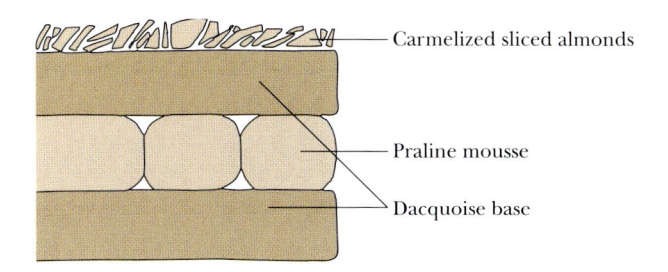

Facing Page: Spiral Cake, Dacquoise

Dacquoise

Spread a layer of special praline mousseline cream (see page 12) between two layers of dacquoise base. Smooth the top with the cream and cover with caramelized sliced almonds. Tie a ribbon around the cake, making an elaborate bow on top.

Dacquoise Base No. 1

almond powder	17.5 oz	500 g
confectioners' sugar	14 oz	400 g
flour	3 oz	80 g
egg whites	20	20
sugar	5.5 oz	150 g

Sift together the almond powder, confectioners' sugar, and flour.

Whip the egg whites to medium peaks with the 5.5 oz/150 g sugar. Gently fold the sifted ingredients into the whipped egg whites.

Moisten a tart ring with water and place it on a buttered and floured sheet pan. With a hand scraper, fill the ring approximately 1/2 in/1 cm high. Remove the ring, twisting and lifting up. Dust with confectioners' sugar and bake on a doubled sheet pan at 320°–350°F/160°–180°C for approximately 40 minutes.

TPT
Tant Pour Tant

TPT, or Tant Pour Tant, is a commonly used French term which literally translates to "as much as," standing for equal weights of two ingredients. It is most often used to refer to equal amounts of almonds and sugar, ground together to form a powder (almond powder can be used, eliminating the need for grinding).

This mixture can be prepared in advance, so that it is ready when needed. Other types of TPTs include those made with blanched or unblanched almonds.

Dacquoise Base No. 2

TPT	35 oz	1,000 g
flour	3.5 oz	100 g
egg whites	20	20
sugar	14 oz	400 g

Combine and sift the TPT and flour. Whip the egg whites to medium peaks, gradually adding 14 oz/400 g sugar. Gently fold the TPT/flour mixture into the whipped egg whites.

With a pastry bag and tip, pipe out the batter in spirals on sheet pans that have been buttered and floured or lined with parchment paper.

Dust with confectioners' sugar. Bake in a moderate oven, 320°–350°F/160°–180°C.

Praline Mousseline Cream
No. 1
Crème Mousseline au Praliné

pastry cream	17.5 oz	500 g
praline paste	21 oz	600 g
butter, softened	28 oz	800 g
Italian meringue	35 oz	1,000 g

Use a whisk to combine the pastry cream and praline paste until smooth and well blended. Whip in the butter. Finish by gently folding in the Italian meringue.

Praline Mousseline Cream
No. 2
Crème Mousseline au Praliné

praline paste	17.5 oz	500 g
pastry cream	17.5 oz	500 g
buttercream	35 oz	1,000 g
Italian meringue	26.5 oz	750 g

Use a whisk to combine the praline paste and pastry cream until smooth and well blended. Gradually whisk in the buttercream until smooth. Gently fold in the Italian meringue.

Use this mousseline shortly after it is prepared.

Caramelized Sliced Almonds
Amandes Effilées Caramélisées

sliced almonds	17.5 oz	500 g
simple syrup, 30° baumé	3.5 oz	100 g
sugar	5.5 oz	150 g

Combine all ingredients. Place the mixture on a sheet pan and set in a moderate oven. Toss occasionally so the nuts roast evenly to a golden brown. Once they have reached the proper color, slide them off the sheet pan and onto a marble or other work surface to stop the cooking and cool quickly.

- Marzipan
- Almond biscuit moistened with cognac simple syrup
- Praline mousse
- Succès base

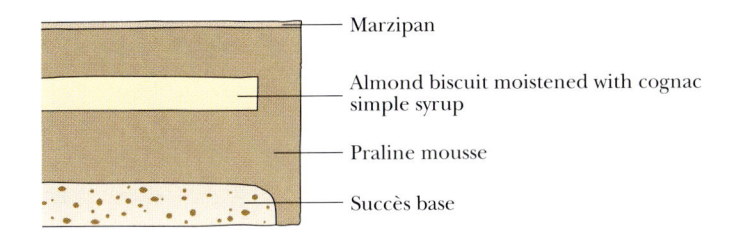

Almond Cognac Cake
Duc de Plessy

This cake is assembled in a 1 1/3 in/3.5 cm high cake ring. Prepare disks of biscuit and succès bases. It is important to cut the biscuit and succès slightly smaller in diameter than the cake ring. When the cake is finished and the ring removed, only the mousse will be seen around the sides.

Place the succès base inside the ring. Fill the ring half-full with praline mousse, spreading it against the inside of the ring. Cover with a layer of almond biscuit, moistened with Cognac simple syrup. Smooth the mousse flush to the top of the ring. Freeze.

Roll out a sheet of white marzipan. With a pastry brush, coat the marzipan with a thin layer of melted cocoa butter. Apply a thin layer of writing chocolate here and there over the cocoa butter. Run a wood grain tool across the marzipan to create a wood grain effect.

Remove the cake ring by heating it with a propane torch. Trim the marzipan to the desired size and place it on top of the cake. Place a pastry shop label on top.

Praline Mousse
Mousse au Praliné

praline paste	17.5 oz	500 g
buttercream	35 oz	1,000 g
Italian meringue	17.5 oz	500 g

Whisk the praline paste with a small amount of the buttercream to soften. Whip in the remaining buttercream until smooth. Gently fold in the Italian meringue.

This cream should be used shortly after it is prepared.

Almond Meringue
Meringue aux Amandes

water	17.5 oz	500 g
sugar	35 oz	1,000 g
egg whites	16	16
almond powder	28 oz	800 g

Prepare an Italian meringue by cooking the sugar and water to 250°F/121°C, while whipping the egg whites to soft peaks. Pour the cooked sugar in a fine stream, whipping it into the egg whites. Continue whipping to firm peaks until it is barely warm, then gently fold in the almond powder.

With a pastry bag and tip 1/3–1/2 in/8–10 mm in diameter, pipe the batter onto sheet pans, buttered and floured or lined with parchment paper.

Bake in a low oven. These bases become crispy after cooling.

Almond Cognac Cake, Checkerboard Cake

14   *Modern French Pastry*

Checkerboard Cake
Damier

This cake is assembled on a standard sheet pan, then cut into smaller cakes.

Prepare two sheets of joconde biscuit, approximately 1/4 in/5 mm thick. Prepare two sheets each of almond génoise and chocolate biscuit, approximately 1/2 in/1 cm thick. It is important that they be the same thickness for a symmetrical checkerboard effect.

Spread a thin layer of coating chocolate on the top (smooth side) of the joconde biscuit. After the chocolate sets, turn the biscuit over and peel off the parchment paper. Moisten the porous side, now on top, with simple syrup flavored with vanilla, rum, Grand Marnier, Cointreau, kirsch, or other liqueur, to taste. Spread a thin layer of buttercream flavored to taste.

Cut the almond and chocolate biscuit sheets into 1 in/3 cm wide strips. It is sometimes necessary to trim the strips so they are even in height. A ruler can be used to measure the height at both ends while trimming with a serrated knife. It is preferable for the strips to be a bit taller as opposed to shorter than intended. Once the strips are cut to size, the cake is ready to be assembled.

Place alternating strips of chocolate and almond biscuit over the layer of joconde biscuit, entirely covering it. Moisten the strips with flavored simple syrup. Spread a thin layer of buttercream. Cover with a second row of alternating strips, this time switching the placement so that a strip of chocolate is set directly over a strip of almond génoise and vice versa. Moisten the strips with simple syrup, then spread a thin layer of buttercream. Repeat these steps, alternating the strips, moistening them with simple syrup, and covering with buttercream, until the desired height is achieved.

Cover with a layer of joconde biscuit, moisten with simple syrup, and spread a thin layer of buttercream. Refrigerate.

Dust the top of the cake with confectioners' sugar and draw diagonal lines in the sugar. Heat a serrated knife with hot water and cut the cake into smaller squares, rectangles, or individual portions. Decorate with molded sugar flowers and leaves.

Special Buttercream
Crème au Beurre Spéciale

egg yolks	15	15
sugar	17.5 oz	500 g
water	14 oz	400 g
vanilla beans	2	2
butter, softened	35 oz	1,000 g
Italian meringue	10.5 oz	300 g

In the bowl of an electric mixer, whisk the egg yolks until pale and aerated.

Place the sugar, water, and scrapings from the vanilla beans along with the pod in a copper sugar pot (poêlon). Cook to 250°F/121°C. Remove the vanilla pod.

Pour the cooked sugar in a fine stream into the egg yolks while whipping. Continue to whip until completely cool.

Whip in the softened butter. Gently fold in the Italian meringue.

Misérable, White Rose

Misérable

This cake is assembled on a standard half- or full-sized sheet pan. The finished cake is then cut into smaller cakes.

Prepare two layers of dacquoise biscuit. Spread the dacquoise batter 1/2–3/4 in/1–1.5 cm thick onto a sheet pan that has been buttered and floured or lined with parchment paper. Dust lightly with confectioners' sugar before baking in a low oven.

After cooling, cover the top of one layer of dacquoise with coating chocolate. After the chocolate has set, turn the dacquoise over and peel off the parchment paper, if used.

Spread a 1/2 in/1 cm layer of the special buttercream (see page 12), flavored to taste. Cover with a second layer of dacquoise. Press the top of the cake lightly with a sheet pan to even it out. Smooth a thin layer of buttercream on top of the cake. Refrigerate.

Chef's Note: *This cake can be assembled in a cake frame 1–1 1/3 in/3–3.5 cm high. The frame makes it easier to obtain very regular, even layers.*

Heat a serrated knife with hot water, cut the cake into smaller cakes such as squares, rectangles, or individual portions.

Dust the cakes with confectioners' sugar. Then dust with cocoa powder, heavily covering one corner, gradually lightening, and stopping at the center diagonal of the cake. Place a pastry shop label on top. Or, instead of forming the cocoa powder diagonal, consider dusting cocoa powder over a decorative stencil.

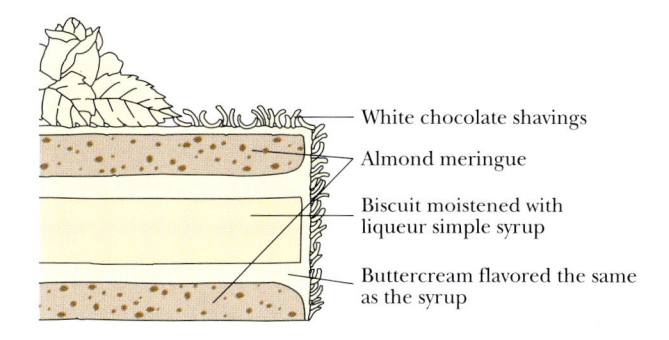

White chocolate shavings
Almond meringue
Biscuit moistened with liqueur simple syrup
Buttercream flavored the same as the syrup

White Rose
Rose Blanche

This cake is assembled in a 2 in/5 cm high cake ring.

Prepare two almond meringue disks (see page 13) approximately 1/2 in/1 cm thick. Also prepare an almond biscuit or almond génoise disk the same diameter as the meringue disks and 1/2–3/4 in/1.5–2 cm thick.

This cake is layered with buttercream flavored with liqueur such as rum, Cointreau, or Grand Marnier.

Place a meringue disk inside the cake ring. Spread a layer of the buttercream, coating the inside of the ring so only the buttercream will be seen when the ring is removed. Cover with the almond génoise or biscuit, moistened liberally with a simple syrup flavored with the same liqueur used in the buttercream. Spread a thin layer of buttercream and cover with the second almond meringue disk, smooth side up. Spread a thin layer of buttercream. Refrigerate.

Remove the cake ring by heating it with a propane torch. Coat the top and sides of the cake with a thin layer of buttercream. Immediately press white chocolate shavings on the top and sides of the cake while the buttercream is soft. Center a white plastic chocolate or molded white chocolate flower on top of the cake.

Coffee Buttercream Cake (Moka)

Coffee Buttercream Cake
Moka

The moka is one of the oldest, most established cakes in the repertoire of French pastry making and is still popular today. Being a classic makes it difficult to alter the cake's basic composition: biscuit or génoise moistened with coffee, vanilla, or rum simple syrup and layered with coffee buttercream. Rather than change this structure, the cake can be modernized by altering its presentation.

The name "moka" is derived from the Arabian coffee bean of the same name. In French, "moka" means coffee flavored and not a combination of coffee and chocolate, as is commonly assumed.

Coffee Buttercream Cake No. 1
Moka

This moka is assembled on a cake cardboard, free form. Cut a génoise horizontally into three equal layers. Place the bottom layer on the cardboard and moisten with simple syrup. Spread a layer of moka buttercream. Repeat the steps génoise, simple syrup, buttercream with the remaining layers. Spread a smooth layer of buttercream over the top and sides of the cake.

Decorate by placing three strips of coffee marzipan approximately 2 in/5 cm wide and 2 in/5 cm apart across the top of the cake. With a pastry bag and fluted tip, pipe decorative lines of buttercream along the sides of the marzipan. This cake has an austere yet elegant style.

In this volume dedicated to nouvelle pastry making, the moka is the only cake assembled by applying buttercream free form with a palette knife. This is an important technique often used in classic pastry making, although it is now considered somewhat antiquated compared to the faster procedures followed today, such as the following:

1. Assembling sheets of cakes in cake frames the size of full or half sheet pans.
2. Assembling cakes in cakes rings of various diameters and heights.

These are perhaps the most expedient procedures for assembling cakes with lighter cream and mousse fillings.

Coffee Buttercream Cake No. 2
Moka

This Moka is assembled in a cake ring 1 1/3–1.5 in/ 3.5–4 cm high.

Place the ring on a cake cardboard. Set a layer of biscuit inside the ring, and moisten with coffee simple syrup. Spread a thin layer of coffee buttercream. Repeat the steps of biscuit, simple syrup, and buttercream until three layers of biscuit are used. Finish by spreading a smooth layer of buttercream flush to the top of the ring. Refrigerate. (Using the ring results in very even layering.)

Glaze the top of the cake with freshly heated coffee fondant that is warm, not hot. Remove the cake ring by heating it with a propane torch. Press candied almonds around the side of the cake. On top, place two flowers and three leaves of molded sugar cooked to the caramel stage. Use a paper cone to write the inscription "Moka" on top of the cake. This is one way of giving a modern touch to a classic cake.

Coffee Buttercream Cake No. 3
Moka

This moka is assembled on a sheet pan. A cake frame may be used to make it easier to achieve very even layering and to unmold.

Superimpose three sheets of biscuit or génoise, each moistened with coffee (or other flavor) simple syrup and layered with buttercream. Refrigerate.

Roll out a sheet of marzipan the same size as the top of the cake and place it on the cake. Unmold the cake. Heat a serrated knife with hot water and cut the cake into smaller square or rectangular cakes, or individual portions. Spread a thin layer of buttercream around the sides of each cake. Decorate by dusting over a plastic stencil with cocoa powder. Remove the stencil and place a pastry shop label on top. Wrap gold paper foil around the side. This is a quick and elegant way to construct and decorate the moka.

Assembling in Cake Rings

Photo 1: Place the ring over a cake cardboard. Use a hand scraper or rubber spatula to spread the filling around and against the inside of the ring. Only the filling is seen around the sides of the finished cake for a clean presentation.

Photo 2: Place a layer of biscuit or génoise inside the cake ring and moisten with simple syrup flavored to taste. Spread a layer of the mousse or cream filling. Cover with a second layer of biscuit or génoise, moistened with simple syrup. Smooth the filling flush to the top of the ring. Refrigerate.

Depending on personal taste and the height of the ring, two or three layers of biscuit or génoise can be used. The top layer is always made with the filling, unless otherwise indicated.

After the cake has set up, remove the ring by heating it with a propane torch.

Diagram labels:
- Italian meringue carmelized with a hot iron and coated with apricot glaze
- A medley of cubed fresh or poached fruit
- Pastry cream
- Puff pastry base

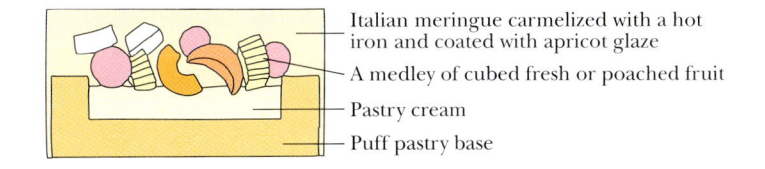

Ingot
Lingot

This cake is prepared in two stages. First, line a tart strip frame with a sheet of fresh puff pastry (puff pastry trimmings may be used).

Dock the dough, then let it rest in the refrigerator for at least one half hour before baking. Line the rested shell with parchment paper and pie weights. Blind bake it three fourths of the way, remove the weights and paper, and finish baking the shell. Cool.

Brush the base of the cooled shell with apricot glaze. Fill with pastry cream lightened with chantilly. Cover with assorted fresh or poached fruit such as apricots, strawberries, peaches, cherries, pears, kiwi, or mandarin orange sections. Cut the strip into cakes serving 4–10. Place each cake on a cake cardboard wider than the shell. Cover the top and sides of each cake with freshly made Italian meringue, smoothing it to obtain very straight sides. Refrigerate the cakes to set the meringue.

After chilling, place the cakes in a very hot oven for a few seconds so the meringue forms a crust. Sprinkle the top and sides with confectioners' sugar. Caramelize the sugar with a hot iron, being careful to maintain the straight edges. Coat with apricot glaze. Place a pastry shop label on top.

Chef's Note: *If using fresh fruit in the ingot and strawberry diablotin cakes, refrigerate but do not freeze. Freezing would break down the texture of the fruit, making the cakes soggy and watery after defrosting.*

Strawberry Diablotin Cake
Diablotin aux Fraises

This cake is assembled on full or half sheet pans and cut into smaller cakes of desired size.

Prepare three sheets of biscuit or mousseline génoise 1/2 in/1 cm thick that have been baked on parchment paper. Spread coating chocolate over one of the sheets of biscuit or génoise. After the chocolate sets, turn the sheet over and peel off the parchment paper. Moisten lightly with a simple syrup flavored to taste with vanilla, rum, or kirsch. Spread a layer of diablotin cream and scatter strawberries over the cream. Cover with a second layer of biscuit or génoise, moistened with simple syrup. Spread a second layer of the cream, scattering strawberries on top. Cover with the third layer of biscuit or génoise, moistened with simple syrup. Spread a thin layer of pastry cream over the top of the cake. Refrigerate, but do not freeze, as noted above.

Heat a serrated knife with hot water and cut the cake into smaller square or rectangular cakes or individual portions. Sprinkle the top of each cake with crystallized sugar. Caramelize the sugar using a propane torch. This step can be repeated if necessary. Place a pastry shop label on top.

Chef's Note: *The strawberries in the diablotin cake can be replaced with wild strawberries, raspberries, or bananas. This cake is delicate, but excellent.*

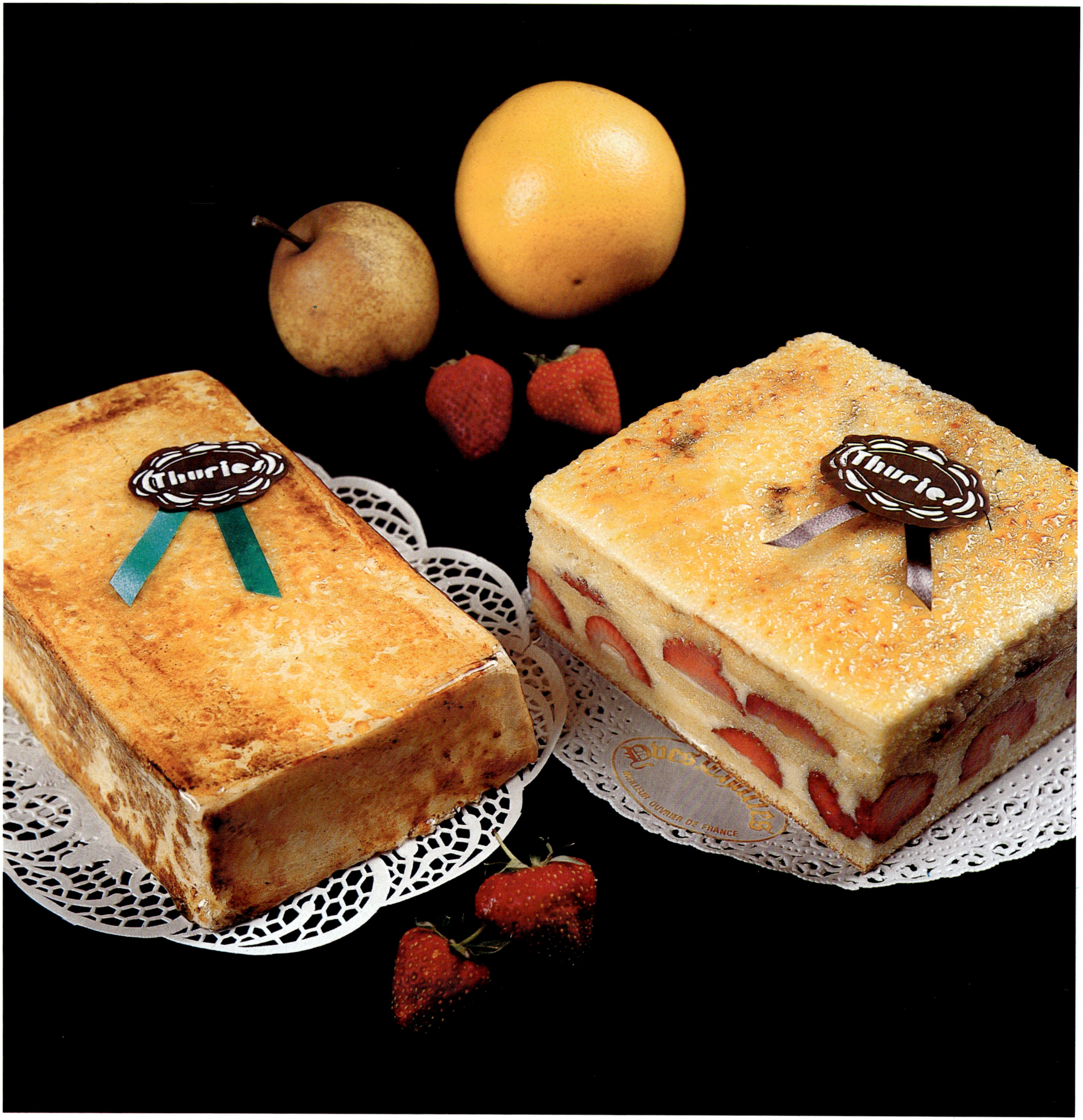
MEILLEUR OUVRIER DE FRANCE

Diablotin Cake Cream
Crème à Diablotin

gelatin sheets	5	5
pastry cream	35 oz	1,000 g
cream, whipped	14 oz	400 g
rum, vanilla, or kirsch to taste		

Cover the gelatin sheets with very cold water to soften. Reheat a finished pastry cream, stirring it constantly over low heat.

Remove the cream from the heat, squeeze the excess water from the gelatin sheets, and stir into the hot cream until melted.

Set the cream aside to cool, stirring occasionally. Just before the cream sets, add the flavoring or liqueur. Gently fold in the whipped cream.

This cream should be used shortly after it is prepared.

Chocolate Cream Cake
Diavolos

This cake is assembled in a cake frame 13.5–21.5 in/ 35–55 cm and 1.5 in/4 cm high. The finished sheet cake is cut into smaller cakes.

Prepare two layers of joconde biscuit. Spread a thin layer of coating chocolate on one joconde layer. After the chocolate sets, turn the joconde over and place it inside the frame. Peel off the parchment paper. Moisten the joconde with vanilla or rum simple syrup. Prepare a chocolate chantilly cream and fill the frame half-full. Refrigerate.

Prepare a vanilla or rum chantilly and fill it to 1/2 in/ 1 cm from the top of the frame. Cover with a second sheet of joconde biscuit, moistened with simple syrup. Spread a layer of chantilly, smoothing it flush to the top of the frame. Freeze.

Chef's Note: *The chantilly will hold up longer by adding two to four gelatin sheets per 34 fl oz/1 L crème fraîche or heavy cream. Melt the softened gelatin in the flavoring heated before whipping.*

Run a knife around the inside of the frame to release the cake. Remove the frame, lifting it straight up. Roll out a sheet of marzipan to cover the top of the cake. Cut the sheet cake into smaller cakes. Place a stencil with a decoration or logo of the pastry shop over the cake. Dust with cocoa powder or use a spray gun filled with chocolate for a velvet-textured finish (see page 35).

Facing Page: Ingot, Strawberry Diablotin Cake

Modern French Pastry

- Special milk chocolate coating
- Coffee mousse
- Almond génoise moistened with coffee simple syrup

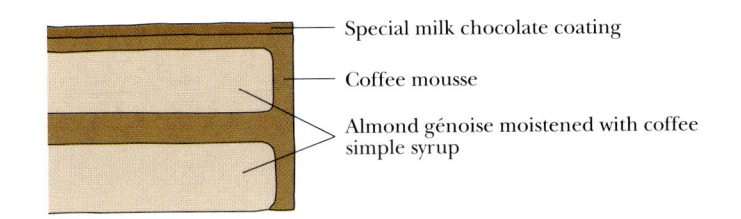

Coffee Almond Cake
Romanoff

This cake resembles a contemporary moka. It is assembled in a 1 1/3 in/3.5 cm high cake ring with two layers of génoise and mousse each, or in a 1.5–2 1/3 in/4–6 cm high ring, with three layers of each.

Prepare two or three layers of almond génoise, trimming them a bit smaller than the diameter of the ring. Place the cake ring on a cake cardboard. Spread a thin layer of coffee mousse on the base and up against the inside the ring. Place a layer of génoise inside the ring, moistened with coffee simple syrup. Spread a fairly thick layer of mousse. Cover with a second layer of génoise, moistened liberally with coffee simple syrup. Spread and smooth a layer of the mousse flush to the top of the ring. For taller rings, follow the same procedure, adding a third layer of mousse and génoise. Refrigerate.

While still in the ring, coat the top of the cake with special milk chocolate coating (see page 5). Using a knife, scrape off any excess coating from the edge of the ring to obtain a clean finish. Remove the ring by heating it with a propane torch. Cut the cardboard base flush to the edge of the cake and place it on a decorative gold-colored cardboard.

Because this cake is decorated simply, it is important to give it a clean, sharp finish. Decorate with piping chocolate using a paper cone. Top with either a pastry shop label or molded sugar flowers and leaves.

Coffee Mousse
Mousse au Café

butter, softened	35 oz	1,000 g
coffee extract	7 oz	200 g
Italian meringue	35 oz	1,000 g

Whisk the softened butter and coffee extract until smooth and well combined. Whisk in one half (17.5 oz/500 g) of the cooled Italian meringue and blend well. With a rubber spatula or whisk, gently fold in the second half of the Italian meringue. This mousse should be used shortly after it is prepared.

Chef's Note: *It is also possible to add all of the Italian meringue in one step, folding it in gently. This will result in a lighter mousse. Although it would be too light for the coffee almond cake, it could be used as a filling for other pastries.*

Facing Page: Chocolate Cream Cake, Coffee Almond Cake

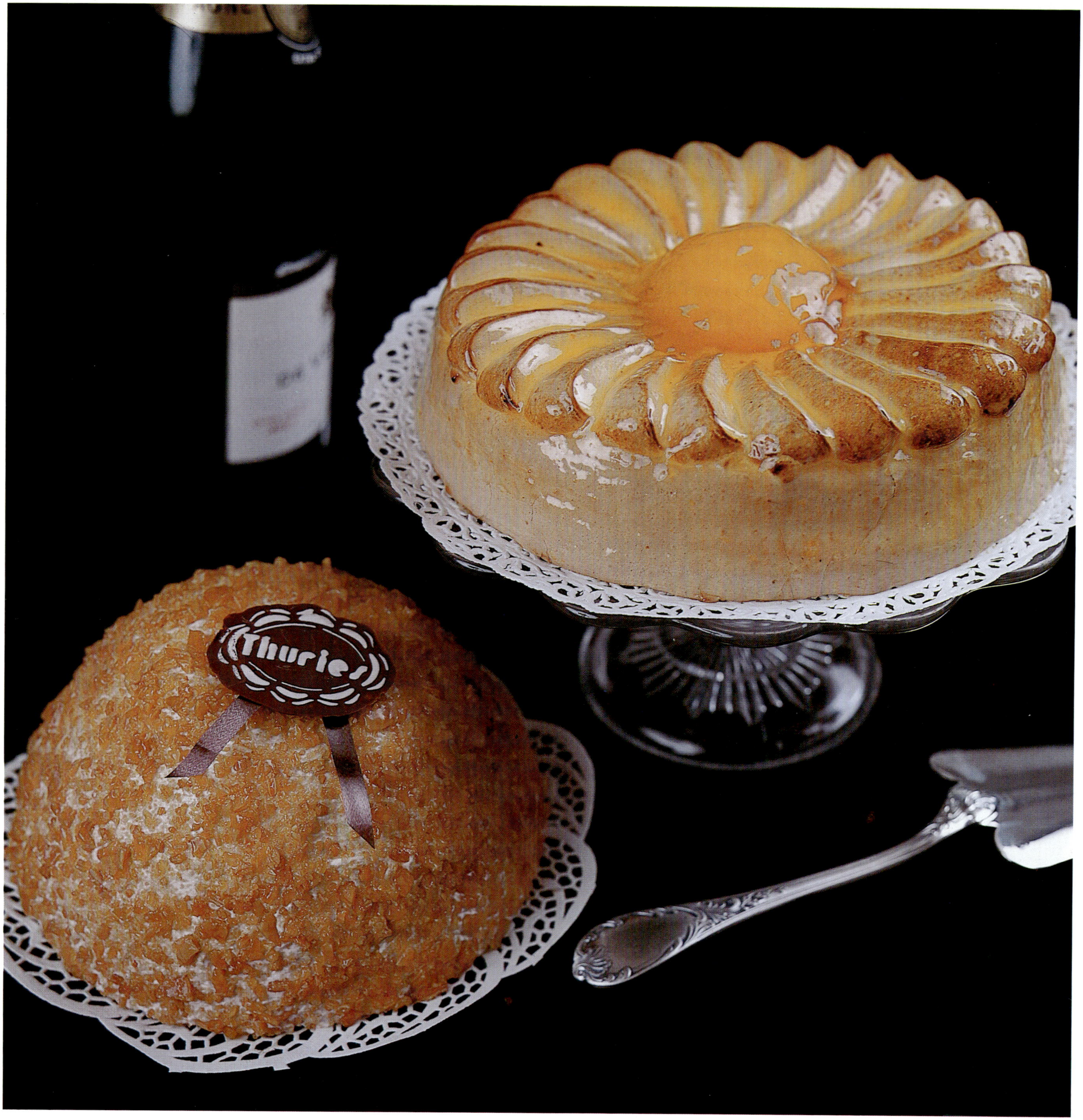
Thuries

Sovereign
Souverain

Cut an almond biscuit or génoise into three layers. Place the bottom layer on a cake cardboard and moisten with peach juice. Use the juice from canned or freshly poached peaches, which can be sweetened and thickened as needed by adding sugar and bringing to a boil.

Spread a layer of sovereign cream (recipe follows). Cover with a second layer of génoise or biscuit, moistened with the peach syrup. Spread a second layer of sovereign cream. Generously scatter slices of thinly sliced poached peaches over the cream. Cover with the third layer of génoise or biscuit, moistened with the syrup. Refrigerate.

Prepare an Italian meringue by cooking sugar and water to 250°F/121°C, while whipping egg whites to soft peaks. Pour the cooked sugar in a fine stream, whipping it into the egg whites.

Spread the Italian meringue over the top and sides of the cake. With a pastry bag and Saint Honoré tip (flat tip with a slit), pipe out a petal pattern on the top of the cake. Place the cake in a hot oven for a few seconds for the meringue to form a crust and brown lightly. Place a poached peach half on top of the cake. Coat with apricot glaze.

Angels' Cake
Pain des Anges

This cake is assembled upside down in a half-sphere mold.

Prepare sheets of mousseline génoise (see page 88) or biscuit; they should be supple and tender enough to conform to the mold without cracking.

Line the mold with the mousseline génoise or biscuit, trimming it flush to the top of the rim. Spread a layer of coffee buttercream inside. Fill with babas (miniature or pieces) macerated in rum syrup. Spread a thin layer of coffee buttercream and cover with biscuit or génoise. Spread a thin layer of coating chocolate. Refrigerate.

Remove the cake by heating the mold with a propane torch or by dipping it in hot water. Spread a thin layer of buttercream and press craquelin onto it. Place a pastry shop label on top.

Sovereign Cream
Crème à Souverain

almond paste	14 oz	400 g
pastry cream	17.5 oz	500 g
kirsch	2 oz	50 g

Combine the almond paste and pastry cream until smooth. Stir in the kirsch.

Facing Page: Angels' Cake, Sovereign

Black Rose, Cherry Almond Cake

Plastic chocolate rose and leaves

Chocolate nonpareils

Chocolate biscuit moistened with Cognac simple syrup

Chocolate mousse

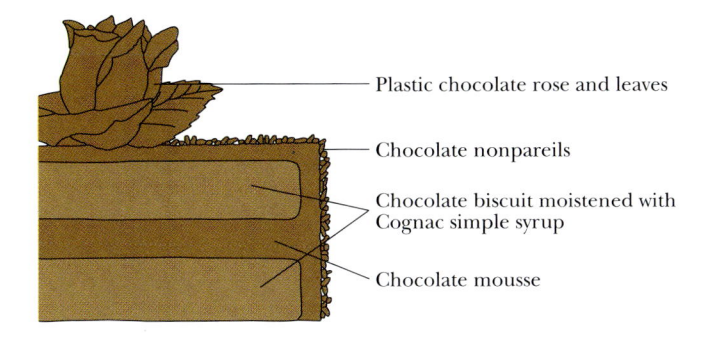

Black Rose
Rose Noire

This cake is assembled in a 1 1/3 in/3.5 cm high cake ring.

Prepare layers of chocolate biscuit slightly smaller than the ring.

Place the cake ring on a cardboard. Spread a thin layer of chocolate mousse on the base and a thick layer around the inside of the ring. Cover with a layer of biscuit, moistened with Cognac simple syrup. Spread a fairly thick layer of the mousse. Cover with a second layer of biscuit, moistened with Cognac simple syrup. Spread and smooth chocolate mousse flush to the rim of the ring. Refrigerate.

Remove the cake ring by heating it with a propane torch. Trim the cardboard even to the base of the cake. Press chocolate nonpareils on the top and sides of the cake. Place the cake on a gold-colored cardboard. Decorate the top with a plastic chocolate rose and leaves and a pastry shop label.

Chocolate Mousse
Mousse au Chocolate

butter, softened	35 oz	1,000 g
ganache	2 lbs 10.5 oz	1,200 g
Italian meringue	28 oz	800 g

Use a whisk to combine the softened butter and ganache. Add 10.5 oz/300 g of the Italian meringue and whisk smooth. Gently fold in the remaining Italian meringue.

Almond Buttercream
Crème au Beurre aux Amandes

marzipan	17.5 oz	500 g
kirsch	3.5 oz	100 g
buttercream	35 oz	1,000 g

Soften the marzipan by beating in the kirsch. Use a whisk to gradually incorporate the buttercream until smooth and aerated.

Cherry Almond Cake
Charleroy

This cake is assembled on full or half sheet pans. The finished cake is then cut into smaller cakes. Prepare two layers of dacquoise biscuit (recipe follows), approximately 1/2–3/4 in/1.5 cm thick. Bake them on sheet pans that have been buttered and floured or lined with parchment paper. Dust with confectioners' sugar just before baking in a low oven.

Coat one dacquoise biscuit with a thin layer of coating or couverture chocolate. After the chocolate has set, turn the dacquoise over and peel off the parchment

(Cherry Almond Cake recipe continued on page 31)

Modern French Pastry

paper. Spread a 1/2 in/1 cm thick layer of almond buttercream. Press candied cherries, macerated in kirsch, into the buttercream. Smooth buttercream over the cherries. Cover with the second layer of dacquoise biscuit.

With a sheet pan, press lightly but firmly on the cake to even out the layers. Spread a smooth layer of buttercream on top using a palette knife. Refrigerate.

Roll out a sheet of marzipan large enough to cover each finished cake. With a pastry brush, coat the marzipan with a thin layer of melted cocoa butter. Apply a thin layer of writing chocolate here and there over the cocoa butter. Run a wood graining tool across the marzipan to create a wood grain effect.

Heat a serrated knife with hot water and cut the sheet cake into smaller cakes of desired size. Cover the cakes with the decorated marzipan. Place a pastry shop label on top of each cake.

Dacquoise Biscuit
Biscuit Dacquoise

egg whites	35 oz	1,000 g
sugar	7 oz	200 g
almond powder	35 oz	1,000 g
confectioners' sugar	35 oz	1,000 g
flour	5.5 oz	150 g

Whisk the egg whites to soft peaks, then gradually add the sugar. Whisk to moderately firm peaks. Sift together almond powder, confectioners' sugar, and flour. Gently fold the sifted mixture into the whipped egg whites.

With a pastry bag and large tip, 1/2 in/1 cm diameter, pipe the batter onto sheet pans with turned-up sides and lined with parchment paper. Dust with confectioners' sugar.

Bake at 320°–350°F/160°–180°C.

Facing Page: Praline Dome, Angels' Hell Cake

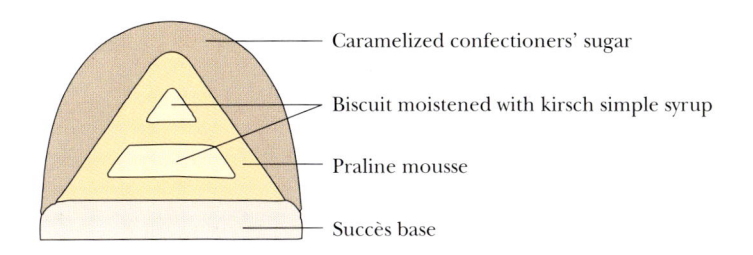

Praline Dome
Dôme au Praliné

Bake biscuit batter in half-sphere molds. Prepare succès bases the same diameter as the bases of the molds.

This cake is assembled in the same molds the biscuit was baked in. Unmold the biscuit and allow it to cool. Return the cooled biscuit to the mold. Using a serrated knife, cut a triangle from the center of the base of the biscuit.

Moisten the inside of the cut biscuit with kirsch simple syrup. Fill the cut sides with praline mousse. Cut off the tip of the biscuit triangle, place it over the mousse, and moisten liberally with kirsch simple syrup. Spread a second layer of mousse. Cover with a second layer of biscuit, moistening with the syrup. Smooth praline mousse to the rim of the mold. Refrigerate.

Unmold the cake onto a succès base the same diameter as the base of the mold. Dust the cake with confectioners' sugar and caramelize with a hot iron.

Chef's Note: *Some biscuit will be left over from each cake; this can be used for other pastries.*

Special Pastry Cream
Crème Pâtissière Spéciale

pastry cream	17.5 oz	500 g
Cointreau	2 oz	50 g
chantilly	7 oz	200 g

Whisk well-chilled pastry cream and Cointreau until smooth. Gently fold the chantilly into the mixture.

Praline Mousse
Mousse au Praliné

praline paste	9 oz	250 g
butter, softened	17.5 oz	500 g
sugar	17.5 oz	500 g
water	5.5 oz	150 g
egg whites	8	8

Whisk the praline paste and butter until smooth and well blended.

Prepare an Italian meringue by cooking the sugar and water to 250°F/121°C, while whipping the egg whites to soft peaks. Pour the cooked sugar in a fine stream, whipping it into the egg whites. Continue whipping until cool. Gently fold the butter/praline paste mixture into the meringue.

This mousse should be used shortly after it is prepared.

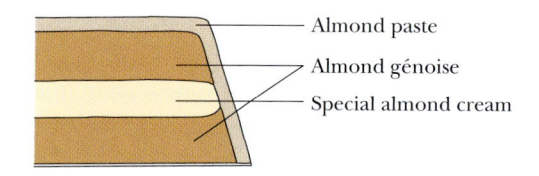

Angels' Hell Cake
Enfer des Anges

Cut an almond génoise in half horizontally. Place the bottom half on a cake cardboard. Moisten with Cointreau or Grand Marnier simple syrup. Spread a layer of special almond cream flavored with the same liqueur used in the simple syrup. Cover with the top half of the génoise and moisten with the simple syrup. Refrigerate.

Using a palette knife, cover the top and sides of the cake with almond paste softened with egg whites (recipe follows). Set the cake in a dry area for 24 hours for the paste to form a crust.

The next day, place the cake in a hot oven for a few minutes to further dry the almond paste and achieve a light golden color. After cooling, caramelize the surface using a propane torch. Brush with apricot glaze to create a sheen.

Almond Paste
Pâte d'Amandes Crue

almond	35 oz	1,000 g
sugar	2 lbs 6.5 oz	1,100 g
egg whites	10	10

Grind the almonds and sugar to a powder. Add the egg whites until well combined.

Chef's Note: *For the angels' hell cake, work just enough additional egg whites into the almond paste recipe above to create a spreadable consistency.*

Special Almond Cream
Crème Spéciale aux Amandes

almond paste	10.5 oz	300 g
butter, softened	5.5 oz	150 g
meringue	3 oz	80 g
Cointreau or Grand Marnier	2 oz	50 g

Whisk the almond paste and softened butter until well combined. Add the liqueur, then gently fold the Italian meringue into the mixture.

This cream should be used shortly after it is prepared.

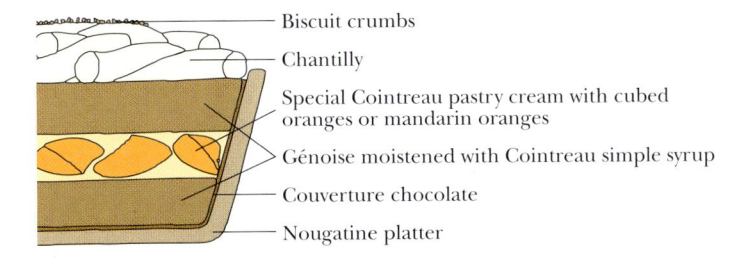

Diagram labels:
- Biscuit crumbs
- Chantilly
- Special Cointreau pastry cream with cubed oranges or mandarin oranges
- Génoise moistened with Cointreau simple syrup
- Couverture chocolate
- Nougatine platter

Milanese Gratin or Macaroni
Gratin Milanais ou Macaroni

Make a nougatine gratin dish by lining a génoise mold with a sheet of warm nougatine to take on the shape of the mold. Form two rounded handles out of nougatine. Use cooked sugar or caramel to attach the handles to opposite ends of the molded nougatine dish. Using a pastry brush, dab the inside bottom and sides with couverture or coating chocolate. The chocolate layer prevents the nougatine from becoming soggy from the moisture of the cake.

Place a 1/2 in/1 cm thick layer of génoise inside the nougatine mold, and moisten with Cointreau simple syrup. Spread a layer of special Cointreau pastry cream (see page 32). Scatter cubes of fresh orange or mandarin orange sections over the cream. Cover with the top layer of génoise, moistened with the simple syrup.

Fill a pastry bag and tip (1/4 in/6 mm diameter) with a firm chantilly. Holding the pastry bag perpendicular to the cake, pipe the chantilly in random curly strands to imitate pasta. Dust the chantilly with biscuit crumbs to simulate grated cheese.

Chef's Note: *The Milanese gratin cake can be made in any flavor. Choose a fruit that will match or complement the liqueur used in the simple syrup. For example, use cubed poached pears with kirsch simple syrup. This cake can also be made with more robust flavors such as coffee, hazelnut, or chocolate.*

Gratin (Variation)
Gratin (Variante)

Prepare a nougatine platter as for the Milanese gratin. Using a pastry brush, dab the interior with couverture or coating chocolate. Place a 1/2 in/1 cm layer of biscuit or génoise inside the nougatine mold. Moisten with kirsch or maraschino simple syrup. Spread a layer of Bavarian cream flavored the same as the simple syrup. Scatter cherries macerated in liqueur or griottes (small sour cherries) macerated in kirsch over the cream. Cover with a layer of génoise or biscuit, moistened with the simple syrup. Spread a second layer of Bavarian cream. Refrigerate.

Pipe chantilly with a pastry bag as for the Milanese gratin, to simulate pasta. Sprinkle with biscuit crumbs to finish.

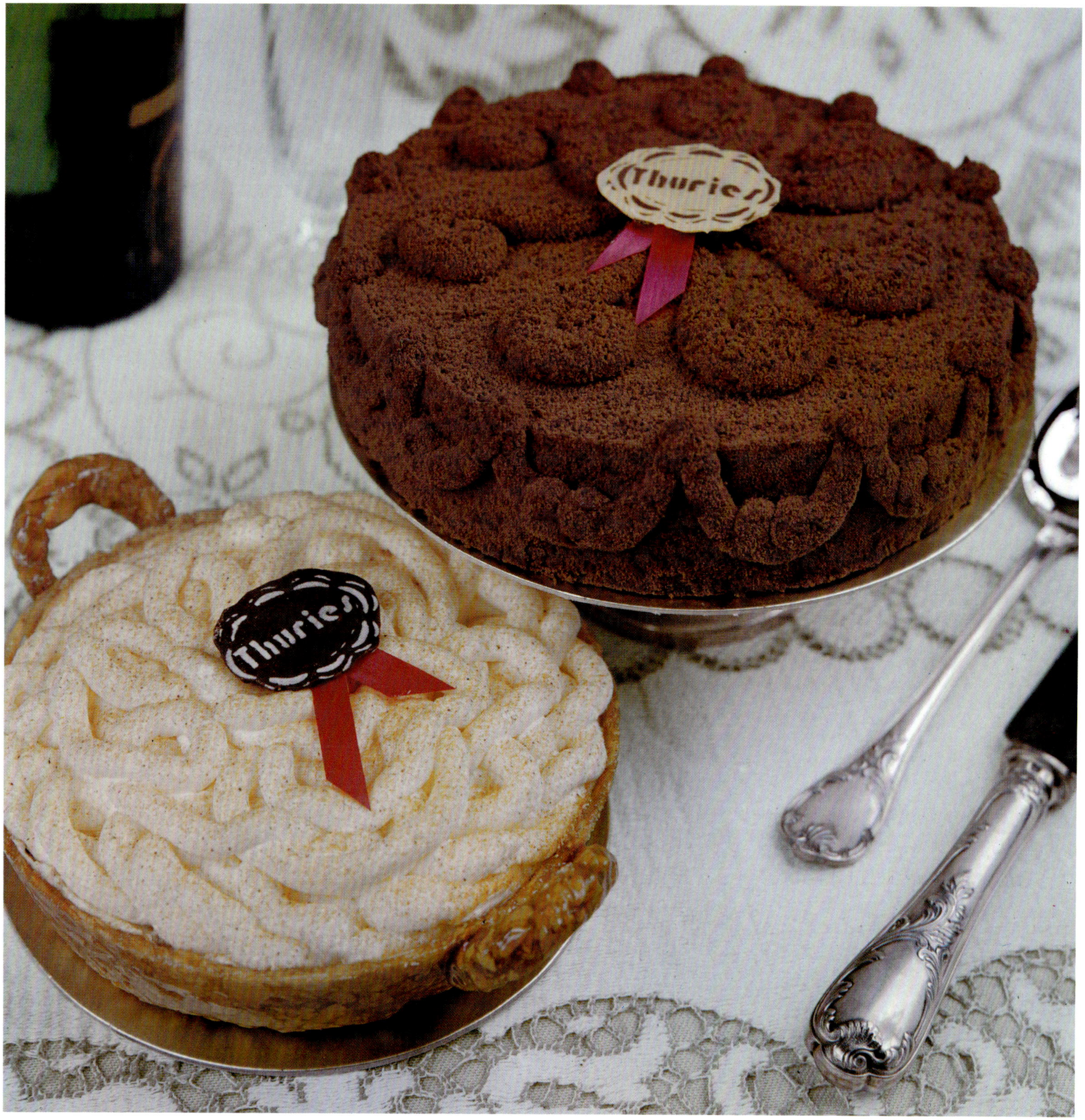
Thuries
Thuries

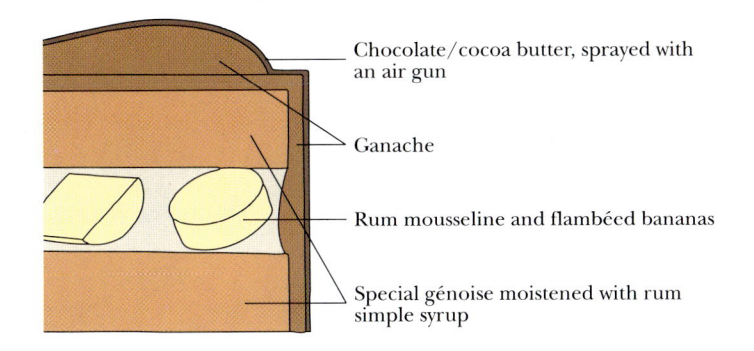

Banana Chocolate Cake
Bananier

Prepare a rum simple syrup by combining 7 oz/200 g rum per 34 fl oz/L simple syrup, 30° baume. Flambé bananas in rum and set them aside to cool.

Cut a special génoise in half horizontally. Moisten the bottom layer with rum simple syrup. Spread a thick layer of rum mousseline. Blanket the mousseline with flambéed bananas. Cover with the second layer of génoise, moistened with the simple syrup. Refrigerate.

Spread and smooth a layer of ganache over the top and sides of the cake. With a pastry bag and plain tip, decorate the top and sides of the cake with additional ganache, if desired. Freeze.

When the cake is frozen, spray it with chocolate/cocoa butter using a spray gun to create a velvet texture. Place a pastry shop label on top.

Special Génoise
Génoise Spéciale

eggs	22	22
sugar	17.5 oz	500 g
flour	17.5 oz	500 g
cornstarch	3.5 oz	100 g
TPT	3.5 oz	100 g
butter, melted	5.5 oz	150 g

Warm the eggs and sugar, whipping until pale and aerated. Sift together the flour, cornstarch, and TPT. Gently fold the sifted ingredients into the whipped egg/sugar batter. Fold a bit of whipped egg and sugar into the butter to lighten before folding it into the batter.

Rum Mousseline Cream
Crème Mousseline au Rhum

marzipan	9 oz	250 g
rum	7 oz	200 g
butter, softened	17.5 oz	500 g
pastry cream	17.5 oz	500 g

In the bowl of an electric mixer, use the paddle attachment to soften the marzipan with the rum. Add the softened butter and pastry cream. After blending, replace the paddle with the whisk attachment and whip until well aerated.

Sprayed Chocolate
Veloutage au Pistolet

Melt couverture chocolate and combine it with half its weight in melted cocoa butter. Strain the mixture through a fine-mesh strainer and place in spray gun. The mixture should be used while very warm for an even coating. It is important that the cake or pastry to be sprayed is frozen to achieve a velvety texture. If the cake is not cold enough, the coating will be smooth. The cake or pastry can be sprayed two to three times until the desired effect is achieved. If applying more than one coating, the pastry must be refrozen between each spraying for a textured appearance.

Facing Page: Milanese Gratin or Macaroni, Banana Chocolate Cake

36 *Modern French Pastry*

Special milk chocolate coating

Meringue disks

Rum baba

Coffee buttercream

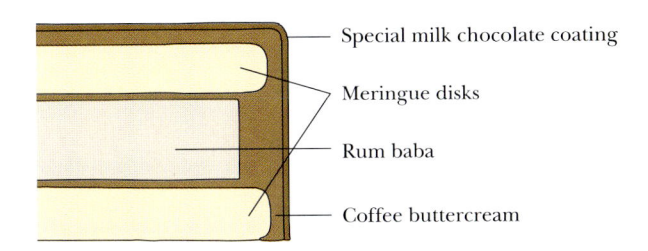

Coffee Rum Cake
Bayard

This cake is assembled in a 2 1/3 in/6 cm cake ring. Prepare two meringue disks the same diameter as the cake ring. Macerate in rum syrup a layer of baba that has been baked in a cake ring 1 in/3 cm smaller than the diameter of the cake ring.

Place the first meringue disk inside the cake ring. Spread a thin layer of coffee buttercream over the disk and add additional buttercream around the inside of the ring. Cover with the macerated baba. Spread a layer of buttercream. Cover with a second meringue disk. Fill the ring with the buttercream, smoothing it flush to the rim. Refrigerate.

Remove the cake ring by heating it with a propane torch. Smooth the buttercream around the sides of the cake, if needed. Coat the top and sides of the cake with special milk chocolate coating (see page 9). Decorate with piping chocolate using a paper cone. Place a pastry shop label on top.

Chef's Note: *The baba layer can be replaced with a layer of brioche mousseline; the procedure remains the same.*

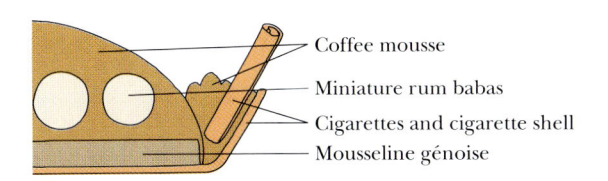

Coffee mousse

Miniature rum babas

Cigarettes and cigarette shell

Mousseline génoise

Saint Hubert
Saint-Hubert

To prepare the base for this cake, spread cigarette batter on a buttered sheet pan to the desired size, allowing an extra 2 in/5 cm for the edge. Bake in a hot oven until golden. Upon removing the disk from the oven, shape it immediately by placing it inside a génoise mold and gently pushing a second, smaller mold on top so that it takes the form of the mold. Remove the base only after it is completely cooled.

Prepare small cigarettes and store them in an airtight container.

Prepare the Saint Hubert coffee mousse (see page 38). Fill a half-sphere or bombe mold (or a small bowl) half full with the mousse. Set miniature babas, macerated in rum syrup, into the mousse. Fill the mold to 1/2 in/1 cm from the top with the mousse. Cover with a layer of génoise the diameter of the base of the mold. Freeze.

Unmold the bombe inside the prepared base. Decorate the side of the cake with alternating chantilly rosettes and cigarettes to imitate a crown.

Facing Page: Coffee Rum Cake, Saint Hubert

Saint Hubert Coffee Mousse
Mousse au Café Saint-Hubert

sugar	14 oz	400 g
water	4 oz	120 g
egg whites	8	8
coffee extract	5.5 oz	150 g
crème fraîche	17.5 oz	500 g

Prepare an Italian meringue by cooking the sugar and water to 250°F/121°C while whipping the egg whites to soft peaks. Pour the cooked sugar in a fine stream, whipping it into the egg whites. Pour in the coffee extract and continue whipping until cool.

Whip the crème fraîche to soft peaks and fold it into the coffee meringue.

This mousse should be used shortly after it is prepared.

Raspberry or Strawberry Saint Hubert
Saint-Hubert aux Framboises ou aux Fraises

The procedure for preparing raspberry or strawberry Saint Hubert is the same as for the coffee Saint Hubert. The coffee mousse is replaced with a fruit mousse of choice. The miniature babas are replaced with fresh raspberries or strawberries. The decorations around the sides are made with chantilly and raspberries or strawberries.

Special Cigarette Batter
Pâte à Cigarettes Spéciale

This batter is especially suitable for making various sized tulips (cups).

flour	17.5 oz	500 g
confectioners' sugar	19.5 oz	550 g
egg whites	10	10
few drops of vanilla extract		

Sift together the flour and confectioners' sugar. With a wooden spoon, stir in the egg whites and vanilla extract. It is best to rest the batter before using it.

Spread a thin circle of batter to the size needed, on a sheet pan. Bake in a hot oven until golden. Shape the cigarettes or tulips upon removing them from the oven, while they are still hot and pliable. If they should cool before molding, return them to the oven for a few seconds until soft to avoid cracking. Store in a cool area in airtight containers.

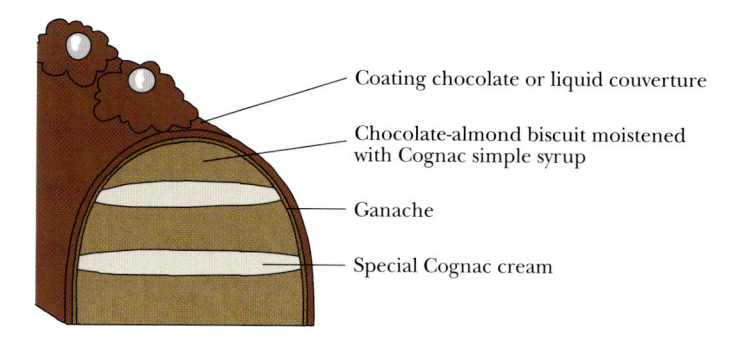

Labels: Coating chocolate or liquid couverture; Chocolate-almond biscuit moistened with Cognac simple syrup; Ganache; Special Cognac cream

Cherub
Angelot

Bake an almond biscuit batter, lightly flavored with chocolate, in long, rounded molds (gouttière). Prepare a ganache and special Cognac cream.

After cooling, use a serrated knife to even out the bottom layer of the biscuit. Spread a dollop of ganache on a cake cardboard to attach the biscuit and prevent it from slipping. Cut the biscuit in three or four layers horizontally, leaving the base on the cardboard. Moisten the base layer with Cognac simple syrup. Spread a layer of Cognac cream. Cover with the second layer of biscuit and moisten with Cognac simple syrup. Spread a layer of Cognac cream. Repeat this step—biscuit, syrup, Cognac cream—finishing by reconstructing the biscuit with the rounded layer on top. Moisten the top rounded layer with Cognac simple syrup. Spread and smooth a layer of ganache over the top and sides of the cake. Refrigerate.

Cut the cake into smaller cakes. Place each cake over a cooling rack and glaze with liquid couverture or coating chocolate. Using a pastry bag and fluted tip, pipe a decoration with ganache.

Almond Biscuit Flavored with Chocolate
Biscuit aux Amandes Parfumé au Chocolate

almond paste	26.5 oz	750 g
confectioners' sugar	17.5 oz	500 g
egg yolks	20	20
eggs	5	5
flour	3.5 oz	100 g
cornstarch	3.5 oz	100 g
cocoa powder	6.5 oz	180 g
butter, melted	5 oz	150 g
egg whites	20	20

In the bowl of an electric mixer, use the paddle attachment to whip the almond paste, confectioners' sugar, and egg yolks. Gradually whip in the whole eggs.

Sift together the flour, cornstarch, and cocoa powder. Add the dry ingredients to the mixer. Pour in the melted, but not hot, butter.

Whip the egg whites to firm peaks and gently fold them into the batter. Fill buttered, floured, rounded (gouttière) molds three quarters full.

Bake in a moderate oven. Unmold immediately after baking.

Special Cognac Cream
Crème Spéciale au Cognac

almond paste	17.5 oz	500 g
Cognac	2.5 oz	75 g
cocoa powder, (optional)	3.5 oz	100 g
butter, softened	3.5 oz	100 g

In the bowl of an electric mixer, use the paddle attachment to soften the almond paste with the Cognac. Add the cocoa powder, if used, then the butter. Whip until smooth.

Chef's Note: *This cream can be made in any flavor, such as Cointreau, kirsch, Grand Marnier, or rum. The cocoa powder is optional; if omitted, the procedure remains the same.*

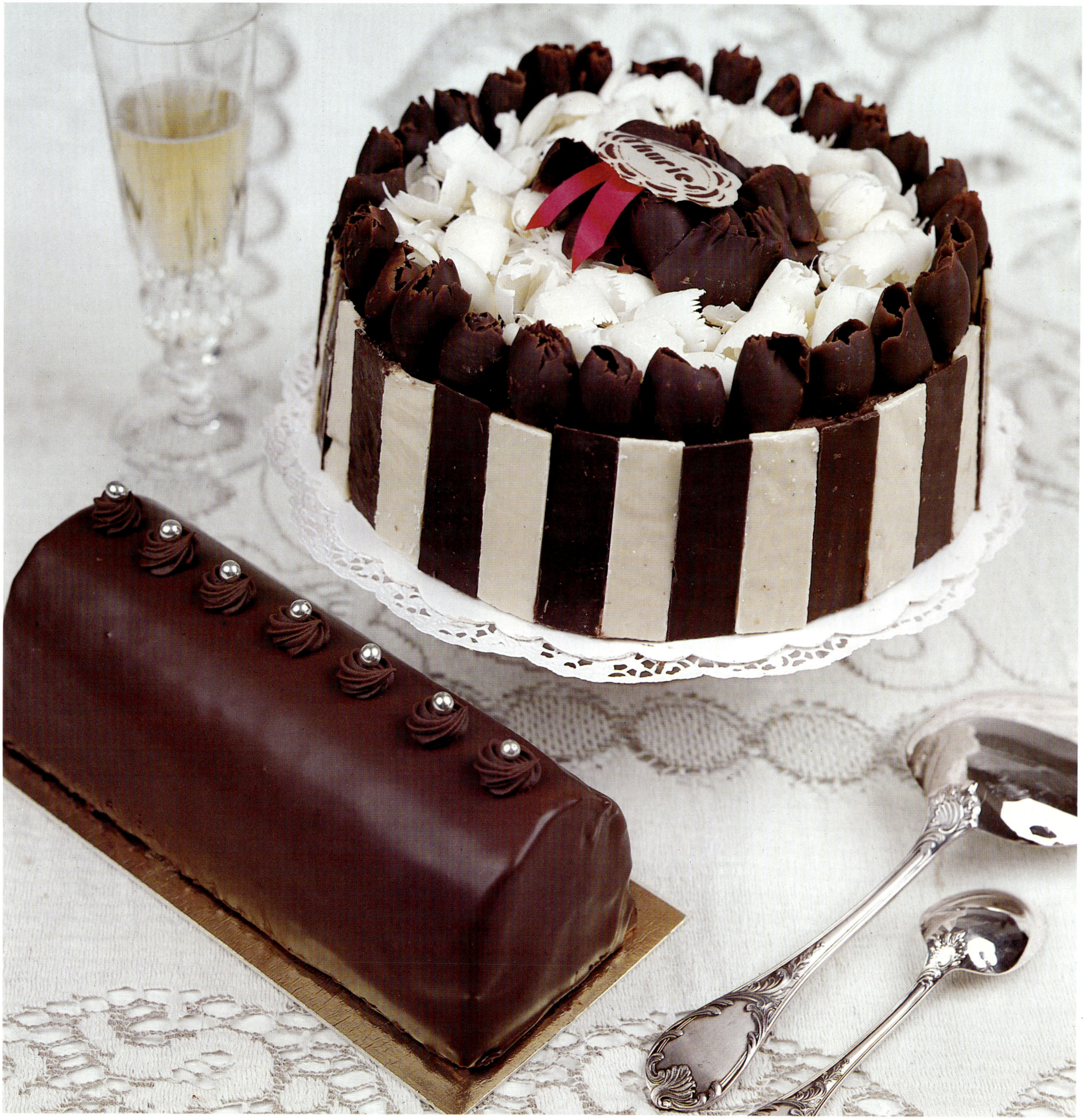
Thurie

Chocolate shavings
Chocolate border
Hazelnut progrès
Biscuit moistened with Cognac simple syrup
Cognac ganache

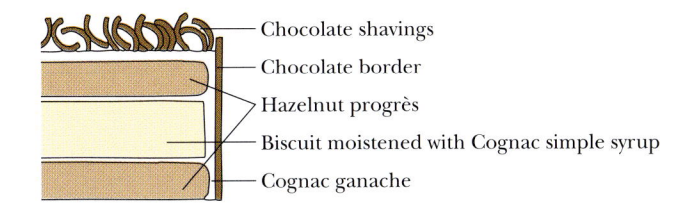

Charlemagne

This cake is assembled most easily in a cake ring, but can be constructed free form, layered with a palette knife. Prepare two hazelnut progrès bases to the size needed. Prepare a layer of biscuit the same size.

Place a progrès base on a cake cardboard. Spread a fairly thick layer of Cognac ganache. Cover with a layer of biscuit, moistened liberally with Cognac simple syrup. Spread a layer of ganache and cover with the second progrès disk, turned over, flat side up. Spread and smooth a layer of ganache over the top and sides of the cake.

On a sheet of clear plastic, spread a 1/16 in/2 mm thick layer of tempered couverture chocolate. As the chocolate begins to set, cut small, even rectangles with a hot knife. Following the same procedure, prepare a second strip of rectangles in white chocolate. After both strips of chocolate are completely set, remove the rectangles from the plastic and attach them around the cake with ganache, alternating the two colors.

Decorate the top of the cake with white and dark chocolate curls prepared using a vegetable peeler (see page 43). Place a pastry shop label on top.

Hazelnut Progrès
Progrès aux Noisettes

TPT	17.5 oz	500 g
progrès trimmings	3.5 oz	100 g
flour	1 oz	25 oz
egg whites	12	12
sugar	1.5 oz	50 g

Combine and sift the TPT (see page 12), progrès trimmings, and flour. Whip the egg whites to soft peaks with the sugar. Gently sprinkle and fold the dry ingredients into the whipped egg whites. Using a pastry bag and 1/2 in/1 cm diameter tip, pipe spirals of batter onto sheet pans that have been buttered and floured or lined with parchment paper.

Bake in a low oven. Store the disks in a cool, dry area.

Special Coating Chocolate
Pâte à Glacer Spéciale

coating chocolate	35 oz	1,000 g
couverture chocolate	14 oz	400 g
peanut oil	5 oz	150 g

Melt the coating and couverture chocolates with the oil. For best results use this coating between 104°–106°F/40°–41°C.

Facing Page: Cherub, Charlemagne

42   *Modern French Pastry*

Chocolate Shavings
Copeaux Chocolate

Chocolate shavings made with a vegetable peeler

Photo 1: The same technique is used for dark, milk, or white chocolate. Slightly warm a block of chocolate. Scrape off curls with the tip of a vegetable peeler.

Photo 2: The shavings are very delicate and should be handled carefully when placing them on the cake or pastry to be decorated.

Shavings made with a pastry cutter

Photo 3: Slightly warm a block of chocolate. Scrape off curls with a pastry cutter. The size of the curl can be adjusted according to the angle made with the cutter while scraping.

Photo 4: Curls made with a pastry cutter tend to be more even, thicker, and stronger than those made with a vegetable peeler.

Regardless of which method is used, the most important step is to warm the block of chocolate to just the right temperature. If the chocolate is too cool, the chocolate will crumble. If too warm, the chocolate will melt. Either way it will be difficult if not impossible to form curls. This procedure does not work in a warm area.

Other procedures: Spread melted couverture chocolate onto a pastry marble. When it begins to set, scrape off curls with a pastry cutter or the tip of a vegetable peeler. This technique offers good results but requires the time to melt and space to spread the chocolate.

Gemini
Gémini

This cake is assembled in a special cone-shaped mold. Prepare sheets of joconde biscuit.

Line the mold with the joconde biscuit, lightly moisten with coffee simple syrup. Fill the base and spread the sides of the mold with coffee mousse. Scatter coffee liqueur-filled candies or sprinkle coffee liqueur over the mousse. Cover with trimmings of joconde biscuit liberally moistened with coffee simple syrup. Spread a second layer of coffee mousse and again scatter liqueur-filled drops or sprinkle with coffee liqueur. Continue to fill the mold to the rim, alternating layers of coffee mousse sprinkled with coffee liqueur drops or liqueur, and biscuit moistened with coffee simple syrup. The last layer is made with biscuit. Refrigerate.

Unmold the cake and smooth the sides with ganache, if necessary. Refrigerate if the ganache is applied. Glaze the cake with special coating chocolate or liquid couverture.

Coffee Mousse
Mousse au Café

butter, softened	35 oz	1,000 g
coffee extract	7 oz	200 g
sugar	35 oz	1,000 g
water	10.5 oz	300 g
egg whites	16	16

Combine the softened butter and coffee extract. Prepare an Italian meringue by cooking the sugar and water to 250°F/121°C, while whipping the egg whites to soft peaks. Pour the cooked sugar in a fine stream, whipping it into the egg whites. Continue whipping until cool. Gently fold the Italian meringue into the coffee/butter mixture.

Modern French Pastry

- Chocolate shavings
- Chocolate border
- Chocolate mousse
- Chocolate biscuit moistened with Cognac simple syrup

Chocodream
Chocorêve

This cake is assembled in a 1 1/3 in/3.5 cm high cake ring.

Prepare chocolate biscuit layers the same size as, or slightly smaller in diameter than, the cake ring.

Place a layer of biscuit inside the cake ring, moistened liberally with Cognac simple syrup. Spread a fairly thick layer of chocolate mousse. Cover with a second layer of chocolate biscuit. Fill the ring flush to the rim with chocolate mousse. Refrigerate.

Cut a strip of plastic 1.5 in/4 cm wide and as long as the circumference of the cake. On pastry marble, cover the plastic strip with tempered couverture chocolate approximately 1/16 in/2 mm thick. When the chocolate begins to set, wrap the strip around the side of the cake so the chocolate adheres to the cake. Wait until the chocolate has completely set before peeling off the plastic. The plastic can be left on to protect the chocolate until the time the cake is served. Cover the top of the cake with chocolate curls made using a pastry cutter or vegetable peeler.

Chocolate Mousse No. 1
Mousse au Chocolat

butter, softened	35 oz	1,000 g
egg yolks	12	12
crème fraîche	24.5 oz	700 g

Facing Page: Gemini, Chocodream, Majestic

couverture chocolate, chopped	35 oz	1,000 g
sugar	26.5 oz	750 g
water	8 oz	225 g
egg whites	12	12

Whip the softened butter and egg yolks until well blended. Bring the crème fraîche to a boil and pour it over the chopped chocolate. Stir until the chocolate is completely melted, then set aside to cool.

Prepare an Italian meringue by cooking the sugar and water to 250°F/121°C, while whipping the egg whites to soft peaks. Pour the cooked sugar in a fine stream, whipping it into the egg whites. Continue whipping until cool.

Combine the egg yolk/butter and chocolate/cream mixtures. Gently fold in the Italian meringue.

This mousse should be used shortly after it is prepared.

Chocolate Mousse No. 2
Mousse au Chocolat

ganache	35 oz	1,000 g
butter, softened	21 oz	600 g
rum or other liqueur	3.5 oz	100 g
egg whites	12	12
sugar	28 oz	800 g
water	8.5 oz	240 g

In the bowl of an electric mixer, use the paddle attachment to whip the ganache and softened butter. Add the rum.

Prepare an Italian meringue by cooking the sugar and water to 250°F/121°C, while whipping the egg whites to soft peaks. Pour the cooked sugar in a fine stream, whipping it into the egg whites. Continue whipping until cool.

Gently fold the cool meringue into the first part.

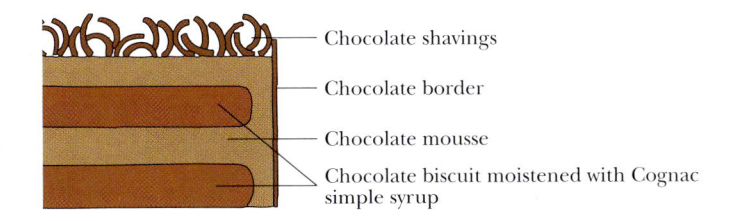

This mousse should be used shortly after it is prepared.

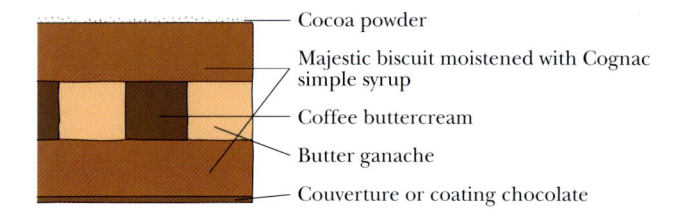

Majestic

This cake is assembled on a full or, more often, half sheet pan. Prepare two equal-sized layers of majestic biscuit.

Place one majestic biscuit layer on a sheet pan, moisten with Cognac simple syrup. Fill a pastry bag and tip (1/2 in/1 cm diameter) with buttered ganache. Fill a second pastry bag and tip (same size as the first) with coffee buttercream. Cover the biscuit by piping alternating lines of buttered ganache and buttercream. Cover with a second layer of biscuit, being careful not to shift the filling below. With a sheet pan, press straight down gently on the biscuit to even the layers. Moisten the top layer of biscuit with Cognac simple syrup. Smooth on a layer of ganache. Refrigerate.

Heat a serrated knife with hot water and cut into smaller square or rectangular cakes, or individual portions.

Dust the top with cocoa powder. Coat the two plain ends with coating or couverture chocolate. Leave the two ends with alternating filling exposed. Draw decorative lines in the cocoa powder on the top and place a pastry shop label at one corner.

Majestic Biscuit
Biscuit Majestic

TPT	35 oz	1,000 g
flour	6 oz	170 g
egg whites	28	28
coffee extract	5.5 oz	150 g

Sift together the TPT (see page 12) and flour.

Whip the egg whites to soft peaks. Add the coffee extract and continue to whip the whites to firm peaks. Gently fold the TPT/flour mixture into the whipped egg whites.

Spread the biscuit batter approximately 1/2 in/1 cm thick onto sheet pans with a raised edge and lined with parchment paper.

Bake at 400°F/200°C. This biscuit barely rises during baking.

After cooling, remove the parchment paper.

Cognac Simple Syrup
Sirop au Cognac

Combine 9 oz/250 g Cognac per 35 oz/1,000 g simple syrup, 30° baume.

Passion Fruit Supreme
Suprême au Fruit de la Passion

This cake is assembled following the same procedure given for the lemon supreme cake. Simply replace the lemon mousse with passion fruit mousse and moisten the biscuit with passion fruit simple syrup.

Decorate, omitting the poached lemon slices, by glazing the top of the cake with gelée containing crushed passion fruit seeds.

Passion Fruit Mousse
Mousse au Fruit de la Passion

gelatin sheets	12	12
passion fruit juice	21 oz	600 g
crème fraîche	14 oz	400 g
egg yolks	20	20
cornstarch	3 oz	80 g
sugar	21 oz	600 g
water	6.5 oz	180 g
egg whites	20	20
sugar	7 oz	200 g

Cover the gelatin sheets with very cold water to soften.

In a saucepan, combine the passion fruit juice, crème fraîche, egg yolks, and cornstarch. Stir constantly over the heat until the first bubbles break the surface then remove the pan from the heat. Squeeze out the excess water from the gelatin and stir into the hot cream until melted.

Prepare an Italian meringue by cooking the first sugar and the water to 250°F/121°C, while whipping the egg whites to soft peaks with the second sugar. Pour the cooked sugar in a fine stream, whipping it into the egg whites.

Gently fold the Italian meringue into the hot cream. This mousse should be used shortly after it is prepared.

Passion Fruit Simple Syrup
Sirop au Fruit de la Passion

passion fruit juice	14 oz	400 g
simple syrup, 30° baumé	21 oz	600 g
water	7 oz	200 g

Combine all ingredients.

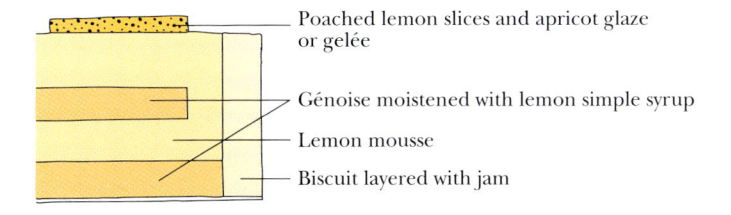

- Poached lemon slices and apricot glaze or gelée
- Génoise moistened with lemon simple syrup
- Lemon mousse
- Biscuit layered with jam

Lemon Supreme
Suprême au Citron

This cake is assembled in a 2 1/3 in/6 cm high cake ring. Line the inside of the ring with slices of biscuit joined with jam or gelée (see page 61). Place a layer of génoise inside the ring, moistened with lemon simple syrup. Fill the ring half-full with lemon mousse. Cover with a layer of génoise slightly smaller than the diameter of the ring, moistened with lemon simple syrup. Smooth the mousse flush to the top of the ring. Freeze.

Remove the cake ring. Place lemon slices poached in syrup on top of the cake. Brush the top and sides of the cake with apricot glaze.

Modern French Pastry

Lemon Mousse
Mousse au Citron

gelatin sheets	12	12
crème fraîche	21 oz	600 g
lemon juice	10.5 oz	300 g
lemon zest	2 oz	50 g
sugar	10.5 oz	300 g
cornstarch	2 oz	60 g
egg yolks	20	20
egg whites	20	20
sugar	12.5 oz	350 g

Cover the gelatin sheets with very cold water to soften. Bring the crème fraîche, lemon juice, and zests to a boil. Whisk the sugar, cornstarch, and egg yolks until thick and pale. Pour half the cream mixture into the egg mixture and return all to the saucepan with the remaining cream. Cook as for a pastry cream, stirring for a few minutes until thickened. Squeeze out the excess water from the gelatin sheets and stir them into the hot cream until melted.

Whip the egg whites with a small portion of the second sugar (12.5 oz/350 g). When the whites have nearly formed firm peaks, add the rest of the sugar. Gently fold the whipped egg whites into the warm cream.

This mousse should be used shortly after it is prepared.

Chef's Note*: It is possible to prepare an Italian meringue by cooking the sugar with 3.5 oz/100 g of water to 250°F/ 121°C and pouring it in gradually to the whipping whites after they have reached soft peaks. Continue whipping until cool. The Italian meringue makes for a more stable mousse.*

Lemon Simple Syrup
Sirop au Citron

lemon juice	12.5 oz	350 g
simple syrup	17.5 oz	500 g
water	5.5 oz	150 g

Combine all ingredients.

Blackcurrant Supreme
Suprême au Cassis

This cake is assembled in a 2 1/3 in/6 cm high cake ring. Line the inside of the ring halfway up with slices of biscuit layered with blackcurrant gelée (see page 61). Follow the diagram given for the borsalino cake (see page 50). Make the appropriate substitutions, replacing the wine mousse with blackcurrant mousse, and moisten the génoise with blackcurrant simple syrup.

Place a layer of génoise inside the lined cake ring. Moisten the génoise with blackcurrant simple syrup. Fill the ring half-full with blackcurrant mousse. Cover with a second layer of génoise slightly smaller in diameter than the ring, moistened liberally with blackcurrant simple syrup. Spread and smooth the mousse flush to the top of the ring. Freeze.

Remove the ring by heating it with a propane torch. Cover the top of the cake with fresh blackcurrants and brush with apricot glaze, or simply brush with blackcurrant gelée.

Chef's Note*: The blackcurrant supreme can also be assembled in a 1–1.5 in/3–4 cm high cake ring, in which case fill with only one bottom layer of génoise and one layer of mousse.*

Facing Page: Borsalino, Blackcurrent Supreme, Lemon Supreme

Blackcurrant Mousse No. 1
Mousse au Cassis

gelatin sheets	15	15
blackcurrant juice	21 oz	600 g
crème fraîche	28 oz	800 g
egg yolks	28	28
sugar	7 oz	200 g
cornstarch	2.5 oz	70 g
sugar	17.5 oz	500 g
water	5.5 oz	150 g
egg whites	28	28
red food coloring, as needed		

Cover the gelatin sheets with very cold water to soften.

Bring the blackcurrant juice, crème fraîche, egg yolks, sugar, and cornstarch to a boil, stirring constantly. Remove from heat.

Squeeze out the excess water from the gelatin sheets and stir them into the cream until completely melted.

Prepare an Italian meringue by cooking the second sugar and the water to 250°F/121°C, while whipping the egg whites to soft peaks. Pour the cooked sugar in a fine stream, whipping it into the egg whites. Add a few drops of red food coloring, whipping it in to the meringue. Gently fold the meringue into the hot cream.

This mousse should be used shortly after it is prepared.

Blackcurrant Mousse No. 2
Mousse au Cassis

gelatin sheets	15	15
blackcurrant juice	31.5 oz	900 g
crème fraîche	17.5 oz	500 g
egg yolks	20	20
cornstarch	2 oz	60 g
sugar	14 oz	400 g
water	4 oz	120 g
egg whites	20	20

Follow the same procedure as for Recipe 1, above.

Blackcurrant Simple Syrup
Sirop au Cassis

blackcurrant juice	17.5 oz	500 g
simple syrup	17.5 oz	500 g
water	10.5 oz	300 g

Combine all ingredients.

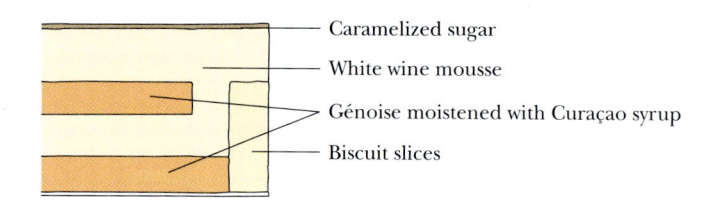

Borsalino

This cake is assembled in a 2 1/3 in/6 cm high cake ring. Line the cake ring two thirds of the way up with slices of biscuit layered with jam, jelly, or apricot glaze (see page 61).

Place a layer of génoise inside the lined ring. Moisten the génoise with Curaçao (or other liqueur) simple syrup. Fill the ring half-full with white wine mousse. Cover with a second layer of génoise, liberally moistened with simple syrup. The génoise can be moistened by dipping the entire layer in a pan of flavored simple syrup and turning it over into the ring, moistened side up. This is a quick way to evenly moisten the génoise. Smooth the mousse flush to the top of the ring. Freeze.

Remove the cake ring by heating it with a propane torch. Sprinkle sugar on the top of the cake and caramelize it with a hot iron. Repeat this step two or three times, using confectioners' sugar the last time, until the surface is well caramelized.

Chef's Note: *The borsalino can be assembled in a shorter ring, 1–1.5 in/3–4 cm high. In this case, use only the bottom layer of génoise and one layer of mousse.*

White Wine Mousse
Mouse au Vin

gelatin sheets	12	12
white wine	34 fl oz	1 L
vanilla beans	2	2
egg yolks	12	12
cornstarch	3 oz	80 g
sugar	7 oz	200 g
lemons, juice	2	2
sugar	17.5 oz	500 g
water	5.5 oz	150 g
egg whites	12	12

Cover the gelatin sheets with very cold water to soften.

Bring the white wine and vanilla to a boil. Whisk the egg yolks, cornstarch, sugar, and lemon juice until thick and pale.

Combine the two mixtures and bring to a boil, cooking as for pastry cream and stirring until thickened. Remove from heat.

Squeeze out the excess water from the gelatin sheets and stir into the cream until melted.

Prepare an Italian meringue by cooking the sugar and water to 250°F/121°C, while whipping the egg whites to soft peaks. Pour the cooked sugar in a fine stream, whipping it into the egg whites. Gently fold the meringue into the hot cream.

This cream should be used shortly after it is prepared.

Chef's Note: *Almost any white wine can be used for this recipe, although a fruity wine such as a muscat works especially well.*

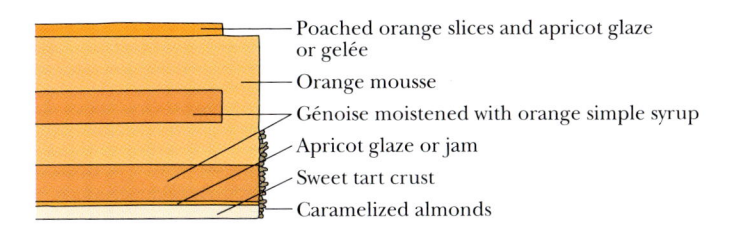

- Poached orange slices and apricot glaze or gelée
- Orange mousse
- Génoise moistened with orange simple syrup
- Apricot glaze or jam
- Sweet tart crust
- Caramelized almonds

Orange Mousse Cake
Andalou

This cake is assembled in a 2 1/3 in/6 cm high cake ring. Prepare and bake disks of sweet tart dough the same diameter as the ring. Prepare layers of génoise and poached orange slices.

Place the sweet tart crust inside the ring. Spread a thin layer of orange marmalade or apricot glaze. Cover with a layer of génoise, moistened with orange simple syrup. The layer of jam will hold the génoise in place and prevent the crust from becoming soggy.

Fill the ring half-full with orange mousse. Cover with a layer of génoise slightly smaller in diameter than the ring. Moisten liberally with orange simple syrup. Smooth the mousse flush to the top of the ring. Freeze.

Decorate with attractive poached orange slices. Brush with gelée or apricot glaze. Remove the cake ring by heating it with a propane torch. Brush a light coating of apricot glaze around the sides on the génoise. Press candied almonds around the base of the cake.

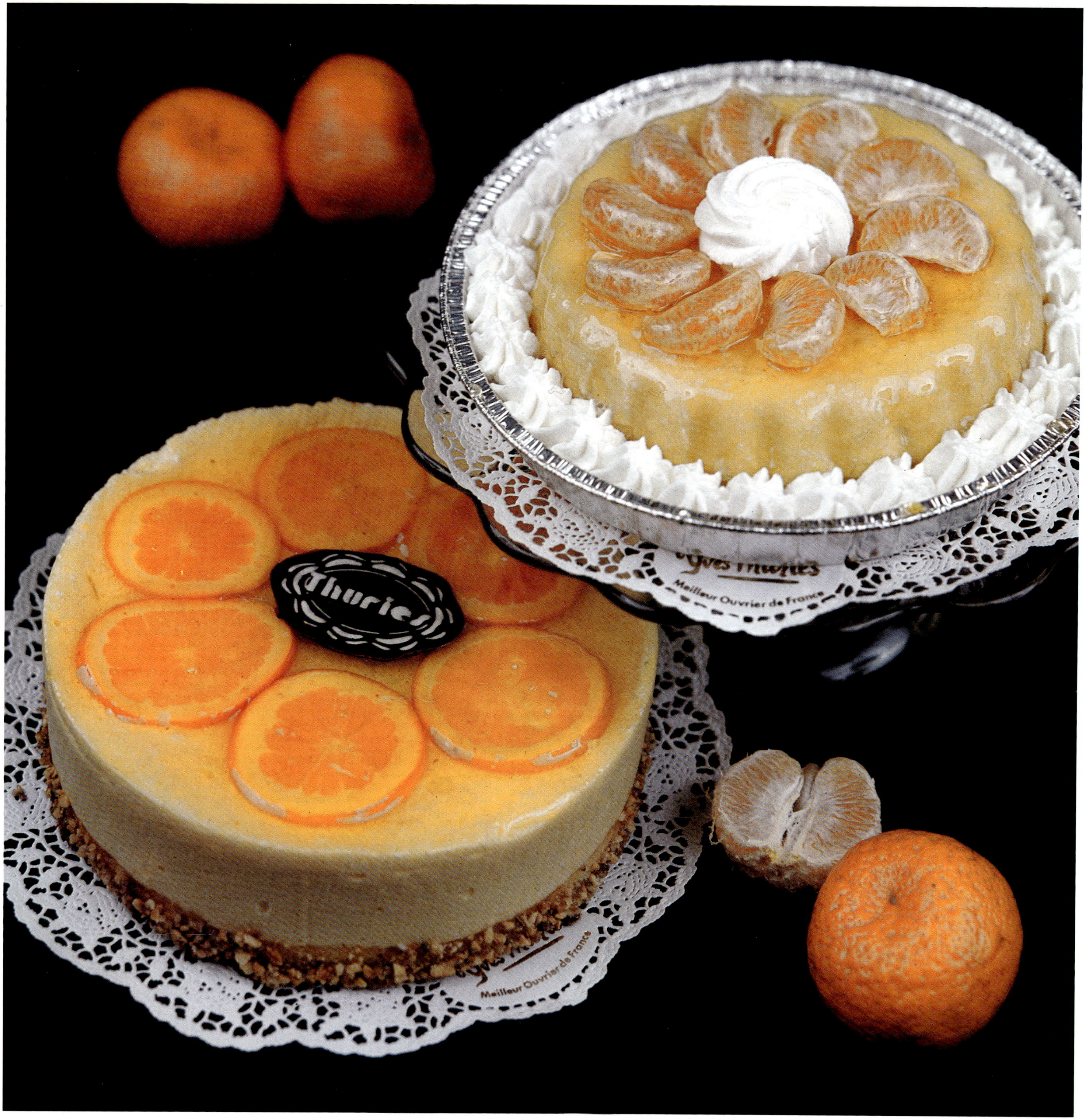
Meilleur Ouvrier de France
Meilleur Ouvrier de France

Orange Mousse
Mousse à l'Orange

gelatin sheets	14	14
crème fraîche	14 oz	400 g
orange juice	21 oz	600 g
orange concentrate	7 oz	200 g
cornstarch	2 oz	60 g
sugar	3.5 oz	100 g
egg yolks	24	24
sugar	17.5 oz	500 g
water	5.5 oz	150 g
egg whites	24	24

Cover the gelatin sheets with very cold water to soften.

Bring the crème fraîche, orange juice, and orange concentrate to a boil.

Whisk together the cornstarch and sugar. Gradually add the egg yolks, whisking until thick and pale. Combine the two mixtures and cook as for pastry cream, stirring constantly until thickened. Remove from heat. Squeeze the excess water from the gelatin sheets and stir into the cream until melted.

Prepare an Italian meringue by cooking the sugar and water to 250°F/121°C, while whipping the egg whites to soft peaks. Pour the cooked sugar in a fine stream, whipping it into the egg whites. Gently fold the meringue into the hot cream.

This cream should be used shortly after it is prepared.

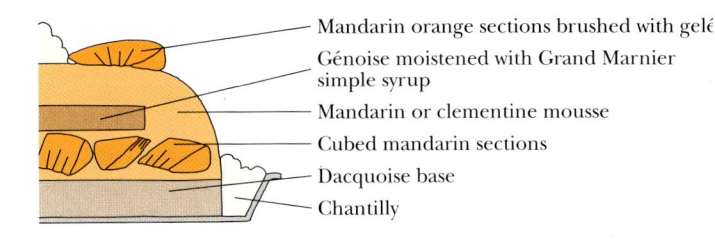

Facing Page: Orange Mousse Cake, Mandarin

Mandarin

- Mandarin orange sections brushed with gelée
- Génoise moistened with Grand Marnier simple syrup
- Mandarin or clementine mousse
- Cubed mandarin sections
- Dacquoise base
- Chantilly

This cake is assembled in a fluted cake mold. Prepare dacquoise bases and génoise layers. Fill the mold half-full with mandarin mousse. Cover with a layer of génoise slightly smaller in diameter than the mold. Moisten with Grand Marnier simple syrup. Spread a thin layer of mousse and scatter chopped mandarin orange sections. Spread and smooth the mousse flush to the rim of the mold. Freeze.

Unmold the cake using a propane torch and place the cake over a dacquoise base. Top with a pinwheel of mandarin orange sections. Return the cake to the freezer, if needed. Brush with gelée or apricot glaze. Place the cake on a high-sided presentation platter. With a pastry bag and fluted tip, decorate by piping a border of chantilly. Pipe a rosette on top of the cake, inside the pinwheel of mandarin orange sections.

Mandarin Orange Mousse
Mousse à la Mandarine

gelatin sheets	12	12
mandarin orange juice	17.5 oz	500 g
crème fraîche	14 oz	400 g
Grand Marnier	3.5 oz	100 g
egg yolks	20	20
cornstarch	1.5 oz	50 g
egg whites	20	20
sugar	21 oz	600 g
water	6.5 oz	180 g

(Mandarin Orange Mousse recipe continued on page 55)

Cakes

Modern French Pastry

Follow the procedure given for the orange mousse (see page 53). Bring the first set of ingredients to a boil. Remove from heat and stir in the softened gelatin until melted. Prepare an Italian meringue by whipping the egg whites and pouring in the cooked sugar in a fine stream. Gently fold the meringue into the hot cream.

This mousse should be used shortly after it is prepared.

Orange Simple Syrup
Sirop à l'Orange

orange juice	10.5 oz	300 g
simple syrup, 30° baume	17.5 oz	500 g
water	10.5 oz	300 g
orange concentrate or orange syrup	5.5 oz	150 g

Combine all ingredients.

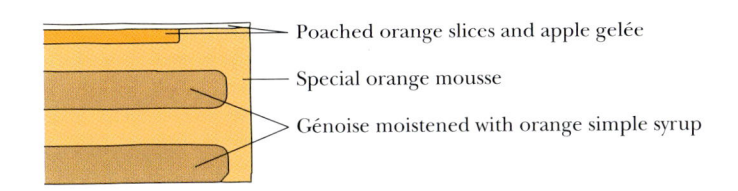

Valencia

This cake is assembled upside down in a 1 1/3 in/ 3.5 cm high cake ring. Poach very thin orange slices in simple syrup, 30° baume. Drain them well before using. Prepare génoise layers slightly smaller in diameter than the cake ring.

Place the cake ring over a sheet of plastic. Decoratively arrange drained poached orange slices on the plastic inside the ring. Fill the ring one third full with the mousse, spreading it against the inside of the ring. Cover with a thin layer of génoise, moistened liberally with orange simple syrup. Fill the ring three quarters full with the mousse. Cover with a second layer of génoise, moistened with orange simple syrup. Smooth the mousse flush to the rim of the ring. Freeze.

Turn the ring over and set it on a cake cardboard so the orange slices are on top. Glaze the top of the cake with orange-flavored apple gelée. Remove the cake ring by heating it with a propane torch.

Special Orange Mousse
Mousse à l'Orange Spéciale

orange juice	14 oz	400 g
oranges, zest of	4	4
lemons, juice	2	2
butter	7 oz	200 g
eggs	10	10
sugar	21 oz	600 g
gelatin sheets	24	24
pastry cream	14 oz	400 g
crème fraîche	5 lbs 4 oz	2,400 g
sugar	7 oz	200 g
orange extract	1 1/4 tsp	5 g

Gently heat the orange juice and zests, lemon juice, butter, eggs, and sugar over moderate heat, stirring constantly. Do not allow this mixture to boil.

Cover the gelatin sheets with very cold water to soften.

Bring the pastry cream to a boil, stirring constantly with a whisk. Remove from heat. Squeeze the excess water from the gelatin sheets and stir them into the hot cream until melted.

Combine the hot orange cream and pastry cream. Set aside to cool.

Prepare a chantilly by whipping the crème fraîche and sugar to soft peaks, then stir in the extract.

When the orange/pastry cream mixture is cool, gently fold in the chantilly.

This mousse should be used shortly after it is prepared.

Facing Page: Valencia, Creole Soufflé

Gelée for the Valencia Cake

gelatin sheets	5	5
apple gelée	14 oz	400 g
orange extract	1 tsp	5 g

Cover the gelatin sheets with very cold water to soften. Squeeze the gelatin sheets to remove the excess water and warm them with the gelée and orange extract until melted. Do not allow the mixture to boil.

Banana Mousse
Mousse aux Bananes

peeled bananas	35 oz	1,000 g
lemons, juice	4	4
heavy cream	35 oz	1,000 g
gelatin sheets	16	16
sugar	28 oz	800 g
water	8.5 oz	240 g
egg whites	12	12

Mash the bananas into a purée with the lemon juice.

Whip the cream to soft peaks. Cover the gelatin with very cold water to soften.

Prepare an Italian meringue by cooking the sugar and water to 250°F/121°C, while whipping the egg whites to soft peaks. Pour the cooked sugar in a fine stream, whipping it into the egg whites. Squeeze the excess water from the gelatine sheets and add them to the hot meringue. Continue whipping the meringue until cool.

Divide the meringue in half. In one half, fold in the banana purée. In the other half, gently fold in the whipped cream. Then fold together the two mixtures.

This mousse should be used shortly after it is prepared.

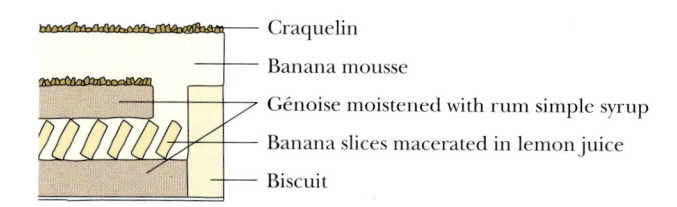

Craquelin
Banana mousse
Génoise moistened with rum simple syrup
Banana slices macerated in lemon juice
Biscuit

Creole Soufflé
Soufflé Créole

Macerate banana slices in lemon juice for several hours.

This cake is assembled in a 2 1/3 in/6 cm high cake ring.

Line the inside of the ring with a strip of biscuit cut to two thirds the height of the ring. Place a layer of génoise inside the ring, moistened with rum simple syrup. Spread a layer of banana mousse. Cover the mousse with the lemon-macerated banana slices. Fill the ring half-full with the mousse. Cover with a layer of génoise, liberally moistened with rum simple syrup. Sprinkle craquelin over the génoise. Smooth a layer of mousse flush to the rim of ring. Freeze.

Sprinkle craquelin on top of the cake. Remove the cake ring by heating it with a propane torch. Brush the biscuit around the side of the cake with apricot glaze. Wrap a ribbon around the side. Place a pastry shop label on top.

Grapefruit Syrup
Sirop de Pamplemousse

simple syrup, 30° baume	17.5 oz	500 g
grapefruit juice	5.5 oz	150 g
kirsch	2 oz	50 g

Combine all ingredients.

Grapefruit Mousse
Mousse au Pamplemousse

gelatin sheets	8	8
grapefruit juice	10.5 oz	300 g
crème fraîche	7 oz	200 g
egg yolks	6	6
cornstarch	2 oz	50 g
sugar	5.5 oz	150 g
crème fraîche, whipped	35 oz	1,000 g
kirsch, (optional)	2 oz	50 g

Cover the gelatin sheets with very cold water to soften. Bring the grapefruit juice, first crème fraîche, egg yolks, cornstarch, and sugar to a boil, stirring constantly with a whisk.

The cream can also be prepared following the method for pastry cream, using the grapefruit and crème fraîche in place of milk.

Remove the cream from the heat. Squeeze the gelatin sheets to remove the excess water. Stir the gelatin into the hot cream until melted. Set aside to cool.

Just before the cream sets up, whip the second crème fraîche to soft peaks and fold it into the cream with the kirsch (if used).

This mousse should be used shortly after it is prepared.

Fill a decorative mold half-full with the mousse. Make sure the mold is lined with stainless steel or other material that will not react to the acidity of the grapefruit. Cover with a thin layer of génoise, moistened with grapefruit simple syrup. Smooth the mousse flush to the top of the mold. Freeze.

Heat the mold slightly and unmold the mousse onto a layer of génoise. Brush with gelée or apricot glaze. Place the cake in a deep serving platter. With a pastry bag and fluted tip, pipe a decorative border at the base and a ring on top of the cake.

Place chocolate curls inside the chantilly ring on top of the cake.

Chef's Note: *The grapefruit mousse can be presented in many ways. Another possibility is to use the method given for pineapple Willy (recipe follows), making the appropriate substitutions.*

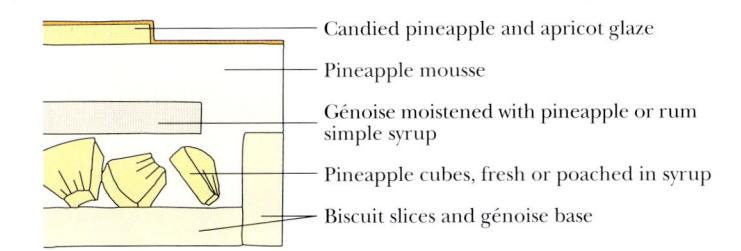

- Candied pineapple and apricot glaze
- Pineapple mousse
- Génoise moistened with pineapple or rum simple syrup
- Pineapple cubes, fresh or poached in syrup
- Biscuit slices and génoise base

Pineapple Willy
Willy Ananas

This cake is assembled in a 2 1/3 in/6 cm high cake ring. Line the sides of the ring half-way up with slices of biscuit layered with jam or apricot glaze (see page 61). Place a layer of génoise inside the ring, moistened with pineapple or rum simple syrup. Fill the ring half-full with pineapple mousse and scatter pineapple cubes on top, fresh or poached in syrup. Cover with a second layer of génoise slightly smaller than the diameter of the ring, moistened with the same simple syrup. Smooth a layer of the mousse flush to the rim of the ring. Freeze.

Place poached pineapple slice, centered, on top of the cake. Coat with gelée or apricot glaze. Remove the ring by heating it with a propane torch. Brush the biscuit slices around the side of the cake with apricot glaze.

Chef's Note: *The pineapple Willy cake can also be prepared in a shorter cake ring, 1–1.5 in/3–4 cm high. In this case, spread one layer of mousse over one layer of génoise. The procedure and presentation remain the same. The pineapple in the mousse can be substituted with other flavors such as strawberry, raspberry, blackcurrant, banana, or passion fruit. Use a complementary simple syrup.*

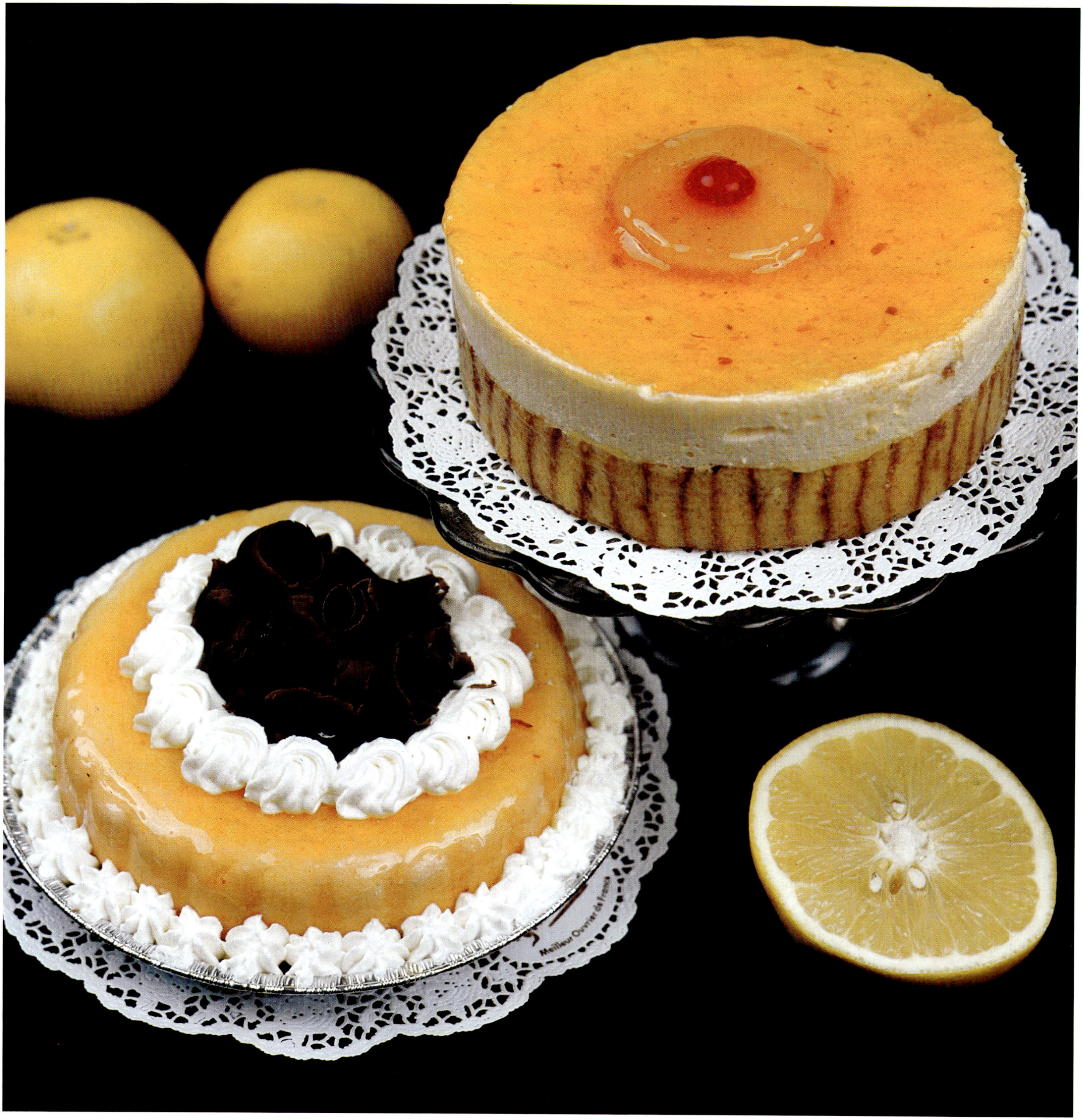
Meilleur Ouvrier de France

Pineapple Mousse
Mousse à l'Ananas

gelatin sheets	16	16
milk	9 oz	250 g
sugar	12.5 oz	350 g
pineapple pulp	35 oz	1,000 g
crème fraîche or heavy cream	4 lbs	1,800 g
kirsch, (optional)	2 oz	50 g

Cover the gelatin sheets with very cold water to soften.

Bring the milk and sugar to a boil. Remove from heat. Squeeze the gelatin sheets to remove the excess water and stir into the hot cream until melted. Strain the pineapple pulp and add it to the cream. Set the cream aside to cool. Just before setting, fold in the whipped cream or crème fraîche and kirsch, if used.

This mousse should be used shortly after it is prepared.

Strawberry or Raspberry Willy
Willy à la Fraise ou à la Framboise

The strawberry and raspberry Willy are assembled and presented following the procedure given for the pineapple Willy (see page 57), making the appropriate substitutions. Use a strawberry or raspberry mousse for the filling and moisten with a kirsch or fruit simple syrup. Glaze with strawberry or raspberry gelée.

Facing Page: Grapefruit Mousse, Pineapple Willy

Strawberry or Raspberry Mousse
Mousse à la Fraise ou à la Framboise

gelatin sheets	16	16
milk	9 oz	250 g
sugar	10.5 oz	300 g
raspberry or strawberry pulp	35 oz	1,000 g
crème fraîche, whipped	4 lbs	1,800 g

Follow the procedure given for the pineapple mousse.

Blackcurrant Willy
Willy au Cassis

This cake is assembled following the same procedure given for the pineapple Willy (see page 57), making the appropriate substitutions. Use a blackcurrant mousse for the filling and moisten with blackcurrant simple syrup. Glaze with blackcurrant gelée.

Blackcurrant Mousse
Mousse au Cassis

gelatin sheets	16	16
milk	9 oz	250 g
sugar	12.5 oz	350 g
blackcurrant pulp	35 oz	1,000 g
crème fraîche, whipped	4 lbs 6 oz	2,000 g

Follow the procedure given for pineapple mousse, making the appropriate substitutions.

60   *Modern French Pastry*

Banana Willy
Willy à la Banane

This cake is assembled following the same procedure given for the pineapple Willy (see page 57), making the appropriate substitutions. Use a banana mousse for the filling and moisten with rum simple syrup. Glaze with apple gelée.

Banana or Melon Mousse
Mousse à la Banane ou au Melon

gelatin sheets	14	14
milk	9 oz	250 g
sugar	9 oz	250 g
banana or melon pulp	35 oz	1,000 g
crème fraîche, whipped	4 lbs 6 oz	2,000 g

Follow the same procedure given for the pineapple mousse (see page 59).

Lining a Cake Ring with Slices of Biscuit Layered with Jam

Photo 1: Bake sheets of biscuit. Superimpose 4–6 layers of baked and cooled biscuit, spreading jam or apricot glaze between the layers. Cut off a strip of biscuit, the width of the strip corresponding to the height needed.

Photo 2: Using a serrated knife, cut 1/4–1/3 in/5–8 mm thick slices from the strip. This step can be accomplished more easily when the strips are very cold or even frozen.

Photo 3: Line the biscuit slices against the inside of the cake ring so that the lines of jam are vertical to the ring.

Photo 4: After lining the cake ring, place a layer of génoise inside the ring as a base for the cake. The génoise layer can be trimmed to fit snugly against the lined biscuit as a support, although a smaller layer can also be used. The cake is now ready to be filled and assembled, as desired.

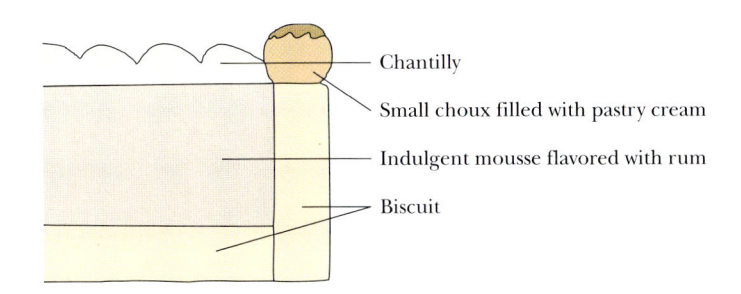

Labels (diagram): Chantilly; Small choux filled with pastry cream; Indulgent mousse flavored with rum; Biscuit

Rum Indulgent
Indulgent au Rhum

This cake is assembled in a 2 1/3 in/3.5 cm high cake ring. Prepare two sheets of biscuit—one layered with red jam, the other with a golden jam or apricot glaze. Line the ring, alternating the two colors of layered biscuit.

Place a layer of biscuit or génoise on the bottom inside the ring, moistened lightly with rum simple syrup. Fill the ring with rum mousse. Cover with a thin layer of biscuit, moistened with rum simple syrup. Refrigerate.

Decoratively cover the top of the cake with chantilly using a pastry bag and fluted tip. Place individual choux, filled with pastry cream and topped with caramel, around the top border of the cake.

Chef's Note: *The choux can also be attached to the biscuit with cooked sugar. The top of the cake is then covered with chantilly. This cake can be flavored using other liqueurs such as Grand Marnier, Cointreau, or kirsch. The procedure and presentation remain the same.*

Indulgent Rum Mousse
Mousse à Indulgent au Rum

sugar	5.5 oz	150 g
glucose	2 oz	50 g
water	7 oz	200 g
egg yolks	24	24

(Indulgent Rum Mousse recipe continued on page 63)

Rum Indulgent, Coffee Indulgent

gelatin sheets	10	10
sugar	10.5 oz	300 g
water	3 oz	90 g
egg whites	16	16
glucose	3.5 oz	100 g
heavy cream, whipped	4 lbs 6 oz	2,000 g
rum	9 oz	250 g

To prepare a bombe batter, make a syrup by bringing the sugar, glucose, and water to a boil. Whisk the syrup into the egg yolks. Heat the mixture, stirring it over a hot water bath. When warm, whisk until completely cool.

Cover the gelatin sheets with very cold water to soften. Prepare an Italian meringue by cooking the sugar, water, and glucose to 250°F/121°C, while whipping the egg whites to soft peaks. Pour the cooked sugar in a fine stream, whipping it into the egg whites. Squeeze the gelatin sheets to remove the excess moisture and whisk them into the hot meringue. Continue whipping the meringue until cool.

Whip the heavy cream to soft peaks. Fold the bombe batter into the meringue, then fold in the whipped cream and rum.

Coffee Indulgent
Indulgent au Café

This cake is assembled in a 2 1/3 in/6 cm high cake ring. Line the ring with layered biscuit slices halfway up. Place a layer of biscuit or génoise into the ring, moistened with coffee simple syrup. Fill the ring half-full with indulgent coffee mousse. Set miniature babas, previously macerated in coffee syrup, into the mousse. Spread a smooth layer of coffee mousse flush to the rim of the ring. Freeze.

Sprinkle craquelin on top of the cake. With a pastry bag and small plain tip, pipe a lattice pattern and border with coffee chantilly over the craquelin. Decorate the border with chocolate coffee beans.

Chef's Note: This cake can also be prepared with other flavors, following the same procedure. The babas can be macerated in any liqueur syrup of choice such as kirsch, Curaçao, Cointreau, maraschino, or vanilla.

Indulgent Coffee Mousse
Mousse à Indulgent au Café

Follow the procedure given for the indulgent rum mousse, (above). Add 5.5 oz/150 g coffee extract. This mousse can also be flavored with chocolate, praline, chestnut, or other flavors according to taste.

Indulgent Liqueur Mousse
Mousse à Indulgent à la Liqueur

Any liqueur of choice can be used, such as Grand Marnier, Cointreau, or kirsch. Follow the procedure given for the indulgent rum mousse, replacing the rum with 9–10.5 oz/250–300 g liqueur.

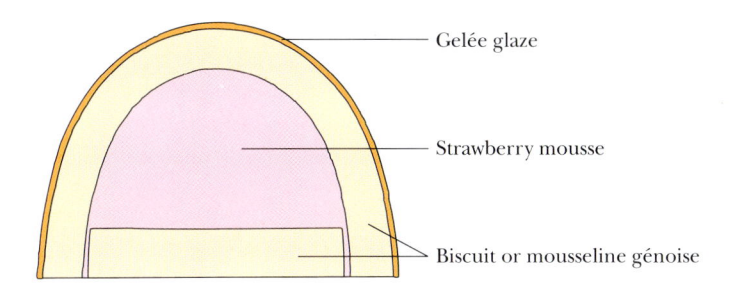

Diagram labels: Gelée glaze; Strawberry mousse; Biscuit or mousseline génoise

Strawberry Colisée
Colisée aux Fraises

The strawberry colisée can be served at Christmas time with appropriate decorations and served as a strawberry yule log.

(Strawberry Colisée recipe continued on page 65)

64 Modern French Pastry

This cake is assembled in a rounded mold (gouttière). Prepare sheets of biscuit or mousseline génoise.

Line the mold with the top side (smooth) of the biscuit touching the mold. Moisten with strawberry liqueur simple syrup.

Fill the mold with strawberry mousse. Although optional, a layer of biscuit moistened liberally with strawberry liqueur simple syrup can be placed between two layers of mousse. Finish with a layer of biscuit cut to fit the base of the mold (now on top). Freeze.

Unmold and brush the cake with gelée or apricot glaze. Cut into smaller cakes. Decorate with macerated strawberries and marzipan leaves.

Variation
Wild strawberries can be scattered in the mousse during assembly. The cake can also be decorated with strawberry gelée or by piping chantilly on the top and sides.

Strawberry Mousse
Mousse aux Fraises

crème fraîche	35 oz	1,000 g
gelatin sheets	16	16
sugar	28 oz	800 g
water	8.5 oz	240 g
egg whites	12	12
strawberry pulp	35 oz	1,000 g

Whip the crème fraîche to soft peaks. Cover the gelatin sheets with very cold water to soften. Prepare an Italian meringue by cooking the sugar and water to 250°F/121°C, while whipping the egg whites to soft peaks. Pour the cooked sugar in a fine stream, whipping it into the egg whites. Squeeze out the excess water from the gelatin sheets and whip them into the hot meringue. Continue to whip the meringue until completely cool.

Divide the meringue into two halves. Gently fold the strawberry pulp into one half. Fold the whipped crème fraîche into the second half. Combine the two.

This mousse should be used shortly after it is prepared.

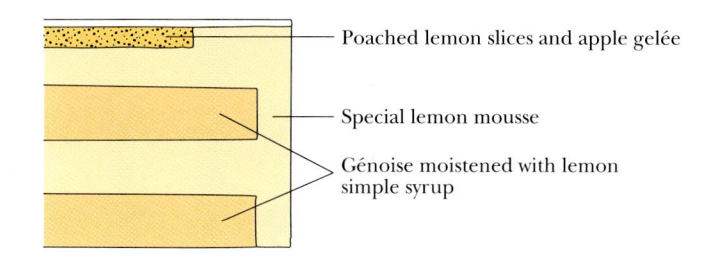

— Poached lemon slices and apple gelée
— Special lemon mousse
— Génoise moistened with lemon simple syrup

Lemon Mousse Cake
Murcia

This cake is assembled upside down in a 1 1/3 in/ 35 mm high cake ring. Poach very thin lemon slices in simple syrup, 30° baume. After poaching, drain the slices well. Prepare layers of génoise slightly smaller in diameter than the ring.

Place the cake ring over a plastic sheet. Place the poached lemon slices decoratively inside the ring on the plastic sheet. Fill the ring one third full with the special lemon mousse, spreading the mousse against the inside of the ring. Cover with a thin layer of génoise, moistened liberally with lemon simple syrup. Fill the ring three quarters full with the mousse. Cover with a second layer of génoise, moistened with simple syrup. Smooth a layer of mousse flush to the rim of the ring. Freeze.

Turn the cake over onto a cake cardboard, so that the lemon slices are now on top. Remove the plastic sheet and glaze the top of the cake with apple gelée. Remove the ring by heating it with a propane torch.

Facing Page: Strawberry Colisée, Lemon Mousse Cake

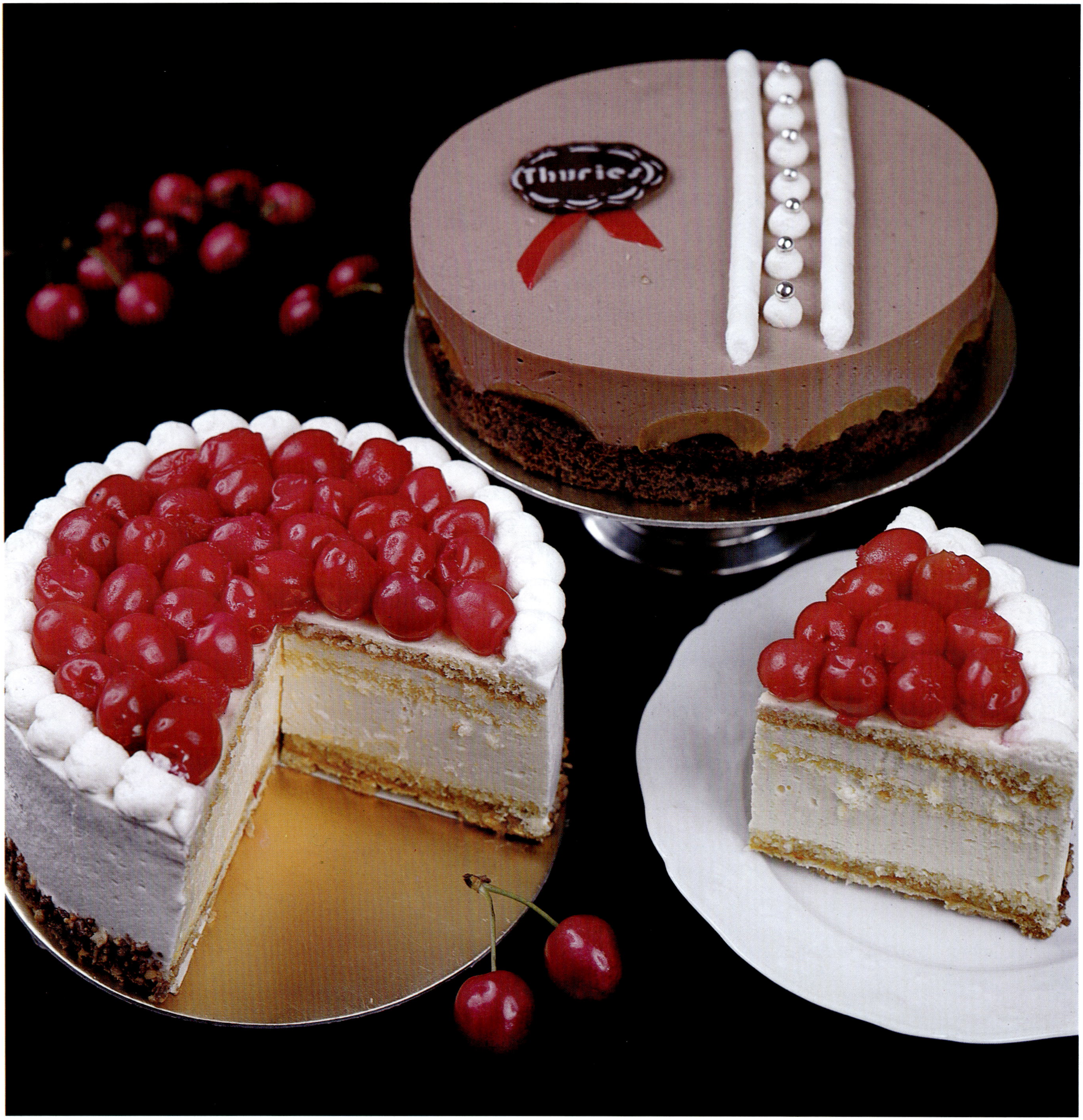
Thuries

Special Lemon Mousse
Mousse au Citron Spéciale

lemon juice	9 oz	250 g
lemons, zest of	2	2
butter	7 oz	200 g
sugar	16 oz	450 g
eggs	10	10
gelatin sheets	24	24
pastry cream	14 oz	400 g
crème fraîche	5 lbs 4 oz	2,400 g
sugar	7 oz	200 g

Without boiling, heat the lemon juice and zest, butter, sugar, and eggs, stirring constantly.

Cover the gelatin sheets with very cold water to soften. Bring the pastry cream to a boil, stirring constantly. Remove from heat. Squeeze the excess water from the gelatin sheets and stir into the hot pastry cream until melted. Combine the lemon mixture and pastry cream while the two are still hot. Set aside to cool.

Whip the crème fraîche and sugar to soft peaks. When the lemon/pastry cream mixture is cool, just before setting, gently fold in the whipped cream.

This mousse should be used shortly after it is prepared.

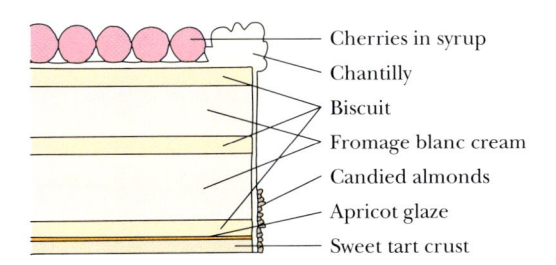

Fromage Blanc Cheese Cake
Gâteau au Fromage Blanc

This cake is assembled in a cake ring 2 1/3 in/6 cm high. Prepare and bake a disk of sweet tart dough the same diameter as the ring. Prepare three layers of biscuit the same diameter as the ring.

Place the sweet tart crust inside the ring and brush with apricot glaze. Cover with a layer of biscuit. Fill the ring half-full with fromage blanc cream. Cover with a second layer of biscuit. Spread on a second layer of fromage blanc cream and cover with a third layer of biscuit. Freeze.

Smooth chantilly on the top and sides of the cake. Press candied almonds around the base of the cake. Pipe a border of chantilly on the top of the cake. Place cherries in syrup on top, inside the chantilly border.

Fromage Blanc Cream
Crème au Fromage Blanc

gelatin sheets	16	16
white wine	9 oz	250 g
egg yolks	10	10
sugar	9 oz	250 g
lemons, zest of	3	3
fromage blanc*	35 oz	1,000 g
crème fraîche, whipped	2 lbs 10 oz	1,200 g

Fromage blanc is a light, fresh cheese. If unavailable, yogurt or a combination of yogurt and sour cream can be substituted.

Cover the gelatin sheets with very cold water to soften. Bring the white wine, egg yolks, sugar, and lemon zest to a boil, stirring constantly. Remove from heat. Squeeze the excess water from the gelatin sheets and stir into the hot mixture until melted. Set the mixture aside to cool.

After cooling, stir the fresh cheese into the wine mixture and gently fold in the whipped crème fraîche.

This mousse should be used shortly after it is prepared.

Facing Page: Fromage Blanc Cheese Cake, Sultan

68 *Modern French Pastry*

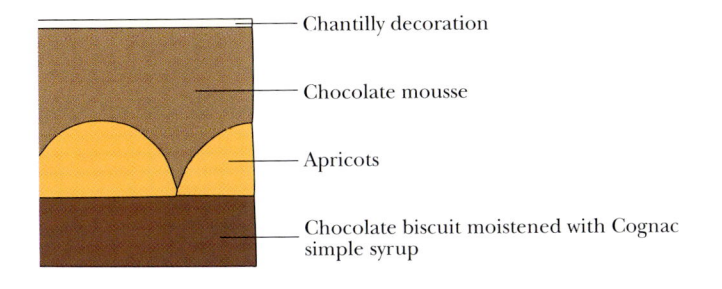

Chantilly decoration
Chocolate mousse
Apricots
Chocolate biscuit moistened with Cognac simple syrup

Sultan

This cake is assembled in a 1.5 in/4 cm high cake ring. Prepare chocolate biscuit layers the same diameter as the cake ring.

Place a layer of biscuit inside the cake ring, moistened with Cognac simple syrup. Place apricot slices on top of the biscuit, and apricot quarters skin side up against the inside of the ring. Fill the ring with chocolate mousse. Freeze.

Remove the ring by heating it with a propane torch. Decorate the top of the cake with chantilly.

Chocolate Mousse
Mousse au Chocolat

gelatin sheets	8	8
milk	9 oz	250 g
sugar	5.5 oz	150 g
cocoa powder	7 oz	200 g
crème fraîche, whipped	35 oz	1,000 g

Cover the gelatin sheets with very cold water to soften.

Bring the milk and sugar to a boil. Add the cocoa powder, stirring until well blended. Remove from heat. Squeeze the excess water from the gelatin sheets and stir them into the hot milk until melted. Set aside to cool. Just before the mixture sets, gently fold in the whipped crème fraîche.

This mousse should be used shortly after it is prepared.

Banana slices brushed with apricot glaze
Rum mousse
Biscuit moistened with rum simple syrup
Chocolate mousse
Biscuit

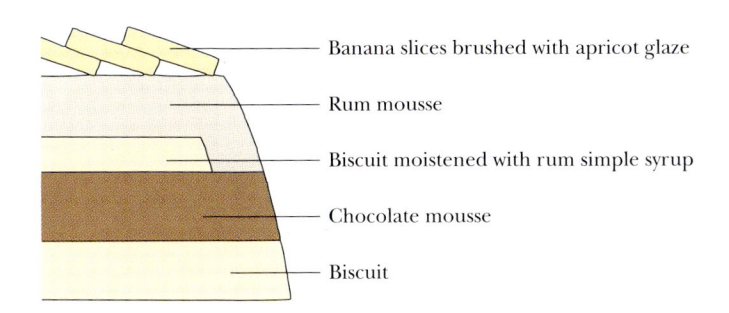

Banania

This cake is assembled in an oval or round génoise mold. Prepare slices of biscuit or génoise. Fill the mold one third full with rum mousse (see maraschino mousse, page 70). Cover with a layer of biscuit slightly smaller in diameter than the ring, moisten with rum simple syrup. Fill three quarters full with chocolate mousse (above). Cover with a layer of biscuit the same diameter as the ring. Freeze.

Unmold the cake by heating the mold with a propane torch. Cover the top of the cake with banana slices previously macerated in lemon juice. Coat the bottom of the cake with chantilly and cover with candied almonds. Brush the bananas with apricot glaze.

Facing Page: Banania, Strawberry-Cherry Mousse Cake, Apple-Cherry Mousse Cake

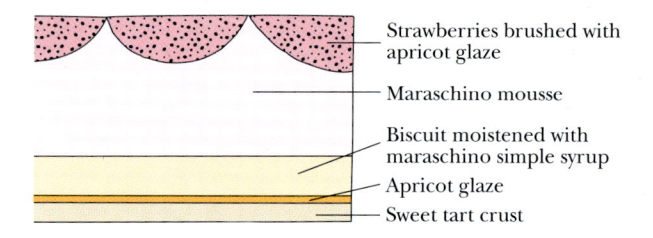

Strawberries brushed with apricot glaze
Maraschino mousse
Biscuit moistened with maraschino simple syrup
Apricot glaze
Sweet tart crust

Strawberry-Cherry Mousse Cake
Fraisilia

This cake is assembled upside down in a 1 1/3 in/ 35 mm high square frame of the size needed. Prepare sheets of biscuit the same size as the frame.

Place the cake frame over a sheet of plastic. Cut strawberries in half and set them, flat side down, on the plastic sheet. The cake will later be turned over and the berries will decorate the finished cake. Fill the frame three quarters full with maraschino mousse. Cover with a layer of biscuit, moistened lightly with maraschino simple syrup.

Refrigerate, but do not freeze, as it would adversely affect the texture of the strawberries.

Place a sheet pan on the cake and turn it over, so the strawberries are now on top. Remove the plastic sheet and the frame. Brush the top of the cake with gelée or apricot glaze. Using a serrated knife, cut the cake into smaller cakes, squares, rectangles, or individual portions.

Roll out and bake a layer of sweet tart dough the same size as the cake frame. After baking, brush the crust with apricot glaze. Set the cakes over the crust. Using a serrated knife, cut the baked sweet tart crust to the size of each cake.

Chef's Note: *The maraschino liqueur used to flavor the mousse can be replaced with the same quantity of kirsch, Cointreau, or rum. Flavor the simple syrup to complement the mousse.*

Maraschino Mousse
Mousse au Marasquin

gelatin sheets	12	12
white wine	9 oz	250 g
sugar	5.5 oz	150 g
egg yolks	5	5
maraschino liqueur	3.5 oz	100 g
crème fraîche, whipped	35 oz	1,000 g

Cover the gelatin sheets with very cold water to soften. Bring the white wine, sugar, and egg yolks to a boil, stirring constantly. Remove from heat. Squeeze the excess water from the gelatin sheets and stir them into the hot wine mixture until melted. Strain and cool. When the mixture begins to set, fold in the maraschino liqueur and whipped crème fraîche.

This mousse should be used shortly after it is prepared.

Chef's Note: *The maraschino liqueur can be replaced with the same quantity of rum, Cointreau, Curaçao, or other liqueur of choice.*

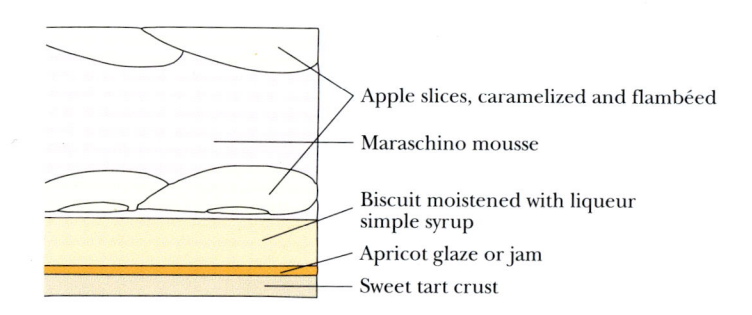

Apple slices, caramelized and flambéed
Maraschino mousse
Biscuit moistened with liqueur simple syrup
Apricot glaze or jam
Sweet tart crust

Apple-Cherry Mousse Cake
Pommélia

This cake is assembled following the same procedure given for the strawberry-cherry mousse cake, making the appropriate substitutions.

Prepare apple slices, caramelizing them in the oven as for the marigny cake (see page 115).

Place a cake frame on a sheet of plastic. Arrange the cooled caramelized apple slices on the plastic in a decorative fashion as they will serve to decorate the finished cake. Fill the frame two thirds full with maraschino mousse. Layer caramelized apple slices over the mousse. Fill the frame three quarters full with the mousse. Cover with a layer of biscuit, moistened with maraschino or other liqueur-flavored simple syrup. Freeze.

Turn the cake over so the apples are on top. Remove the cake frame and the plastic sheet. Brush the top of the cake with apricot glaze or apple gelée. Cut the cake into smaller cakes. Place each cake over a layer of sweet tart crust brushed with jam or apricot glaze.

Chef's Note: *The sweet tart crust can be omitted by spreading a layer of coating chocolate or liquid couverture on the bottom of the biscuit base.*

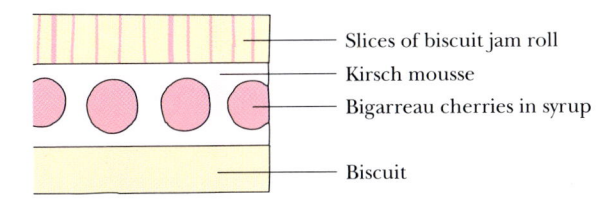

- Slices of biscuit jam roll
- Kirsch mousse
- Bigarreau cherries in syrup
- Biscuit

Little Duke
Petit Duc

This cake is assembled in a stainless steel cake frame 15 in/38 cm by 23 in/58 cm and 2 in/5 cm high. Cover a sheet pan with a plastic sheet and place the cake frame on top. If a cake frame is not available, use a straight-sided square cake pan. Prepare biscuit rolled with raspberry jam (see page 91). Prepare biscuit sheets.

Line the bottom of the cake frame with slices of the biscuit/jam roll. Moisten with kirsch simple syrup. Fill the frame half full with kirsch mousse. Scatter well-drained bigarreau cherries over the mousse. Fill the frame three quarters full with the mousse. Cover with a layer of biscuit. Refrigerate.

Turn the cake over so the rolled biscuit is on top. Remove the frame by heating it with a propane torch. Brush the top of the cake with gelée or apricot glaze. Cut the cake into smaller square, rectangular, or individual cakes. Place the cakes on cake cardboards. Place a pastry shop label on top.

Kirsch Mousse
Mousse au Kirsch

gelatin sheets	10	10
white wine	6 oz	170 g
sugar	5.5 oz	150 g
egg yolks	5	5
kirsch	3 oz	80 g
crème fraîche	35 oz	1,000 g

Cover the gelatin sheets with very cold water to soften. Bring the white wine, sugar, and egg yolks to a boil. Remove from heat. Squeeze out the excess water from the gelatin sheets and stir into the hot wine mixture until melted. Strain through a fine mesh sieve and set aside to cool. Just as the mixture begins to set, stir in the kirsch and fold in the whipped crème fraîche.

This mousse should be used shortly after it is prepared.

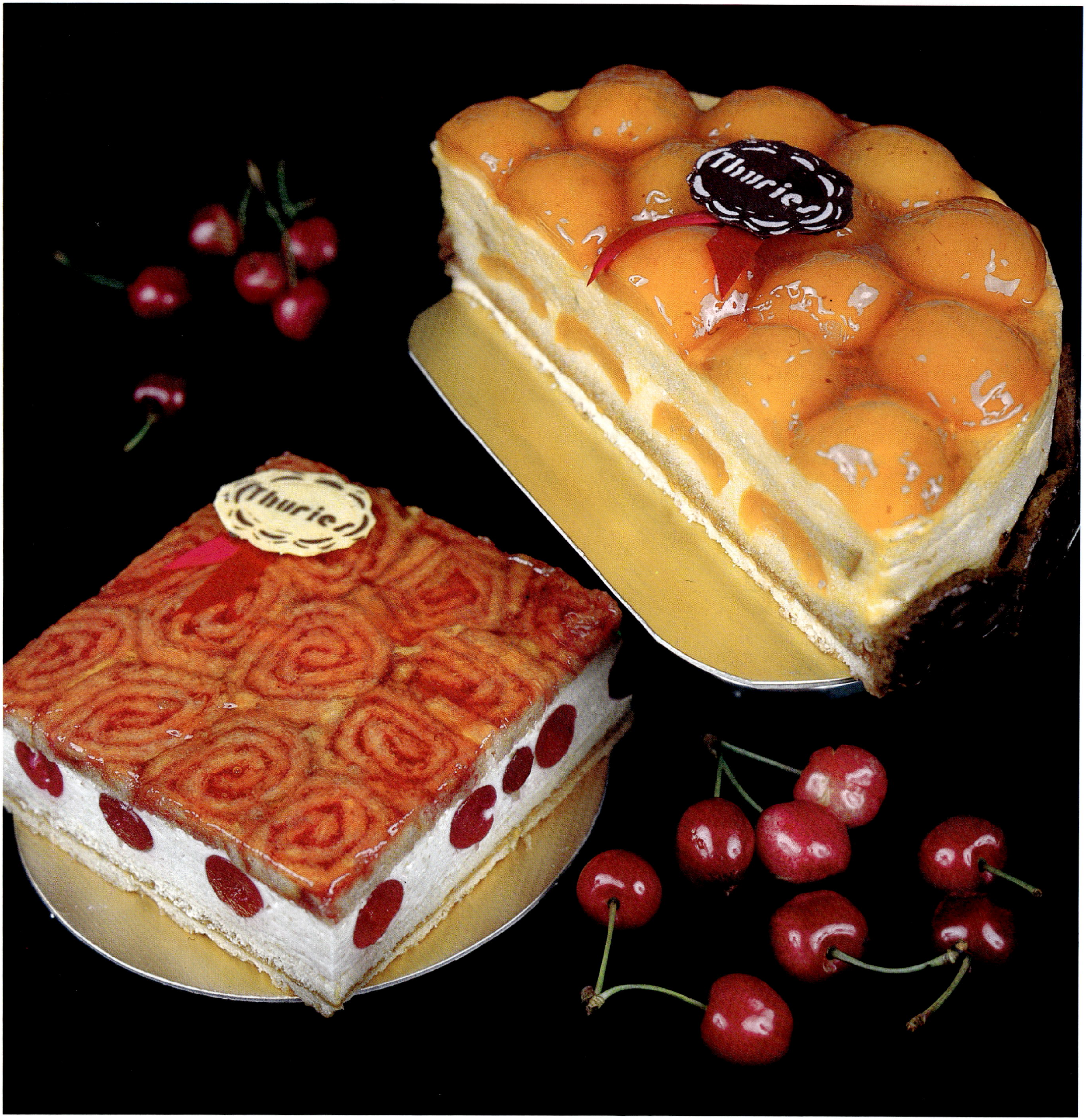
Thuries
Thuries

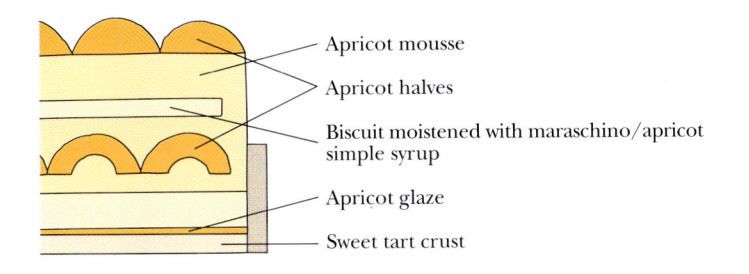

Apricot mousse
Apricot halves
Biscuit moistened with maraschino/apricot simple syrup
Apricot glaze
Sweet tart crust

Cupid
Cupidon

This cake is assembled in a 2 1/3 in/6 cm high cake ring. Place a disk of sweet tart crust inside the ring. Spread a thin layer of apricot glaze. Cover with a layer of biscuit the same diameter as the ring. Moisten with maraschino/apricot simple syrup. Spread a layer of apricot mousse. Cover with apricot halves. Spread a second layer of mousse. Cover with a layer of biscuit slightly smaller in diameter than the ring, moistened with the maraschino/apricot syrup. Smooth the mousse flush to the top of the ring. Freeze.

Remove the ring by heating it with a propane torch. Cover the top of the cake with apricot halves in syrup, cut side down. Press either candied almonds or half-moon cookies coated with tempered couverture chocolate around the cake.

This cake can be presented whole or cut in half to reveal the decorative filling. Place a pastry shop label on top.

Apricot Mousse
Mousse à l'Abricot

apricot pulp	17.5 oz	500 g
sugar	3.5 oz	100 g
egg yolks	6	6
cornstarch	2 oz	50 g
gelatin sheets	10	10
sugar	14 oz	400 g
water	5.5 oz	150 g
egg whites	16	16

Strain the apricot pulp and combine it with the sugar, egg yolks, and cornstarch. Bring the mixture to a boil, stirring constantly.

Cover the gelatin sheets with very cold water to soften. Prepare an Italian meringue by cooking the sugar and water to 250°F/121°C, while whipping the egg whites to soft peaks. Pour the cooked sugar in a fine stream, whipping it into the egg whites.

Squeeze the excess water from the gelatin sheets and add them to the hot cream. Gently fold the hot cream into the meringue.

This mousse should be used shortly after it is prepared.

Maraschino/Apricot Simple Syrup
Sirop Marasquin Abricot

Combine 25.5 fl oz/750 ml. apricot juice with 8.5 fl oz/250 ml maraschino liqueur.

Facing Page: Little Duke, Cupid

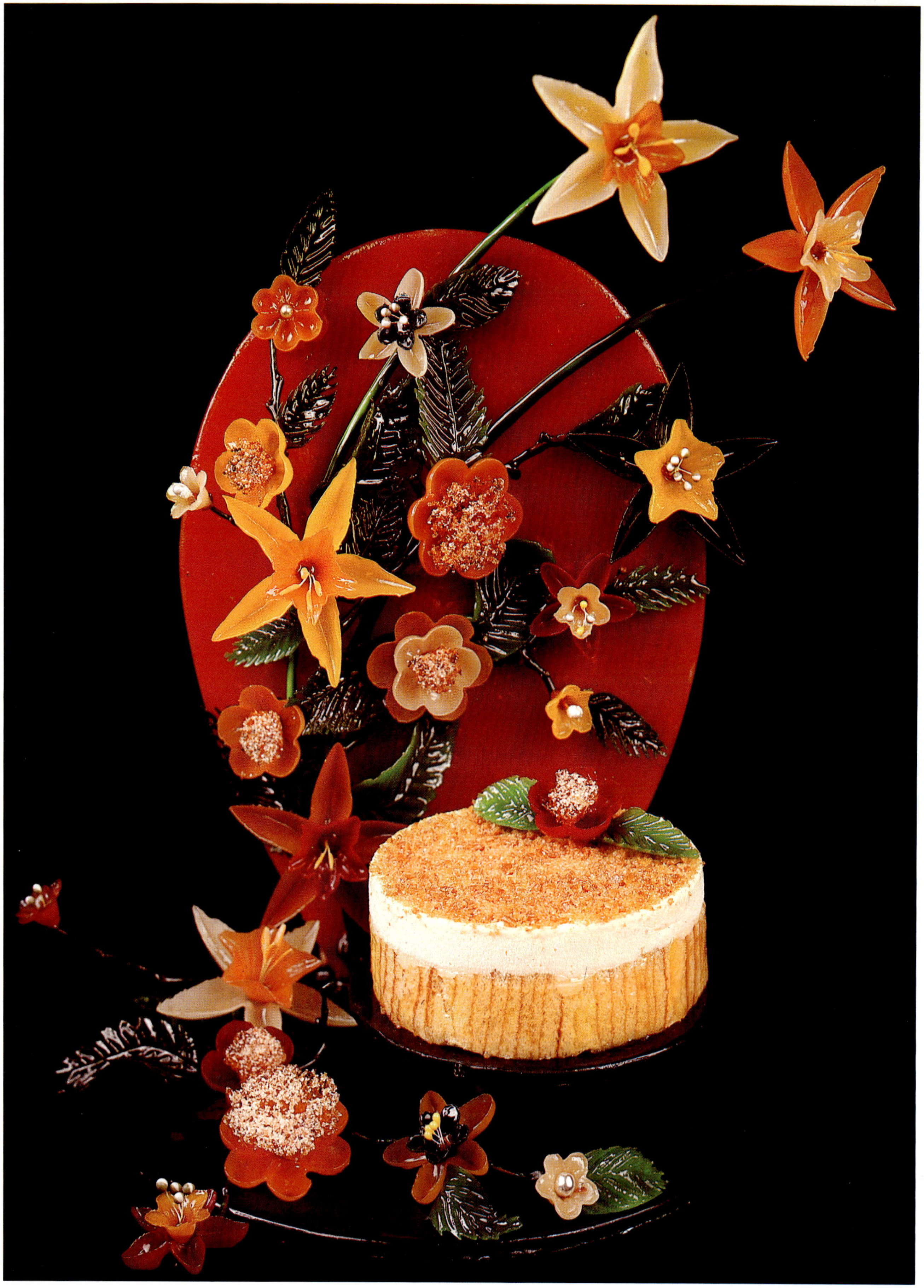

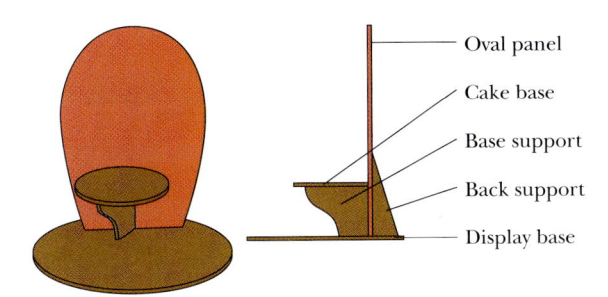

Diagram of Assembled Presentation Pedestal

- Oval panel
- Cake base
- Base support
- Back support
- Display base

Cake Presentation Pedestal

The most appealing and elegant cakes are usually decorated simply. However, special occasions such as weddings, birthdays, and holidays may call for more elaborate presentations. In the past, decorations were placed directly on the cake. Although the ornaments were attractive on their own, the colors and decorations often created a garish-looking cake.

Now, cakes are presented rather modestly, so they are more appetizing, and the decorations are displayed separately. Ornaments and decorations are always prepared from edible materials such as sugar, chocolate, or marzipan. These display pieces give the pastry chef a chance to display his or her talent and creativity.

This presentation piece is made from poured sugar (see pages 330–333) and molded sugar flowers (see pages 286–293). The cake is set on a pedestal constructed from a round disk of poured sugar raised on a support. A large, poured sugar oval panel with a flat end that allows it to be attached to the base plate is decorated with molded flowers and leaves. It stands upright, supported by the back and base plates. All pieces are prepared separately and affixed with caramel.

Facing Page: Cake Presentation Pedestal

- Sliced poached pears brushed with apricot glaze
- Pear brandy mousse
- Biscuit or génoise moistened with pear simple syrup
- Chantilly and candied almonds

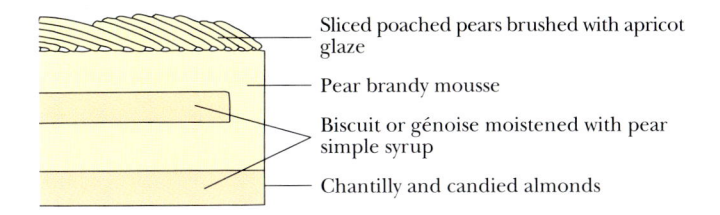

Pear Caprice
Caprice aux Poires

This cake is assembled in a 1 1/3 in/35 mm high cake ring.

Place a layer of biscuit the same diameter as the ring inside, moistened lightly with pear simple syrup. Fill the ring half-full with pear mousse. Cover with a second layer of biscuit slightly smaller in diameter than the ring, moistened with pear simple syrup. Smooth a layer of the mousse flush to the rim of the ring. Refrigerate.

Remove the ring by heating it with a propane torch. Cover the top of the cake with sliced poached pears. Brush with apricot or other light-colored glaze. Coat the sides with chantilly and press on candied almonds.

Cakes

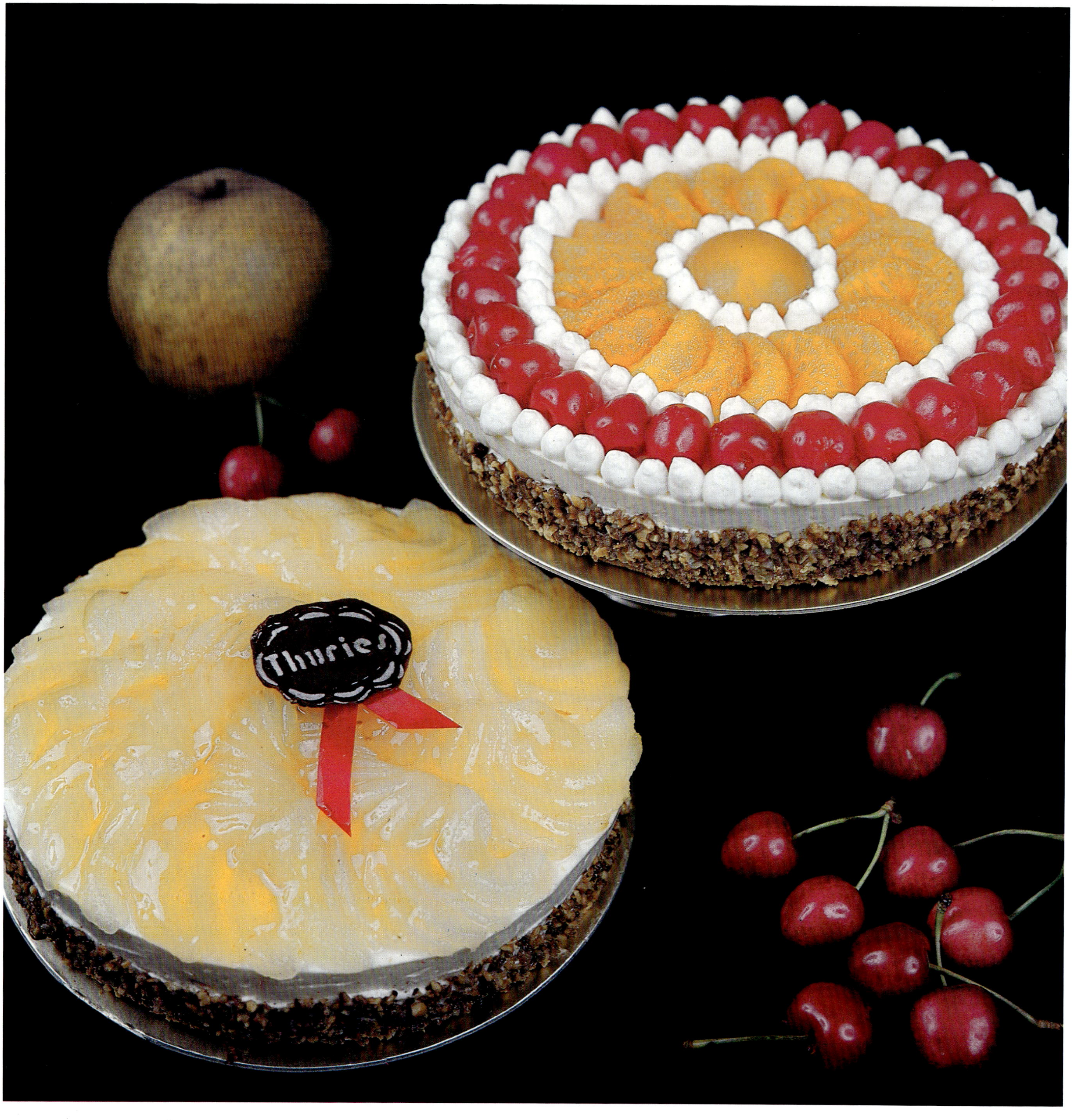
Thuries

Pear Brandy Mousse
Mousse à l'Alcool de Poires

pear brandy, Williamine	5.5 oz	150 g
sugar	4 oz	120 g
gelatin sheets	10	10
crème fraîche, whipped	35 oz	1,000 g

Cover the gelatin sheets with very cold water to soften. Bring the pear brandy and sugar to a boil. Remove from heat. Squeeze the excess water out of the gelatin sheets and stir into hot brandy until melted. Strain and set aside to cool. Just before setting, quickly fold in the whipped crème fraîche.

This mousse should be used shortly after it is prepared.

Fruit Caprice
Caprice aux Fruits

Follow the diagram given for pear caprice (see page 75). This cake is assembled in a 1 1/3 in/35 mm high cake ring. Place a layer of biscuit inside the ring and moisten with kirsch simple syrup. Fill the ring half-full with kirsch mousse. Cover with a second layer of biscuit, moisten with kirsch simple syrup. Smooth a layer of the mousse flush to the rim of the ring. Freeze.

Remove the ring by heating it with a propane torch. Decorate the top of the cake with assorted fresh or poached fruit and chantilly. Coat the sides with chantilly and press candied almonds around the bottom half of the cake.

Facing Page: Pear Caprice, Fruit Caprice

Kirsch Mousse No. 1
Mousse au Kirsch

See recipes for kirsch mousse and little duke on page 71.

Kirsch Mousse No. 2
Mousse au Kirsch

gelatin sheets	12	12
milk	7 oz	200 g
sugar	5.5 oz	150 g
egg yolks	4	4
kirsch	3.5 oz	100 g
crème fraîche, whipped	35 oz	1,000 g

Cover the gelatin sheets with very cold water to soften. Stirring constantly, cook the milk, sugar, and egg yolks to 176°–185°F/80°–85°C. Remove from heat. Squeeze the excess water from the gelatin sheets and stir into the hot liquid until melted. Set aside to cool.

Just before the mixture sets, stir in the kirsch, then fold in the whipped crème fraîche.

This mousse should be used shortly after it is prepared.

Modern French Pastry

- Blackcurrant gelée
- Biscuit moistened with blackcurrant simple syrup
- Blackcurrant mousse

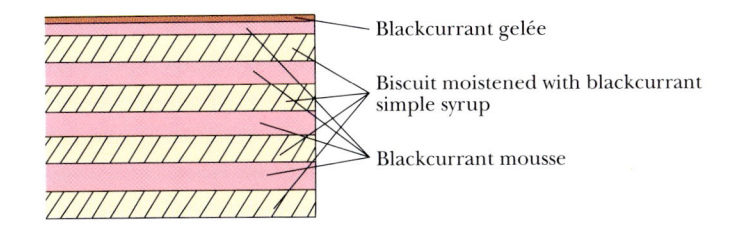

Blackcurrant Saint Ange
Saint-Ange Cassis

This cake is assembled in a 2 in/5 cm high, 15 in/38 cm by 23 in/58 cm stainless steel cake frame. Prepare four layers of biscuit baked on sheet pans approximately 1 in/2.5 cm larger in width and length than the frame. Set the frame over a sheet pan. Place a layer of biscuit inside the frame, turned over with the porous side up (the side touching the sheet pan during baking). Moisten the biscuit with blackcurrant simple syrup. Spread a layer of blackcurrant mousse. Cover with a second layer of biscuit, moistened with the blackcurrant simple syrup. Spread a layer of blackcurrant mousse. Cover with a third layer of biscuit and moisten with the simple syrup. Spread a third layer of mousse, cover with biscuit and moisten with the simple syrup. Smooth a layer of mousse flush to the rim of the frame. Refrigerate.

Spread blackcurrant gelée over the top of the cake. Heat the frame using a propane torch. Run a knife around the inside against the frame and lift it straight off. Heat a serrated knife in hot water and cut the cake into square, rectangular, or individual cakes.

Blackcurrant Mousse
Mousse au Cassis

dessert gelée*	5.5 oz	150 g
blackcurrant pulp	28 oz	800 g
sugar	7 oz	200 g
crème fraîche, whipped	51 fl oz	1.5 L
blackcurrant extract to taste		

*Dessert gelée is a prepared gelatin product available from purveyors. If this is not available, 10–15 gelatin sheets can be substituted. Soak the gelatin sheets in cold water. Then squeeze out the excess water before adding to the hot liquid. Stir until melted.

Bring the blackcurrant pulp, sugar, and dessert gelée to a boil. Remove from heat and set aside to cool.

After the mixture has cooled, stir in the extract and fold in the whipped crème fraîche.

This mousse should be used shortly after it is prepared.

Chef's Note: The quantity above is the amount needed for a cake made in a frame approximately 15 in/38 cm by 23 in/58 cm This mousse works equally well for cakes assembled in cake rings.

Blackcurrant Simple Syrup
Sirop au Cassis

Combine 25.5 fl oz/750 ml. blackcurrant juice with 8.5 fl oz/250 ml. simple syrup, 30° baume.

Blackcurrant Gelée No. 1
Gelée de Cassis

gelatin sheets	15	15
water	17.5 oz	500 g
sugar	17.5 oz	500 g
blackcurrant juice	17.5 oz	500 g

Facing Page: Raspberry Saint Ange, Blackcurrant Saint Ange, Strawberry Saint Ange

(Blackcurrant Gelée No. 1 recipe continued on next page)

Cover the gelatin sheets with very cold water to soften. Bring the water, sugar, and blackcurrant juice to a boil. Remove from heat. Squeeze the excess water from the gelatin sheets and stir into the syrup until melted. Strain through a fine mesh strainer.

Blackcurrant Gelée No. 2
Gelée de Cassis

gelatin sheets	8	8
blackcurrant juice	17.5 oz	500 g
sugar	9 oz	250 g

Cover the gelatin sheets with very cold water to soften. Squeeze the excess water from the gelatin sheets and melt them without boiling. Combine the blackcurrant juice and sugar, and stir in the melted gelatin. Strain through a fine mesh strainer.

Raspberry Saint Ange
Saint-Ange Framboise

Follow the procedure for the blackcurrant Saint Ange (see page 79) using a 1.5 in/4 cm high, 15 in/38 cm by 23 in/58 cm cake frame. As the frame is slightly lower than the blackcurrant Saint Ange, only three layers of biscuit are needed.

Place a cake frame on a sheet pan larger than the frame. Place a layer of biscuit with the porous side up (that which was touching the sheet pan during baking). Moisten the biscuit with raspberry simple syrup. Spread on a layer of raspberry mousse. Cover with a second layer of biscuit, moisten with the syrup, and spread on a layer of mousse. Repeat this step until there are three layers of biscuit and three layers of mousse, the final layer being the mousse spread flush to the rim of the frame. Refrigerate.

Glaze the top of the cake with raspberry gelée. Remove the frame (see page 79). Using a serrated knife, cut into square, rectangular, or individual cakes.

Raspberry Mousse
Mousse Framboise

The following recipe provides the quantity of mousse needed to prepare the raspberry Saint Ange cake, above.

raspberry pulp	24.5 oz	700 g
sugar	5.5 oz	150 g
dessert gelée*	5.5 oz	150 g
crème fraîche, whipped	42 fl oz	1.25 L
raspberry brandy to taste		

*Dessert gelée is a prepared gelatin product available from purveyors. If this is not available, 10–15 gelatin sheets can be substituted. Soak the gelatin sheets in cold water. Then squeeze out the excess water before adding to the hot liquid. Stir until melted.

Bring the raspberry pulp, sugar, and dessert gelée to a boil, stirring constantly. Remove from heat. Before the mixture cools completely, stir in the brandy and fold in the whipped crème fraîche. This mousse should be used shortly after it is prepared.

Raspberry Simple Syrup
Sirop à la Framboise

raspberry brandy	10.5 oz	300 g
raspberry juice	10.5 oz	300 g
simple syrup, 30° baume	10.5 oz	300 g

Combine all ingredients.

Raspberry Gelée
Gelée de Framboises

gelatin sheets	15–20	15–20
apple gelée	35 oz	1,000 g
raspberry juice	9 oz	250 g

Cover the gelatin sheets with very cold water to soften. Bring the raspberry juice to a boil, add the apple gelée and bring the mixture back to a boil. Remove from heat. Squeeze the excess water from the gelatin sheets and stir into the hot mixture until melted.

Strawberry halves brushed with gelée
Strawberry mousse
Biscuit moistened with strawberry simple syrup

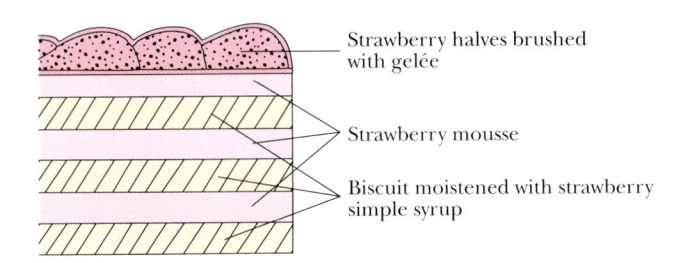

Strawberry Saint Ange
Saint-Ange Fraise

This cake is assembled in a cake frame following the procedure given for the blackcurrant Saint Ange (see page 79). Make the appropriate substitutions, using strawberry mousse and moistening the biscuit with strawberry simple syrup. Decorate the finished cake with strawberry halves and coat with strawberry gelée. Cut into portions.

Strawberry Mousse
Mousse aux Fraises

The following recipe provides the quantity of mousse needed to prepare the Strawberry Saint Ange cake, above.

gelatin sheets	15	15
strawberry pulp	26.5 oz	750 g
sugar	5.5 oz	150 g
crème fraîche, whipped	51 fl oz	1.5 L
natural strawberry extract to taste		

Cover the gelatin sheets with very cold water to soften. Bring the strawberry pulp and sugar to a boil, stirring constantly. Remove from heat. Squeeze the excess water from the gelatin sheets and stir into the hot mixture until melted. Just before the mixture completely cools, stir in the extract and fold in the whipped crème fraîche.

Strawberry Simple Syrup
Sirop à la Fraise

kirsch	10.5 oz	300 g
Strawberry juice	10.5 oz	300 g
Simple syrup, 30° baumé	10.5 oz	300 g

Combine all ingredients.

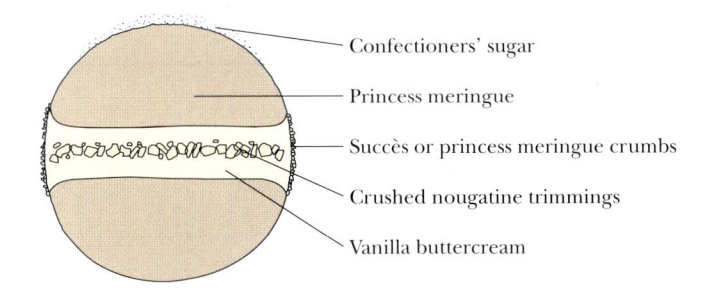

Confectioners' sugar
Princess meringue
Succès or princess meringue crumbs
Crushed nougatine trimmings
Vanilla buttercream

Princess Meringue Cake
Peltier

Bake and cool a princess meringue. Turn it over, flat side up. The bottom can be trimmed so that it sits level

(Princess Meringue Cake recipe continued on page 83)

Cakes

82 Modern French Pastry

on a cardboard. With a pastry bag and flat yule log tip, pipe a layer of vanilla buttercream. Sprinkle a layer of coarsely ground nougatine. Cover with a second layer of buttercream and place another princess meringue on top, rounded (top) side up. Use a metal spatula to smooth buttercream around the sides of the cake where the two layers meet. Cover the buttercream with succès or princess meringue crumbs. Dust the top with confectioners' sugar and wrap a ribbon from underneath, making a bow on top.

Special Buttercream
Crème au Beurre Spéciale

butter	17.5 oz	500 g
Italian meringue	17.5 oz	500 g
vanilla extract, several drops		

Whip the butter until it is light and aerated. Fold in the Italian meringue and vanilla, smoothing with a whisk.

Princess Meringue
Princesse

The princess meringue is a type of almond meringue similar to the succès, though more stable, giving it the advantage of maintaining its classic dome shape.

almond paste	19.5 oz	550 g
milk (approximately)	5.5 oz	150 g
egg whites	21 oz	600 g
sugar	17.5 oz	500 g

Soften the almond paste, gradually stirring in the milk.

Facing Page: Princess Meringue Cake, Sully, Peteroff

At the same time, in the bowl of an electric mixer, whip the egg whites, along with 5.5 oz/150 g of the sugar, to soft peaks. When the egg whites have nearly obtained firm peaks, whip in the remaining sugar.

Gently fold the meringue into the almond paste/milk mixture.

With a hand scraper, drop mounds of meringue of the size needed onto a sheet pan covered with parchment paper. Use a metal spatula, shape the mounds into domes. For individual cakes, pipe the meringue using a pastry bag without a tip to prevent the batter from breaking down.

Bake for 4 hours, at 250°F/120°C.

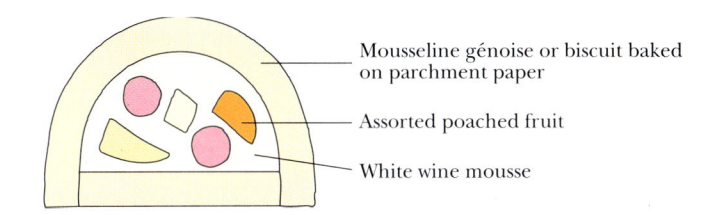

Mousseline génoise or biscuit baked on parchment paper
Assorted poached fruit
White wine mousse

Sully

This cake is assembled upside down in a wide, rounded mold (gouttière), although a narrower mold can be used. Prepare layers of mousseline génoise or sheets of biscuit. Prepare an assortment of well-drained, poached or canned fruit such as cherries, peaches, pears, or apricots.

Line the gouttière with a layer of génoise or biscuit, with the smooth side touching the mold. Fill the bottom of the mold with white wine mousse. Scatter assorted fruit over the mousse. Spread a second layer of mousse and scatter fruit on top. Spread a third layer of mousse. Finish by covering with a strip of génoise or biscuit trimmed to the rim of the mold. Freeze.

Unmold. Dust with confectioners' sugar. Cut into smaller cakes.

White Wine Mousse
Mousse au Vin Blanc

gelatin sheets	10–12	10–12
white wine	12.5 oz	350 g
sugar	14 oz	400 g
egg yolks	12	12
lemons, juice	5	5
crème fraîche, whipped	4 lbs 6 oz	2,000 g

Cover the gelatin sheets with very cold water to soften. Bring the white wine, sugar, eggs yolks, and lemon juice to a boil, whisking constantly. Remove from heat.

Squeeze the excess water from the gelatin sheets and stir into the wine mixture until melted. Set aside to cool. Just when the mixture begins to set, fold in the whipped crème fraîche.

This mousse should be used shortly after it is prepared.

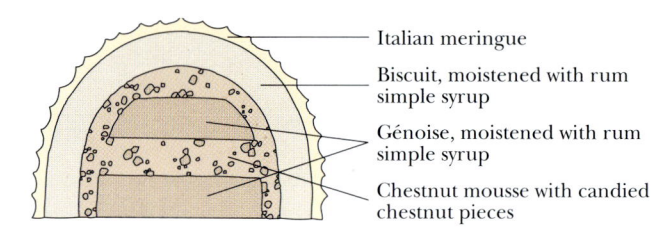

Peteroff

This cake is assembled in a half-sphere mold.

Prepare biscuit or mousseline génoise sheets to line the mold. Prepare thicker layers of génoise for layering. Line the mold with the thinner biscuit or génoise, moistened with rum simple syrup. Fill the base and sides with chestnut mousse and sprinkle with pieces of chestnuts. Cover with a layer of génoise, moistened liberally with rum simple syrup. Spread a second layer of the chestnut mousse and scatter more chestnut pieces. Cover with a second layer of génoise, moistened liberally with rum simple syrup. Smooth the mousse flush to the rim of the mold. Refrigerate.

Unmold the cake onto a cardboard. Moisten with rum simple syrup. Coat the cake with a layer of Italian meringue. With a pastry bag and fluted tip, pipe small stars of Italian meringue over the surface of the cake. Freeze.

Dust the cake with confectioners' sugar and place it in a very hot oven for just a few seconds to brown the tips of the meringue stars. A propane torch can be used to brown the meringue tips or enhance the browning after removing the cake from the hot oven.

Chestnut Mousse
Mousse de Marrons

butter, softened	17.5 oz	500 g
chestnut paste	17.5 oz	500 g
Italian meringue	17.5 oz	500 g

Whip the butter and chestnut paste until light and aerated. Gently fold in the Italian meringue.

This mousse should be used shortly after it is prepared.

Coffee Chestnut Mousse
Mousse de Marrons au Café

chestnut paste	35 oz	1,000 g
butter, softened	17.5 oz	500 g
water, boiling	5.5 oz	150 g
coffee extract	5.5 oz	150 g
Italian meringue	17.5 oz	500 g

In the bowl of an electric mixer, use the paddle attachment to whip the chestnut paste and butter until light and aerated. Gradually add boiling water and coffee extract. Gently fold in the Italian meringue.

Chestnut Paste
Pâte de Marrons

candied chestnut pieces	35 oz	1,000 g
rum or simple syrup, 30° baume	3.5 oz	100 g

Grind the chestnuts pieces with rum or simple syrup to a paste.

Poached Pears

water	34 fl oz	1 L
sugar	24.5 oz	700 g
vanilla beans	2	2

Prepare a light syrup, 20° baume. To do this, bring the above ingredients to a boil, then lower the heat so the syrup is barely simmering. Poach pear halves in the simmering syrup for 1 hour or until tender.

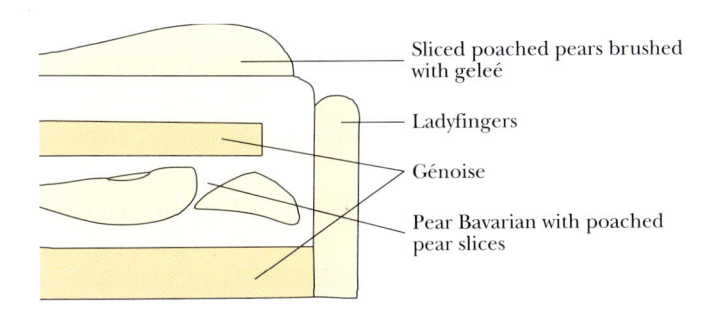

Diagram labels: Sliced poached pears brushed with geleé; Ladyfingers; Génoise; Pear Bavarian with poached pear slices

Pear Charlotte
Charlotte aux Poires

Prepare 4.5 in/12 cm long ladyfingers. Cut them in half crosswise, after baking. Line a cake ring 2.5 in/6 cm high with the ladyfingers, placing the flat, cut side on the bottom. Place a layer of génoise inside the ring so it fits snugly against the ladyfingers. Moisten the génoise with pear simple syrup. Fill the ring half-full with pear charlotte cream. Generously scatter cubes of poached pear over the cream. Cover with a thin layer of génoise, moistened liberally with pear simple syrup. Fill the charlotte to the top with the cream. Freeze.

Remove the cake ring. Cover and decorate the top of the cake with sliced poached pears. Brush with apricot or other light glaze.

Pear Coulis
Coulis aux Poires

pears, canned with syrup	6 lbs 10 oz	3 kg
pears, canned without syrup	4 lbs 6.5 oz	2 kg
sugar	3 lbs 5 oz	1.5 kg
lemons, juice	6	6
pear brandy	2 oz	60 g

Blend all ingredients in a food processor. Store in refrigerator.

Pear Charlotte Cream No. 1
Crème à Charlotte aux Poires

gelatin sheets	18	18
pear poaching syrup	34 fl oz	1 L
dried milk	3.5 oz	100 g
vanilla bean	1	1
egg yolks	20	20
sugar	7 oz	200 g
egg whites	8	8
sugar	17.5 oz	500 g
water	5.5 oz	150 g
pear brandy	9 oz	250 g
crème fraîche	42 fl oz	1.25 L

(Pear Charlotte Cream No. 1 recipe continued on page 87)

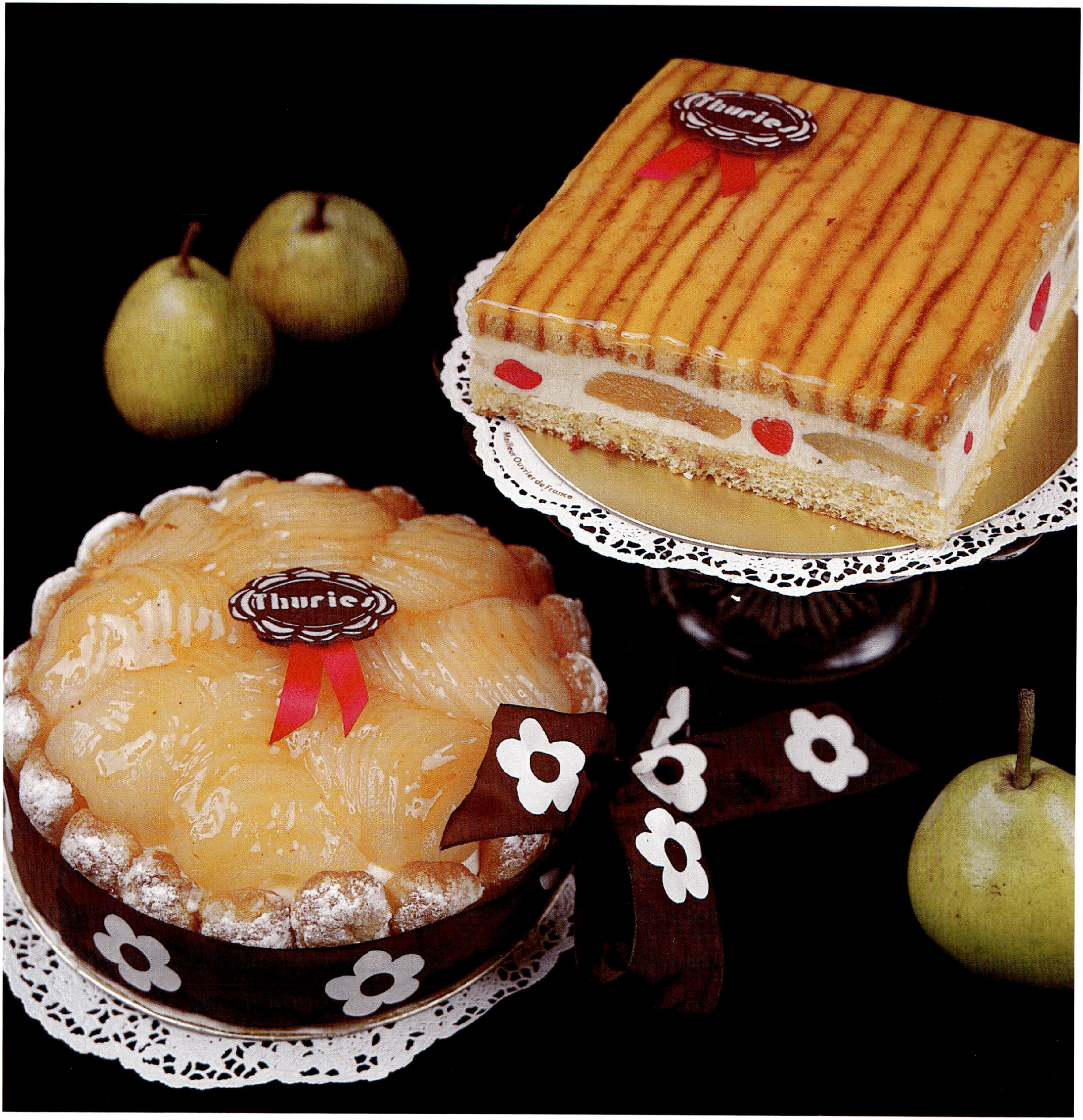
Thuries
Meilleur Ouvrier de France
Thuries

Cover the gelatin sheets with very cold water to soften. Bring the pear syrup, dried milk, and vanilla bean to a boil. Whisk the egg yolks and sugar until thick and pale. Whisk half the syrup mixture into the eggs, then add this mixture to the remaining syrup in the saucepan. Stir continuously until it naps the spatula as for crème anglaise, 185°F/85°C. Remove from heat.

Squeeze the excess water from the gelatin sheets and stir into the hot mixture until melted. Whip the crème fraîche to soft peaks.

Prepare an Italian meringue by cooking the sugar and water to 250°F/121°C, while whipping the egg whites to soft peaks. Pour the cooked sugar in a fine stream, whipping it into the egg whites.

When the pear mixture has cooled, but before setting, whisk in the pear brandy, then fold in the whipped crème fraîche. Finish by gently folding in the Italian meringue.

This cream should be used shortly after it is prepared.

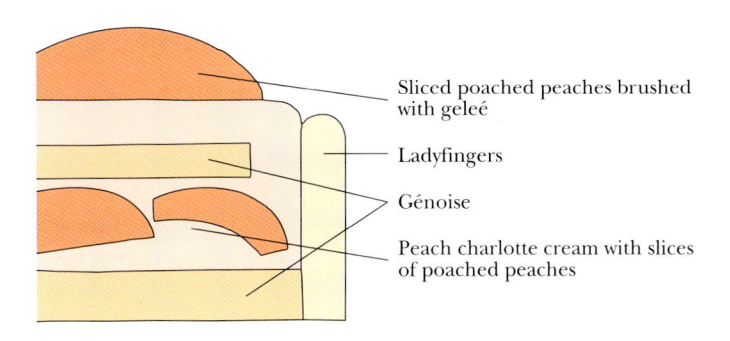

Peach Charlotte
Charlotte aux Pêches

This cake is assembled following the procedure given for the pear charlotte (see page 85), making the appropriate substitutions. Fill with peach charlotte cream. Scatter slices or cubes of poached peaches over the cream. Moisten the biscuit or génoise with peach simple syrup based on the pear simple syrup recipe, but using peach juice and peach brandy.

Pear Simple Syrup
Sirop de Poires

poaching pear liquid, or pear juice	7 oz	200 g
pear brandy	7 oz	200 g
simple syrup	14 oz	400 g

Combine all ingredients.

Peach Charlotte Cream
Crème à Charlotte aux Pêches

peach juice	35 oz	1,000 g
dried milk	3.5 oz	100 g
vanilla bean	1	1
egg yolk	16	16
sugar	7 oz	200 g
gelatin sheets	18	18
peach or maraschino liqueur	7 oz	200 g
crème fraîche	52.5 oz	1,500 g
egg whites	8	8
sugar	17.5 oz	500 g

Follow the procedure given for pear charlotte cream (see page 85).

Facing Page: Pear Charlotte, Gentleman's Whiskey

- Mousseline génoise, layered with jam
- Whiskey mousse with poached fruit
- Biscuit
- Coating chocolate

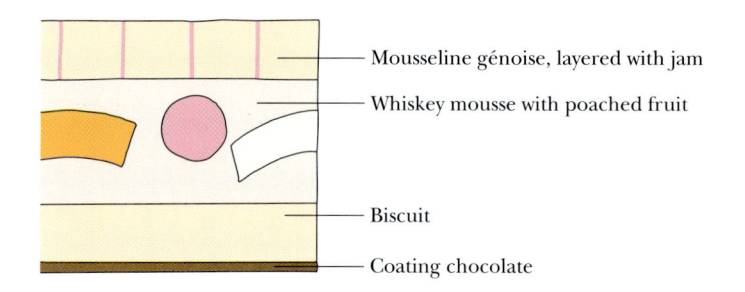

Gentleman's Whiskey
Gentleman au Whiskey

This cake is assembled upside down in a 2 in/5 cm high stainless steel cake frame 15 in/38 cm by 23 in/58 cm. Cover a sheet pan with a sheet of plastic and place the frame over the sheet pan. The sheet pan should be approximately 1 in/2.5 cm longer and wider than the frame. If a cake frame is not available, use a straight-sided sheet pan.

Superimpose 4–5 layers of mousseline génoise each coated with raspberry or other flavored jam. Cut 1/2 in/ 1 cm slices and line them flat on the bottom inside the frame with the layering face up (this recipe follows the technique used for the Alhambra cake). Moisten with whiskey simple syrup. Fill the frame half-full with whiskey mousse. Alternate layers of bigarreau cherries and cubes of poached peaches and pears over the mousse. Spread a second layer of mousse, filling the frame three quarters full. Cover with a fairly thick layer of biscuit, moistened with whiskey simple syrup. Brush on a layer of coating chocolate or liquid couverture. Freeze.

Turn the cake over onto a sheet pan so the layered biscuit is showing. Remove the frame by heating it with a propane torch. Brush the top of the cake with apple gelée or apricot glaze. Cut into squares, rectangles, or individual portions. Place a pastry shop label on top of each cake.

Mousseline Génoise
Génoise Mousseline

eggs	20	20
egg yolks	20	20
sugar	17.5 oz	500 g
flour	7 oz	200 g
cornstarch	7 oz	200 g
butter, melted	3.5 oz	100 g

Whisk the whole eggs, egg yolks, and sugar over a hot water bath or directly over a gas burner until the mixture is warm and aerated. Remove from heat and continue to whip the mixture until it has completely cooled. Sift the flour and cornstarch together and fold them into the egg mixture. Finish by folding in the cool, melted butter. Quickly spread the batter into buttered and floured cake pans or onto sheet pans lined with parchment paper. This recipe fills four sheet pans.

Whiskey Mousse
Mousse au Whiskey

whiskey	5.5 oz	150 g
sugar	5.5 oz	150 g
gelatin sheets	8	8
crème fraîche, whipped	35 oz	1,000 g

Cover the gelatin sheets with very cold water to soften. Bring the whiskey and sugar to a boil. Remove from heat. Squeeze the excess water from the gelatin sheets and stir into the hot liquid until melted. Strain and set aside to cool. Just before setting, fold in the whipped crème fraîche.

This mousse should be used shortly after it is prepared.

Whiskey Simple Syrup
Sirop au Whiskey

Combine 17.5 oz/500 g simple syrup, 30° baume, with 5.5 oz/150 g whiskey.

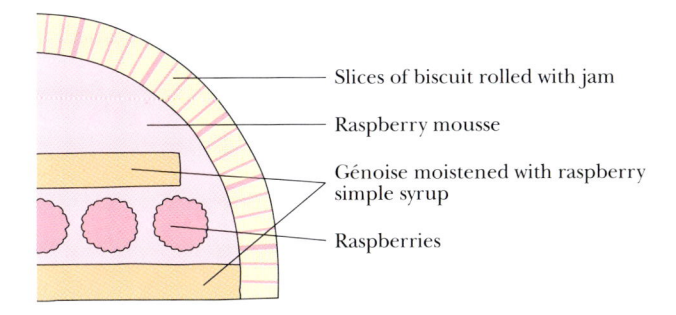

Slices of biscuit rolled with jam
Raspberry mousse
Génoise moistened with raspberry simple syrup
Raspberries

Raspberry Saint Christopher
Saint-Christophe à la Framboise

This cake is assembled in a half-sphere mold of any size. Prepare biscuit rolled with raspberry jam. Prepare génoise layers. Line the mold with slices of biscuit rolled with raspberry jam (see photos on page 91). Spread a layer of raspberry mousse inside the mold. Cover with a layer of génoise, moistened with raspberry simple syrup. Spread a second layer of mousse. Scatter raspberries over the mousse. Spread a third layer of mousse. Cover with a layer of génoise the same diameter as the top of the mold (this becomes the base when the cake is turned out). Freeze.

Unmold. Brush with raspberry gelée or apricot glaze.

Raspberry Mousse
Mousse à la Framboise

gelatin sheets	12	12
white wine	7 oz	200 g
sugar	3.5 oz	100 g
egg yolks	5	5
raspberry purée	12.5 oz	350 g
lemons, juice	4	4
crème fraîche, whipped	35 oz	1,000 g

Cover the gelatin sheets with very cold water to soften. Bring the white wine, sugar, and egg yolks to a boil, stirring constantly. Remove from heat. Squeeze the excess water from the gelatin sheets and stir into the hot mixture until melted. Strain and set aside to cool. Just before the mixture sets, stir in the raspberry purée and lemon juice. Fold in the whipped crème fraîche.

This mousse should be used shortly after it is prepared.

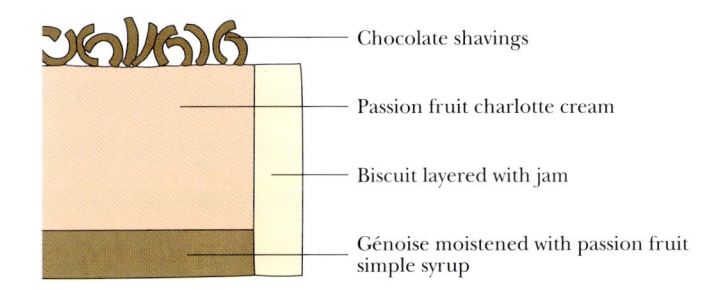

Chocolate shavings
Passion fruit charlotte cream
Biscuit layered with jam
Génoise moistened with passion fruit simple syrup

Passion Fruit Charlotte
Charlotte au Fruit de la Passion

This cake is assembled in a 2 1/3 in/6 cm high cake ring. Line the entire height of the ring with jam-layered biscuit slices. Place a layer of génoise inside the ring, trimmed to fit snugly against the layered biscuit. Moisten the génoise with passion fruit simple syrup. Fill the ring with passion fruit charlotte cream. A second layer of génoise can be added, placing it between two layers of charlotte cream as for the pear charlotte (see page 85, Recipe 1). Freeze.

Remove the cake ring and brush apricot glaze on the layered biscuit around the side of the cake. Decorate the top of the cake with chocolate curls. Place a pastry shop label on top.

Chef's Note: *As an alternative presentation, omit the chocolate curls and brush on a layer of gelée with chopped passion fruit seeds.*

Raspberry Saint Christopher, Passion Fruit Charlotte, Pear Charlotte

Lining a Mold with Rolled Biscuit

Photo 1: Bake a layer of biscuit on a sheet pan lined with parchment paper. Remove the paper, spread a layer of raspberry or other jam or gelée to taste. Tightly roll the biscuit, jelly-roll style. Wrap the roll firmly with plastic wrap. Refrigerate or freeze.

Photo 2: Cut 1/4 in/5 mm thick slices off the roll using a serrated knife. It is easier to cut clean slices if the roll is frozen.

Photo 3: Use the slices to line any cake mold (gouttière or half-sphere) or a cake ring. If a mold is used, the cake is constructed upside down. Evenly distribute the slices, pressing them snugly together starting at the base of the mold and working upward around the sides. The finished cake is unmolded, revealing the slices which decorate the cake.

Passion Fruit Charlotte Cream
Crème à Charlotte au Fruit de la Passion

gelatin sheets	16	16
passion fruit pulp	34 fl oz	1 L
dried milk	3.5 oz	100 g
egg yolks	20	20
sugar	7 oz	200 g
sugar	14 oz	400 g
water	4 oz	120 g
egg whites	8	8
crème fraîche or heavy cream, whipped	3 lbs 5 oz	1,500 g
passion fruit purée	7 oz	200 g

Cover the gelatin sheets with very cold water to soften. Bring the fruit pulp and dried milk to a boil. Whisk the egg yolks and sugar until thick and pale. Stir half of the hot liquid into the egg mixture, then stir the egg mixture into the saucepan with the remaining liquid. Cook the mixture slowly, stirring constantly until it coats a spoon, 185°F/85°C. Immediately remove it from the heat. Squeeze the excess water from the gelatin sheets and stir into the hot mixture until melted.

Prepare an Italian meringue by cooking the sugar and water to 250°F/121°C, while whipping the egg whites to soft peaks. Pour the cooked sugar in a fine stream, whipping it into the egg whites. Continue whipping until cool.

Whip the crème fraîche or heavy cream to soft peaks.

When the passion fruit mixture has cooled, just before it sets, stir in the passion fruit purée. Fold in the cooled meringue, then the whipped cream or crème fraîche.

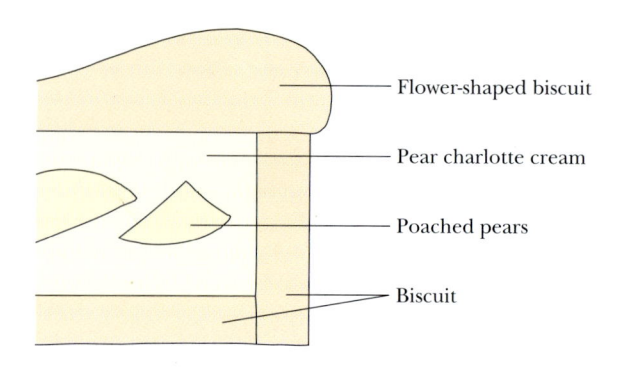

Pear Charlotte
Charlotte aux Poires

This cake is assembled in a 2 1/3 in/6 mm high cake ring. Prepare a strip of ladyfingers, sprinkling them with confectioners' sugar before baking. Trim the baked strips to the height of the ring.

Line the inside of the cake ring with the ladyfingers. Place a layer of génoise inside the ring, moistened with pear simple syrup. Fill the ring half-full with pear charlotte cream. When the cream begins to set, place sliced poached pears on top so that they do not fall to the bottom. Smooth the cream flush to the top of the ring. Freeze.

Remove the cake ring. Cover the top of the cake with a flower-shaped biscuit layer. Wrap a ribbon around the side of the cake.

Chef's Note: This is one of the most expedient ways to prepare a charlotte. Traditionally, this type of charlotte is served with a raspberry or pear coulis.

Pear Charlotte Cream No. 2
Crème à Charlotte aux Poires

gelatin sheets	16	16
pear juice	34 fl oz	1 L
egg yolks	16	16

Place the flower shaped biscuit on top of the cake.

pear brandy	5.5 oz	150 g
crème fraîche	24.5 oz	700 g
Italian meringue	24.5 oz	700 g

Cover the gelatin sheets with very cold water to soften. Whisk the egg yolks until thick and pale. Bring the pear juice to a boil and combine it with the egg yolks. Cook the mixture until it coats the spoon, 185°F/85°C, then remove it from the heat. Squeeze the excess water from the gelatin sheets and stir into the hot mixture until melted. Stir in the pear brandy. Set aside to cool.

Whip the crème fraîche. When the mixture is almost cool, just before it sets, divide it in half.

Fold the whipped cream into one half of the mixture and the Italian meringue into the other half, then gently fold the two mixtures together.

This mousse should be used shortly after it is prepared.

Pear Charlotte Cream No. 3
Crème à Charlotte aux Poires

gelatin sheets	18	18
milk	35 fl oz	1 L
vanilla bean	1	1
egg yolks	20	20
sugar	16 oz	450 g
pear brandy	9 oz	250 g
crème fraîche, whipped	3 lbs 5 oz	1,500 g

Follow the same procedure given for Recipe 2.

Strawberry Sublime Cake
Sublime à la Fraise

This cake can also be flavored with raspberry by replacing the strawberry purée with raspberry purée; the procedure remains the same.

This cake is assembled in a 2 in/5 cm high, 15 in/38 cm by 23 in/58 cm stainless steel cake frame. Cover a sheet pan with a sheet of plastic and place the cake frame on top. If a cake frame is not available, use a high, straight-sided sheet pan or cake pan.

Superimpose 4–5 sheets of biscuit layered with apricot glaze or jam. Cut 1/2 in/1 cm wide strips. Place the strips in the bottom of the cake frame or mold, layered side down. Fill the mold three quarters full with strawberry mousse. Strawberries may be scattered over the mousse, although this would prevent the cake from being stored in the freezer, because freezing adversely affects the texture of the berries. Cover with a fairly thick layer of biscuit, moistened lightly with kirsch simple syrup. Brush on a layer of coating chocolate or liquid couverture. Freeze or refrigerate appropriately.

Place a sheet pan on top of the frame and turn the cake over so the decorative layered biscuit is now on top. Remove the frame. Brush the top of the cake with gelée or apricot glaze. Cut the cake into square, rectangular, large, or individual cakes. Place each cake on a serving cardboard. Place a pastry shop label on top.

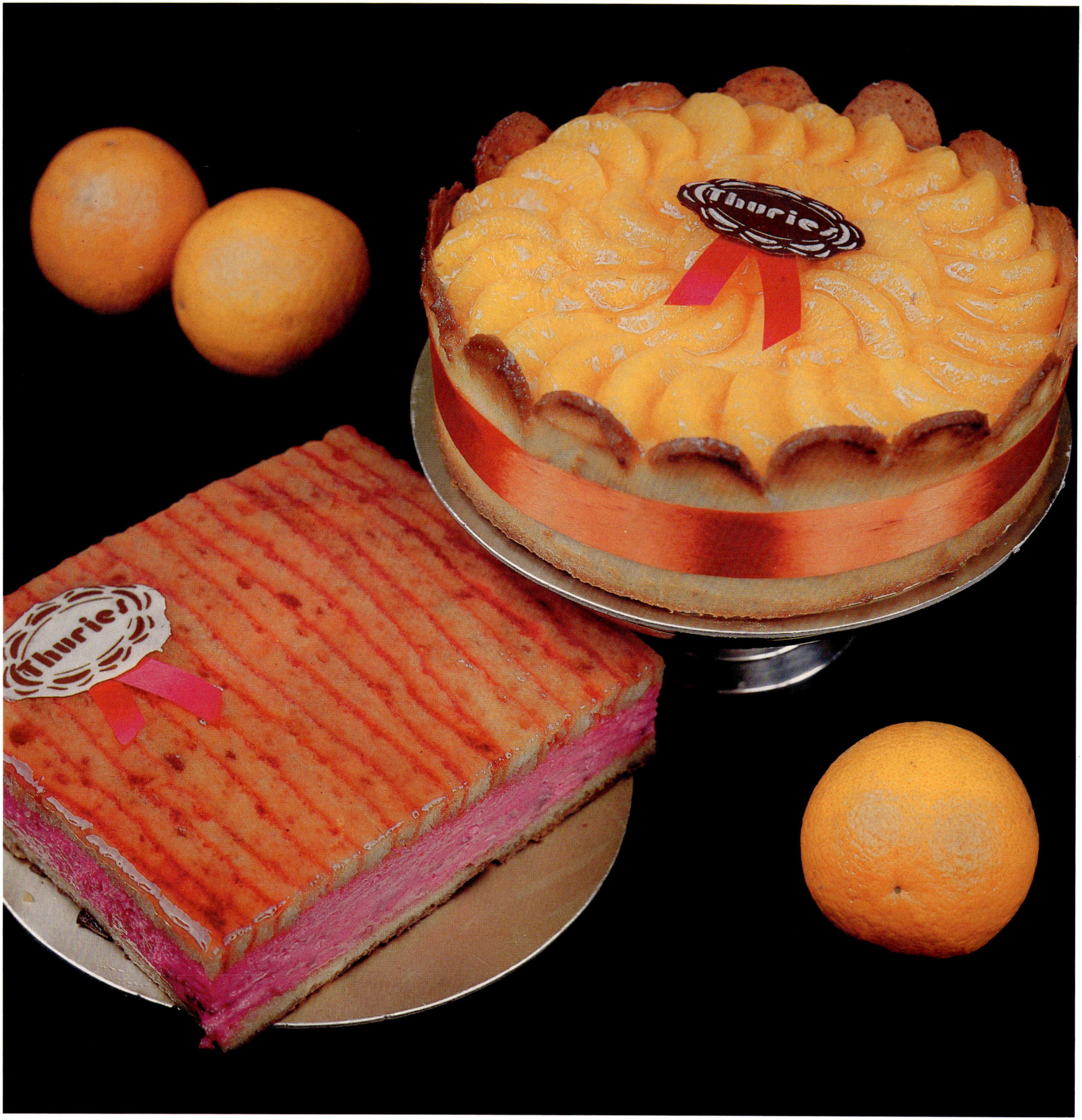
Thuries
Thuries

Strawberry or Raspberry Mousse
Mousse à la Fraise ou à la Framboise

gelatin sheets	12	12
strawberry pulp	17.5 oz	500 g
sugar	5.5 oz	150 g
kirsch or other liqueur	2 oz	50 g
crème fraîche, whipped	35 oz	1,000 g

Cover the gelatin sheets with very cold water to soften.

Bring the fruit pulp and sugar to a boil, stirring constantly. Remove from heat. Squeeze the excess water from the gelatin sheets and stir them into the hot liquid until melted. Just before the mixture has completely cooled, stir in the liqueur, and fold in the whipped crème fraîche.

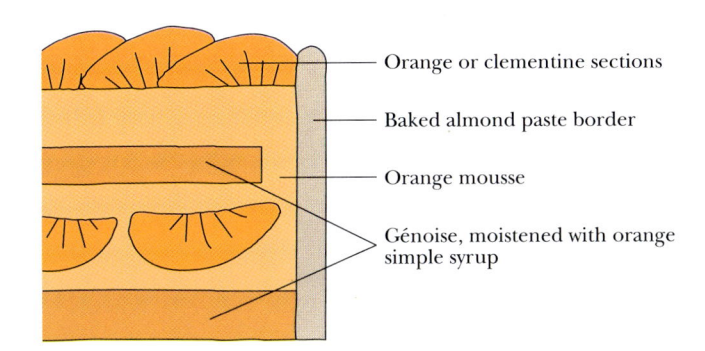

Valencia

A special almond paste border is made for the side of the cake (recipe follows). Use a 1/8 in/3 mm thick stencil, the length of which corresponds to the circumference of the cake ring.

Line the cake ring with the special almond paste. Place a layer of génoise inside the ring, moistened lightly with orange simple syrup. Fill the ring one third full with orange mousse. Scatter cubed orange sections over the mousse. Spread a second layer of mousse. Cover with a layer of génoise liberally moistened with the orange simple syrup. Cover the biscuit with a layer of mousse. Refrigerate.

Remove the ring. Arrange orange or clementine sections on top of the cake to form a pinwheel. Brush with apricot glaze. Wrap a ribbon around the side of the cake and place a pastry shop label on top.

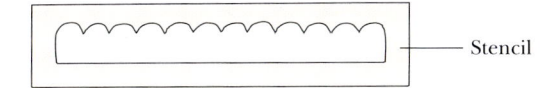

Special Almond Paste
Pâte d'Amandes Spéciale

almond paste	17.5 oz	500 g
egg whites	3	3
crème fraîche	3.5 oz	100 g
flour	4 oz	120 g

This recipe will prepare five medium-sized strips.

Blend all ingredients until well combined.

Place the stencil on a buttered sheet pan and spread the batter over it. Remove the stencil and bake the almond paste strips in a hot oven. Upon removing the strips from the oven, while they are still hot and malleable, line them against the inside of the cake ring.

Orange or Mandarine Mousse
Mousse à l'Orange ou à l'Mandarine

gelatin sheets	18	18
orange juice	34 fl oz	1 L
oranges, zest of	5	5

Facing Page: Strawberry Sublime Cake, Valencia

(Orange or Mandarine Mousse Recipe continued on page 97)

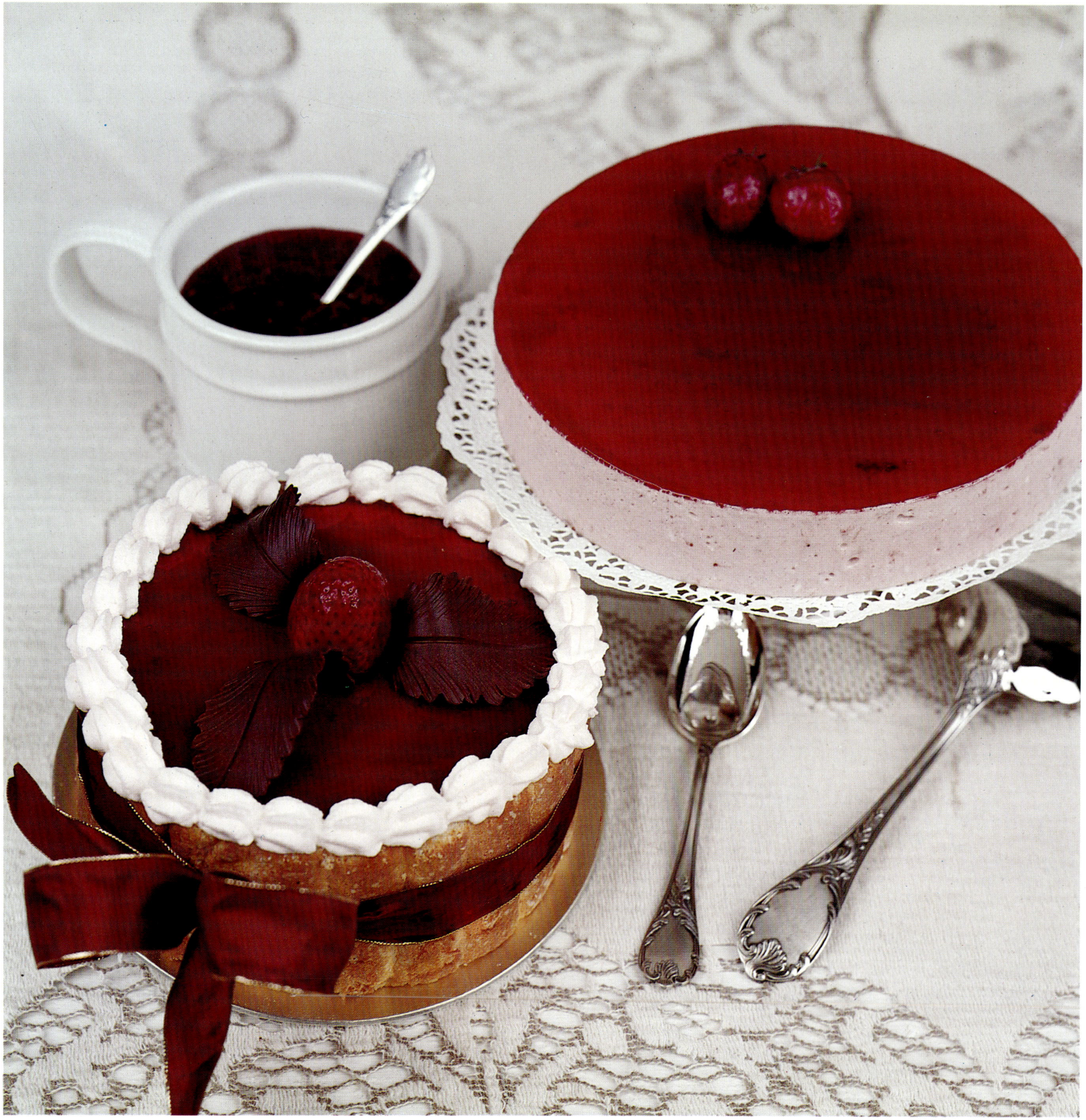

egg yolks	12	12
sugar	14 oz	400 g
Cointreau	3.5 oz	100 g
orange syrup	5 oz	150 g
crème fraîche	51 fl oz	1.5 L

Cover the gelatin sheets with very cold water to soften. Bring the orange juice and zests to a boil. Whisk the egg yolks and sugar until pale and thick. Combine the egg yolk/sugar mixture with the juice and bring them to a simmer, stirring constantly. Remove from heat. Squeeze the gelatin sheets to remove the excess water and stir into the hot mixture until melted. Set aside to cool.

Whip the crème fraîche to soft peaks and fold it along with the orange syrup and the Cointreau into the cool mixture just before it sets.

This mousse should be used shortly after it is prepared.

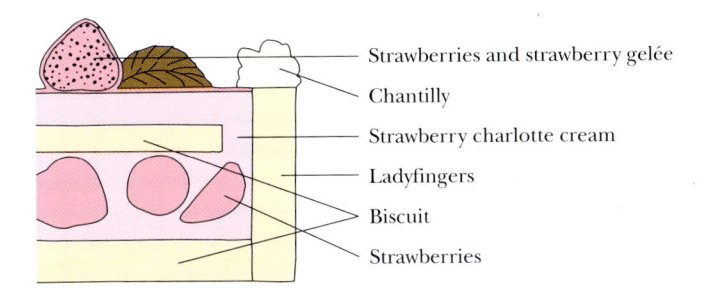

Strawberry Charlotte
Charlotte aux Fraises

This cake is assembled in a 2 1/3 in/6 cm high cake ring. Prepare joined ladyfingers, sprinkling them with confectioners' sugar before baking. Cut the baked, cooled strips 2 1/3 in/6 cm high. Line the ladyfinger strips around the inside of the ring. Place a layer of génoise inside the bottom of the ring, moistened with strawberry simple syrup. Fill the ring one third full with strawberry charlotte cream. Wait until the cream begins to set, then scatter strawberries generously over the cream. Spread a second layer of cream. Cover with a layer of biscuit, moistened liberally with strawberry simple syrup. Smooth the mousse flush to the top of the ring. Refrigerate.

Remove the cake ring. Cover the top of the cake with strawberry gelée. Dip one whole strawberry in the gelée and place it on top of the cake. Surround the strawberry with three plastic chocolate leaves. Pipe a chantilly border on the top edge of the cake. Wrap a ribbon around the side.

Strawberry Charlotte Cream
Crème à Charlotte aux Fraises

gelatin sheets	15	15
strawberry pulp	34 fl oz	1 L
lemons, juice	2	2
extract to taste		
crème fraîche	34 fl oz	1 L
sugar	14 oz	400 g
water	4 oz	120 g
egg whites	8	8

Cover the gelatin sheets with very cold water to soften.

Warm, but do not boil, the strawberry pulp, lemon juice, and extract. Remove from heat. Squeeze the excess water from the gelatin sheets and stir into the hot mixture until melted.

Whip the crème fraîche to soft peaks.

Prepare an Italian meringue by cooking the sugar and water to 250°F/121°C, while whipping the egg whites to soft peaks. Pour the cooked sugar in a fine stream, whipping it into the egg whites.

Just before the strawberry mixture sets, gently fold in the whipped crème fraîche, then the Italian meringue.

This mousse should be used shortly after it is prepared.

Facing Page: Strawberry Charlotte, Strawberry Mirror

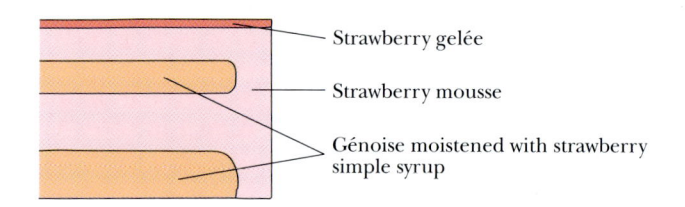

Strawberry Mirror
Miroir aux Fraises

This cake is assembled in a 1 in/3 cm high cake ring. Prepare two layers of génoise slightly smaller in diameter than the cake ring.

    Place a layer of génoise inside the bottom of the cake ring, moistened with strawberry simple syrup. Fill the ring half-full with strawberry mousse. Cover with a second layer of génoise, moistened with strawberry simple syrup. Smooth the mousse flush to the top of the ring. Freeze.

    It is also possible to assemble the cake with three layers of génoise and three layers of mousse.

    Place the cake on a cake cardboard and coat the top with strawberry gelée. Remove the ring by heating it with a propane torch. Decorate the cake with two strawberries dipped in gelée and place them on top of the cake.

Strawberry Simple Syrup
Sirop de Fraises

kirsch	7 oz	200 g
strawberry juice	14 oz	400 g
simple syrup, 30° baumé	14 oz	400 g

Combine all ingredients.

Strawberry Mousse
Mousse aux Fraises

gelatin sheets	16	16
strawberry juice	35 oz	1,000 g
egg yolks	12	12
sugar	7 oz	200 g
strawberry liqueur	9 oz	250 g
crème fraîche or heavy cream, whipped	35 oz	1,000 g
egg whites	8	8
sugar	14 oz	400 g
water	4 oz	120 g

    Follow the procedure given for raspberry mousse (see page 95).

Chocolate Chantilly
Chantilly au Chocolat

Crème fraîche or heavy cream	35 oz	1,000 g
Confectioners' sugar	3.5 oz	100 g
Chocolate, melted	10.5 oz	300 g

    Whip the crème fraîche or heavy cream with confectioners' sugar to soft peaks. Melt the chocolate to 104°F/40°C and fold it into the cream immediately after whipping. It is important to work quickly and stop promptly after combining the two ingredients to prevent the mixture from becoming grainy.

    This mousse should be used shortly after it is prepared.

Chef's Note: *It is also possible to substitute cocoa powder for the chocolate.*

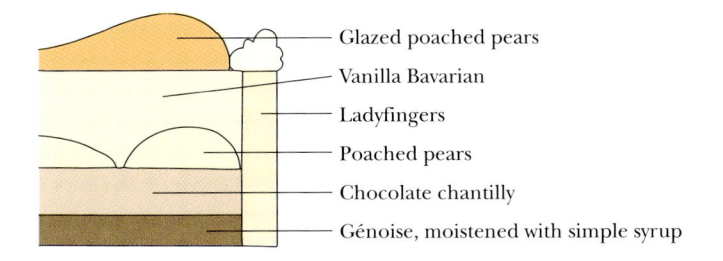

Diagram labels (top to bottom):
- Glazed poached pears
- Vanilla Bavarian
- Ladyfingers
- Poached pears
- Chocolate chantilly
- Génoise, moistened with simple syrup

Belle Hélène Charlotte
Charlotte Belle Hélène

This cake is assembled in a 2 1/3 in/6 cm high cake ring. Prepare joined ladyfingers. Cut the ladyfingers to the height of the ring, 2 1/3 in/6 cm, and line them around the inside of the ring. Place a layer of génoise on the bottom inside the ring, moistened with vanilla or rum simple syrup. Spread a 1/2 in/1 cm layer of chocolate chantilly. Scatter poached pear slices over the chocolate chantilly. Smooth vanilla Bavarian flush to the top of the ring. Freeze.

Remove the cake ring. Place poached pear halves on top of the cake. Brush a drop of red-colored apricot glaze on the center of each pear to create a blush effect. Brush the top of the cake, including the pears, with plain apricot or clear glaze. With a pastry bag and fluted tip, pipe chantilly around the top edge and in the center of the cake. Wrap a ribbon around the cake.

Chef's Note: *To vary this charlotte, replace the pears with other poached or fresh fruit such as apricots, peaches, and cherries.*

Vanilla Bavarian Cream
Crème Bavaroise à la Vanille

gelatin sheets	15	15
milk	34 fl oz	1 L
vanilla beans	2	2
egg yolks	16	16
sugar	12.5 oz	350 g
crème fraîche	26.5 oz	750 g

Cover the gelatin sheets with very cold water to soften. Split the vanilla beans lengthwise. Bring the milk and beans to a boil. Whisk the egg yolks and sugar until thick and pale. Add the egg/sugar mixture to the hot milk. Cook the mixture, stirring constantly, until it coats the spoon, 185°F/85°C, and strain. Squeeze the excess water from the gelatin sheets and stir into the hot mixture until melted. Set the cream aside to cool, stirring occasionally.

Whip the crème fraîche to soft peaks. Just before the cream sets, gently fold in the whipped crème fraîche.

This mousse should be used shortly after it is prepared.

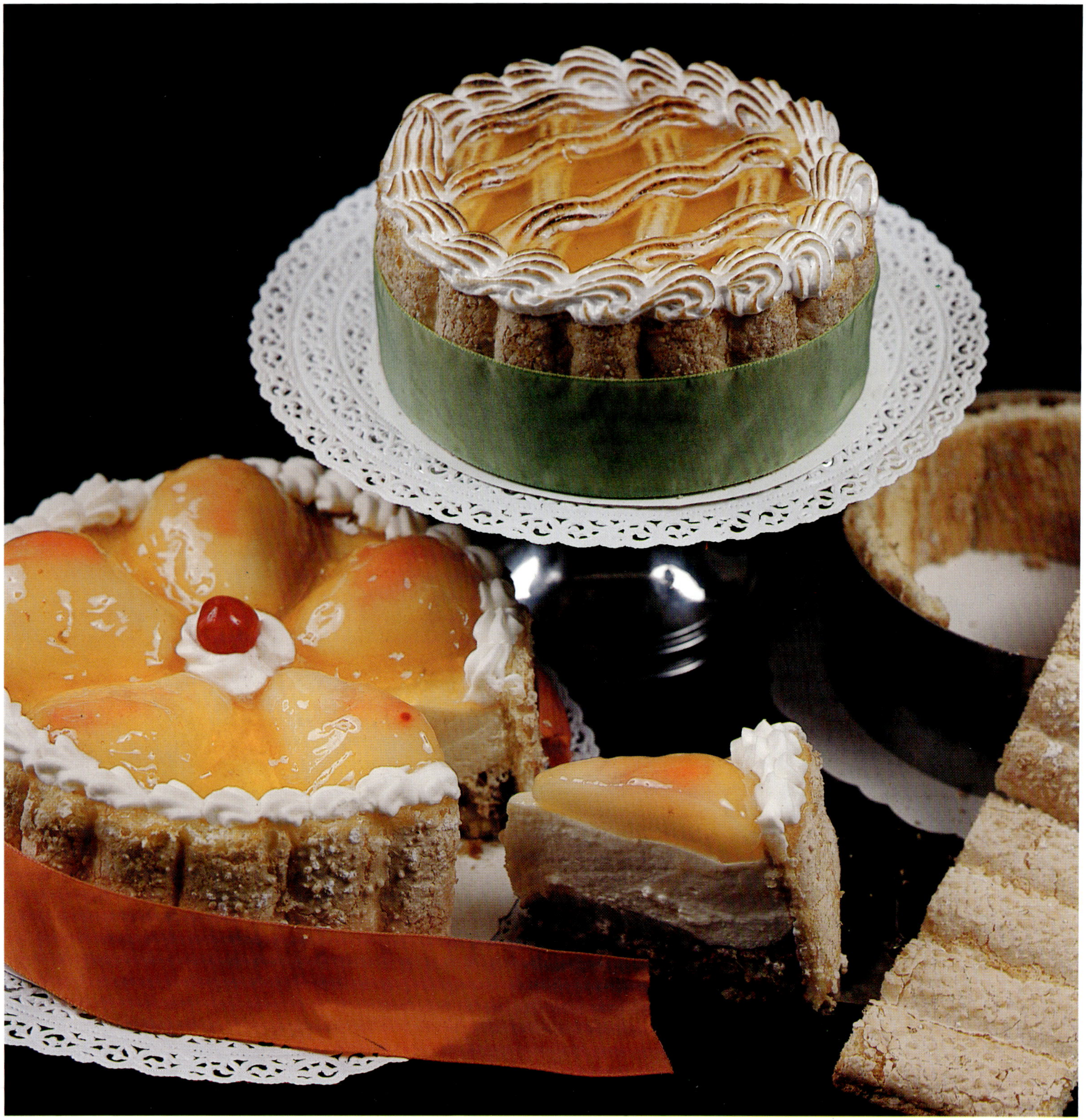

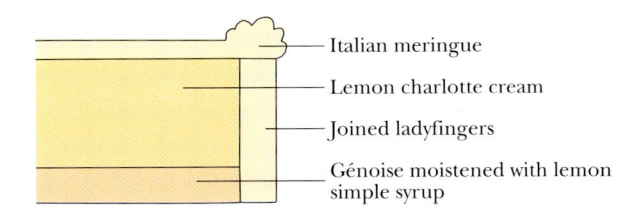

- Italian meringue
- Lemon charlotte cream
- Joined ladyfingers
- Génoise moistened with lemon simple syrup

Lemon Charlotte
Charlotte au Citron

This cake is assembled in a 2 1/3 in/6 cm high cake ring. Prepare joined ladyfingers. Trim the ladyfingers to the height of the cake ring and line them around the inside of the ring. Place a layer of génoise inside the ring, moistened with lemon simple syrup. Fill the ring flush to the rim with lemon charlotte cream. Freeze.

Remove the ring. With a pastry bag and fluted tip, pipe a lattice of Italian meringue on top of the cake and a border around the top edge. Use a propane torch to lightly brown the Italian meringue. Inside each diamond of meringue, pour lemon gelée or glaze thinned with simple syrup, 30° baume. Wrap a ribbon around the side of the cake.

Lemon Charlotte Cream
Crème à Charlotte au Citron

gelatin sheets	18	18
pineapple or apricot syrup*	10.5 oz	300 g
lemon juice	24.5 oz	700 g
lemons, zest of	6	6
sugar	28 oz	800 g
crème fraîche	68 fl oz	2 L

*The poaching syrup from other fruits can also be used.

Cover the gelatin sheets with very cold water to soften.
Bring the lemon juice and zests, syrup, and sugar to a boil. Remove from heat.
Squeeze the excess water from the gelatin sheets and stir them into the hot liquid until melted.
Whip the crème fraîche to soft peaks. Just before the first mixture sets, gently fold in the whipped crème fraîche. This cream should be used shortly after it is prepared.

Raspberry Simple Syrup
Sirop de Framboises

raspberry juice	17.5 oz	500 g
raspberry brandy	3.5 oz	100 g
simple syrup, 30° baume	17.5 oz	500 g

Combine all ingredients.

Raspberry Charlotte Cream
Crème à Charlotte aux Framboises

Prepare the recipe and procedure for strawberry charlotte cream (see page 97), replacing the strawberries with raspberries.

Facing Page: Belle Hélène Charlotte, Lemon Charlotte

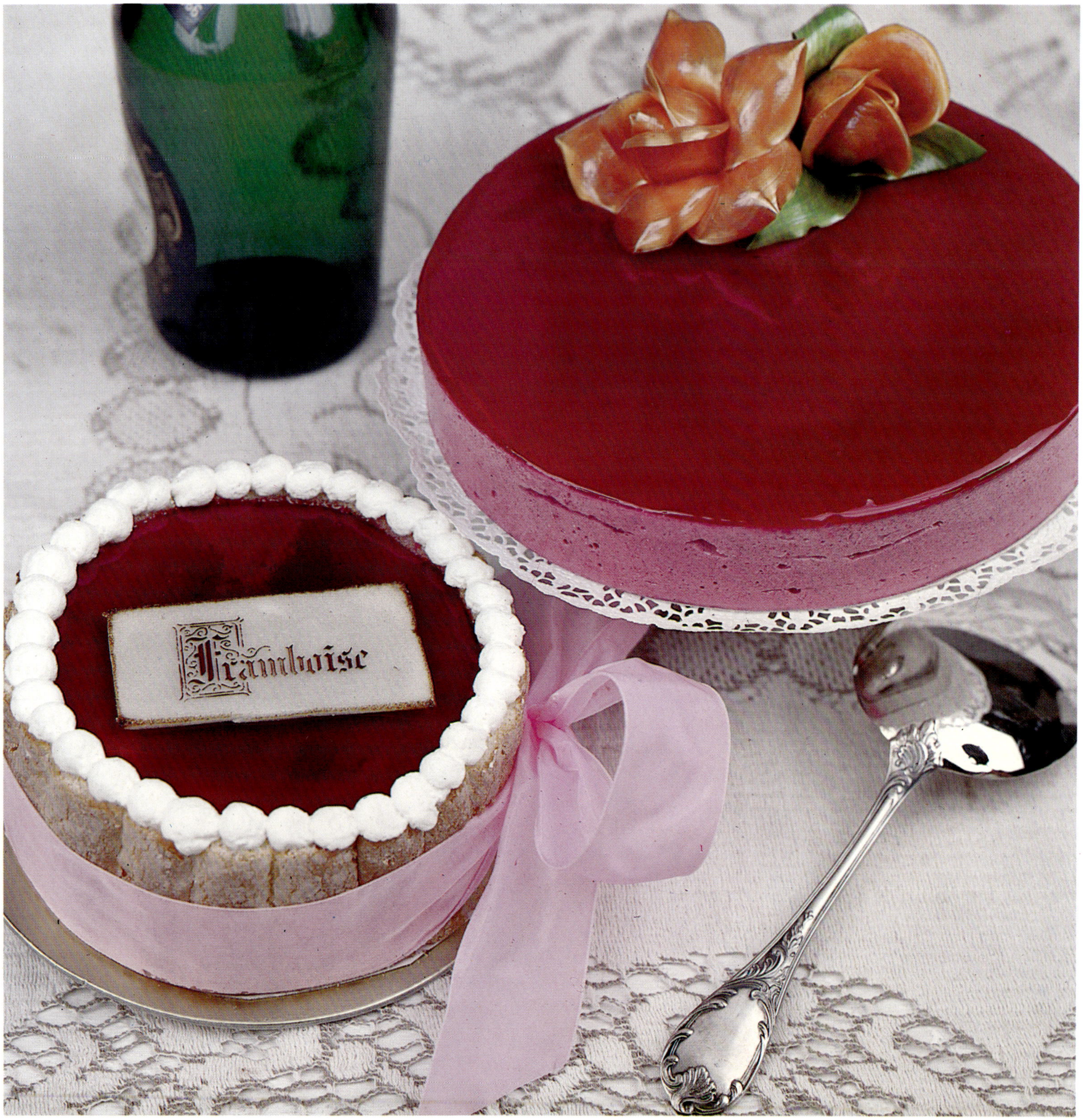
Framboise

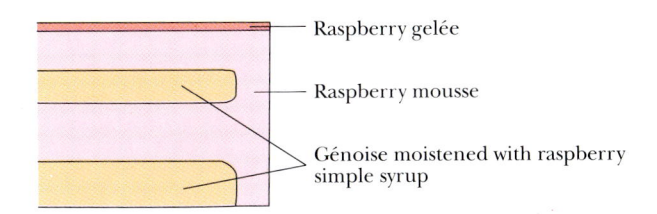

Raspberry Mirror
Miroir à la Framboise

This cake is assembled in a 1 in/3 cm high cake ring. Prepare génoise layers slightly smaller in diameter than the ring, so that only the mousse will be seen around the sides of the finished cake.

Place a layer of génoise inside the cake ring, moistened with raspberry simple syrup. Fill the ring half-full with raspberry mousse, spreading it against the inside of the ring. Cover with a second layer of génoise, moistened liberally with raspberry simple syrup. Smooth the mousse flush to the top of the ring.

It is possible to assemble this cake using three layers of génoise and three layers of mousse. Freeze.

Place the mirror on a cake cardboard. Cover the top of the cake with raspberry gelée. Remove the ring by heating it with a propane torch. Decorate the cake with pulled sugar or marzipan flowers and leaves.

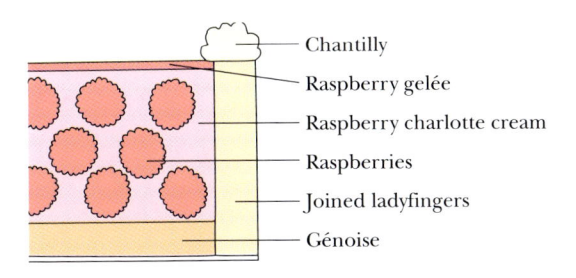

Raspberry Charlotte
Charlotte aux Framboises

This cake is assembled in a 2 1/3 in/6 cm high cake ring. The cake is prepared following a procedure similar to the one used for the strawberry charlotte. Line joined ladyfingers trimmed to the height of the cake ring around the inside of the ring. Place a layer of génoise inside the ring, moistened with raspberry simple syrup. Fill one third full with raspberry charlotte cream. Scatter raspberries generously over the cream. Spread a second layer of raspberry cream. Repeat this procedure, scattering raspberries and covering with the cream until reaching the rim of the ring. A layer of biscuit, moistened liberally with raspberry simple syrup, can be placed in the cake after the first layer of mousse. Refrigerate, do not freeze.

Remove the cake ring and coat the top of the cake with raspberry gelée. With a pastry bag and plain tip, pipe a border of chantilly around the top edge of the cake. Place a decorated marzipan plaque on top of the cake.

Variation
This cake can also be decorated by covering the top of the cake with raspberries and brushing them with raspberry gelée.

Raspberry Mousse
Mousse à la Framboise

gelatin sheets	15	15
raspberry juice	34 fl oz	1 L
dried milk	3.5 oz	100 g
egg yolks	16	16
sugar	7 oz	200 g
crème fraîche or heavy cream	34 fl oz	1 L
sugar	17.5 oz	500 g
water	5.5 oz	150 g
egg whites	10	10
raspberry brandy	9 oz	250 g

Cover the gelatin sheets with very cold water to soften. Bring the raspberry juice and dried milk to a boil. Whisk the egg yolks and sugar until thick and pale.

Facing Page: Raspberry Charlotte, Raspberry Mirror

(Raspberry Mousse recipe continued on next page)

Combine the two mixtures and cook gently as for a crème anglaise, without boiling, and stirring constantly. Remove from heat. Squeeze the gelatin sheets to remove the excess water and stir into the hot mixture until melted.

Whip the crème fraîche or heavy cream to soft peaks.

Prepare an Italian meringue by cooking the sugar and water to 250°F/121°C, while whipping the egg whites to soft peaks. Pour the cooked sugar in a fine stream, whipping it into the egg whites. Continue whipping until cool.

When the first mixture has cooled, and just before it sets, stir in the raspberry brandy. Gently fold in the whipped cream, then the cooled Italian meringue.

This mousse should be used shortly after it is prepared.

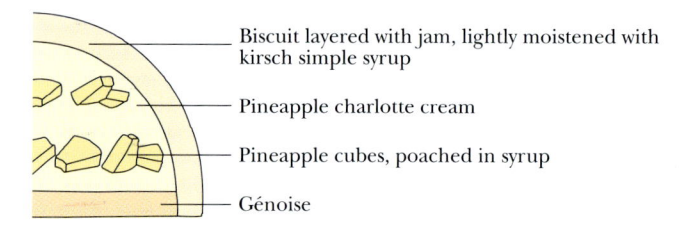

- Biscuit layered with jam, lightly moistened with kirsch simple syrup
- Pineapple charlotte cream
- Pineapple cubes, poached in syrup
- Génoise

Pineapple Charlotte
Charlotte à l'Ananas

This cake is assembled upside down in a half-sphere mold. Prepare sheets of biscuit baked on parchment paper. Layer 4–5 sheets with raspberry or other flavored jam, or apricot glaze.

Refer to page 109 to see how the mold is lined with the biscuit, which decorates the finished cake. When cutting the layered biscuit to form the points, the angle of the point is determined by the depth of the mold. Line the mold, placing the points of the biscuit strips in the center of the bottom of the mold. Lightly moisten the biscuit with kirsch simple syrup. Fill the mold one third full with pineapple charlotte cream. Scatter cubes of pineapple, canned or poached, over the cream. Spread a second layer of cream, filling the mold two thirds full. Again, scatter pineapple cubes over the cream. Fill the mold to 1/2 in/1 cm from the top with the cream. Cover with a layer of génoise the same diameter as the base of the mold. Freeze.

Turn the mold over onto a cake cardboard. Unmold the cake and brush it with clear or apricot glaze.

Pineapple Charlotte Cream
No. 1
Crème à Charlotte à l'Ananas

gelatin sheets	18	18
pineapple juice	34 fl oz	1 L
vanilla bean	1	1
egg yolks	20	20
sugar	7 oz	200 g
crème fraîche or heavy cream	50.5 fl oz	1.5 L
kirsch	3.5 oz	100 g

Cover the gelatin sheets with very cold water to soften.

Bring the pineapple juice and vanilla bean, split lengthwise, to a boil. Whisk the egg yolks and sugar until thick and pale. Combine and gently cook the two mixtures until it coats the spoon as for crème anglaise. Be careful not to let the mixture boil at any time. Remove from heat.

Squeeze the gelatin sheets to remove the excess water and stir into the hot mixture until melted. Whip the crème fraîche or heavy cream to soft peaks. Just before the mixture sets, stir in the kirsch and fold in the whipped cream.

This mousse should be used shortly after it is prepared.

Pineapple Charlotte Cream

No. 2

Crème à Charlotte à l'Ananas

gelatin sheets	18	18
pineapple juice	34 fl oz	1 L
dried milk	3.5 oz	100 g
egg yolks	24	24
sugar	7 oz	200 g
crème fraîche	42 fl oz	1.25 L
Italian meringue	17.5 oz	500 g
kirsch (optional)	3.5 oz	100 g

Follow the same procedure as for Recipe 1 above, with the additional last step of folding in the Italian meringue.

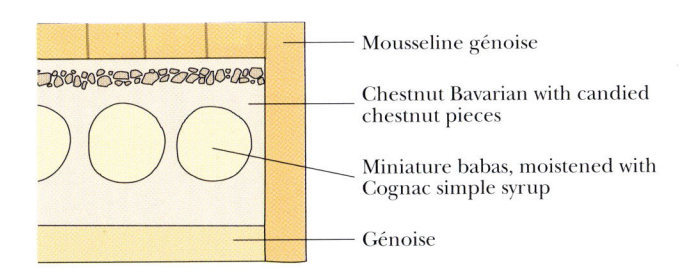

Chestnut Charlotte

Charlotte aux Marrons

This cake is assembled upside down in a 2 1/3 in/6 mm high cake ring. Prepare sheets of mousseline génoise or biscuit baked on parchment paper. Refer to the photograph on page 109 for the method of preparing the biscuit/jam spiral.

It important to line the base of the ring carefully, as the rolled biscuit serves to decorate the finished cake. Cover a sheet of biscuit with a layer of jam or apricot glaze and cut off 1/2 in/1 cm strips. Starting at one end, roll the strips jelly-roll style into a large spiral.

Place the cake ring over a cake cardboard. Line the inside of the the ring with a band of biscuit the same height as the ring. Place the biscuit/jam spiral on the bottom, inside the ring, so it fits snugly against the band of biscuit around the ring. Lightly moisten with Cognac simple syrup. Spread a layer of chestnut charlotte cream. Scatter pieces of chestnuts over the cream. Cover with miniature babas moistened in Cognac simple syrup. The babas can be replaced with a layer of mousseline génoise. Fill the ring four fifths full with the cream. Cover with a layer of génoise the same diameter as the ring. Freeze.

Place a cake cardboard over the cake and turn it over so the decorative spiral is now facing up. Remove the cake ring. Brush the top and sides of the cake with apricot or other flavored glaze. Wrap a ribbon around the side of the cake. Place a pastry shop label on top.

Chef's Note: The chestnut charlotte is further enhanced by serving chocolate sauce or peach coulis on the side. This cake can also be assembled following the procedure given for the strawberry or raspberry charlotte (see pages 97 and 103). Use rum or Cognac simple syrup to moisten the biscuit. Coat the top of the cake with chestnut gelée, and decorate with two glazed chestnuts and two marzipan leaves.

Chestnut Gelée

Gelée de Marrons

gelatin sheets	5	5
simple syrup, 30° baume	14 oz	400 g
chestnut cream	28 oz	800 g

Cover the gelatin sheets with very cold water to soften. Bring the simple syrup to a boil. Remove from heat. Squeeze the gelatin sheets to remove the excess water and stir into the hot syrup until melted. Whisk in the chestnut cream until smooth.

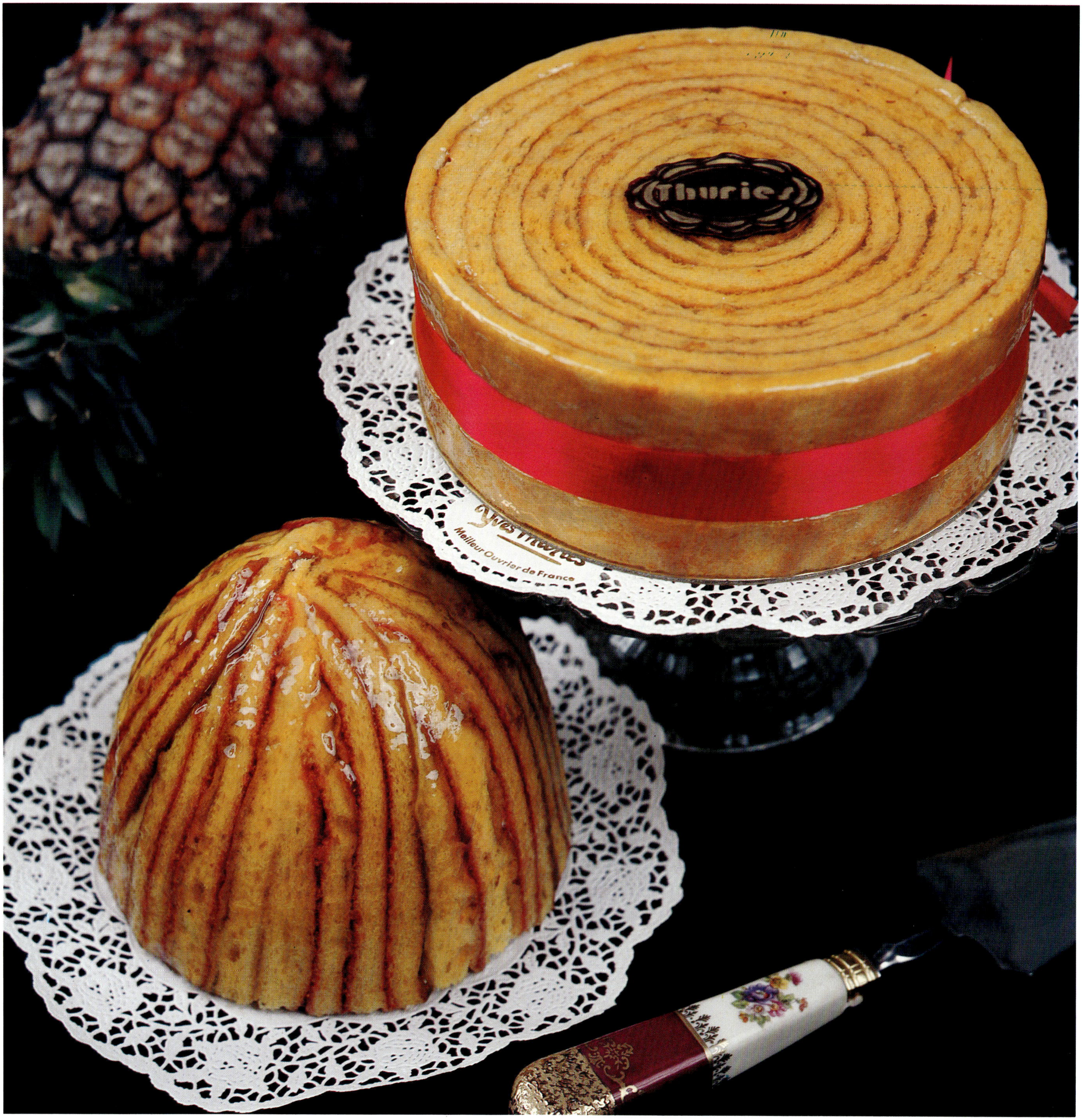
Thuries
Yves Thuries
Meilleur Ouvrier de France

Chestnut Charlotte Cream

No. 1

Crème à Charlotte aux Marrons

gelatin sheets	6	6
milk	17.5 oz	500 g
chestnut paste	17.5 oz	500 g
rum or Cognac	7 oz	200 g
bombe batter	14 oz	400 g
crème fraîche or heavy cream	35 oz	1,000 g
Italian meringue	17.5 oz	500 g

Cover the gelatin sheets with very cold water to soften. Bring the milk to a boil. Whisk in the chestnut paste until smooth. Remove from heat. Squeeze the gelatin sheets to remove the excess water and stir into the hot mixture until melted. Set aside to cool.

Just before the mixture sets, stir in the rum or Cognac, then fold in the bombe batter.

Whip the crème fraîche or heavy cream to soft peaks. Fold the whipped cream into the Italian meringue, then fold the two into the chestnut batter.

This cream should be used shortly after it is prepared.

Chef's Note: *The above recipe can be prepared without the bombe batter.*

Chestnut Charlotte Cream

No. 2

Crème à Charlotte aux Marrons

gelatin sheets	10	10
milk	17.5 oz	500 g
egg yolks	12	12
sugar	5.5 oz	150 g
chestnut paste	17.5 oz	500 g
rum	3.5 oz	100 g
crème fraîche, whipped	35 oz	1,000 g

Cover the gelatin sheets with very cold water to soften. Prepare a crème anglaise by first bringing the milk to a boil. Whisk the egg yolks and sugar until thick and pale. Combine the two mixtures and cook gently, stirring constantly until it coats the spoon, never boiling. Remove from heat. Squeeze the gelatin sheets to remove the excess water and stir into the hot mixture until melted. Set aside to cool.

Soften the chestnut paste by stirring in the rum. Just before the first mixture sets, stir in the chestnut paste. Whip the crème fraîche to soft peaks and gently fold it into the cream.

This cream should be used shortly after it is prepared.

Chef's Note: *As an alternative procedure, soften the chestnut paste by stirring in the rum, fold in the chantilly, then fold in the crème anglaise.*

Rum or Cognac Simple Syrup

Sirop au Rhum ou au Cognac

Combine 34 oz/1,000 g simple syrup (30° baume) with 9 oz/250 g rum or Cognac. The amount of liquor used can be increased, according to taste, for a stronger syrup.

Facing Page: Pineapple Charlotte, Chestnut Charlotte

108   *Modern French Pastry*

Lining a Cake Ring with a Biscuit or Génoise Spiral

Photo 1: Bake sheets of biscuit or mousseline génoise on parchment paper. After cooling, remove the parchment paper and spread apricot or other flavored glaze or jam on the porous side (that which was touching the parchment paper).

Photo 2: Spread the jam or glaze evenly over the surface.

Photo 3: Cut 1/3–1/2 in/7–10 mm wide strips off the biscuit or génoise. Begin forming the spiral, rolling one of the strips around itself. Attach another strip beginning where the first left off and continue to add on strips until the desired circumference is reached.

Photo 4: Place the spiral on a cake cardboard. Place a cake ring around the spiral. Cut a plain strip of biscuit the same width as the height of the cake ring and line the inside of the ring. Moisten the biscuit with simple syrup flavored according to taste. Assemble the cake and chill to set.

Once the cake has set up, turn it over so the spiral is on top of the cake. Remove the cake ring and brush the top and sides of the cake with apricot or other glaze.

Lining a Half-Sphere Mold with Layered Biscuit

Photo 1: Superimpose 4–6 layers of biscuit baked on parchment paper, each covered with raspberry or other flavored jam. Refrigerate. Cut 1/4–1/3 in/5–8 mm wide strips from the long side of the stacked layers.

Photo 2: Cut triangles of layered biscuit; the length is determined by the depth of the mold. The points of the sections meet the bottom of the mold. After lining the mold, use a serrated knife to trim any uneven ends flush to the top of the mold.

Charlottes

For many years, mostly savory rather than sweet charlottes were prepared. Jean Millet, a highly regarded French pastry chef, has brought the charlotte back to the pastry kitchen. He knew how to adapt and present this cake, making it one of the most popular cakes in French pastry making.

Charlottes can be presented and decorated in a variety of ways according to the flavors used in the cake, such as pineapple, chestnut, passion fruit, strawberry, pear, or lemon. They should be eaten at a moderately cool temperature, between 40°–50°F/4°–10°C.

Charlottes are best when accompanied with a coulis (pronounced coo-lee) or other sauce on the side.

Strawberry Coulis
Coulis de Fraises

This recipe can be used with almost any fruit, such as fresh raspberries or blackcurrants, poached pears, or peaches. Simply substitute the desired fruit with the same quantities below.

strawberry purée	35 oz	1,000 g
confectioners' or granulated sugar	17.5 oz	500 g
lemon, juice	1	1
fruit brandy or liqueur to taste		

Combine all ingredients.

Sauces for Charlottes

Sauce Anglaise

milk	34 fl oz	1 L
vanilla bean	1	1
egg yolks	10	10
sugar	12.5 oz	350 g

Follow the same technique used for a classic crème anglaise. If a thicker sauce is desired, one or more softened gelatin sheets can be stirred into the cream just after it has been removed from heat, before straining.

Caramel Sauce

Cook 35 oz/1,000 g sugar to an amber caramel, add 35 oz/1,000 g boiling hot crème fraîche being careful to avoid splattering. Stir until well blended.

Chocolate Sauce

Chop 17.5 oz/500 g couverture or ganache chocolate and place it in a bowl. Pour 9 oz/250 g boiling water over the chocolate and stir with a whisk until smooth.

Coffee Charlotte Cream
Crème à Charlotte au Café

gelatin sheets	16	16
milk	34 fl oz	1 L
vanilla bean	1	1
egg yolks	16	16
sugar	10.5 oz	300 g
instant coffee	1 oz	30 g
sugar	17.5 oz	500 g
water	5.5 oz	150 g
egg whites	8	8
crème fraîche	34 fl oz	1 L

Cover the gelatin sheets with very cold water to soften. Bring the milk and vanilla bean, split lengthwise, to a boil. Whisk the egg yolks and sugar until thick and pale. Combine the two mixtures. Stir constantly over low heat until it coats the spoon, 185°F/85°C. Remove from heat. Stir in the instant coffee or the same quantity of coffee extract. Squeeze the gelatin sheets to remove the excess water and stir into the hot mixture until melted. Strain.

Prepare an Italian meringue by cooking the sugar and water to 250°F/121°C, while whipping the egg whites to soft peaks. Pour the cooked sugar in a fine stream, whipping it into the egg whites. Continue whipping until cool. Whip the crème fraîche to soft peaks.

Just before the anglaise mixture sets, gently fold in the Italian meringue, then the whipped crème fraîche.

This cream should be used shortly after it is prepared.

Praline Charlotte Cream
Crème à Charlotte Pralinée

Follow the recipe and procedure given for the coffee charlotte cream above, replacing the instant coffee with 10.5 oz/300 g praline paste, stirring it into the crème anglaise mixture while hot, just after removing it from the heat.

Chocolate Charlotte Cream
Crème à Charlotte au Chocolat

Follow the recipe and procedure given for the coffee charlotte cream above, replacing the instant coffee with 9 oz/250 g cocoa powder or 10.5 oz/300 g unsweetened chocolate, stirring it into the anglaise mixture while hot, just after removing it from the heat.

Vanilla Charlotte Cream
Crème à Charlotte à la Vanille

Follow the recipe and procedure given for the coffee charlotte cream above, replacing the instant coffee with 5 vanilla beans, split lengthwise and scraped. Place the scrapings and pods into the cold milk, bringing them to a boil together.

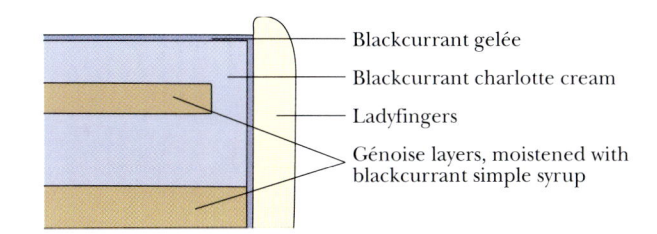

Blackcurrant gelée
Blackcurrant charlotte cream
Ladyfingers
Génoise layers, moistened with blackcurrant simple syrup

Blackcurrant Charlotte
Charlotte au Cassis

This cake can be assembled in two ways.

Procedure 1
Line the inside of a cake ring with ladyfingers. Place a layer of génoise inside the ring, moistened with blackcurrant simple syrup. Fill the ring half-full with blackcurrant charlotte cream. Cover with a second layer of génoise, liberally moistened with blackcurrant simple syrup. Smooth the cream flush to the top of the ring. Freeze.

Remove the ring and coat the top of the cake with blackcurrant gelée. Wrap a ribbon around the side of the cake. Place a pastry shop label on top.

Procedure 2
Place a layer of génoise inside a cake ring of the same diameter. Moisten the génoise with blackcurrant simple syrup. Fill the ring half-full with blackcurrant charlotte cream. If desired, cover with a second layer of génoise, moistened liberally with blackcurrant simple syrup. Smooth the cream flush to the top of the ring. Freeze.

Remove the cake ring by heating it with a propane torch. Coat the top and sides of the cake with blackcurrant gelée. Immediately after, press ladyfingers, cut in half crosswise, around the cake with the cut side on the bottom. Wrap a ribbon around the side of the cake to help support the ladyfingers and decorate the cake. This method produces a particularly neat presentation.

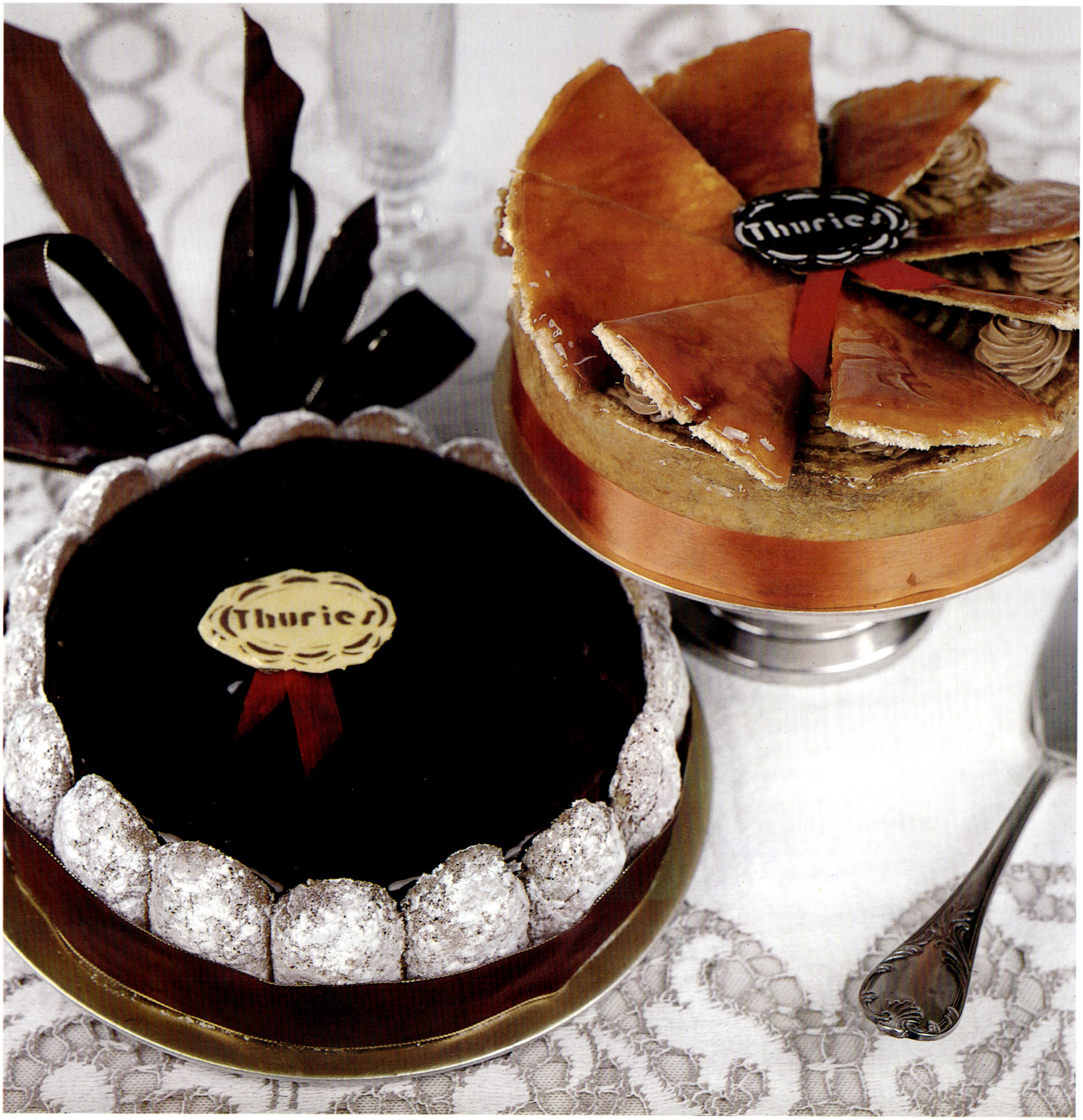
Thuries
Thuries

Blackcurrant Charlotte Cream

Crème à Charlotte au Cassis

gelatin sheets	18	18
blackcurrant juice	34 fl oz	1 L
powdered milk	3.5 oz	100 g
vanilla bean	1	1
egg yolks	18	18
sugar	7 oz	200 g
crème fraîche, whipped	3 lbs 4.5 oz	1,500 g
sugar	17.5 oz	500 g
water	5 oz	150 g
egg whites	8	8
blackcurrant liqueur	7 oz	200 g

Cover the gelatin sheets with very cold water to soften. Bring the blackcurrant juice, powdered milk, and vanilla bean, split lengthwise, to a boil. Whisk the egg yolks and sugar until thick and pale. Combine the two mixtures and return to the heat, cooking as for a crème anglaise until it coats the spoon. Remove from heat. Squeeze the gelatin sheets to remove the excess water and stir into the hot cream until melted. Set aside to cool. Prepare an Italian meringue by cooking the sugar and water to 250°F/121°C, while whipping the egg whites to soft peaks. Pour the cooked sugar in a fine stream, whipping it into the egg whites. Continue whipping until cool.

Whip the crème fraîche to soft peaks. When the cream is cool, just before setting, stir in the liqueur. Gently fold in the Italian meringue, then the whipped crème fraîche.

This cream should be used shortly after it is prepared.

Facing Page: Blackcurrant Charlotte, Caramel Délice

Blackcurrant Gelée

Gelée au Cassis

gelatin sheets	32	32
water	34 fl oz	1 L
sugar	35 oz	1,000 g
blackcurrant juice	34 fl oz	1 L

Cover the gelatin sheets with very cold water to soften. Bring the water, sugar, and blackcurrant juice to a boil. Remove from heat. Squeeze the gelatin sheets to remove the excess water and stir into the hot liquid until melted. Strain.

Blackcurrant Simple Syrup

No. 1

Sirop au Cassis

blackcurrant pulp	17.5 oz	500 g
confectioners' sugar	17.5 oz	500 g
lemon, juice of	1/2	1/2

Combine all ingredients.

Blackcurrant Simple Syrup

No. 2

Sirop au Cassis

blackcurrant juice	17.5 oz	500 g
simple syrup, 30° baume	35 oz	1,000 g

Combine both ingredients. The amount of blackcurrant juice used can be increased or decreased according to taste.

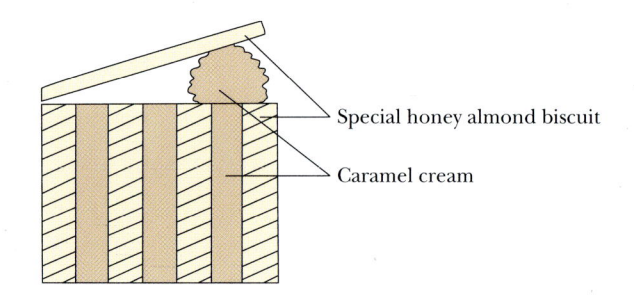

Caramel Délice
Délice au Caramel

Cakes are most often assembled horizontally with layers of génoise and/or biscuits and filling. The caramel délice is an exception. The biscuit and filling are assembled jelly-roll style. The roll is then cut to the size needed. The width of the slice determines the height of the cake, which is turned flat on its side so the spiral is facing up.

Prepare 2–4 sheets of special honey almond biscuit baked on parchment paper, depending on the size and quantity of cakes needed. Remove the parchment paper and moisten the porous side (side touching the paper) with caramel simple syrup. Spread a layer of caramel cream on a sheet of biscuit and roll it as for a yule log or jelly roll, starting with the narrow end. Wrap the roll tightly in plastic wrap and freeze.

While the first layer is setting, prepare the second layer, spreading the cream on top. Then roll it around the first chilled layer. Continue in this fashion, adding to the original roll until the desired circumference is reached.

Always store the rolled section in the freezer while preparing the next layer, to prevent it from unrolling or deforming. Freeze the finished roll. Heat a serrated knife with hot water and cut off slices, the thickness of which will determine the height of the cake. Set the cut section flat on its side so the spiral is upright.

Cut a circle the same size as the spiral from the sheet of plain honey biscuit. Spread a thin layer of amber caramel on top. Cut the circle into 8–10 triangular sections (depending on the size of the cake); each represents one portion.

Brush the top border and side of the cake lightly with apricot glaze. With a pastry bag and fluted tip, pipe rosettes on top of the cake; one rosette per portion. Position one triangle of caramel-coated biscuit at an angle over each rosette. Place a pastry shop label on top. Wrap a ribbon around the side of the cake.

Caramel Simple Syrup
Sirop au Caramel

Combine 5 oz/150 g hot, fluid caramel and 34 fl oz/ 1 L simple syrup, 30° baume.

Special Honey Almond Biscuit
Biscuit Spécial aux Amandes et au Miel

almonds, unblanched*	17.5 oz	500 g
sugar	17.5 oz	500 g
candied orange peel	2 oz	60 g
egg whites	5	5
honey	2 oz	60 g
TPT	4.5 oz	125 g
flour	4.5 oz	125 g
egg whites	20	20
sugar	5.5 oz	150 g

*Almonds with skin.

In a food processor, grind the almonds, sugar, and candied orange peel. Soften this mixture with the egg whites and honey. Add the TPT (equal weights ground almonds and sugar) and flour.

Whisk the egg whites to soft peaks before gradually adding the sugar. Continue to whisk to firm peaks. Fold the whipped egg whites into the batter.

Spread or pipe the batter 1/2 in/1 cm thick on sheet pans lined with parchment paper.

Bake in a moderate oven, approximately 350°F/180°C.

Caramel Cream
Crème au Caramel

sugar	17.5 oz	500 g
crème fraîche	14 oz	400 g
butter, softened	17.5 oz	500 g

Cook the sugar to a dark brown caramel. Add the crème fraîche carefully to avoid splattering. Combine the two until smooth. Set aside to cool. After cooling, add the softened butter and whip until light and aerated.

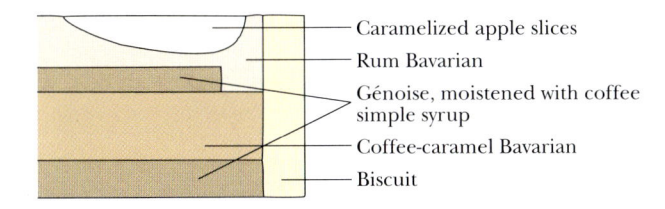

Caramelized apple slices
Rum Bavarian
Génoise, moistened with coffee simple syrup
Coffee-caramel Bavarian
Biscuit

Marigny

This cake is assembled upside down in a 2 1/3 in/6 mm high cake ring. Cut strips of biscuit equal to the height of the ring. Peel and cut the apples into 12 even slices. Arrange the slices on a buttered sheet pan. Dot with butter and dust with confectioners' sugar. Bake in a hot oven. When the apples are caramelized to a golden brown, sprinkle lightly with rum and flambé (this step is optional). The apples can be prepared in advance and set aside. They must be cool before assembling the cake.

Place the cake ring over a sheet of plastic. Line a strip of biscuit around the inside of the ring with the porous side (originally touching the parchment paper) against the cake ring. Place the caramelized apple slices inside the ring in a decorative fashion, such as a pinwheel. The apples will decorate the finished cake. Spread a thin layer of rum Bavarian cream over the apples. Cover with a layer of génoise, moistened liberally with coffee simple syrup. Fill the ring four fifths full with coffee-caramel Bavarian cream. Cover with a layer of génoise so it lies flush to the top of the ring. Freeze.

Cover the cake with a cake cardboard and turn the cake over so the apple slices are on top. Remove the ring. Coat the top of the cake with apricot glaze or apple gelée. Wrap a ribbon around the side of the cake.

Chef's Note: *The layer of rum Bavarian can be replaced with coffee-caramel Bavarian. The strip of biscuit that lines the side of the cake can be replaced with a strip of joined ladyfingers.*

Coffee-Caramel Bavarian Cream
Crème Bavaroise au Café-Caramel

milk	34 fl oz	1 L
vanilla bean	1	1
coffee beans, coarsely ground	3.5 oz	100 g
sugar	17.5 oz	500 g
gelatin sheets	12	12
egg yolks	12	12
cornstarch	1 oz	30 g
crème fraîche	3 lbs 4.5 oz	1,500 g

Bring the milk and vanilla bean, split lengthwise, to a boil. Add the coarsely ground coffee beans and infuse for 30 minutes, off the heat.

Cook 14 oz/400 g of the sugar to a dark caramel. Add the milk, vanilla, and coffee, bringing all to a boil. Strain.

Cover the gelatin sheets with very cold water to soften. Combine the cornstarch with the remaining 3.5 oz/100 g

(Coffee-Caramel Bavarian Cream recipe continued on page 117)

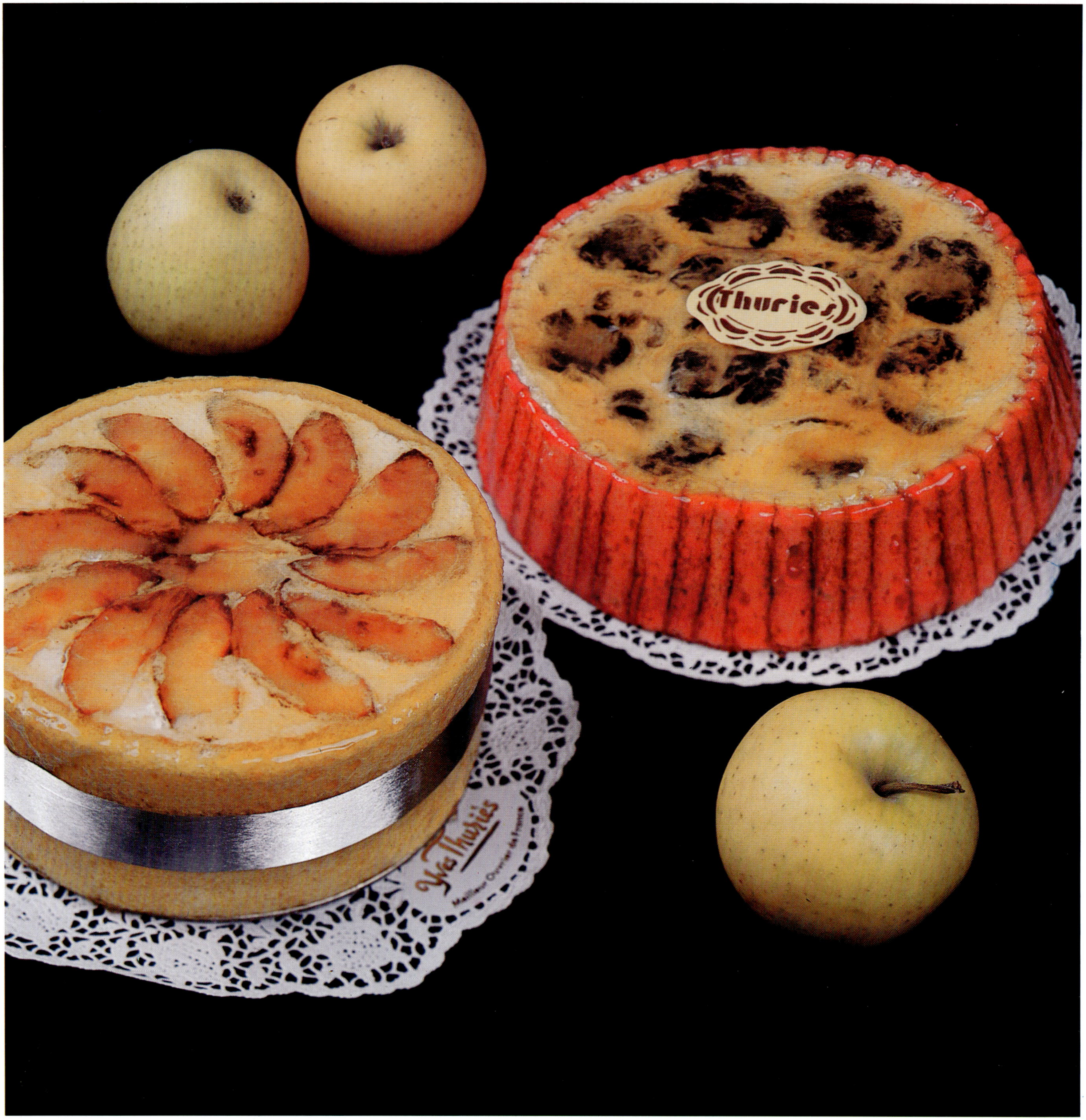
Thuries
Yves Thuries

of sugar, and egg yolks, whisking until thick and pale. Add the egg yolk mixture to the hot milk and cook as for pastry cream. Remove from heat. Squeeze the gelatin sheets to remove the excess water and stir into the hot cream until melted. Set aside to cool.

Whip the crème fraîche to soft peaks. Once cool, just before the cream sets, fold in the whipped crème fraîche.

This mousse should be used shortly after it is prepared.

- Dried prunes macerated in armagnac
- Armagnac Bavarian cream
- Génoise, moistened with Armagnac syrup
- Biscuit layered with jam
- Prune mousse
- Génoise

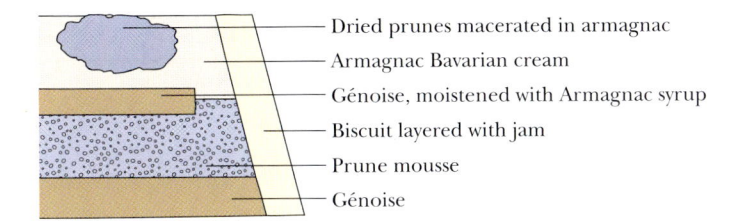

Gascony Prince
Prince de Gascogne

This cake is assembled upside down in a stainless steel génoise mold or cake pan. Prepare sheets of biscuit and layer them with jam or apricot glaze, following the procedure shown on page 118.

Line the sides of the mold with slices of layered biscuit. Spread a thin layer of armagnac Bavarian cream on the bottom of the mold. Press prunes, previously macerated in Armagnac, into the cream. Spread a layer of Bavarian over the prunes. Cover with a layer of génoise, moistened with Armagnac simple syrup. Fill the mold to 1/4 in/1/2 cm from the top of the mold with prune mousse. Cover with a layer of génoise the same diameter as the mold. Freeze.

Dip the bottom of the mold in hot water for just a few seconds. Unmold the cake, turning it over so the prunes are on top. Coat the top of the cake with apricot or other golden glaze. Brush the side of the cake with a red glaze.

Facing Page: Marigny, Gascony Prince

Bavarian Cream
Crème Bavaroise

Flavor vanilla or plain Bavarian with 3.5 oz/100 g Armagnac per 34 fl oz/1 L of milk.

Prune Mousse
Mousse aux Pruneaux

gelatin sheets	6	6
sugar	14 oz	400 g
water	4 oz	120 g
egg whites	8	8
crème fraîche or heavy cream	17.5 oz	500 g
prune paste*	17.5 oz	500 g

*Prepare prune paste by grinding pitted prunes in a food processor.

Cover the gelatin sheets with very cold water to soften. Prepare an Italian meringue by cooking the sugar and water to 250°F/121°C, while whipping the egg whites to soft peaks. Pour the cooked sugar in a fine stream, whipping it into the egg whites. Squeeze the gelatin sheets to remove the excess water and add them to the hot Italian meringue, just after adding the cooked sugar. Continue whipping until cool.

Whip the crème fraîche or heavy cream to soft peaks. Divide the cool meringue in half. Fold one half into the prune paste and the other half into the whipped cream. Combine the two batters.

This mousse should be used shortly after it is prepared.

Lining a Cake Mold for Gascony Prince

Photo 1: Superimpose sheets of biscuit coated with jam. Cut strips off the long side, equal in width to the height of the mold. Freeze. Cut 1/4–1/3 in/5–8 mm slices, cutting across the strips.

Photo 2: Line the sides of the mold with the slices of layered biscuit. If necessary, use a serrated knife to even the tops of the slices flush to the rim of the mold.

Photo 3: Place previously macerated prunes on the bottom of the mold. Spread on a thin layer of Bavarian cream without disturbing the placement of the prunes. Continue assembling the cake as indicated on the previous page.

Banana Cream Filling Flavored with Rum
Crème Garniture à la Banane Parfumée au Rhum

banana	28 oz	800 g
sugar	2 oz	50 g
butter	1 oz	30 g
rum	2 oz	50 g
sugar	9 oz	250 g
glucose	2 oz	50 g
crème fraîche	7 oz	200 g
rum	2 oz	50 g
butter	7 oz	200 g

Procedure 1
Peel the bananas (weigh them after peeling) and place them whole in a baking dish. Sprinkle with 2 oz/50 g sugar and dot with 1 oz/30 g butter. Bake in a moderate oven for 7–8 minutes or until tender. Upon removing them from the oven, sprinkle with rum and flambé. Purée the bananas and set aside to cool.

Cook the second sugar and glucose to an amber caramel. Bring the crème fraîche and rum to a boil. Immediately after boiling, while still hot, combine the rum/crème fraîche and caramel. Bring all to a boil, then set aside to cool.

Whip the second butter in the bowl of an electric mixer using the whisk attachment. Add the cooled caramel cream and banana purée. Whip until well blended.

Procedure 2
Prepare the banana purée as in Procedure 1 above, with the bananas, 2 oz/50 g sugar, 1 oz/30 g butter, and 2 oz/50 g rum. After the purée has cooled, whip the banana mixture with 24.5 oz/700 g mousseline cream until light and aerated.

Procedure 3
Prepare the banana purée as in Procedure 1 above. In the bowl of an electric mixer, whip 17.5 oz/500 g pastry cream and 7 oz/200 g butter, softened, until light and aerated. Combine the two mixtures.

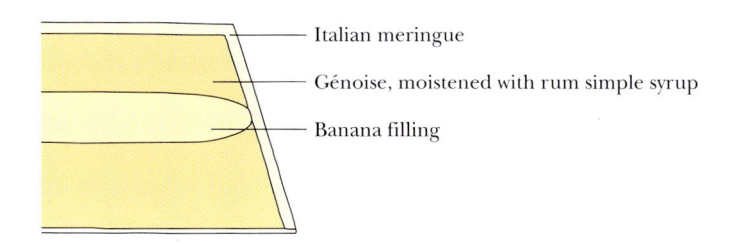

— Italian meringue
— Génoise, moistened with rum simple syrup
— Banana filling

Banana Rum Cake
Vahiné aux Bananes

Secure a square génoise to a cake cardboard by spreading a small bit of apricot glaze on the cardboard before setting the génoise on top. Cut the génoise in half horizontally. Set the top half aside. Moisten the bottom half with rum simple syrup and spread a layer of banana rum filling. Cover with the top half of the génoise, moistened with rum simple syrup. Refrigerate.

Use a palette knife to cover the top and sides of the cake with Italian meringue. Place the cake in a hot oven for a few seconds to set the meringue. Use a propane torch or hot iron to lightly brown the top and sides of the cake. Coat with apricot glaze. Place a pastry shop label or marzipan roses and leaves on top of the cake.

Banana Rum Cake, Duchess Anne, Prince Albert

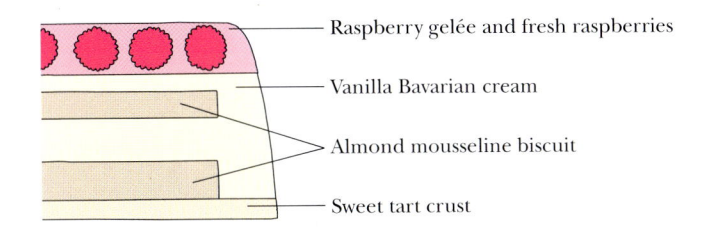

Raspberry gelée and fresh raspberries
Vanilla Bavarian cream
Almond mousseline biscuit
Sweet tart crust

Duchess Anne
Duchesse Anne

This cake is assembled upside-down in a non-stick cake mold. The finished cake is turned over and set on a disk of sweet tart crust of the same diameter.

Pour a 1/16 in/2 mm thick layer of raspberry gelée into the mold. Generously scatter fresh raspberries over the gelée. Allow the gelée to set before going to the next step. Pour a second layer of raspberry gelée, covering the raspberries. The mold should be approximately one third full. Allow the gelée to set. Spread a thin layer of vanilla Bavarian cream (see page 99). Cover with a layer of almond mousseline biscuit slightly smaller in diameter than the cake. Moisten the biscuit with straight liquor, liqueur, or raspberry simple syrup. Spread a layer of Bavarian cream. Cover with a layer of the biscuit. Refrigerate.

Unmold the cake by dipping the base of the mold in hot water, and turn it out onto a disk of sweet tart crust. Spread a layer of apricot glaze over the crust to prevent it from becoming soggy. Coat the Bavarian section, the bottom two thirds, around the side of the cake, with chantilly. Press candied almonds around the base of the cake.

Chef's Note: *The same procedure used for the Duchess Anne cake can be followed using fruit other than bananas such as wild strawberries, blackcurrants, and blueberries.*

Raspberry Syrup
Sirop de Framboises

raspberry purée	17 fl oz	500 ml
simple syrup, 30° baume	34 fl oz	1 L
lemons, juice	2	2

Combine and strain all ingredients.

Almond Mousseline Biscuit
Biscuit Mousseline aux Amandes

egg yolks	35	35
sugar	35 oz	1,000 g
eggs	10	10
almond powder	17.5 oz	500 g
flour	17.5 oz	500 g
egg whites	35 oz	35
sugar	9 oz	250 g

Whisk the egg yolks and first sugar until thick and pale. Gradually whisk in the whole eggs.

Sift the flour and almond powder and add them to the egg/sugar mixture.

Whip the egg whites to firm peaks with the second sugar. Gently fold the two mixtures together.

Immediately pour the batter into either buttered cake pans or cake rings on sheet pans lined with parchment paper. Bake in a moderate oven.

Raspberry Gelée
Gelée de Framboises

gelatin sheets	25	25
water	8.5 fl oz	250 ml

(Raspberry Gelée recipe continued on next page)

sugar	17.5 oz	500 g
raspberry pulp	25.5 fl oz	750 ml

Cover the gelatin sheets with very cold water to soften. Bring the water and sugar to a boil. Remove from heat. Squeeze the gelatin sheets to remove the excess water and add to the hot syrup, stirring until melted. Stir in the raspberry pulp. Strain.

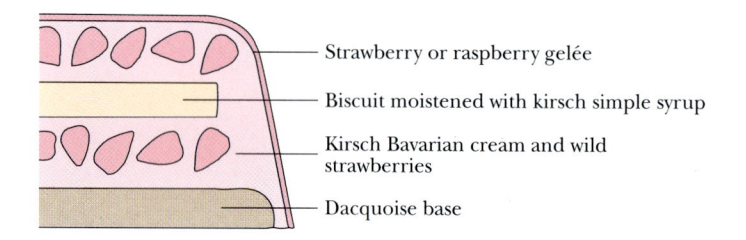

- Strawberry or raspberry gelée
- Biscuit moistened with kirsch simple syrup
- Kirsch Bavarian cream and wild strawberries
- Dacquoise base

Prince Albert

This cake is molded following the procedure given for the Duchess Anne cake (see page 121), in a non-stick cake pan.

Spread a thin layer of Bavarian cream on the bottom of a mold. Scatter wild strawberries over the cream. Spread a second layer of Bavarian cream, enough to cover the berries. Cover with a layer of biscuit, moistened with kirsch simple syrup. Spread a layer of Bavarian cream and scatter wild strawberries on top. Cover the berries with a layer of cream. Cover with a dacquois base slightly smaller in diameter than the mold. Freeze.

To unmold the cake, dip the bottom of the mold in hot water and stick a fork into the center of the cake, pulling it out of the mold. Coat the cake with strawberry gelée.

Chef's Note: *This cake can be made by substituting raspberries for the stawberries, following the same procedure. In this case, flavor the cream with raspberry brandy and moisten the biscuit with raspberry simple syrup or straight raspberry brandy. The cake can also be made with blackcurrant, blueberry, or other fruits of choice, making the appropriate substitutions. Regardless of the fruit used, this cake is often served with a raspberry coulis.*

Almond Génoise
Génoise aux Amandes

almond paste	17.5 oz	500 g
eggs	32	32
sugar	23 oz	650 g
emulsifier (optional)	2 oz	60 g
flour	31.5 oz	900 g
butter, melted	9 oz	250 g

Soften the almond paste by whisking in a few eggs. In the bowl of an electric mixer, use the whisk attachment to whip the remaining eggs, sugar, and emulsifier until light and aerated. No heat is needed for this step.

Sift the flour and fold it into the egg mixture. Then fold in the melted butter after combining it with a small portion of the batter.* Pour the batter into buttered and floured cake pans. Bake in a moderately hot oven, 390–425°F/200–220°C.

*It is best not to incorporate the melted butter directly into the génoise batter; rather, first fold the butter, melted but not hot, into a small amount of the génoise batter. Gently fold this mixture into the batter. This will prevent the batter from falling when the butter is added.

Diagram labels:
- Coffee chantilly
- Coffee gelée
- Layered biscuit
- Miniature babas macerated in coffee simple syrup
- Coffee Bavarian cream
- Biscuit, lightly moistened with coffee simple syrup

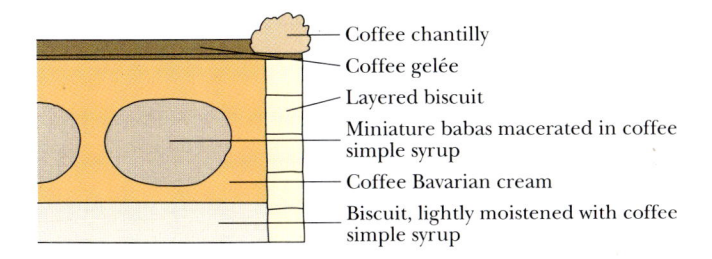

Brazilian Charlotte
Charlotte Brésilienne

This cake is assembled in a 2–2 1/3 in/5–6 cm high cake ring. Line the ring with one strip of biscuit layered horizontally with jam or apricot glaze (see page 109). Place a layer of plain or coffee génoise on the bottom, inside the ring, moistened with coffee simple syrup. Fill the ring half-full with coffee Bavarian. Cover the cream with miniature babas macerated in coffee simple syrup. Smooth the Bavarian flush to the top of the ring. Freeze.

Remove the cake ring by heating it with a propane torch. Coat the top of the cake with coffee gelée. Brush the sides of the cake with apricot glaze. With a pastry bag and plain tip, pipe coffee chantilly, forming a lattice decoration. With a fluted tip, pipe a border of chantilly around the top edge of the cake.

Coffee Bavarian Cream
Crème Bavaroise au Café

gelatin sheets	16	16
milk	35 oz	1,000 g
vanilla bean	1	1
coffee beans, ground	9 oz	250 g
egg yolks	20	20
sugar	9 oz	250 g
cream, whipped	4 lbs 6 oz	2,000 g
coffee extract*	2 oz	50 g

Cover the gelatin sheets with very cold water to soften. Bring the milk, vanilla, and ground coffee to a boil. After boiling, set aside to infuse off the heat for approximately 15 minutes. Strain.

Whisk the egg yolks and sugar until thick and pale. Add the egg/sugar mixture to the saucepan of milk. Return it to the heat, stirring constantly until it coats the spoon as for crème anglaise. Remove from heat. Squeeze the gelatin sheets to remove the excess water and stir into the hot liquid until melted.

Whip the cream to soft peaks. Just before the cream sets, stir in the coffee extract. Fold in the whipped cream.

This Bavarian should be used shortly after it is prepared.

The quantity of coffee extract can vary according to the strength of the extract and how much coffee flavor is desired.

Coffee Simple Syrup for Miniature Babas
Sirop au Café pour Mini-Babas

Combine coffee extract and simple syrup, 30° baume, according to taste and the desired depth of color.

Coffee Gelée
Gelée au Café

Combine apple or other high-pectin jelly to coffee extract according to taste and the desired depth of color.

124   Modern French Pastry

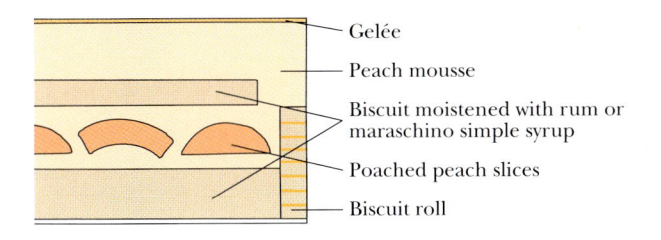

Gelée
Peach mousse
Biscuit moistened with rum or maraschino simple syrup
Poached peach slices
Biscuit roll

Peach Brillat Savarin
Brillat Savarin aux Pêches

This cake is assembled in a 2 1/3 in/6 cm high cake ring. Line the sides of the ring halfway up with slices of biscuit rolled with strained peach jam. Place a layer of génoise large enough to cover the bottom inside the ring, moistened with maraschino or rum simple syrup. Fill the ring half-full with peach mousse. Scatter cubes of lightly poached fresh or canned peaches over the mousse. Cover with a layer of génoise smaller in diameter and moistened with the same syrup. Smooth the mousse flush to the top of the ring. Freeze.

Slice one or two poached or canned peach halves. Spread the slices neatly across the top of one side of the cake. Coat the top of the cake with gelée. Remove the cake ring by heating it with a propane torch. Brush the side of the cake, including the rolled biscuit, with apricot glaze. Place a pastry shop label on top.

Peach Mousse
Mousse à la Pêche

peach pulp	46.5 oz	1,300 g
rum	3.5 oz	100 g
meringue reinforced with gelatin	35 oz	1,000 g
cream, whipped	35 oz	1,000 g

Purée the fresh or canned peaches in a food processor. Add the rum. Gently fold in the meringue and whipped cream. The meringue should be folded in when cool or when barely warm, but before setting. If too warm, it will break down the whipped cream; if too cool, it will not blend into the mixture.

This mousse should be used shortly after it is prepared.

Italian Meringue Reinforced with Gelatin
Meringue Gélatinée

gelatin sheets	15	15
sugar	35 oz	1,000 g
water	14 oz	400 g
egg whites	15	15

This meringue is prepared as for regular Italian meringue, but with the addition of gelatin.

Cover the gelatin sheets with very cold water to soften. Prepare an Italian meringue by cooking the sugar and water to 250°F/121°C, while whipping the egg whites to soft peaks. Pour the cooked sugar in a fine stream, whipping it into the egg whites. Squeeze the gelatin sheets to remove the excess water and add to the hot whipped egg whites. It is important to incorporate the gelatin into the hot meringue immediately after the cooked sugar, to be sure they melt. Whip until barely warm, but before setting.

The quantity of gelatin can vary depending on the thickness and stability required of the mousse.

Facing Page: Brazilian Charlotte, Peach Brillat Savarin

Vatel, Pineapple Cake

126   *Modern French Pastry*

Diagram labels:
- Chocolate/cocoa butter, sprayed with an air gun—or cocoa powder
- White marzipan
- Chocolate mousse with banana slices and orange sections
- Chocolate biscuit moistened with liqueur simple syrup
- Coating chocolate

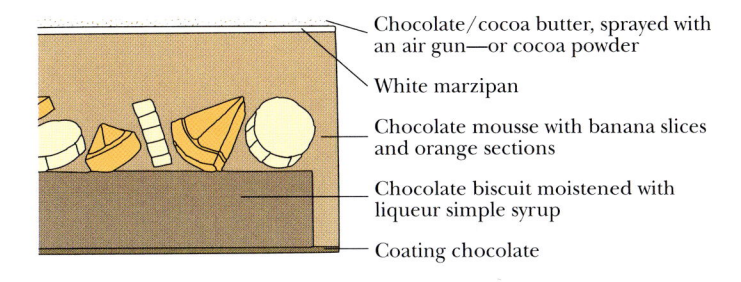

Vatel

This cake is assembled in a 1–1 1/3 in/30–35 mm high cake ring. Prepare chocolate biscuit layers slightly smaller in diameter than the cake ring. After unmolding, only the mousse will be seen around the side of the cake.

Coat the bottom of one layer of chocolate biscuit with coating chocolate or liquid couverture. After the chocolate has set, place it inside the cake ring turned over with the chocolate side down. Moisten the biscuit with Grand Marnier, Cointreau, or other liqueur simple syrup. Fill the ring half-full with special chocolate mousse. Macerate banana slices and cubed orange sections in simple syrup flavored with the liqueur used to moisten the biscuit. Scatter the fruit over the chocolate mousse. Smooth the mousse flush to the top of the ring. Refrigerate.

Procedure 1
Place a disk of white marzipan over the top of the cake. Using a stencil with the name of the pastry shop or restaurant or other appropriate decoration, dust with cocoa powder. Remove the stencil to reveal the design.

Procedure 2
Place a disk of white marzipan over the top of the cake. Place the cake in the freezer. When the cake is frozen, decorate with a spray gun filled with chocolate to obtain a velvet texture.

Chef's Note: *If following Procedure 2, replace the bananas and oranges with candied, macerated orange peel, as the fresh fruit would break down after defrosting.*

Chocolate Mousse
Mousse au Chocolat

unsweetened chocolate	*9 oz*	*250 g*
chocolate	*26.5 oz*	*750 g*
butter, softened	*26.5 oz*	*750 g*
liqueur	*7 oz*	*200 g*
sugar	*3.5 oz*	*100 g*
water	*3.5 oz*	*100 g*
egg yolks	*8*	*8*
sugar	*10.5 oz*	*300 g*
water	*3 oz*	*90 g*
egg whites	*8*	*8*

Melt the two chocolates. Add the softened butter and liqueur such as Grand Marnier, Cointreau, or rum, and stir gently until smooth.

Prepare a bombe batter by bringing the sugar and water to a boil, and whisking in the egg yolks. Whisk the mixture over a water bath until warm, then remove from heat and whip until cool and aerated.

Prepare an Italian meringue by cooking the sugar and water to 250°F/121°C, while whipping the egg whites to soft peaks. Pour the cooked sugar in a fine stream, whipping it into the egg whites. Whip until completely cool.

While still malleable, fold the chocolate mixture into the bombe mixture, then fold in the meringue.

This mousse should be used shortly after it is prepared.

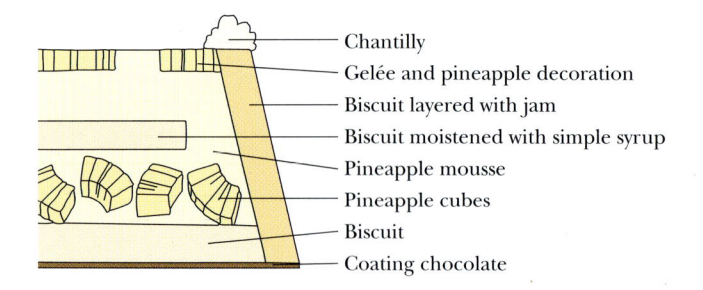

- Chantilly
- Gelée and pineapple decoration
- Biscuit layered with jam
- Biscuit moistened with simple syrup
- Pineapple mousse
- Pineapple cubes
- Biscuit
- Coating chocolate

Pineapple Cake
Fruty à l'Ananas

This cake is assembled upside down in a stainless steel cake pan or génoise mold. Prepare sheets of biscuit layered with jam or apricot glaze (see page 118). Line the slices of layered biscuit around the inside of the mold. Place pineapple slices on the bottom, inside the mold, to decorate the finished cake. Fill the mold half-full with pineapple mousse or pineapple charlotte cream. Cover with a thin layer of biscuit, moistened with pineapple juice or kirsch simple syrup. Spread a second layer of mousse and scatter fresh or canned pineapple cubes on top. Cover with a layer of biscuit, and spread a layer of coating chocolate. Freeze.

Unmold the cake by heating with a propane torch, and turn it over so the pineapple slices are on top. Coat the top and sides of the cake with gelée or apricot glaze. With a pastry bag and fluted tip, pipe a chantilly border around the top edge of the cake. Place a pastry shop label on top.

Pineapple Mousse
Mousse à l'Ananas

pineapple pulp	21 oz	600 g
gelatin sheets	10	10
sugar	17.5 oz	500 g
egg whites	8	8
water	5 oz	150 g
crème fraîche, whipped	21 oz	600 g
kirsch (optional)	3 oz	80 g

Purée the pineapple pulp in a food processor. Cover the gelatin sheets with very cold water to soften.

Prepare an Italian meringue reinforced with gelatin by cooking the sugar and water to 250°F/121°C, while whipping the egg whites to soft peaks. Pour the cooked sugar in a fine stream, whipping it into the egg whites. Squeeze the gelatin sheets to remove the excess water and add them to the meringue immediately after the cooked sugar.

Whip the crème fraîche to soft peaks. Gently fold the Italian meringue into the pineapple pulp, then fold in the whipped crème fraîche.

This mousse should be used shortly after it is prepared.

Seville
Séville

This cake is assembled upside down in a long, rounded (gouttière) mold. Prepare sheets of biscuit and thin lemon slices poached in syrup.

Line the mold with the most attractive of the poached lemon slices, as they decorate the finished cake.

Fill the mold half-full with lemon mousse. Cover with a strip of biscuit narrower than the mold, moistened with lemon simple syrup. Spread on a second layer of mousse. Cover with a strip of biscuit the same size as the mold. Freeze.

Unmold either using a propane torch or by dipping the mold into hot water. Coat the cake with gelée or apricot glaze. Cut the cake into smaller cakes and set them on cake cardboards. Place a pastry shop label at one end on top of each cake.

Chef's Note*: This cake can be made with orange or kiwi following the same procedure. A white rum syrup can be used in place of the lemon syrup. This cake, when decorated appropriately, can be presented as a yule log.*

Lemon Syrup
Sirop Citron

Combine 17.5 oz/500 g simple syrup, 30° baume with 5.5 oz/150 g lemon juice.

Lemon Mousse
Mousse au Citron

gelatin sheets	8	8
lemon juice	7 oz	200 g
sugar	7 oz	200 g
cream, whipped	35 oz	1,000 g
kirsch (optional)	2 oz	50 g

Cover the gelatin sheets with very cold water to soften. Bring the lemon juice and sugar to a boil. Remove from heat. Squeeze the gelatin sheets to remove the excess water and stir into the hot lemon juice until melted. Set aside to cool.

Whip the cream to soft peaks. Just before the lemon mixture sets, whisk in the kirsch (if used), then fold in the whipped cream.

This mousse should be used shortly after it is prepared.

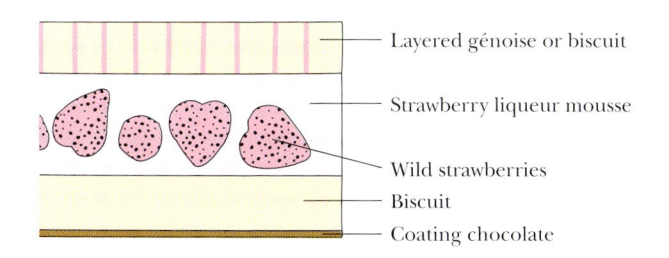

— Layered génoise or biscuit
— Strawberry liqueur mousse
— Wild strawberries
— Biscuit
— Coating chocolate

Imperial
Impérial

This cake is assembled upside down in a stainless steel cake frame 15 in/38 cm by 23 in/58 cm and 2 in/5 cm high. Other sized frames can be used as needed. If a cake frame is not available, a straight, high-sided cake pan can be used, although it is more difficult to unmold.

Cover a sheet pan, approximately 2 in/5 cm longer and wider than the frame, with a sheet of plastic.

Superimpose 4–5 sheets of biscuit coated with strawberry, raspberry, or red currant jam or glaze. Cut 1/2 in/1 cm strips and place them flat against the plastic (see photo page 109) or inside the base of a cake pan. Lightly moisten the biscuit with strawberry simple syrup. Fill the frame or mold half-full with strawberry liqueur mousse. Scatter wild strawberries over the mousse. Fill the frame three quarters full with the mousse. Cover with a sheet of biscuit, moistened lightly with the strawberry simple syrup. Use a pastry brush to cover the biscuit with coating chocolate. Freeze.

Place a sheet pan over the cake frame and turn the cake over so the layered biscuit is facing up. Remove the frame by heating it with a propane torch or by running a knife against the inside of the frame. Brush the top of the cake with gelée or apricot glaze. Cut the sheet cake into rectangles, squares, or individual cakes. Place each cake onto a cake cardboard. Place a pastry shop label at one corner on top of each cake.

(Imperial recipe continued on page 131)

Seville, Imperial

Chef's Note: This cake can also be prepared substituting the stawberries with other fruit such as blueberries or raspberries. The mousse and liqueur are flavored to complement the berries. The procedure remains the same.

Strawberry Simple Syrup
Sirop à la Fraise

Combine 17.5 oz/500 g simple syrup, 30° baume with 3.5 oz/100 g strawberry brandy or liqueur.

Strawberry Liqueur Mousse
Mousse à la Liqueur de Fraises

gelatin sheets	8	8
strawberry brandy or liqueur	7 oz	200 g
sugar	6.5 oz	180 g
cream, whipped	35 oz	1,000 g

Cover the gelatin sheets with very cold water to soften. Bring the liqueur and sugar to a boil. Remove from heat. Squeeze the gelatin sheets to remove the excess water and stir into the hot liquid until melted. Strain and set aside to cool.

Whip the cream to soft peaks. Just before the mixture sets, fold in the whipped cream.

This mousse should be used shortly after it is prepared.

Chapter 2

Mousse and Cream Fillings for Cakes and Pastries

Very Light Chocolate Mousse
Mousse au Chocolat Très Légère

Ganache chocolate	35 oz	1,000 g
Crème fraîche	7 oz	200 g
Egg yolks	15	15
Egg whites	24	24
Sugar	17.5 g	500 g

Melt the chocolate over a warm water bath. Remove from heat. Whisk the crème fraîche and egg yolks into the melted chocolate.

Whisk the egg whites to soft peaks, gradually adding the sugar. Continue whisking to medium peaks. Gently fold the egg whites into the chocolate mixture.

This mousse should be used shortly after it is prepared.

Chocolate Mousse No. 1
Mousse au Chocolat

butter	17.5 oz	500 g
ganache*	35 oz	1,000 g
egg yolks	8	8
sugar	14 oz	400 g
water	4 oz	120 g
egg whites	8	8
rum or Cognac (optional)	3.5 oz	100 g

*for information and recipes on ganache, see page 151

Blend the butter and ganache until soft. Whisk in the egg yolks.

Prepare an Italian meringue by cooking the sugar and water to 250°F/121°C, while whipping the egg whites to soft peaks. Pour the cooked sugar in a fine stream, whipping it into the egg whites. When the meringue is cool, gently fold it into the chocolate mixture.

This mousse should be used shortly after it is prepared.

Chocolate Mousse No. 2
Mousse au Chocolat

ganache*	17.5 oz	500 g
butter, softened	17.5 oz	500 g
Italian meringue	17.5 oz	500 g

*for information and recipes on ganache, see page 151

Whip the ganache and butter until soft and well blended. Gently fold in the Italian meringue.

Chocolate Mousse No. 3
Mousse au Chocolat

couverture chocolate	7 oz	200 g
chocolate paste or unsweetened chocolate	2 oz	50 g
butter, softened	17.5 oz	500 g
egg yolks	8	8
Italian meringue	17.5 oz	500 g

Melt the couverture and unsweetened chocolates. Combine, by whisking the melted chocolates with the softened butter and egg yolks. Gently fold in the Italian meringue.

Coffee Mousse
Mousse au Café

butter, softened	17.5 oz	500 g
coffee extract	2 oz	50 g
egg yolks	8	8
sugar	14 oz	400 g
water	4 oz	120 g
egg whites	8	8
coffee extract	1 tbsp 2 tsp	20 g

(Coffee Mousse recipe continued on next page)

Whip the softened butter with the coffee extract and egg yolks until aerated.

Prepare an Italian meringue by cooking the sugar and water to 250°F/121°C, while whipping the egg whites to soft peaks. Pour the cooked sugar in a fine stream, whipping it into the egg whites. Add the coffee extract. Continue whipping until cool.

Fold the Italian meringue into the coffee/butter mixture.

Craquelin Mousse
Mousse au Craquelin

butter, softened	35 oz	1,000 g
praline paste	5.5 oz	150 g
Italian meringue	14 oz	400 g
nougatine, ground (craquelin)	17.5 oz	500 g
Italian meringue	21 oz	600 g

Whip the softened butter and praline paste until aerated. Fold the ground nougatine (craquelin) into the first Italian meringue, then fold both into the butter mixture, smoothing with a whisk.

Gently fold the remaining Italian meringue into the batter. This mousse should be used shortly after it is prepared.

Chocolate Craquelin Mousse
Mousse au Craquelin Parfumée au Chocolat

dark chocolate	17.5 oz	500 g
butter, softened	17.5 oz	500 g
craquelin	9 oz	250 g
Italian meringue	17.5 oz	500 g

Melt the chocolate over a hot water bath. Whip the butter to soften and aerate. Combine the butter, melted chocolate, and craquelin with a whisk. Gently fold in the Italian meringue.

This mousse should be used shortly after it is prepared.

Blackcurrant Mousse
Mousse au Cassis

butter, softened	17.5 oz	500 g
blackcurrant pulp	9 oz	250 g
egg yolks	8	8
Italian meringue	17.5 oz	500 g

Whip the butter until aerated. Add the blackcurrant pulp and egg yolks, blending well. Gently fold in the Italian meringue.

This mousse should be used shortly after it is prepared.

Chestnut Mousse
Mousse aux Marrons

butter, softened	17.5 oz	500 g
chestnut paste	12.5 oz	350 g
egg yolks	8	8
rum	2 oz	50 g
Italian meringue	17.5 oz	500 g

Whip the butter until soft and aerated. Add the chestnut paste, egg yolks, and rum to the butter, blending well. Gently fold in the Italian meringue.

This mousse should be used shortly after it is prepared.

Pistachio Mousse No. 1
Mousse à la Pistache

butter, softened	17.5 oz	500 g
pistachio paste	4.5 oz	125 g
marzipan	4.5 oz	125 g
egg yolks	8	8
sugar	17.5 oz	500 g
water	5 oz	150 g
egg whites	8	8

Whip the butter until soft and aerated. Blend the pistachio and marzipan and add them to the butter along with the egg yolks, whisking until smooth.

Prepare an Italian meringue by cooking the sugar and water to 250°F/121°C, while whipping the egg whites to soft peaks. Pour the cooked sugar in a fine stream, whipping it into the egg whites. Continue whipping until cool. Gently fold the cool meringue into the batter.

This mousse should be used shortly after it is prepared.

Walnut Mousse
Mousse aux Noix

walnuts	9 oz	250 g
butter, softened	14 oz	400 g
egg yolks	8	8
sugar	17.5 oz	500 g
water	5.5 oz	150 g
egg whites	8	8
Cointreau (optional)	3 oz	80 g

Use a food processor to finely grind the walnuts. Combine the ground nuts with the softened butter and egg yolks until well blended.

Prepare an Italian meringue by cooking the sugar and water to 250°F/121°C, while whipping the egg whites to soft peaks. Pour the cooked sugar in a fine stream, whipping it into the egg whites. Continue whipping until cool. Gently fold the meringue into the batter.

This mousse should be used shortly after it is prepared.

Pistachio Mousse No. 2
Mousse à la Pistache

buttercream	21 oz	600 g
pistachio paste	5.5 oz	150 g
sugar	17.5 oz	500 g
water	5.5 oz	150 g
egg whites	8	8

Whip the buttercream and pistachio paste until well aerated.

Prepare an Italian meringue by cooking the sugar and water to 250°F/121°C, while whipping the egg whites to soft peaks. Pour the cooked sugar in a fine stream, whipping it into the egg whites. Continue whipping until cool. Gently fold the cool meringue into the batter.

This mousse should be used shortly after it is prepared.

Orange Mousse
Mousse à l'Orange

candied orange peel	10.5 oz	300 g
marzipan	14 oz	400 g
Cointreau	3.5 oz	100 g
butter, softened	24.5 oz	700 g
egg whites	8	8
sugar	17.5 oz	500 g
water	5.5 oz	150 g

Use a food processor to grind the candied orange peel. Blend the ground peel with the marzipan and Cointreau. Whip in the butter until smooth and aerated.

Prepare an Italian meringue by cooking the sugar and water to 250°F/121°C, while whipping the egg whites to soft peaks. Pour the cooked sugar in a fine

(Orange Mousse recipe continued on next page)

stream, whipping it into the egg whites. Gently fold the meringue into the batter.

This mousse should be used shortly after it is prepared.

Vanilla Milk Cream Filling
Crème Garniture au Lait

milk	17.5 oz	500 g
sugar	24.5 oz	700 g
glucose	7 oz	200 g
vanilla bean	1	1
butter	35 oz	1,000 g

Warm the milk, sugar, glucose, and vanilla to 220°F/104°C. Set aside to cool. Whip the cooled mixture with the butter on medium speed for 10 minutes.

This cream can be flavored to taste.

Almond Cream
Crème aux Amandes

marzipan	17.5 oz	500 g
kirsch	2 oz	50 g
butter	14 oz	400 g

In the bowl of an electric mixer, use the paddle attachment to whip the marzipan and kirsch until soft and well blended. Remove the paddle and put on the whisk attachment. Gradually whip in the butter until light and smooth.

Caramel Cream
Crème au Caramel

sugar	17.5 oz	500 g
milk	3.5 oz	100 g
crème fraîche	3.5 oz	100 g
butter	17.5 oz	500 g

Cook the sugar to an amber caramel. Add the milk and crème fraîche to deglaze. In the bowl of an electric mixer, whip the cream with the whisk attachment until completely cool. While whipping, gradually add the butter and continue to whip until smooth.

Orange Buttercream No. 1
Crème au Beurre Parfumée à l'Orange

candied orange peel	9 oz	250 g
marzipan	17.5 oz	500 g
Curaçao	3.5 oz	100 g
butter	21 oz	600 g
buttercream	3 lbs 4.5 oz	1,500 g

Use a food processor to grind the candied orange peel. Whip the marzipan and Curaçao (or other orange liqueur of choice) into the ground orange peel. Whisk in the butter until light and aerated. Finish by whipping in the buttercream until smooth.

Orange Buttercream No. 2
Crème au Beurre Parfumée à l'Orange

candied orange peel	9 oz	250 g
marzipan	17.5 oz	500 g
Curaçao	3.5 oz	100 g
butter	28 oz	800 g
Italian meringue	28 oz	800 g

Use a food processor to grind the candied orange peel. Whip the marzipan and Curaçao into the ground orange peel. Whisk in the butter. Gently fold in the Italian meringue until smooth.

Orange Buttercream No. 3
Crème au Beurre Parfumée à l'Orange

milk	17.5 oz	500 g
sugar	17.5 oz	500 g
eggs	5	5
orange juice	9 oz	250 g
oranges, zest of	3	3
lemons, zest of	2	2
butter	35 oz	1,000 g

Bring the milk to a simmer. Whisk the sugar and eggs until thick and pale. Combine this mixture with the juice and zests, stirring constantly and cooking as for crème anglaise until it coats the spoon. Strain and cool.

Whisk the butter gradually into the cream.

Lemon Cream for Tarts
Crème au Citron pour Tartes

eggs	10	10
sugar	35 oz	1,000 g
lemons, juice and zest of	6	6
butter	17.5 oz	500 g

Whisk all ingredients in a saucepan. Warm slowly over low heat, whisking constantly until the cream thickens. Set aside to cool and use as needed.

Lemon Cream Filling No. 1
Crème Garniture au Citron

lemons	5	5
sugar	17.5 oz	500 g
butter	2 oz	50 g
butter	17.5 oz	500 g

Use a food processor to finely grind the lemons. Cook the ground lemons with the sugar and first butter for several minutes. Set aside to cool.

In the bowl of an electric mixer, whip the cream and second butter on high speed for 10 minutes.

Lemon Cream Filling No. 2
Crème Garniture au Citron

butter	9 oz	250 g
sugar	17.5 oz	500 g
lemons, juice and zest of	4	4
eggs	3	3

In a sugar copper pot (poêlon), bring the butter, sugar, lemon juice, and zests to a boil. Remove from heat. Whip the eggs lightly and add them to the hot mixture. Strain. Return the mixture to the heat and cook to 221°F/105°C. Set aside to cool.

Chef's Note: This recipe can be used as is or lightened with pastry cream or mousseline cream.

Nougatine Cream
Crème Nougatine

nougatine, ground	12.5 oz	350 g
butter, softened	17.5 oz	500 g
Italian meringue	17.5 oz	500 g

Grind the nougatine to a powder. Whip the nougatine powder into the butter along with the Italian meringue, smoothing with a whisk.

Modern French Pastry

Nougatine Mousse
Mousse Nougatine

Use the list of ingredients given for the nougatine cream on page 139. Whip the butter with the nougatine, then gently fold in the Italian meringue, maintaining its lightness so the batter is more aerated than the nougatine cream.

This mousse should be used shortly after it is prepared.

Buttercream (Quick Method)
No. 1
Crème au Beurre

butter, softened	17.5 oz	500 g
flavor to taste		
Italian meringue	17.5 oz	500 g

Whip the butter until light and aerated. Add the flavoring, such as coffee, praline, chocolate, or liqueur. Add the Italian meringue, whisking until smooth.

Buttercream (Quick Method)
No. 2
Crème au Beurre

butter	17.5 oz	500 g
confectioners' sugar	14 oz	400 g
flavor to taste		

In the bowl of an electric mixer, use the whisk attachment to whip the butter, confectioners' sugar, and flavoring until smooth.

Facing Page: Yule Logs

Chef's Note: *This buttercream should be used only in a pinch. It is quick to prepare but does not have the finesse of better quality buttercreams.*

Yule Logs
Bûches de Noël

Traditional yule logs generally contain buttercream fillings; modern versions replace the buttercream fillings with lighter creams and mousses. Other than maintaining the characteristic long, rounded log shape, yule logs do not follow any particular recipe. They can be designed according to personal taste using almost any cream or mousse of choice. These cakes are also prepared without the apparent holiday decorations. At Christmas, holiday decorations can simply be added.

As lighter fillings make it difficult to roll the yule log according to the standard technique, they are most often assembled upside down in molds called gouttière. The molds are lined with sheets of biscuit cut to size; mousseline biscuit is recommended for its flexibility. The filling is added, along with any garniture or additional biscuit layer. A final layer of biscuit is trimmed to fit the top of the mold, which becomes the bottom after the cake is turned out.

Alhambra Yule Log
Bûche Alhambra

Line a gouttière mold with slices of biscuit layered with jam. Fill with a grapefruit, lemon, orange, or pineapple cream or mousse. Cover with a layer of biscuit trimmed to fit the top of the mold. Freeze.

Unmold and coat with gelée or light glaze. Cut into smaller cakes. Decorate with a plaque inscribed with "Merry Christmas," chocolate holly leaves, and marzipan figures.

Coffee Yule Log
Bûche au Café

This cake can be varied by changing the flavor of the filling and moistening with a complementary simple syrup. The procedure remains the same.

Line a gouttière mold with a layer of biscuit and moisten lightly with coffee simple syrup. Fill half-full with coffee mousse or coffee charlotte cream. Cover with a layer of biscuit liberally moistened with coffee simple syrup.

Fill the mold with the same filling and cover with biscuit trimmed to size. Freeze.

Unmold. With a pastry bag and fluted tip, pipe coffee chantilly, covering the entire cake. Decorate according to taste.

Whiskey or White Wine Mousse Yule Log
Bûche au Whiskey ou au Vin Blanc

Line a gouttière mold with a layer of mousseline biscuit. Fill half-full with whiskey or white wine mousse. Scatter cubes of poached fruit, such as bigarreau cherries, peaches, and pears, over the mousse. Fill with the same mousse. Cover with biscuit trimmed to size. Freeze.

Unmold and cut into smaller cakes. With a pastry bag and fluted tip, cover with Italian meringue. Sprinkle with confectioners' sugar and brown lightly with a propane torch. Decorate according to taste.

Whether the log is assembled in a gouttière or rolled by hand, it is possible to trim the two ends, leaving them exposed to reveal the filling and fruit as part of the decoration. However, to prevent the ends from drying out, they can be covered with marzipan disks rolled thinly and cut slightly smaller than the circumference of the cake. Cut off a section from each disk to create a flat edge. Dust with confectioners' sugar and brown lightly with a propane torch. Press the disks, one at each end, with the flat edge on the bottom. This technique can be used to protect and decorate all types of yule logs, including the more traditional rolled yule log filled with buttercream.

Domino Yule Log
Bûche Domino

Line a gouttière mold with slices of biscuit rolled with jam. Fill the mold with kirsch Bavarian. Cover with a strip of biscuit cut to fit the top of the mold. Freeze.

Unmold and coat the cake with gelée or apricot glaze. Decorate according to taste.

White Wine Bavarian Cream
Bavaroise au Vin Blanc

gelatin sheets	8	8
white wine	17.5 oz	500 g
egg yolks	12	12
sugar	5.5 oz	150 g
crème fraîche, whipped	35 oz	1,000 g

Cover the gelatin sheets with very cold water to soften.

Bring the white wine to a boil. Whisk the egg yolks and sugar until thick and pale. Combine the wine and egg mixture, stirring constantly over the heat, cooking as for crème anglaise until it coats the spoon. Remove from heat.

Squeeze the gelatin sheets to remove the excess water and stir into the wine mixture until melted. Set aside to cool.

Whip the crème fraîche to soft peaks and gently fold it into the cooled cream just before it sets.

This cream should be used shortly after it is prepared.

Chestnut Charlotte Cream
Crème à Charlotte aux Marrons

gelatin sheets	8	8
milk	17.5 oz	500 g
chestnut paste	17.5 oz	500 g
egg yolks	8	8
sugar	3.5 oz	100 g
rum	3.5 oz	100 g
crème fraîche	17.5 oz	500 g

Follow the procedure given for the charlotte creams on this page.

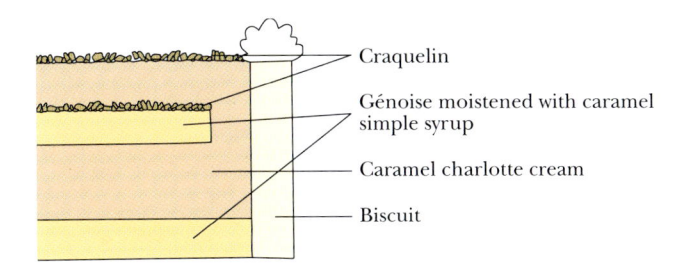

Caramel Charlotte
Charlotte au Caramel

This cake is assembled following the procedure used for the Saint Gaston cake.

Charlotte Caramel Cream
Crème à Charlotte au Caramel

gelatin sheets	16	16
sugar	17.5 oz	500 g
milk	34 fl oz	1 L
egg yolks	10	10
crème fraîche	3 lbs 4.5 oz	1,500 g
Italian meringue	10.5 oz	300 g

Cover the gelatin sheets with very cold water to soften.

Cook the sugar to an amber caramel. Bring the milk to a boil and whisk it into the caramel. Whisk the egg yolks and add them to the milk/caramel mixture, stirring constantly until it coats the spoon as for crème anglaise. Remove from heat.

Squeeze the gelatin to remove the excess water and stir into the cream until melted. Set aside to cool.

Whip the crème fraîche to soft peaks and fold it into the cream just before it sets up. Fold in the Italian meringue.

This cream should be used shortly after it is prepared.

Charlotte Coffee Cream
Crème à Charlotte au Café

gelatin sheets	8	8
milk	17.5 oz	500 g
vanilla bean	1/2	1/2
coffee, ground	3.5 oz	100 g
egg yolks	12	12
sugar	3.5 oz	100 g
crème fraîche, whipped	35 oz	1,000 g
Italian meringue*	14 oz	400 g

*See next page for Italian meringue recipe

Cover the gelatin sheets with very cold water to soften.

Bring the milk, vanilla, and ground coffee to a boil. Remove from heat, and set aside to infuse for approximately 15 minutes. Strain.

Whisk the egg yolks and sugar until thick and pale. Combine the egg mixture with the milk and cook, stirring constantly until it coats the spoon as for a crème anglaise. Remove from heat. Squeeze the gelatin to remove the excess water and stir into the cream until melted. Set aside to cool.

Whip the crème fraîche to soft peaks and fold it into the cream just before it sets. Fold in the Italian meringue.

Diagram labels: Craquelin; Génoise moistened with caramel simple syrup; Caramel charlotte cream; Biscuit

Italian Meringue

sugar	12.5 oz	350 g
water	3.5 oz	100 g
egg whites	6	6
coffee extract	1 tbsp 2 tsp	20 g

Prepare an Italian meringue by cooking the sugar and water to 250°F/121°C, while whipping the egg whites to soft peaks. Pour the cooked sugar in a fine stream, whipping it into the egg whites. Pour in the coffee extract and continue whipping until cool.

Chocolate Charlotte Cream
Crème à Charlotte au Chocolat

gelatin sheets	8	8
milk	17.5 oz	500 g
vanilla bean	1	1
cocoa powder	5.5 oz	150 g
egg yolks	8	8
sugar	5.5 oz	150 g
gelatin sheets	8	8
crème fraîche, whipped	17.5 oz	500 g
cocoa powder, sifted	2 oz	50 g
Italian meringue	17.5 oz	500 g

Cover the gelatin sheets with very cold water to soften.

Bring the milk, vanilla bean, and cocoa powder to a boil. Whisk the egg yolks and sugar until thick and pale. Combine the two mixtures and cook as for crème anglaise, stirring constantly until it coats the spoon. Remove from heat.

Squeeze the gelatin sheets to remove the excess water and stir into the cream until melted. Strain and set aside to cool.

Whip the crème fraîche to soft peaks, and fold it into the cream when it begins to set. Combine the second cocoa powder with the Italian meringue then fold the meringue into the batter.

This mousse should be used shortly after it is prepared.

Mandarin Orange Mousse or Charlotte Cream
Mousse à la Mandarine ou Crème à Charlotte à la Mandarine

gelatin sheets	8	8
mandarin pulp	17.5 oz	500 g
vanilla bean	1	1
egg yolks	12	12
sugar	3.5 oz	100 g
powdered milk	2 oz	50 g
mandarine liqueur	3.5 oz	100 g
crème fraîche, whipped	26.5 oz	750 g
Italian meringue	14 oz	400 g

Cover the gelatin sheets with very cold water to soften.

Bring the mandarin pulp and vanilla bean to a boil. Whisk the egg yolks, sugar, and powdered milk so they are thick and pale. Combine the two mixtures and cook, stirring constantly, until it coats the spoon. Remove from heat.

Squeeze the gelatin sheets to remove the excess water and stir into the mandarine mixture until melted. Set aside to cool.

Just before the cream sets, stir in the liqueur, fold in the whipped crème fraîche and Italian meringue.

This mousse should be used shortly after it is prepared.

Liquor Mousse or Charlotte Cream
Mousse à l'Alcool ou Crème à Charlotte à l'Alcool

gelatin sheets	16	16
milk	35 oz	1 L
sugar	10.5 oz	300 g
egg yolks	18	18
cornstarch	1.5 oz	40 g
liquor (of choice)	7 oz	200 g

sugar	14 oz	400 g
water	4 oz	120 g
egg whites	8	8
crème fraîche or heavy cream	3 lbs 4.5 oz	1,500 g

Cover the gelatin sheets with very cold water to soften.

Bring the milk to a boil. Whisk the sugar, egg yolks, and cornstarch until thick and pale. Combine the egg yolk mixture with the milk and cook as for a crème anglaise, stirring constantly until it coats the spoon. Remove from heat.

Squeeze the gelatin sheets to remove the excess water and stir into the hot cream until melted. Set aside to cool. Just before the cream sets up, stir in the liquor.

Prepare an Italian meringue by cooking the sugar and water to 250°F/121°C, while whipping the egg whites to soft peaks. Pour the cooked sugar in a fine stream, whipping it into the egg whites. Continue whipping until cool.

Whip the crème fraîche or heavy cream to soft peaks. Fold the cool meringue into the anglaise mixture, then fold in the whipped cream.

This mousse should be used shortly after it is prepared.

Chef's Note: *This recipe can be made without cornstarch. If it is omitted, prepare the milk, sugar, and egg yolks as for crème anglaise. Stir in 18 softened gelatin sheets just after the mixture has been removed from the heat. Follow the remaining procedure as above.*

Chocolate Mousse for Fillings
Mousse au Chocolat pour Garnitures

milk	35 oz	1 L
baking chocolate	7 oz	200 g
butter	1 oz	30 g
egg yolks	8	8
sugar	12.5 oz	350 g
cornstarch	2.5 oz	70 g
crème fraîche	17.5 oz	500 g

Bring the milk, chocolate, and butter to a boil. Whisk the egg yolks, sugar, and cornstarch until thick and pale. Combine the milk and egg mixtures and cook as for a crème anglaise until it coats the spoon. Set aside to cool.

Whip the crème fraîche to soft peaks. Whisk the chocolate mixture until smooth and fold in a small portion of the whipped crème fraîche, blending well. Gently fold in the remaining whipped crème fraîche.

This mousse should be used shortly after it is prepared.

Fruit Mousse No. 1— Blackcurrant, Strawberry, Raspberry
Mousse aux Fruits—Cassis, Fraises, Framboises

gelatin sheets	6	6
water	2.5 oz	75 g
fruit pulp	9 oz	250 g
sugar	7 oz	200 g
crème fraîche, whipped	35 oz	1,000 g

Cover the gelatin sheets with very cold water to soften. Squeeze the gelatin sheets to remove the excess water; discard the water. Put the sheets in 2.5 oz/75 g fresh water, heating without boiling until melted.

Whisk together the fruit pulp, sugar, and melted gelatin. Whip the crème fraîche to soft peaks and fold it into the pulp mixture.

This mousse should be used shortly after it is prepared. To be used for the Mirror, Saint Ange, Charlottes or any cake.

Fruit Mousse No. 2—Blackcurrant, Strawberry, Raspberry
Mousse aux Fruits—Cassis, Fraises, Framboises

gelatin sheets	14	14
milk	7 oz	200 g
sugar	7 oz	200 g
fruit pulp	17.5 oz	500 g
crème fraîche, whipped	35 oz	1,000 g

Cover the gelatin sheets with very cold water to soften.

Bring the milk and sugar to a boil. Remove from heat. Squeeze the gelatin sheets to remove the excess water and stir into the hot milk. Stir in the fruit pulp. Strain and set aside to cool.

Whip the crème fraîche to soft peaks and fold it into the mixture just before it sets.

This mousse should be used shortly after it is prepared.

Hazelnut Mousse for Fillings
Mousse Noisette pour Garnitures

gelatin sheets	8	8
milk	17.5 oz	500 g
egg yolks	5	5
sugar	3.5 oz	100 g
cornstarch	2 oz	50 g
hazelnut praline paste	7 oz	200 g
crème fraîche, whipped	35 oz	1,000 g

Cover the gelatin sheets with very cold water to soften.

Prepare a pastry cream by heating the milk, and whisking together the egg yolks, sugar, and cornstarch. Combine and cook until thickened. Remove from heat. Squeeze the gelatin sheets to remove the excess water and stir into the pastry cream until melted. Whisk in the hazelnut praline paste. Set aside to cool. When the pastry cream is cool, whisk until smooth.

Whip the crème fraîche to soft peaks. Whisk in one third of the whipped crème fraîche to lighten the pastry cream, then gently fold in the remaining crème fraîche, being careful to maintain lightness.

Chocolate Suzanne Cream
Crème Suzanne au Chocolat

dark chocolate or couverture chocolate	9 oz	250 g
pastry cream	5.5 oz	150 g
chantilly	9 oz	250 g

Melt the chocolate. Whisk in the pastry cream until smooth. Gently fold in the chantilly.

This cream should be used shortly after it is prepared.

Chantilly Cream
Crème Chantilly

Chantilly cream is made by whipping crème fraîche or heavy cream to soft peaks, sweetening with sugar. The quantity of sugar used depends on how the chantilly will be used and the clients' taste.

As a guideline, use 3.5–6.5 oz/100–180 g of sugar per 35 oz/1,000 g of crème fraîche or heavy cream.

Chantilly can be sweetened differently according to how it will be used and personal taste:

1. Confectioners' sugar or granulated sugar can be mixed into the crème fraîche before adding it to the machine or whipping in an electric mixer.

2. A simple syrup, 30° baume, can be whisked into the heavy cream. For every 35 oz/1,000 g heavy cream, add

approximately 10.5 oz/300 g simple syrup. Then pour it into the machine or whip in an electric mixer.

3. Glucose or trimoline can be used by preparing a heavy syrup. Bring 35 oz/1,000 g glucose or trimoline and 9 oz/250 g water to a boil. Sweeten each 35 oz/1,000 g crème fraîche or heavy cream with 5.5 oz/150 g of the syrup and put it into the machine or whip in an electric mixer.

Chantilly cream can be flavored with vanilla; use a few drops of extract per liter of cream.

Whipped Cream
Crème Fouettée

This is simply crème fraîche or heavy cream that is whipped, usually to soft peaks. With the addition of sugar and vanilla it becomes chantilly (see preceding recipe).

Orange Mousse
Mousse à l'Orange

gelatin sheets	10	10
oranges, juice and zest of	4	4
egg yolks	6	6
sugar	5.5 oz	150 g
lemon, juiced	1	1
crème fraîche, whipped	35 oz	1,000 g

Cover the gelatin sheets with very cold water to soften.
Cook the orange juice and zest, egg yolks, sugar, and lemon juice until it is thick and coats the spoon.
Squeeze the gelatin sheets to remove the excess water and stir them into the orange cream until melted. Strain and set aside to cool. Just before setting, fold in the whipped cream.
This mousse should be used shortly after it is prepared.

Chef's Note: *The quantity of gelatin in the orange mousse can be decreased or eliminated altogether according to personal taste and the amount of stability required.*

Lemon Mousse
Mousse au Citron

gelatin sheets	8	8
lemons, juice and zest of	4	4
egg yolks	6	6
sugar	5.5 oz	150 g
white wine	5.5 oz	150 g
crème fraîche, whipped	35 oz	1,000 g

Cover the gelatin sheets with very cold water to soften.
Cook the lemon juice and zest, egg yolks, sugar, and white wine, whisking constantly until it coats the spoon. Remove from heat. Squeeze the gelatin sheets to remove the excess water and stir into the hot mixture until melted. Strain and set aside to cool. Just before the mixture sets, fold in the whipped crème fraîche.
This mousse should be used shortly after it is prepared.

- Gelée
- Almond paste
- Almond glaze
- Almond biscuit, moistened with maraschino simple syrup
- Almond paste filling

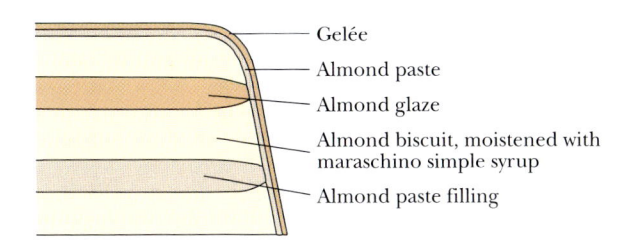

Mogador

Place an almond biscuit baked in a mold on a cake cardboard. With a serrated knife, cut the biscuit into 3 layers, horizontally. Moisten the bottom layer with maraschino simple syrup. Spread a layer of almond

(Mogador recipe continued on page 149)

Fillings for Cakes and Pastries

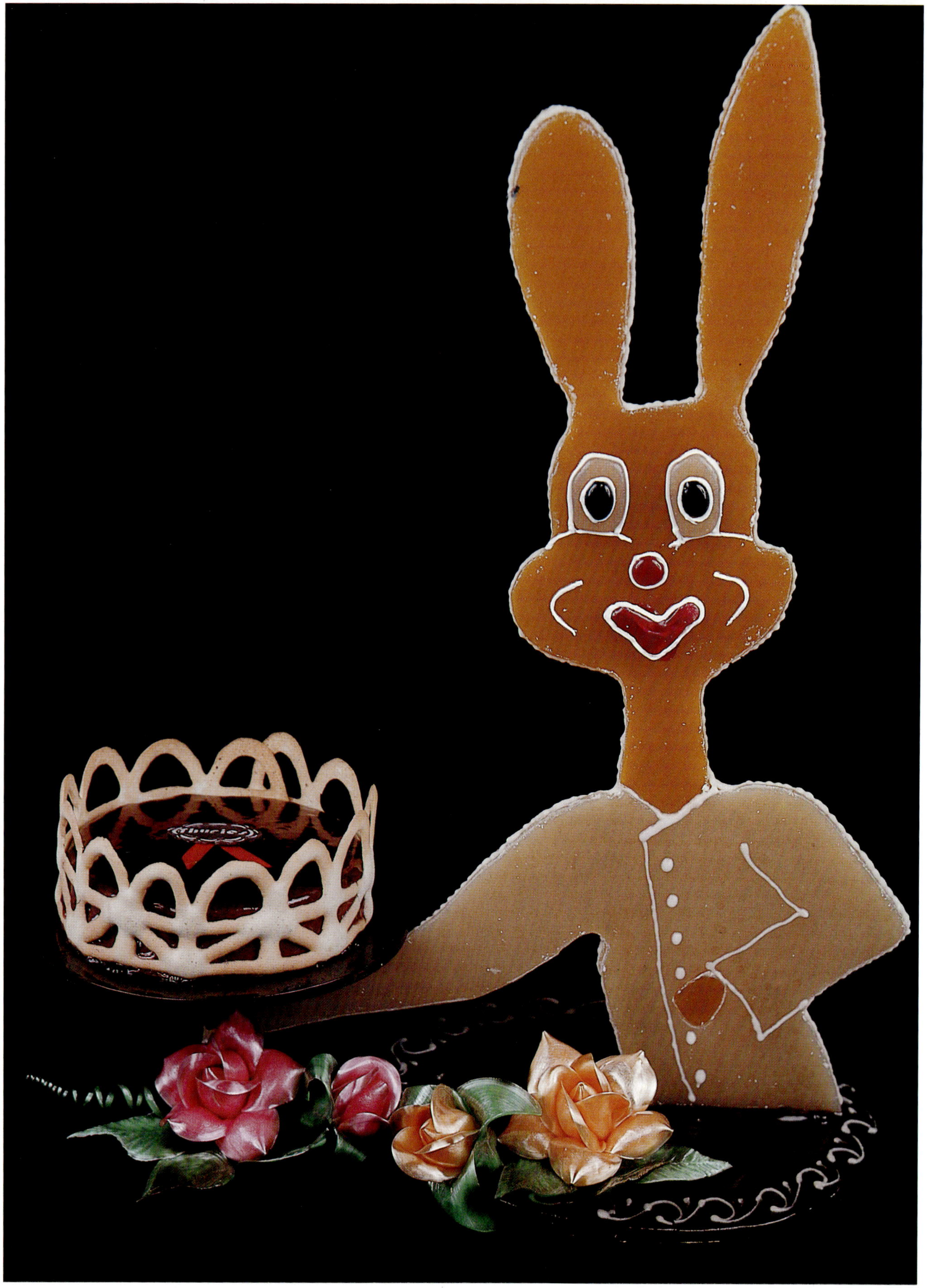

paste filling. Cover with the second layer of biscuit, moistened with maraschino simple syrup. Spread a layer of almond glaze, cover with the third layer of biscuit, and moisten with the maraschino simple syrup.

Coat the top and sides of the cake with almond paste softened with egg whites to a spreadable consistency. Place the cake in a moderate oven for a few seconds or until the almond paste forms a protective crust. Brush the top and sides with gelée.

Almond Glaze
Nappage aux Amandes

Combine 17.5 oz/500 g apricot glaze with 3.5 oz/100 g almond powder.

Almond Paste Filling
Garniture à la Pâte d'Amandes

Soften marzipan with a liquor of choice. Add buttercream (half the weight of the marzipan). Whip until light and aerated.

If using raw almond paste, follow the same procedure, but adding more buttercream—up to 100 percent of the weight of the almond paste.

Coffee Extract
Extrait de Café

sugar	35 oz	1,000 g
water	10.5 oz	300 g
water	35 oz	1,000 g
instant coffee	7 oz	200 g

Facing Page: Mogador, displayed on a poured sugar presentation piece

Cook the sugar and first water to an amber caramel. Bring the second water to a simmer and add the instant coffee, stirring to dissolve. Gradually add the hot water to the caramel, stirring with a whisk.

Chef's Note: To determine whether the caramel is properly cooked, dribble several drops of the caramel into a bowl of cold water. The caramel is ready if it immediately rises to the surface of the water.

Coffee Simple Syrup No. 1
Sirop au Café

Combine simple syrup, 30° baume, with strong coffee or coffee extract according to taste and use.

Coffee Simple Syrup No. 2
Sirop au Café

Combine 35 oz/1,000 g boiling water with 10.5 oz/300 g instant coffee and 35 oz/1,000 g simple syrup, 30° baume.

Strong Coffee for Flavoring

Combine 35 oz/1,000 g ground coffee beans with 2 qt 3.5 fl oz/2 L boiling water. Set aside to infuse for 24 hours. Strain through a coffee filter after infusing.

Fillings for Cakes and Pastries

Simple Syrup for Moistening Cakes

Chocolate Simple Syrup

water	34 fl oz	1 L
cocoa powder	10.5 oz	300 g
simple syrup, 30° baume	34 fl oz	1 L

Bring the water and cocoa powder to a boil. Stir in the simple syrup.

Liquor Simple Syrup

water	17.5 oz	500 g
simple syrup	17.5 oz	500 g
liquor of choice	17.5 oz	500 g

Combine the water, simple syrup, and liquor such as Cointreau, Grand Marnier, rum, Curaçao, or kirsch.

Almond Syrup

sugar	35 oz	1,000 g
water	21 oz	600 g
almond	3.5 oz	100 g
bitter almond*	1 tsp	5 g
water	3.5 oz	100 g
confectioners' sugar	9 oz	250 g
few drops orange flower water		

*Bitter almond can be difficult to obtain, so if necessary, substitute with a few drops bitter almond extract or oil, or use an equal amount almond paste containing bitter almond.

Bring the sugar and water to a boil.
Use a food processor to grind the almonds and bitter almonds to a powder. In a blender, mix the powdered almonds with the second water and confectioners' sugar. Pour the boiling water over the almonds. Bring to a boil and maintain a temperature of 176°F/80°C for 20 minutes. Remove from heat and add a few drops orange flower water.
Store in the refrigerator in an airtight container.

Coating Cakes and Pastries with Liquid Couverture

Recipe No. 1

coating chocolate	17.5 oz	500 g
dark couverture chocolate	17.5 oz	500 g

Melt the two chocolates together in a hot water bath to 100.5°–104°F/38°–40°C.

Recipe No. 2

dark couverture chocolate	24.5 oz	700 g
butter, softened	10.5 oz	300 g

Melt the chocolate over a warm water bath. Remove from heat and stir in the softened butter until smooth and melted.

Recipe No. 3

milk	17.5 oz	500 g
ganache chocolate, chopped	26.5 oz	750 g
butter, softened	12.5 oz	350 g

Bring the milk to a boil. Pour it over the chopped chocolate. Remove from heat and stir in the softened butter until smooth.

Recipe No. 4

It is possible to purchase certain types of coating chocolates that do not require tempering.

Recipe No. 5

dark couverture chocolate	17.5 oz	500 g
butter, softened	7 oz	200 g
simple syrup, 30°baume	10.5 oz	300 g
glucose	7 oz	200 g

Melt the chocolate over a warm water bath. Add the softened butter, simple syrup, and glucose, stirring until smooth.

Basic Ganache

crème fraîche	35 oz	1,000 g
chocolate, chopped or melted	3 lbs 8.5 oz	1,600 g

Bring the crème fraîche to a boil in a poêlon. Remove from heat and stir it into the chocolate until smooth.

Chef's Note: The chocolate can be replaced with 28 oz/ 800 g couverture chocolate and 28 oz/800 g chocolate.

Easter Nest Cakes
Nid de Pâques

Easter nests do not follow any particular recipe. All cakes filled with buttercream or ganache can be used. Generally, the génoise or biscuit is baked in a savarin, kougloff, or bundt mold so the cake will have a hollow center on top to imitate a bird's nest. The génoise or biscuit is cut into three layers horizontally, moistened with flavored simple syrup, and layered with a filling of choice.

The cakes are decorated with buttercream Morning Glories or other flowers and leaves, chocolate curls, or tuiles. Place chocolate, liqueur, or nougatine eggs in the hollow center along with plaques inscribed "Happy Easter."

Ganaches

A basic ganache is composed of crème fraîche or evaporated milk and chocolate or couverture chocolate. The preparation and flavorings can be varied according to taste and application. By raising the quantity of chocolate, the resulting ganache is firmer and has a better storage life. Conversely, if the quantity of chocolate is diminished, the ganache will be softer.

Almost any type of chocolate can be used, although it will affect the color, taste, and texture of the finished ganache. The better quality chocolates offer a deeper, less sweet ganache. The crème fraîche can be replaced with heavy cream or evaporated milk. The proportions remain the same. The glucose can be replaced with inverted sugar (trimoline), as they both help to prevent crystallization.

Praline Ganache
Ganache Pralinée

crème fraîche or heavy cream	14 oz	400 g
couverture chocolate, chopped or melted	35 oz	1,000 g
praline paste	27 oz	200 g
butter, softened	17.5 oz	500 g
flavor of choice	3 oz	80 g

Bring the cream to a boil. Pour it over the chopped or melted chocolate. Add the praline paste, butter, and flavor, stirring until smooth.

152   Modern French Pastry

Pistachio Ganache
Ganache Pistache

evaporated milk or crème fraîche	14 oz	400 g
white chocolate couverture, chopped or melted	35 oz	1,000 g
pistachio paste	7 oz	200 g
butter, softened	10.5 oz	300 g

Bring the milk or crème fraîche to a boil. Pour it over the chopped or melted chocolate. Stir in the pistachio paste and smooth with a whisk. Set aside to cool. Stir the butter into the cool mixture until smooth.

Bitter Ganache
Ganache Amère

ganache chocolate	24.5 oz	700 g
chocolate paste or unsweetened chocolate	9 oz	250 g
crème fraîche	17.5 oz	500 g
vanilla bean	1	1

Chop or melt the chocolates. Bring the crème fraîche and vanilla bean (split lengthwise) to a boil. Pour the hot cream over the chocolates. Remove the vanilla bean. Stir until smooth.

Facing Page: Easter Nest Cakes

154 *Modern French Pastry*

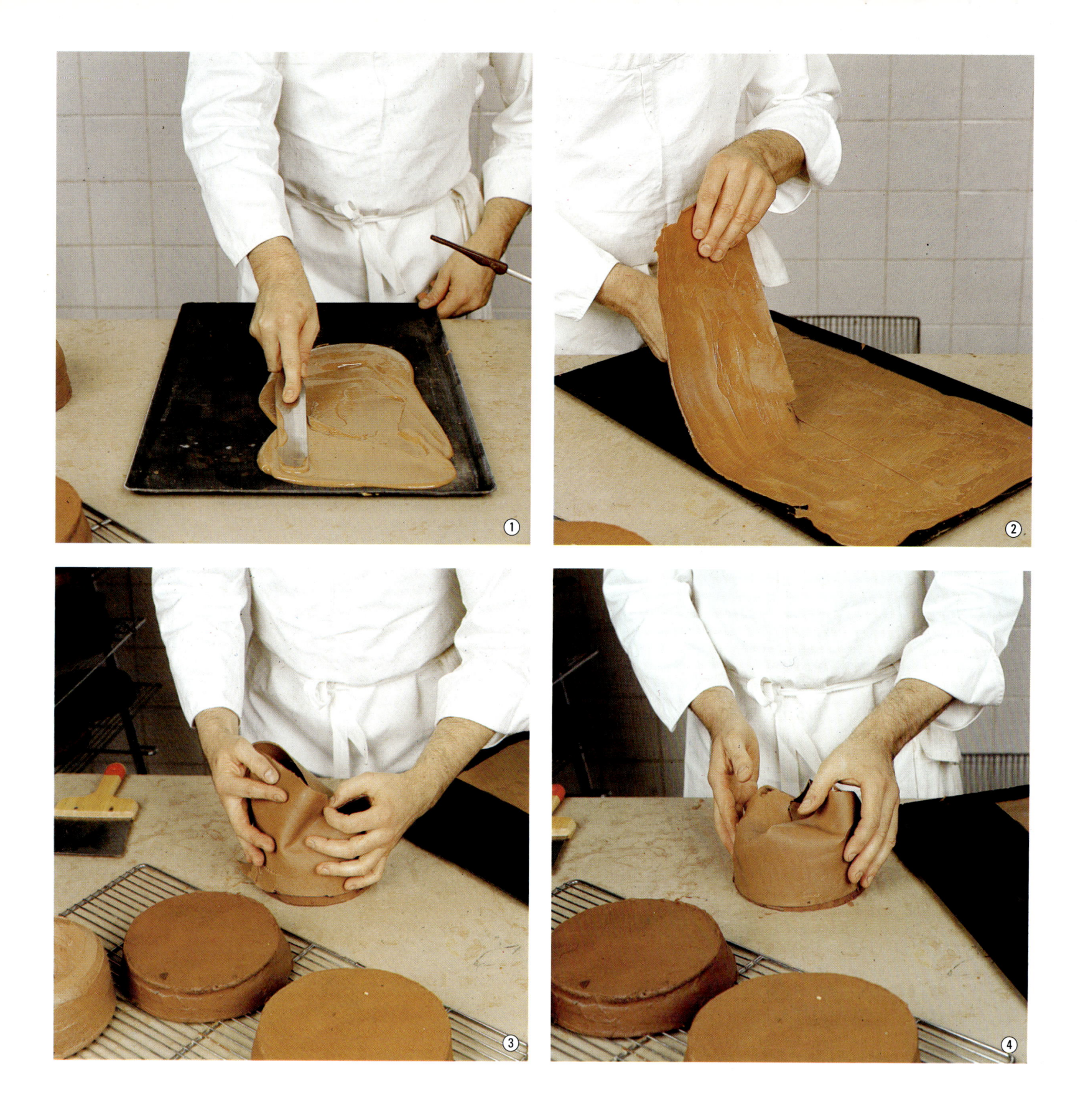

Chocolate Strips, Heating and Chilling Technique

Photo 1: Spread melted, not tempered, chocolate over a very cold sheet pan that has been taken immediately from the freezer. With a metal spatula, work quickly to spread the chocolate in an even layer, approximately 1/16 in./2 mm thick, over the sheet pan.

Photo 2: A few seconds later, after the chocolate has set, cut strips to the size needed using the corner of a pastry triangle. Hold the triangle with one hand scraping it against the sheet pan to release the strip of chocolate while lifting the loosened edge with the other hand.

Photo 3: Wrap the strip around the cake to be decorated. It is important that the chocolate strip not be too firm but rather supple enough so it will adhere to the cake and be shaped without cracking.

Photo 4: Fold the chocolate inward on the top, making sure it is still malleable enough not to crack during this step.

Chef's Note: *Any size strip can be made using this technique. The procedure remains the same for milk chocolate and couverture chocolate.*

Chocolate Cigarettes

Photo (page 155): Spread tempered chocolate, approximately 1/16 in/2 mm thick, on a room temperature or warm sheet pan. Wait for the chocolate to partially set. Before the chocolate is completely firm, use the corner of a pastry triangle to cut strips to the length desired for the cigarettes. Scrape the triangle approximately 1/2 in/1 cm from the end forward to form the cigarettes. The thickness can be varied by scraping closer or farther away from the end.

Variation
Spread a layer of tempered chocolate, approximately 1/16 in/2 mm thick, on a marble or other work surface. When the chocolate is partially set, run the corner of the triangle down the chocolate to cut the width needed. This will determine the length of the cigarettes. Scrape the triangle forward to form the cigarettes to the thickness needed. By cutting wider strips, longer cigarettes can be made. These cigarettes can then be cut into smaller ones.

CHAPTER 3

Biscuits and Génoises— Bases for Cakes and Pastries

Génoise Mousseline
Mousseline Génoise

eggs	20	20
egg yolks	16	16
sugar	16 oz	450 g
flour	9	250 g
cornstarch	5.5 oz	150 g

Whip the eggs, egg yolks, and sugar over a hot water bath or other heat source until warm. Remove from heat and continue whipping until the batter has completely cooled.

Sift together the flour and cornstarch. Gently fold them into the batter. Pour or pipe the batter onto sheet pans lined with parchment paper or into buttered and floured molds.

Bake in a moderate oven, 390°F/200°C.

Special Butter Génoise
Génoise Beurrée Spéciale

eggs	16	16
sugar	14 oz	400 g
flour	12.5 oz	350 g
cornstarch or potato starch	3.5 oz	100 g
almond powder	3.5 oz	100 g
butter, melted	7 oz	200 g

Whip the eggs and sugar over a hot water bath or other heat source until warm. Remove from heat and continue whipping until the batter has completely cooled.

Sift together the flour, cornstarch, and almond powder. Gently fold them into the batter. Combine a small amount of batter with the melted butter to lighten, then fold it into the batter. Pour the batter onto sheet pans lined with parchment paper or into buttered and floured molds.

Bake in a moderate oven, 390°F/200°C.

Chocolate Génoise
Génoise au Chocolat

eggs	16	16
sugar	17.5 oz	500 g
flour	10.5 oz	300 g
cornstarch	5.5 oz	150 g
cocoa powder	3.5 oz	100 g
hazelnut powder	3.5 oz	100 g

Whip the eggs and sugar over a hot water bath or other heat source until warm. Remove from heat and continue whipping until the batter has completely cooled.

Sift together the flour, cornstarch, cocoa powder, and hazelnut powder. Gently fold into the batter. Pour or pipe the batter onto sheet pans lined with parchment paper or into buttered and floured molds.

Bake in a moderate oven, 390°F/200°C.

Coconut Génoise No. 1
Génoise à la Noix de Coco

eggs	20	20
sugar	21 oz	600 g
flour	19.5 oz	550 g
coconut, grated	3.5 oz	100 g

Whip the eggs and sugar over a hot water bath or other heat source until warm. Remove from heat and continue whipping until the batter has completely cooled.

Sift the flour and combine it with the grated coconut. Gently fold into the batter. Pour or pipe the batter onto sheet pans lined with parchment paper or into buttered and floured molds.

Bake in a moderate oven, 390°F/200°C.

Coconut Génoise No. 2
Génoise à la Noix de Coco

eggs	20	20
sugar	16 oz	450 g
almond powder	5.5 oz	150 g
flour	9 oz	250 g
cocoa powder	3.5 oz	100 g
coconut, grated	3.5 oz	100 g
butter, melted	7 oz	200 g

Whip the eggs, sugar, and almond powder over a hot water bath or other heat source until warm. Remove from heat and continue whipping until the batter has completely cooled.

Sift together the flour and cocoa powder and add the grated coconut. Gently fold into the batter. Combine a small amount of batter with the melted butter to lighten, then fold it into the batter. Pour or pipe the batter onto sheet pans lined with parchment paper or into buttered and floured molds.

Bake in a moderate oven, 390°F/200°C.

Hazelnut Génoise
Génoise à la Noisettes

eggs	12	12
sugar	14 oz	400 g
flour	10.5 oz	300 g
hazelnuts, roasted and ground	5.5 oz	150 g
butter, melted	1.5 oz	50 g

Whip the eggs and sugar over a hot water bath or other heat source until warm. Remove from heat and continue whipping until the batter has completely cooled.

Sift together the flour and roasted hazelnut powder. Gently fold into the batter. Combine a small amount of batter with the melted butter to lighten, then fold it into the batter. Pour or pipe the batter onto sheet pans lined with parchment paper or into buttered and floured molds.

Bake in a moderate oven, 390°F/200°C.

Almond Biscuit No. 1
Biscuit aux Amandes

almond powder	12.5 oz	350 g
sugar	17.5 oz	500 g
egg yolks	16	16
eggs	2	2
flour	11.5 oz	325 g
egg whites	16	16
sugar	3.5 oz	100 g
butter, melted (optional)	3.5 oz	100 g

Whip together the almond powder, first sugar, egg yolks, and eggs. Sift the flour and fold it into the batter.

Whip the egg whites to firm peaks adding the second sugar at the end of whipping. Fold the whites into the batter.

Combine a small amount of batter with the melted butter to lighten, then fold it into the batter. Pour or pipe the batter onto sheet pans lined with parchment paper or into buttered and floured molds.

Bake in a moderate oven, 390°F/200°C.

Almond Biscuit No. 2
Biscuit aux Amandes

TPT	17.5 oz	500 g
eggs	10	10
egg whites	10	10
sugar	3.5 oz	100 g
flour	7 oz	200 g

Whip the TPT and eggs. Whisk the egg whites to soft peaks before gradually adding the sugar. Continue whisking to firm peaks. Fold the flour, then the whipped egg whites, into the egg mixture.

Pour or pipe the batter onto sheet pans lined with parchment paper or into buttered and floured molds.

Bake in a moderate oven, 390°F/200°C.

Almond Biscuit No. 3
Biscuit aux Amandes

Eggs	4	4
Egg yolks	12	12
Sugar	26.5 oz	750 g
Flour	7 oz	200 g
Almond powder	17.5 oz	500 g
Butter, melted	7 oz	200 g
Egg whites	12	12

Whip the eggs, egg yolks, and sugar. Sift the flour and fold it and the almond powder into the batter.

Whip the egg whites to firm peaks. Fold them into the batter.

Combine a small amount of batter with the melted butter to lighten, then fold it into the batter. Pour or pipe the batter onto sheet pans lined with parchment paper or into buttered and floured molds.

Bake in a moderate oven, 390°F/200°C.

Chocolate Biscuit
Biscuit au Chocolat

egg yolks	20	20
sugar	14 oz	400 g
flour	14 oz	400 g
cocoa powder	3.5 oz	100 g
egg whites	20	20
sugar	5.5 oz	150 g

Whip the egg yolks and first sugar to aerate. Sift together the flour and cocoa powder and fold them into the batter.

Whip the egg whites to firm peaks adding the second sugar at the end of whipping. Fold the egg whites into the batter.

Pour or pipe the batter onto sheet pans lined with parchment paper or into buttered and floured molds.

Bake in a moderate oven, 390°F/200°C.

Coffee Biscuit
Biscuit au Café

Follow the recipe and procedure for chocolate biscuit above, omitting the cocoa powder, increasing the flour to 17.5 oz/500 g, and adding 2 oz/50 g instant coffee.

Coffee Almond Biscuit
Biscuit Café aux Amandes

TPT	17.5 oz	500 g
egg yolks	20	20
instant coffee	2 oz	50 g
egg whites	20	20
sugar	7 oz	200 g
flour	5.5 oz	150 g
butter, melted (optional)	7 oz	200 g

Whip the TPT, egg yolks, and instant coffee.

Whisk the egg whites to soft peaks before gradually adding the sugar. Continue whisking to firm peaks. Fold the whites into the batter. Alternately fold in the flour and melted butter.

Pour or pipe the batter onto sheet pans lined with parchment paper or into buttered and floured molds.

Bake in a moderate oven, 390°F/200°C.

Almond Chocolate Biscuit
Biscuit Chocolat aux Amandes

TPT	35 oz	1,000 g
sugar	17.5 oz	500 g
egg yolks	24	24
eggs	8	8
egg whites	24	24
sugar	5.5 oz	150 g
flour	7 oz	200 g
butter, melted	10.5 oz	300 g
chocolate paste or unsweetened chocolate, melted	10.5 oz	300 g

Whip the TPT, first sugar, egg yolks, and eggs.

Fold in the flour, then the melted butter and chocolate. Whisk the egg whites to soft peaks before gradually adding the second sugar. Continue whisking to firm peaks. Fold the whipped egg whites into the batter.

Pour or pipe the batter onto sheet pans lined with parchment paper or into buttered and floured molds.

Bake in a moderate oven, 390°F/200°C.

Orange Biscuit No. 1
Biscuit à l'Orange

almonds, blanched and ground	9 oz	250 g
sugar	17.5 oz	500 g
candied orange peel	3.5 oz	100 g
oranges, zest of	3	3
egg yolks	16	16
flour	9 oz	250 g
butter, melted	5.5 oz	150 g
egg whites	16	16
sugar	5.5 oz	150 g

Grind together the almonds, first sugar, candied orange peel, and orange zest. Whisk in the egg yolks. Sift in the flour and stir in the melted butter.

Whisk the egg whites to soft peaks before gradually adding the second sugar. Continue whisking to firm peaks. Fold the whipped egg whites into the batter.

Pour or pipe the batter onto sheet pans lined with parchment paper or into buttered and floured molds.

Bake in a moderate oven, 390°F/200°C.

Orange Biscuit No. 2
Biscuit à l'Orange

egg yolks	30	30
confectioners' sugar	17.5 oz	500 g
candied orange peel, ground	3.5 oz	100 g
egg whites	30	30
sugar	5.5 oz	150 g
flour	26.5 oz	750 g
butter, melted	5.5 oz	150 g

Whip the egg yolks, confectioner's sugar, and candied ground orange peel.

Whisk the egg whites to soft peaks before gradually adding the second sugar. Continue whisking to firm peaks. Fold the whipped egg whites into the batter. Fold in the flour, then the melted butter.

Pour or pipe the batter onto sheet pans lined with parchment paper or into buttered and floured molds.

Bake in a moderate oven, 390°F/200°C.

Cherry Biscuit
Biscuit aux Cerises

candied bigarreau cherries	5.5 oz	150 g
TPT	24.5 oz	700 g
eggs	6	6
egg yolks	16	16
egg whites	16	16

sugar	3.5 oz	100 g
flour	12.5 oz	350 g

Use a food processor to grind the bigarreau cherries. Whip the TPT, bigarreau cherries, eggs, and egg yolks.

Whisk the egg whites to soft peaks before gradually adding the sugar. Continue whisking to firm peaks. Fold the whipped egg whites into the batter. Fold in the flour.

Pour or pipe the batter onto sheet pans lined with parchment paper or into buttered and floured molds.

Bake in a moderate oven, 390°F/200°C.

Pistachio Biscuit
Biscuit Pistache

egg yolks	20	20
sugar	14 oz	400 g
flour	9 oz	250 g
pistachio powder	9 oz	250 g
almond powder	5.5 oz	150 g
egg whites	12	12
sugar	7 oz	200 g
butter, melted	1.5 oz	100 g

Whisk the egg yolks and first sugar until thick and pale. Sift the flour, pistachio powder, and almond powder.

Whisk the egg whites to soft peaks before gradually adding the second sugar. Continue whisking to firm peaks. Fold the whipped egg whites into the batter simultaneously with the flour and nut powders. Combine a small amount of batter with the melted butter to lighten, then fold it into the batter.

Pour or pipe the batter onto sheet pans lined with parchment paper or into buttered and floured molds.

Bake in a moderate oven, 390°F/200°C.

Dobos Biscuit

egg yolks	24	24
sugar	12.5 oz	350 g
flour	10.5 oz	300 g
hazelnut powder	3.5 oz	100 g
butter, melted	5.5 oz	150 g
egg whites	24	24

Whisk the egg yolks and sugar until thick and pale. Sift the flour and hazelnut powder and combine them with the egg/sugar mixture. Combine a small amount of batter with the melted butter to lighten, then fold into the batter.

Whisk the egg whites to medium peaks and gently fold them into the batter.

Pour or pipe the batter onto sheet pans lined with parchment paper or into buttered and floured molds.

Bake in a moderate oven, 390°F/200°C.

Nougat Biscuit
Biscuit au Nougat

egg yolks	15	15
almond paste	17.5 oz	500 g
egg whites	15	15
sugar	5.5 oz	150 g
nougat, ground	14 oz	400 g
biscuit crumbs	14 oz	400 g
flour	3.5 oz	100 g
butter, melted	2 oz	50 g

Whisk the egg yolks and almond paste until thick and pale.

Whisk the egg whites to soft peaks before gradually adding the sugar. Continue whisking to firm peaks. Fold into the egg mixture, adding the ground nougat, biscuit crumbs, and sifted flour. Combine a small

(Nougat Biscuit recipe continued on next page)

amount of batter with the melted butter to lighten, then fold into the batter.

Pour or pipe the batter onto sheet pans lined with parchment paper or into buttered and floured molds.

Bake in a moderate oven, 390°F/200°C.

Walnut Biscuit
Biscuit aux Noix

This biscuit is a bit heavier than other biscuits, but is particularly flavorful.

TPT, walnut	17.5 oz	500 g
sugar	5.5 oz	150 g
honey (optional)	3.5 oz	100 g
egg yolks	30	30
flour	14 oz	400 g
butter, melted	14 oz	400 g
egg whites	20	20
sugar	3.5 oz	100 g

Whisk the walnut TPT, first sugar, honey, and egg yolks until thick and pale. Sift the flour and add it to the egg mixture. Combine a small amount of batter with the melted butter to lighten, then fold into the batter.

Whisk the egg whites to soft peaks before gradually adding the second sugar. Continue whisking to firm peaks. Fold into batter.

Pour or pipe the batter onto sheet pans lined with parchment paper or into buttered and floured molds.

Bake in a moderate oven, 390°F/200°C.

Hazelnut Biscuit
Biscuit aux Noisettes

eggs	8	8
egg yolks	30	30
TPT, hazelnut	3 lbs 10 oz	1,650 g
flour	9 oz	250 g
egg whites	30	30

In the bowl of an electric mixer whisk the egg yolks, hazelnut TPT, and flour until thick and pale. Gradually whisk in the eggs.

Whisk the egg whites to medium peaks and fold them into the batter.

Pour or pipe the batter onto sheet pans lined with parchment paper or into buttered and floured molds.

Bake in a moderate oven, 390°F/200°C.

Chef's Note: *The quantity of flour may be increased or decreased in proportion to the hazelnut TPT, according to taste. Roasted hazelnuts are preferred.*

Hazelnut Chocolate Biscuit
Biscuit Noisette au Chocolat

egg yolks	26	26
sugar	17.5 oz	500 g
flour	9 oz	250 g
hazelnut powder	7 oz	200 g
cocoa powder	5.5 oz	150 g
butter, melted	5.5 oz	150 g
egg whites	16	16

Whisk the egg yolks and sugar until thick and pale. Sift together the flour, hazelnut powder, and cocoa powder. Combine them with the egg/sugar mixture. Combine a small amount of batter with the melted butter to lighten, then fold into the batter.

Whisk the egg whites to medium peaks and gently fold into the batter.

Pour the batter into génoise molds or pullman molds that have been buttered and floured.

Bake in a moderate oven, 390°F/200°C.

Sacher Biscuit

almond paste	35 oz	1,000 g
confectioners' sugar	12.5 oz	350 g
egg yolks	30	30
eggs	8	8
flour	10.5 oz	300 g
cocoa powder	9 oz	250 g
egg whites	30	30
sugar	12.5 oz	350 g
butter, melted	9 oz	250 g

In the bowl of an electric mixer, whisk the almond paste, confectioners' sugar, egg yolks, and eggs until light and aerated.

Sift together the flour and cocoa powder and fold into the egg mixture.

Whisk the egg whites to soft peaks before gradually adding the sugar. Continue whisking to firm peaks. Gently fold the whipped egg whites into the batter.

Combine a small amount of batter with the butter (melted but not hot) to lighten, then fold into the batter.

Pour or pipe the batter onto sheet pans lined with parchment paper and bake in a hot oven, 460°F/240°C; or pour into buttered and floured cake pans and bake in a moderate oven, 390°F/200°C.

Orange Biscuit
Biscuit à l'Orange

almond paste	17.5 oz	500 g
candied orange peel, ground	3.5 oz	100 g
orange, zest of	1	1
eggs	5	5
egg yolks	12	12
flour	10.5 oz	300 g
egg whites	12	12
sugar	5.5 oz	150 g

Whisk the almond paste, ground candied orange peel, orange zest, eggs, and egg yolks until thick and pale. Sift the flour and add it to the batter.

Whisk the egg whites to soft peaks before gradually adding the sugar. Continue whisking to firm peaks. Gently fold the whipped egg whites into the batter.

Pour or pipe the batter onto sheet pans lined with parchment paper or into buttered and floured molds.

Bake in a moderate oven, 390°F/200°C.

CHAPTER 4

Croquembouches

168 *Modern French Pastry*

Croquembouches

Croquembouches, which translates literally as "crunch in mouth", are traditional French cakes served to celebrate weddings, anniversaries, and other special occasions. Croquembouches (pronouced: krow-kam-booch) are often shaped into structures relating to the event celebrated such as a church for a wedding or a basket for a baptism.

Today, more inventive and unusual forms are being created. The following chapter on Croquembouches presents a selection of both the more traditional as well as original designs. Croquembouches can be decorated with marzipan or pulled sugar flowers. Here, included is the more modern method of using molded sugar flowers which are more adventageous than marzipan. They are simple to prepare, can be made in an assortment of colors, and offer a lower production cost (see pages 285–293). Molded flowers are not meant to take the place of the artistic work of pulled sugar flowers, which are time consuming and require a considerable ability and practice better suited for the experienced professional.

Croquembouches are made of small filled choux balls (or cream puffs) joined with sugar cooked to hard crack stage, minimum 311°F/155°C.

The choux are filled through an opening made on the bottom or flat side with a small round pastry tip. The most common fillings are pastry cream or mousseline cream flavored to taste. The size of the cakes vary according on the needs of the client. On average, count 3–5 choux per person.

Regardless of the size of the choux, the procedure for assembling the cakes remains the same. Croquembouches can be made into almost any shape although the conical form is most often requested and one of the easiest to prepare.

Facing Page: Croquembouches

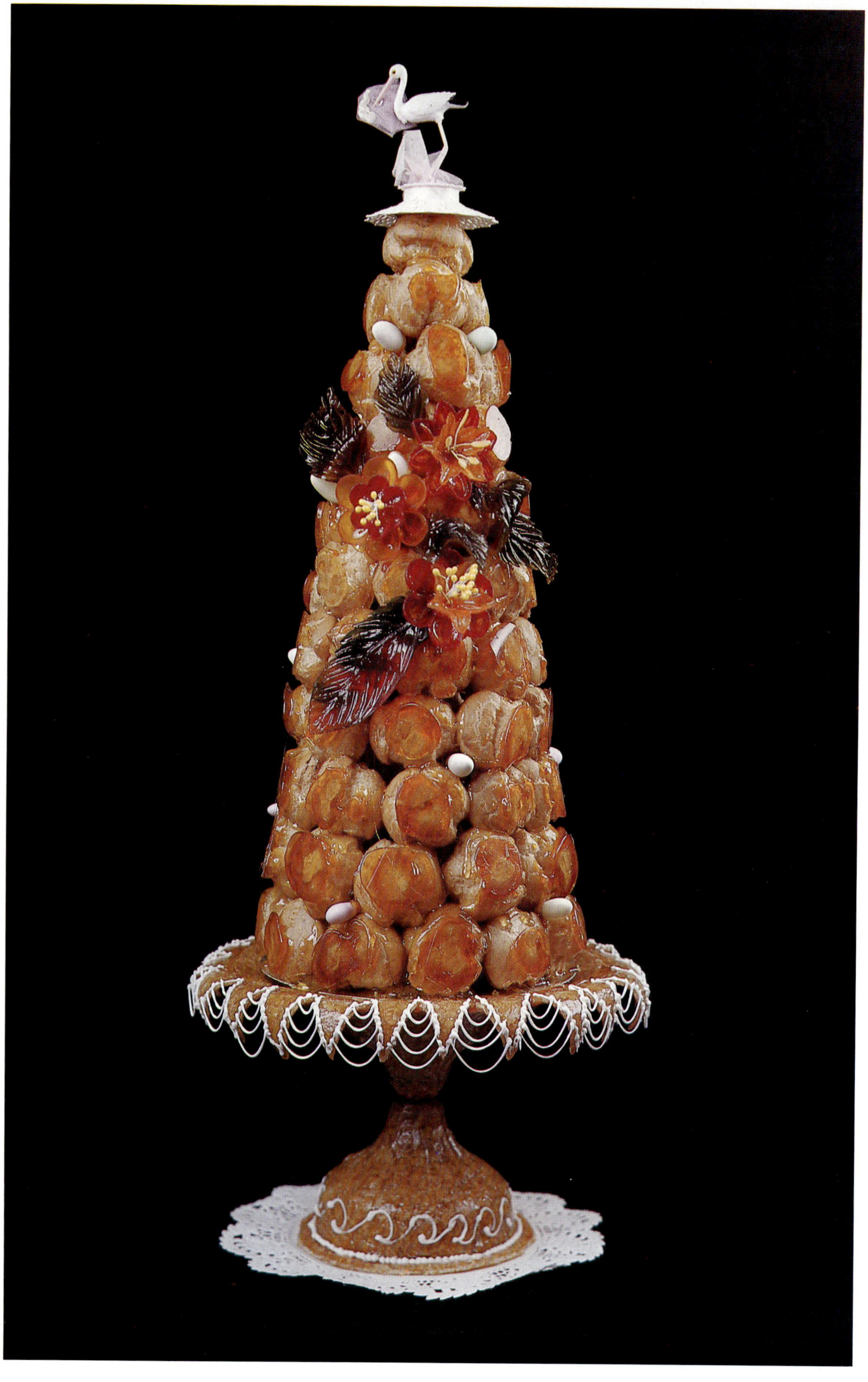

Conical Croquembouche

Method 1—Freeform, Without a Mold

This procedure requires some practice, but it is the fastest and one of the more practical ways to assemble a conical croquembouche.

Coat the top of the choux with caramel. Begin the first row, by placing the choux on their side and attaching them with caramel to to a rigid cardboard or nougatine base. The croquembouche can also be prepared on an oiled stand, then attached with caramel to a base or pedestal after being assembled.

The number of choux for the first base ring is determined by the number of choux to be used. For an especially even conical shape, you can use a conical mold made for this work. Each successive row is diminished by one as the piece is built.

Examples:
If 45 choux are used: The first row is made with 9 choux, the second with 8, the third with 7, and so on until all the choux are used.

For 50 choux, double up the fifth row using larger choux on the first row and smaller choux on the second.

For 55 choux, begin the first row with 10 choux and build from there.

For 60 choux, begin the first row with 10 choux and double the fifth row.

Before attaching the first row, it is important to decide how many choux will be used, remembering each subsequent row will be one less then the previous row, and it might be necessary to double a row to achieve an even, conical shape.

Method 2—Constructed Outside a Mold

This procedure requires a cone-shaped mold. The choux are assembled either outside or inside the mold. To assemble the choux on the exterior, oil the mold with a light oil such as corn, canola, or sunflower.

After the individual choux are caramelized, assemble them over an oiled sheet pan. Attach the choux on their sides with cooked sugar supporting them against the mold. Continue to build to the top. Once the piece has set, gently remove the mold. Attach the piece to a nougatine or rigid cardboard base with cooked sugar.

The conical mold can be made out of nougatine. The nougatine can be prepared in advance and rolled out with a dough sheeter. Attach the nougatine cone onto a solid base and affix the choux around the cone. This procedure produces a solid but somewhat more costly piece.

Method 3—Constructed Inside a Mold

The croquembouche can be assembled inside a metal cone. Oil the inside of the cone. Coat the top of the choux with caramel and attach them starting at the inside point of the mold. The caramelized top of each choux should face outward, touching the mold. Use as many choux as needed.

When the piece has set and the sugar cooled, turn the mold over and gently remove the cone, attaching the piece onto a nougatine or rigid cardboard base. Stabilize the croquembouche with extra choux.

Facing Page: Croquembouche on Nougatine Base

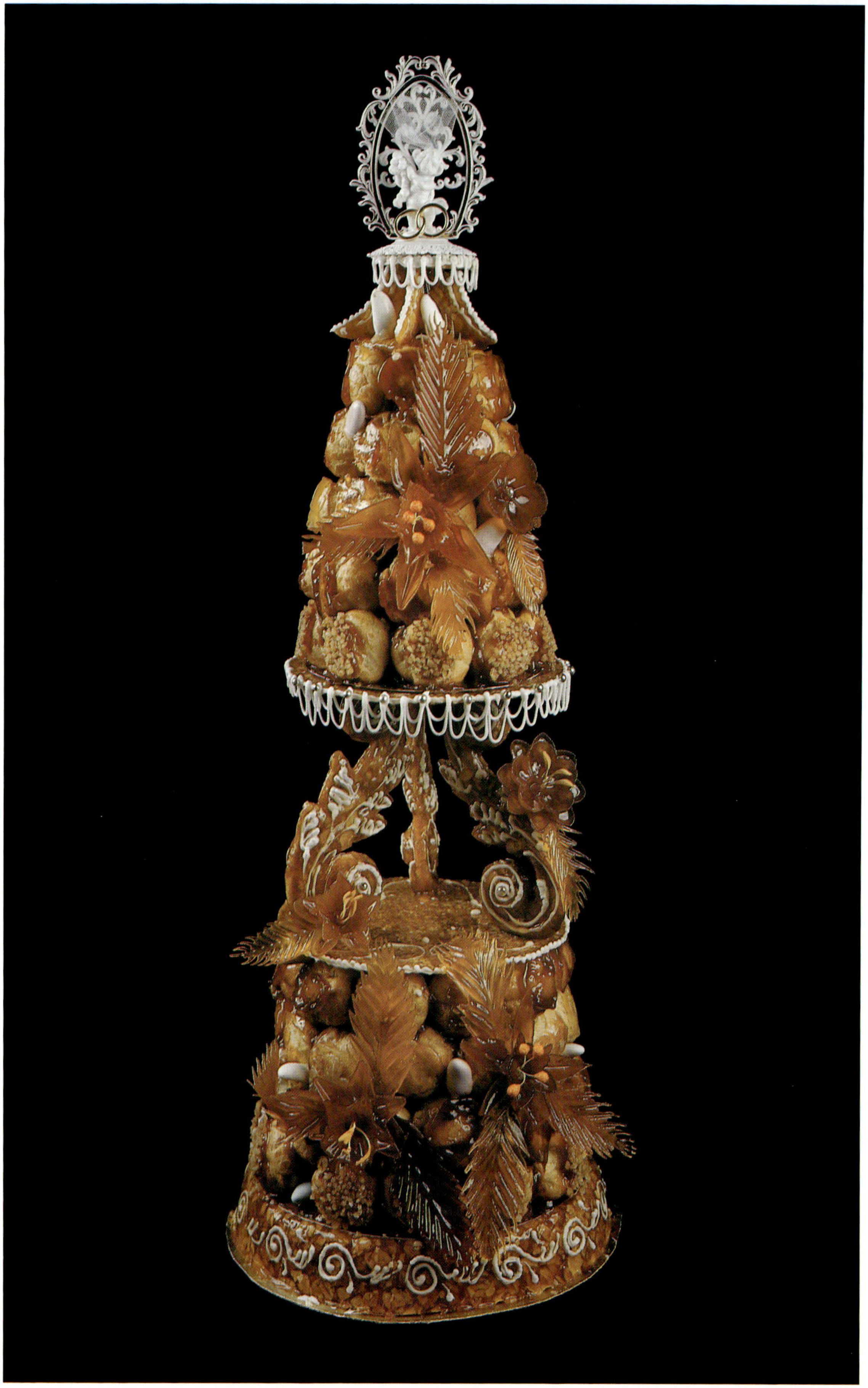

Decorating and Presenting Croquembouches

Croquembouches can be presented simply, or they can be decorated with dragées (candied coated almonds) and molded nougatine. Pulled sugar or marzipan flowers can be used for more elaborate pieces and figurines that symbolize the occasion can be placed on top.

Nougatine Bases

Nougatine can be formed into any shape or size to create a base. For the most basic presentation, line a sheet of nougatine in a génoise mold to the size needed. see page 193 for a step-by-step presentation of this procedure. The base may be decorated with nougatine wolf's teeth (dents de loup) and royal icing.

Nougatine Molds

A special mold can be used to give the nougatine a more ornate form. After molding, assemble the pieces with caramel, if necessary. Decorate with nougatine wolf's teeth and royal icing. Since the decorations can be fragile, finish assembling the top pieces after transporting. Work directly on the presentation table from which the croquembouche will be served to avoid moving it after assembly.

Original Croquembouches

Each professional will decorate croquembouches in his or her own personal style, although some basic shapes and steps are often followed. One of the more popular methods is to divide the piece in two sections. To accomplish this, construct two sections separately and prepare nougatine columns or other type of division. It is important that the two nougatine bases, one for each section, be as even as possible so the finished piece will stand erect.

For transport, prepare three parts separately:

1. A nougatine base, molded inside an oiled génoise or cake pan to the size needed. Decorate with piped royal icing.

2. The bottom section, held together with caramel and decorated with dragées, pulled sugar, or marzipan flowers, and to which the middle section is secured with caramel.

3. The top section, with a decoration made to symbolize the celebrated event.

Transporting the croquembouches in three smaller segments rather than one large piece lessens the risk of breakage. Simply attach the pieces, assembling the croquembouche directly on the presentation table.

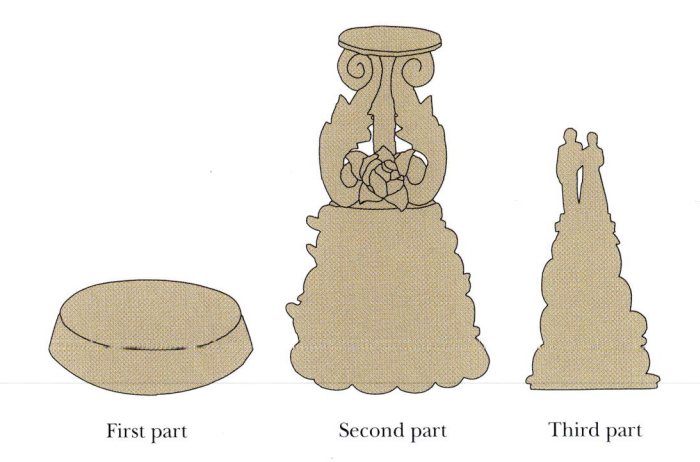

First part   Second part   Third part

Facing Page: Croquembouche Presentation Piece

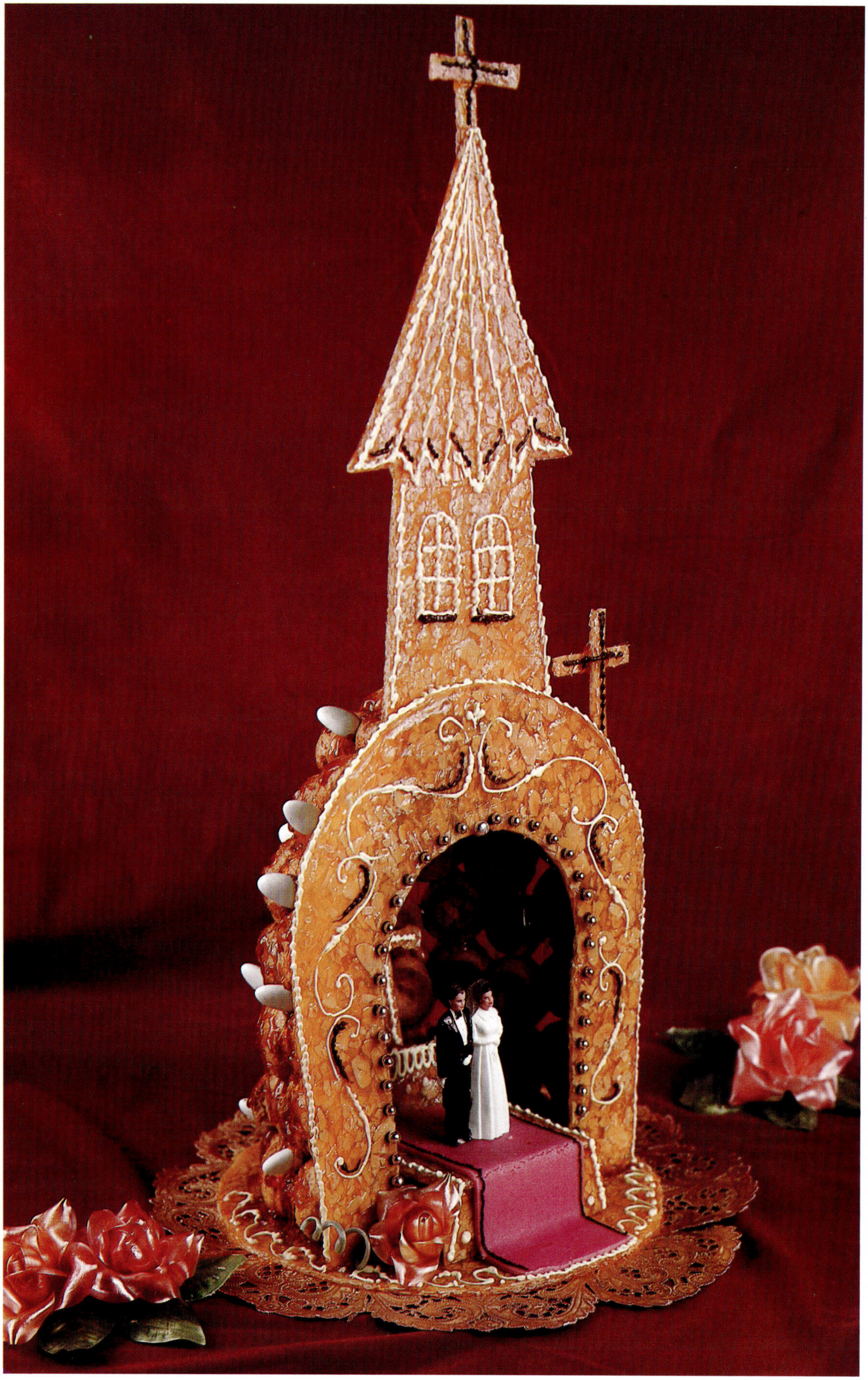

Chapel
Chapelle

This chapel-shaped croquembouche, fairly easy and quick to construct, is often used for communions and weddings. The piece is prepared in two sections and set on a round or rectangular nougatine base. The size of the base is determined by the number of choux used. Cut the facade of the church and the steeple from a sheet of nougatine. Use the cut-out from the facade for the interior, stairs, and altar.

Attach the facade to the base with caramel. Arrange a half-circle of choux behind the facade. Build rows of choux on top of the half-circle. When the rows of choux reach half the height of the facade, begin reducing the number of choux to create a half-dome to the height of the facade. This will serve as the back of the chapel.

Affix the steeple to the back of the facade and attach choux behind it for support. Place a few choux inside the chapel to make a floor and cover them with strips of nougatine to form a step. Position the altar inside with a nougatine cross on top.

Roll and cut out a strip of marzipan for the runner. Decorate it with white and/or chocolate royal icing. A bride and bridegroom or other appropriate figurines can be placed inside.

Chef's Note: *Variations of the chapel can be made with a nougatine roof and more elaborate facades with nougatine doors, see pages 196 and 222.*

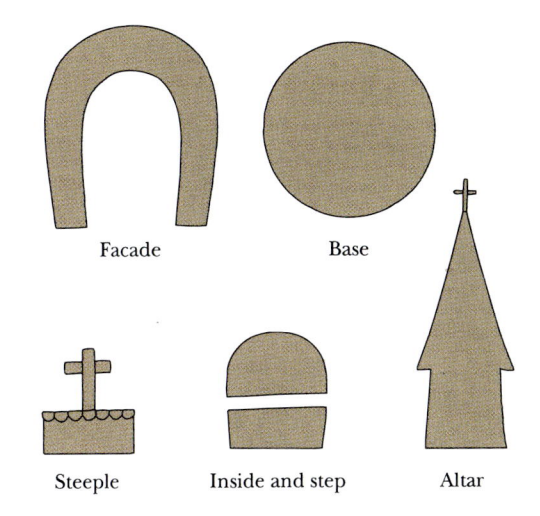

Facade   Base

Steeple   Inside and step   Altar

Presentation Bases

It is preferable to assemble the croquembouche on cardboard rather than a nougatine disk. The cardboard is supple but strong, and gives the piece added security during transport. The nougatine disk would be more likely to crack, causing the whole piece to weaken and become unstable.

Nougatine bases can be made in an assortment of shapes and sizes. It is possible to put one base on top of another. Wolf's teeth or curved triangles are often attached around the edge to hide the seam. They are then decorated with royal icing. The base can also be made out of poured sugar in various forms and colors. These bases are decorated with flowers and leaves molded from leftover caramel which was used to assemble the piece. This is a fairly easy and cost-effective method that offers excellent results.

Facing Page: Chapel

Croquembouches

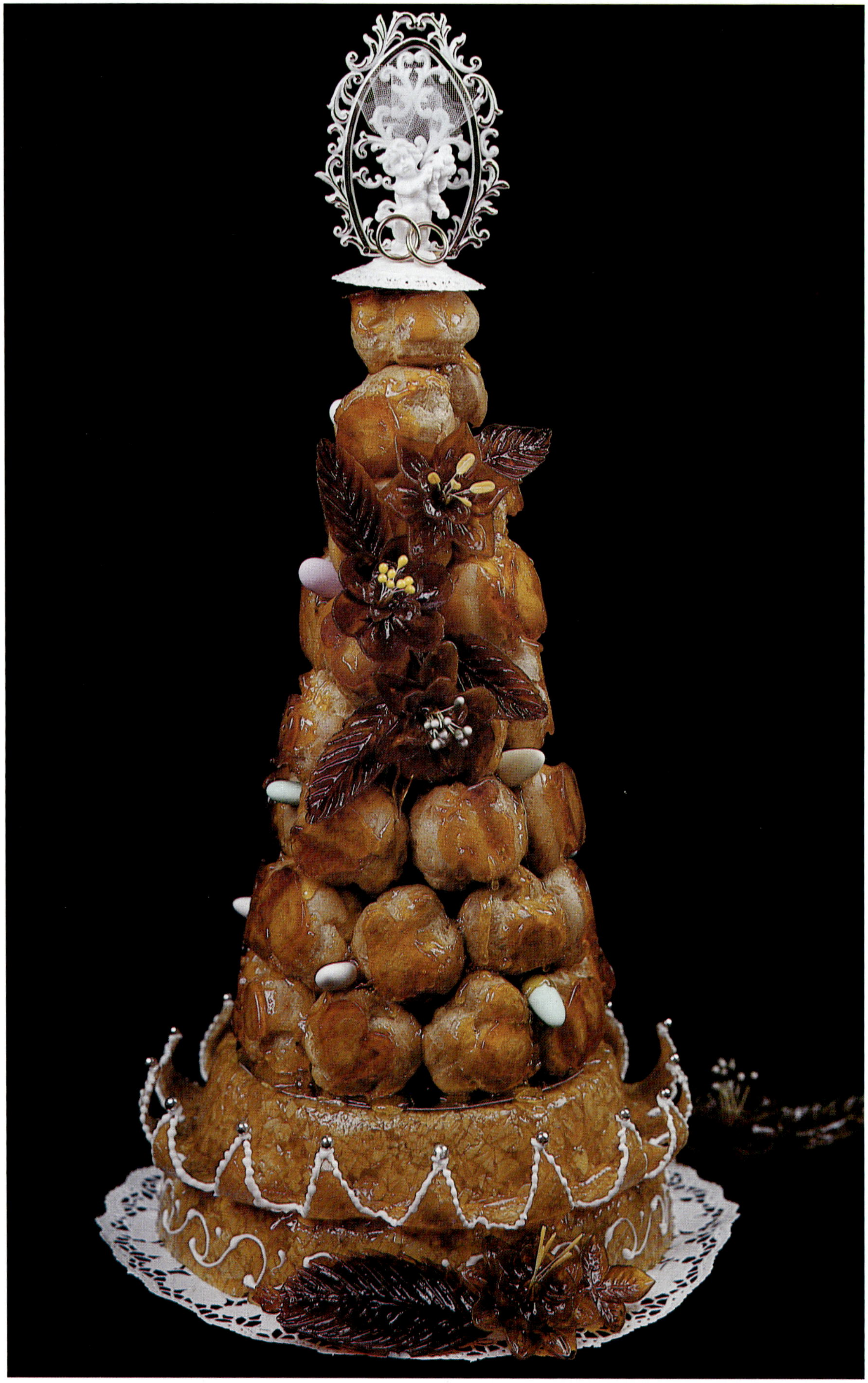

Molded Caramel Flowers

Magyfleur are solid bronze molds that can be used for chocolate and, as presented here, caramel flowers. For more information, see pages 285–293.

Photo 1: Use the caramel prepared for assembling the croquembouche. Make certain the bronze molds are well chilled and dip them two thirds to three fourths of the way into the caramel.

Photo 2: Quickly remove the mold and scrape off any excess caramel with a wooden spatula.

Photo 3: With the tip of a paring knife, push the flower off onto foam or other soft surface; the flower will release easily. It is important that the molds be clean and very cold. They can be stored in their container in the freezer. Use the melted caramel to assemble the flowers; several layers can be attached to form simple to elaborate flowers.

Facing Page: *Classic Croquembouche on a Nougatine Pedestal*

Croquembouches

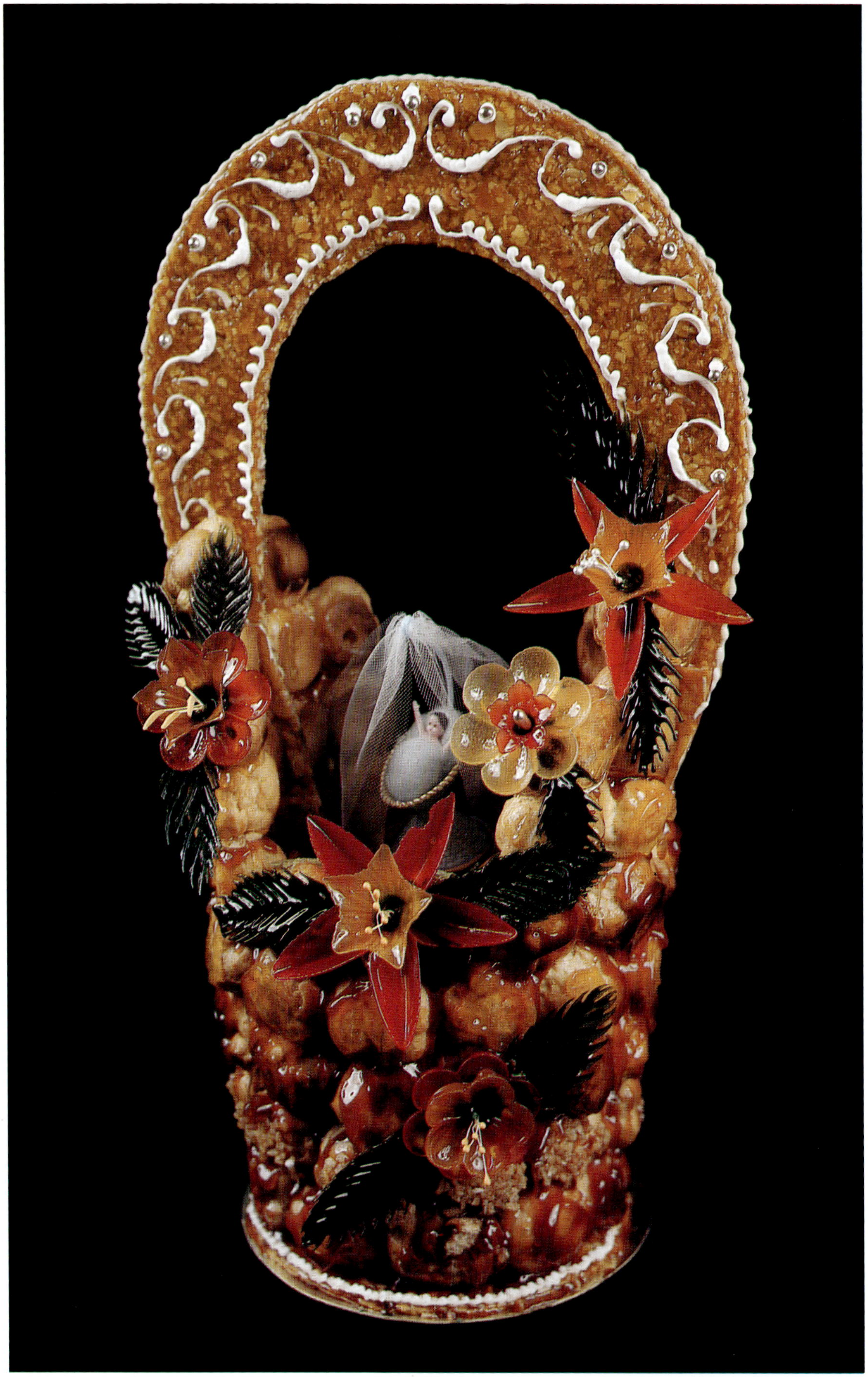

Flower Basket
Panier Fleuri

This croquembouche flower basket is particularly appropriate for engagement parties, weddings, or anniversaries.

Prepare a basket handle and base out of nougatine. The assembly can be prepared in one of the two ways indicated below.

Method 1
Attach the choux directly to the nougatine base. Increase the number of choux per row by one so the basket widens as it is built up. This form requires good stability, so it is important that the choux be dry, and the caramel be allowed to set after each row is applied before attaching the next.

Place the nougatine handle on top, affixing and supporting it to the inside of the basket with choux and caramel. Wolf's teeth (curved nougatine triangles) can be placed around the basket. Affix a strip of nougatine across the inside of the basket, near the top, which will serve to support the flowers. Attach sugar or marzipan flowers and leaves with caramel.

The handle is very fragile, especially where it adjoins the basket. It can be reinforced with small choux and caramel at both ends.

Method 2
Assemble the basket upside down on a lightly oiled sheet pan or nougatine disk. Reduce the number of choux by one for each proceeding row until the desired number of choux are used. Turn the basket over, upright, and attach it to a nougatine base.

Affix the nougatine handle, wolf's teeth (curved nougatine triangles), and sugar flowers as for the first method.

Facing Page: Flower Basket

Chef's Note: The nougatine handle can be replaced with a handle made out of braided or twisted pulled sugar. It is attached following the same procedure above.

Choux Paste for Croquembouches
Pâte à Choux pour Croquembouches

There are two important aspects required of choux prepared for croquembouches: a very even rounded shape with a flat bottom, and a hollow interior. Care should be taken in baking the choux. It should be well dried out but not brittle.

There are numerous recipes for choux; regardless which is used, the procedure remains the same.

Choux Paste No. 1

water	17.5 oz	500 g
milk	17.5 oz	500 g
butter	16 oz	450 g
salt	1 tbsp 2 tsp	20 g
flour	21 oz	600 g
eggs	18–20	18–20

Bring the water, milk, butter, and salt to a boil. Choose a saucepan large enough to eventually include the flour. Remove from heat just before adding sifted flour.

Sift the flour and add all at once to the hot mixture. Return it to the heat, stirring constantly with a wooden spoon to prevent the batter from sticking to the bottom of the pan and scorching. Lower the heat and continue to dry out the batter until it no longer sticks to the side of the saucepan.

(Choux Paste No. 1 recipe continued on page 181)

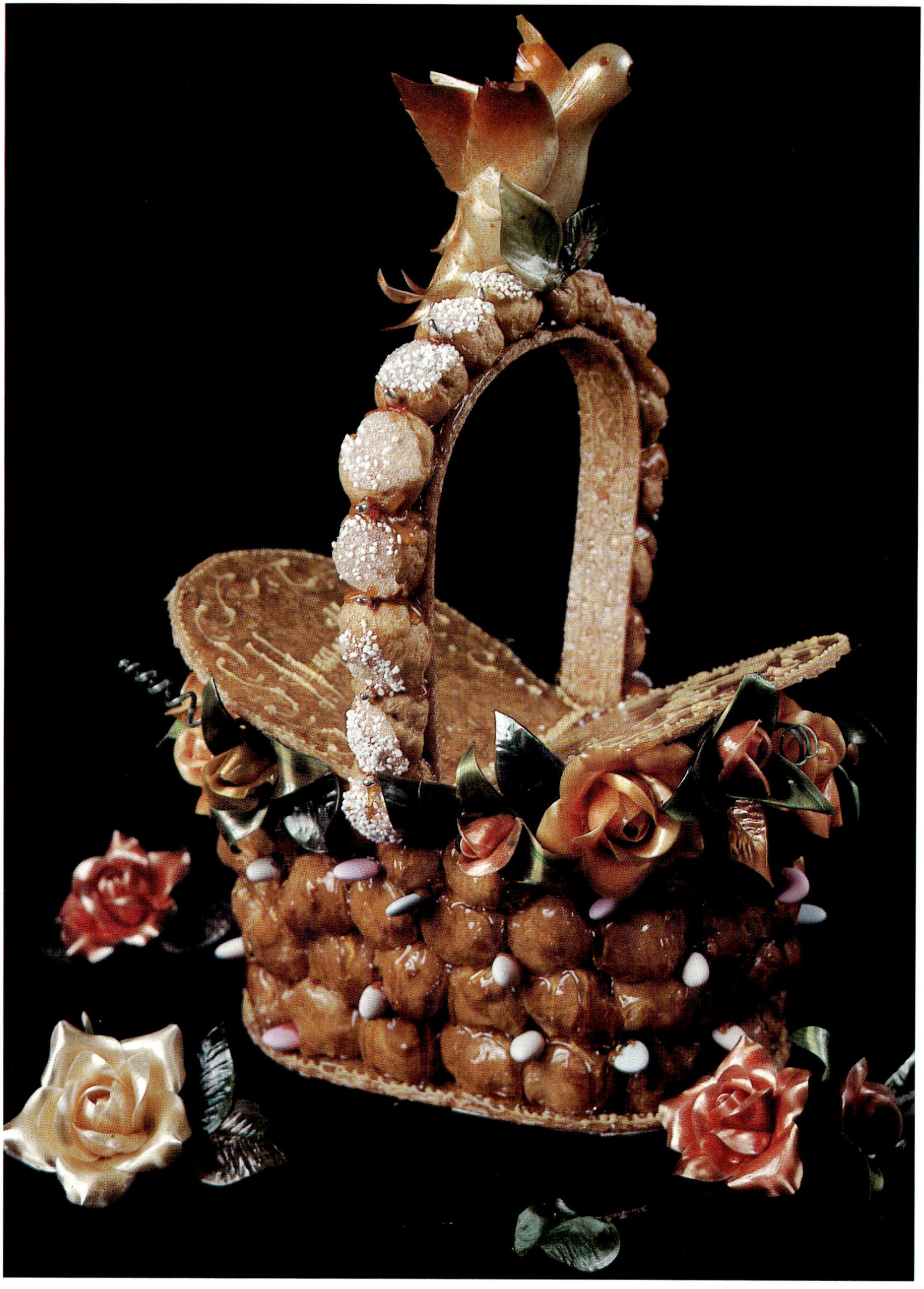

Either by hand, or in the bowl of an electric mixer using the paddle attachment, beat two or three eggs into the batter at a time, waiting until they are incorporated before adding more. The total number of eggs needed can vary depending on the type of flour used and how much the batter was dried out. The batter should have body without being too liquid or dry, and slowly fall from the spoon.

With a pastry bag and 1/3–1/2 in/8–10 mm diameter tip, pipe out the batter to the size needed onto a lightly buttered sheet pan. Brush each choux with egg wash and even the tops by gently pressing with the prongs of a fork, barely making an indentation.

Bake in a hot oven with the door ajar until the choux are dried, hollow inside, and golden brown all around the outside so they will not fall. If necessary, the oven can be lowered or the nearly finished choux can be transferred to a cooler oven to dry.

Choux Paste No. 2

water	35 oz	1,000 g
salt	1 tbsp 2 tsp	20 g
sugar	1 tbsp 2 tsp	20 g
butter	16 oz	450 g
flour	19.5 oz	550 g
eggs	18–20	18–20

Follow the procedure given for Recipe 1.

Grandmother's Basket
Panier de Grand-Mère

This croquembouche is especially appropriate for silver or golden wedding anniversaries.

Prepare an oval nougatine base. The size depends on the number of choux to be used. Prepare a second, slightly larger oval and cut it in half for the basket's flap covers.

Cut a strip of nougatine the same circumference as the larger oval, and curve it to form the handle.

Assemble the choux directly on the nougatine base, making each row wider by one choux so the basket flares outward slightly. Reinforce the basket by attaching a row of choux inside at the top for double thickness.

Attach the handle to the basket with caramel. Affix the flaps to the inside of the handle. Set them slightly open, and either prop them on a strip of nougatine or place a small chou at each corner of the flaps where they meet at the handle. These supports can be hidden with sugar flowers. Reinforce the handle by attaching choux decorated with pearl sugar on the outside.

Position pulled sugar or marzipan flowers so they appear to emerge from the basket flaps, supporting them open. Decorate with piped royal icing and dragées.

Chef's Note: If marzipan flowers are used, it is important they be prepared several days in advance so they are thoroughly dried when needed.

Jewelry Box
Coffret

This croquembouche is fairly simple to construct and allows space for an inscription, making it suitable for any occasion.

Prepare two rectangles of nougatine, making the top slightly larger than the base. The size of the rectangles is determined by how many choux are to be used. Prepare wolf's teeth (nougatine triangles).

Assemble the choux directly on the base in even-numbered, staggered rows. The number of rows of choux is determined by the height of the box, although

(Jewelry Box recipe continued on page 185)

Facing Page: Grandmother's Basket

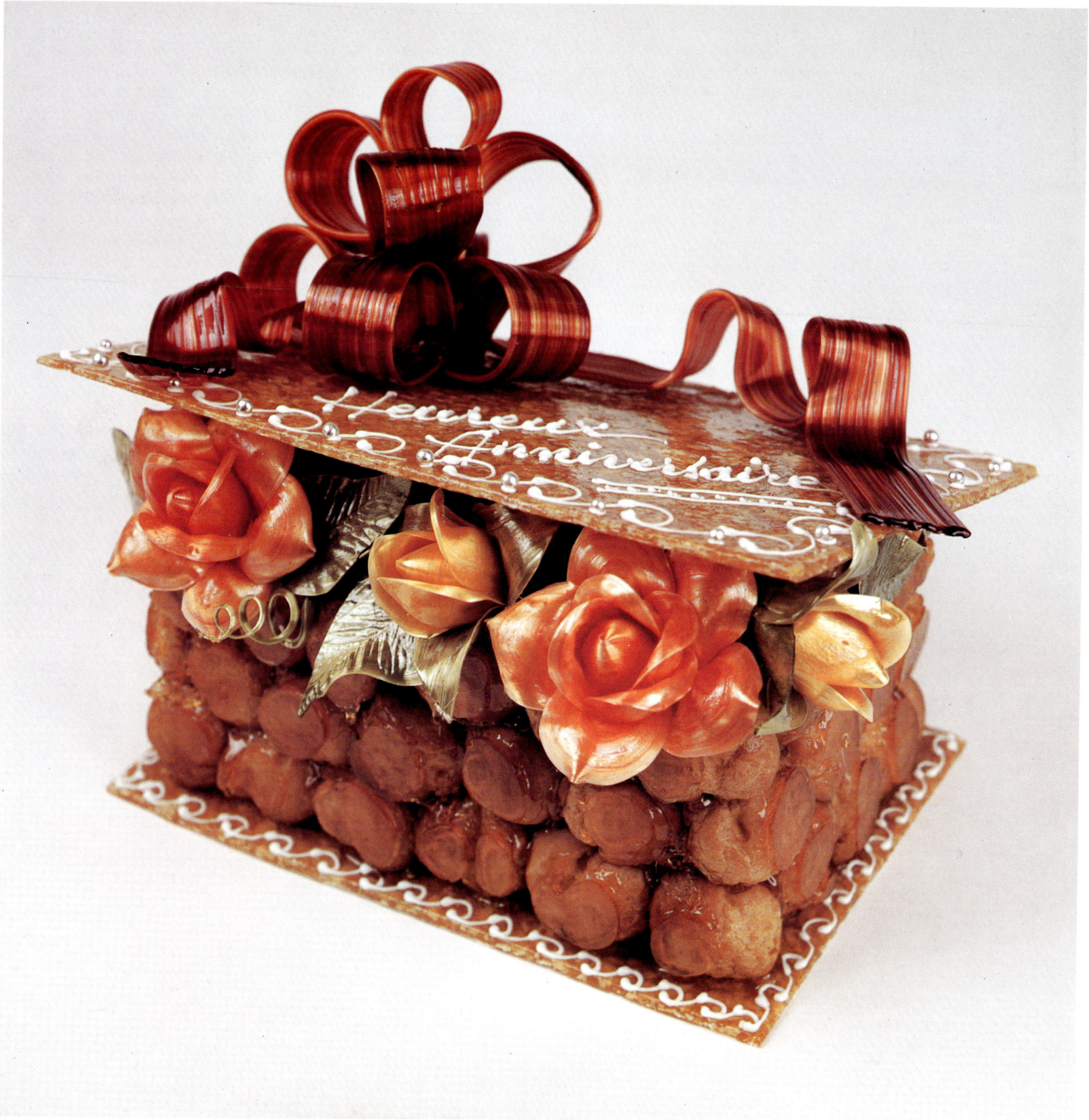
Heureux Anniversaire

Cutting Nougatine

Photo 1: On lightly oiled marble, roll out a layer of nougatine with a rolling pin to the desired thickness. The marble should be warm, not refrigerated.

Photo 2: Avoid cracking and breaking by working quickly; cut the nougatine while warm into the shapes needed. Use a lightly oiled knife.

Photo 3: Prepare the curved triangles, called wolf's teeth (dents de loup in French). Cut small triangles from a sheet of malleable nougatine and immediately place them in a gouttière or tuile mold to form the curved shape.

Small crescents are cut out with a lightly oiled round cutter, placing one-fourth to one-half of the cutter over the edge of the nougatine, depending on the size needed.

Chef's Note: *It is easiest to work in a warm area so the nougatine stays softer longer before becoming brittle and cracking. This can be accomplished by working under a heat lamp or on a sheet pan that can be quickly taken in and out of the oven to maintain the proper temperature.*

Facing Page: Jewelry Box

Croquembouches

184   *Modern French Pastry*

the proportion between length and width should be considered. Attach the wolf's teeth to the top of the box. Place the cover on top, attaching it slightly askew with cooked sugar or caramel. Support the angle of the cover with a strip of nougatine or several small choux which can be hidden by decorations.

Use caramel to attach pulled sugar or marzipan flowers and leaves around the side, under the cover. Affix a pulled sugar or fabric ribbon to the top of the cover.

Pipe an inscription and decorations with royal icing.

Chef's Note: *The jewel box can be shaped square, round, or oval. Cut the base and cover to the chosen shape and assemble as above.*

Drum
Tambour

This croquembouche is wonderfully amusing and especially appropriate for a child's birthday.

Prepare two nougatine disks to serve as the top and bottom of the drum. Cut two strips of nougatine 3/4–1 in/2–3 cm wide and long enough to wrap around the disks. Cut shorter strips of nougatine to criss-cross from the top to bottom disks to imitate cords.

Assemble the choux directly on the bottom nougatine disk. Each row contains the same number of choux, so the diameter does not vary. Place the second disk on top, attaching it with caramel.

Place the two large strips in the oven for a few seconds, just long enough for them to become malleable. Wrap one around the top and the other around the bottom disk, attaching them with caramel.

Place the shorter strips, criss-crossing them from top to bottom, around the side of the drum, attaching them with caramel.

Decorate with royal icing and piping chocolate, and place dragées around the sides and silver candied pearls around the nougatine bands.

Facing Page: Drum

Pastry Cream for Croquembouches
Crème Pâtissière pour Croquembouches

Pastry cream is the most commonly-used filling for croquembouche choux. However, the milk in the cream releases humidity that tends to soften the choux, which makes it best to fill them at the last moment. It is possible to avoid this problem by preparing a pastry cream enriched with butter.

Pastry Cream for Croquembouches No. 1
Crème Pâtissière pour Croquembouches

milk	34 fl oz	1 L
vanilla bean, split lengthwise	1	1
sugar	9–10.5 oz	250–300 g
egg yolks	10	10
cornstarch	3 oz	80 g
butter, softened	5.5 oz	150 g

Bring the milk and split vanilla bean to a boil.

Whisk the sugar and egg yolks until thick and pale. Lightly whisk in the cornstarch until smooth. Add the egg mixture to the hot milk. Bring the milk back to a boil, whisking constantly for 30 seconds. Remove the pastry cream from heat and set it aside to cool in a stainless steel bowl.

When the cream is cool, whisk it in the bowl of an electric mixer with the whip attachment on high speed, gradually adding the butter.

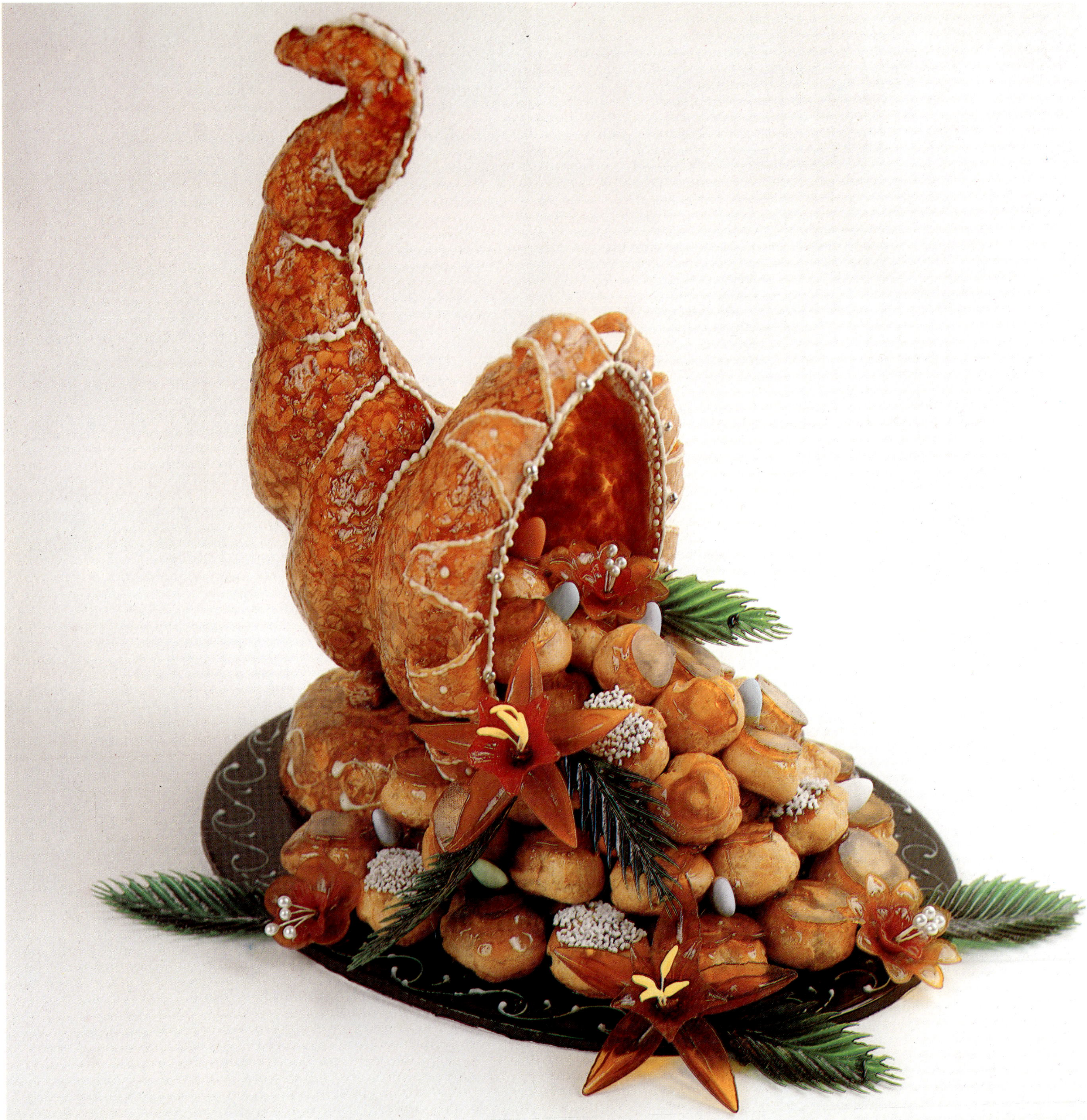

Pastry Cream for Croquembouches No. 2
Crème Pâtissière pour Croquembouches

This recipe is somewhat more cost effective.

milk	34 fl oz	1 L
sugar	10.5 oz	300 g
egg yolks	6	6
cornstarch	3 oz	80 g
butter	3.5 oz	100 g

Follow the procedure given for Recipe 1.

Pastry Cream for Croquembouches No. 3
Crème Pâtissière pour Croquembouches

pastry cream	35 oz	1,000 g
butter, softened	9 oz	250 g

In the bowl of an electric mixer, whip cool, not cold, pastry cream with the whisk attachment, gradually adding the butter. Whip until well blended and smooth, then add any flavor or liqueur of choice.

Flavoring for Pastry Cream
Parfum pour Crème Pâtissière

The following measurements are recommended to flavor 35 oz/1,000 g pastry cream or mousseline cream. The liqueurs are 80–100 proof/40°–50°:

rum	2 oz	50 g
Cointreau	2 oz	50 g
Grand Marnier	2 oz	50 g
kirsch	2 oz	50 g
maraschino liqueur	2 oz	50 g
coffee extract	1 oz	25 g

Grand Prize
Gros Lot

Use caramel to attach a nougatine horn of plenty to a nougatine base molded in a génoise or cake pan. Attach the two pieces to a large disk of poured sugar or nougatine and decorate with royal icing. Place choux inside and around the horn as though they were tumbling out. Decorate with sugar or marzipan flowers and leaves. Iced petit four cakes and/or candied fruit can also be used to garnish the horn.

Glazing Choux for Croquembouches

There are several methods for glazing choux for croquembouches with cooked sugar or caramel. Regardless of the method used, it is essential that the choux be filled before glazing.

Method 1
With one chou in each hand, dip the top of one in a pot of golden caramel. Scrape the second chou against the first to glaze it and remove the excess caramel at the same time. Place the two choux on a rack. This method makes it possible to glaze two choux at the same time.

Method 2
Dip the top of a chou in a pot of caramel and remove the excess by lightly scraping it against the edge of the

(Grand Prize recipe continued on page 189)

Facing Page: Grand Prize

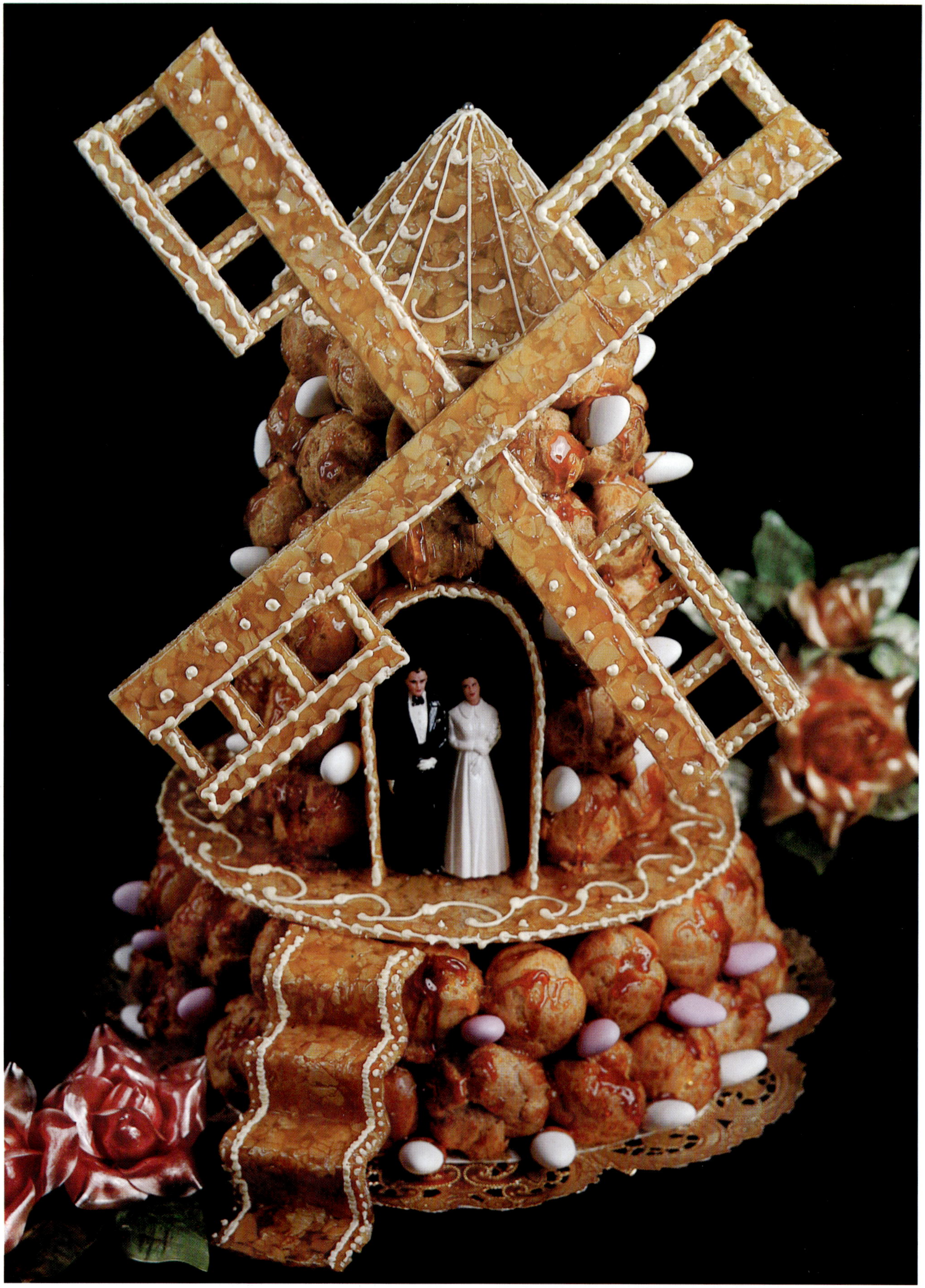

pot. Place the chou, caramel side down, on a non-stick or lightly oiled sheet pan. When the caramel has set, turn the chou upright. The caramel will be flat and even. This technique tends to result in a thick layer of caramel and should therefore be prepared carefully.

Method 3

Dip the choux in caramel and set them, caramel side down, on a layer of pearl sugar. When the caramel has set, the sugar will adhere. Turn the choux over, right-side up, onto a rack.

This procedure is used to vary and brighten up a croquembouche, but some feel it diminishes the flavor of the choux.

Method 4

Assemble the croquembouche with unglazed choux. When the piece is finished, dip a metal spatula in caramel and dab it lightly onto each choux.

Clearly this procedure offers the most inconsistent results and is most suitable when the caramel layer is not an important part of the decoration. Also, this can be a valuable method for especially large pieces, as it is the most expedient.

Lovers' Windmill
Moulin des Amours

This croquembouche is most often used for engagements, weddings, or anniversaries. The piece is assembled in two steps: preparing and trimming the nougatine, and attaching the sections with caramel.

Cut out a round nougatine base; the size is determined by the number of choux used. Bend a strip of nougatine to form the door opening. Cut out the four arms of the windmill. Warm a strip of nougatine, 2 1/3–3 in/6–8 cm wide, until malleable and bend it to form the stairway. The length of the stairway is determined by the height of the bottom section.

Facing Page: Lovers' Windmill

For the roof, cut out a disk of nougatine and remove a 90° section. Bring the two ends of the larger piece together, warming it and shaping it over a cone.

Assemble the bottom section of choux on a rigid cardboard or nougatine disk. This section should be wide, but not high (about two rows). Attach the nougatine base, then the strip that represents the doorway. Attach choux around and over the door, decreasing the rows by one chou. Affix the roof and windmill arms. Decorate with royal icing and dragées.

Nougatine for Croquembouches

Any nougatine recipe can be used for croquembouches and other presentation pieces. However, to assure a greater resistance to humidity, it is best to use a nougatine prepared with fondant.

Nougatine for Croquembouches No. 1

glucose	14 oz	400 g
fondant	21 oz	600 g
sliced or chopped almonds	17.5 oz	500 g
butter*	2 oz	50 g

the butter can be replaced with an equal amount of cocoa butter

In a copper sugar pot (poêlon), melt the glucose, then add the fondant. Cook the two ingredients to the desired color caramel, light or amber. The caramel doesn't need to be stirred constantly as is done in other recipes.

When the caramel has reached the desired color, add the almonds, stirring them in with a wooden spoon to blend well. Stir in the butter or cocoa butter.

(Nougatine for Croquembouches No. 1 recipe continued on next page)

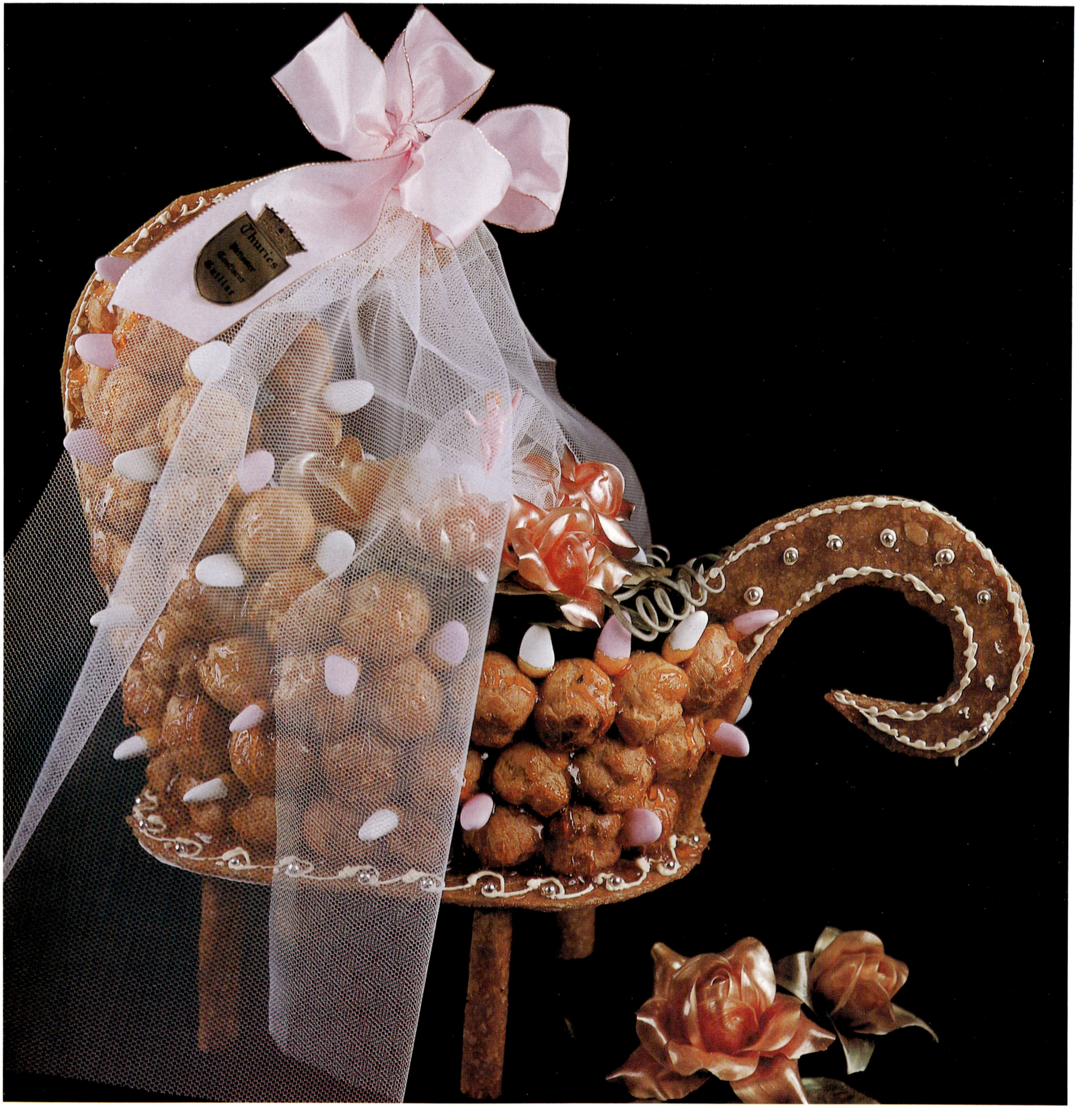
Thuriès

Pour the nougatine out onto a lightly oiled marble. With a triangle, turn the nougatine over from the edge toward the center to help promote even cooling. Place the nougatine in a mound on an oiled sheet pan, rolling, trimming, and cutting to the size and shape needed.

It is important to work quickly, while the nougatine is still soft. It can be placed in the oven to resoften as needed. The nougatine can also be worked near an open oven door or under a heat lamp.

Have all tools ready in advance; clean, dry, and lightly coated with oil. These usually include a pastry triangle, metal rolling pin, knife, and cutters.

The nougatine trimmings can be softened on a lightly oiled sheet pan and used again. Store the nougatine in a cool area in airtight containers.

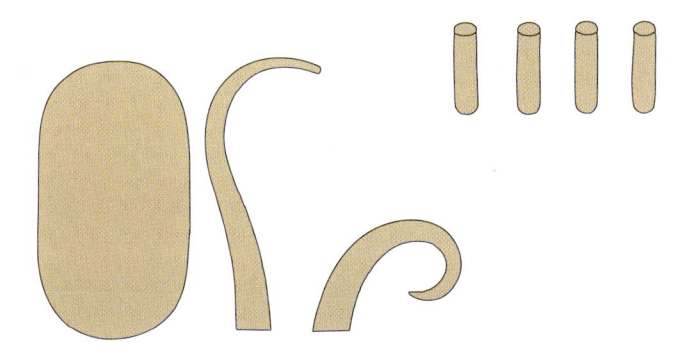

Baby's Bassinet
Berceau

Prepare an oval nougatine base. Cut out the handle and canopy support to which tulle will be attached. Shape four cylinders for the feet.

Assemble the bassinet directly on the base. Attach the canopy support at one end and the handle at the opposite end. Assemble staggered, even-numbered rows of choux to the desired height. Continue mounting the choux around the canopy support to form the canopy.

Attach a few strips of nougatine across the bassinet to support a baptismal figurine and pulled sugar or marzipan flowers and leaves. On the top of the canopy, use caramel to attach tulle and a ribbon. Finish decorating with royal icing and dragées.

This piece can be fairly easily transported, the most delicate part being the handle. Affix the four feet on the presentation table. It is also possible to bond the four feet to a base beforehand then place the bassinet on top.

Temple of Love
Temple d'Amour

This croquembouche is particularly suitable for weddings and engagements. It is fairly easy to transport, and is assembled in two steps: preparing and cutting the nougatine, and assembling the piece with caramel.

Cut out a nougatine disk; the size is determined by the number of choux used. Prepare wolf's teeth (curved nougatine triangles). The base of the kiosk is molded in a génoise or cake pan. Prepare four nougatine columns. The top of the kiosk is made from a nougatine disk the same diameter as the base; a second disk the same size is warmed and pressed in a oiled bowl to form a dome.

To assemble the kiosk, attach the four columns to the base. Join the disk to the top of the columns, then cover with the dome.

Assemble the choux in staggered rows, with each row containing the same number of choux so the sides are straight. As a decorative touch, every other row of choux can be glazed with caramel as usual, and the alternative row caramelized and coated with pearl sugar (see page 189).

Place the larger disk on top of the bottom choux section and attach the nougatine wolf's teeth around it. Join the kiosk on top. Decorate with royal icing and pulled sugar or marzipan flowers.

Facing Page: Baby's Bassinet

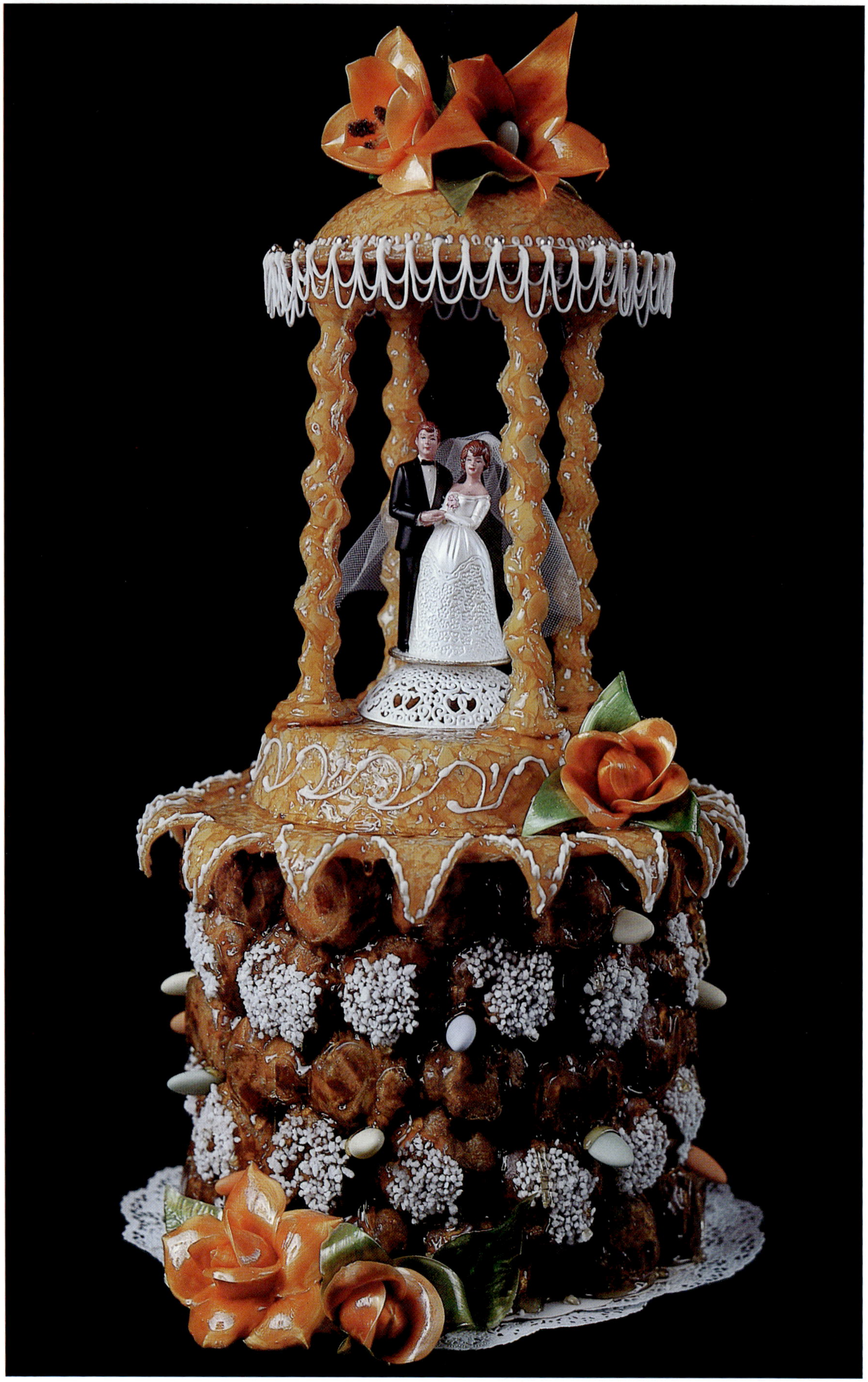

Molding Nougatine

Photo 1: Roll out a layer of nougatine to the desired thickness and place it in a lightly oiled mold, pressing against the sides. A second warm mold can be placed inside to help the nougatine take form.

Photo 2: Using a serrated knife, trim any excess nougatine flush to the rim of the mold.

Photo 3: As soon as the nougatine begins to set, remove the second mold, but leave the nougatine inside until completely cooled so it does not lose shape.

Follow this procedure regardless of the mold used.

Facing Page: Temple of Love

Croquembouches

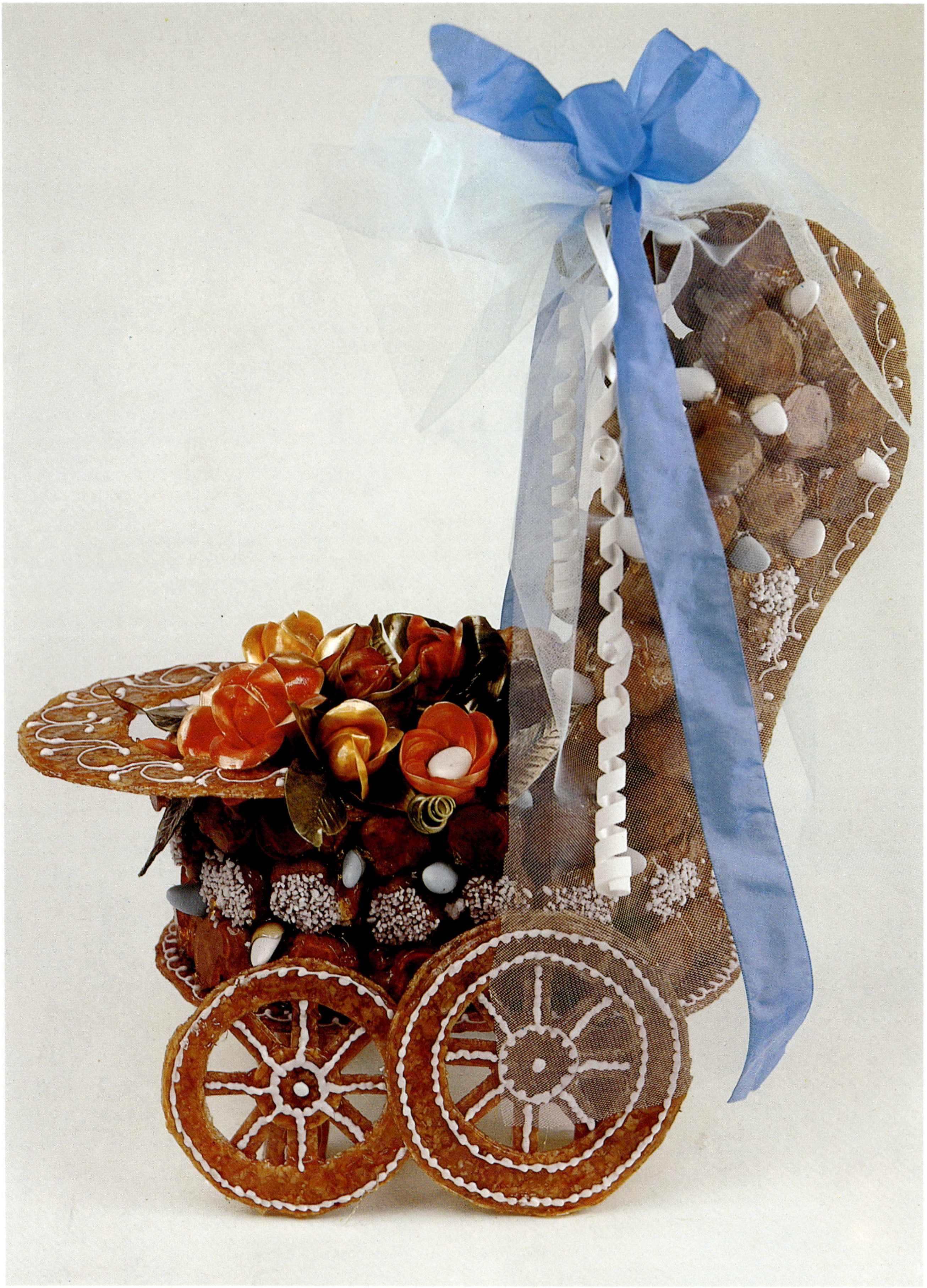

Baby Buggy
Landau

This croquembouche is assembled following a method similar to that used for the bassinet. Place four nougatine columns on the presentation table. Attach the baby buggy on top. Affix a nougatine wheel to each column, which can often be set in place without caramel.

Caramel for Croquembouches

water	14 oz	400 g
glucose	9 oz	250 g
sugar	35 oz	1,000 g

In a copper sugar pot (poêlon), cook the water, glucose, and sugar to 311°–329°F/155°–165°C. When the sugar begins to caramelize, remove it from the heat and stop the cooking by dipping the bottom of the pot in cold water for a few seconds.

During assembly, it is sometimes necessary to reheat the caramel so it remains fluid enough to work with.

Reasons Caramel Softens

1. Humidity. The most common cause of caramel softening.
2. Choux paste that was not thoroughly baked and then filled with a regular pastry cream, because the milk will be absorbed by the choux, then the caramel.
3. Caramel that is overcooked.

Facing Page: Baby Buggy

How to Prevent Caramel from Softening

Although it is difficult to prevent humid conditions, it is possible to take precautions and achieve excellent results.

Carefully bake the choux so it is well dried out. Fill the choux with mousseline cream or butter-enriched pastry cream, flavored to taste. The humidity of these creams is not absorbed by the choux but rather by the butter. Use a caramel especially prepared for croquembouches (below) made with fondant and glucose.

Special Caramel for Croquembouches

In a copper sugar pot (poêlon) melt 17.5 oz/500 g glucose then add 35 oz/1,000 g fondant. Cook to a light blond caramel without adding water, 311°F/155°C.

This caramel can be used to join all parts of the croquembouches and will hold for several hours. Just before presenting the piece, caramelize the choux with a spatula, then attach dragées and other decorations.

The fondant-based caramel is especially advantageous for large presentation pieces.

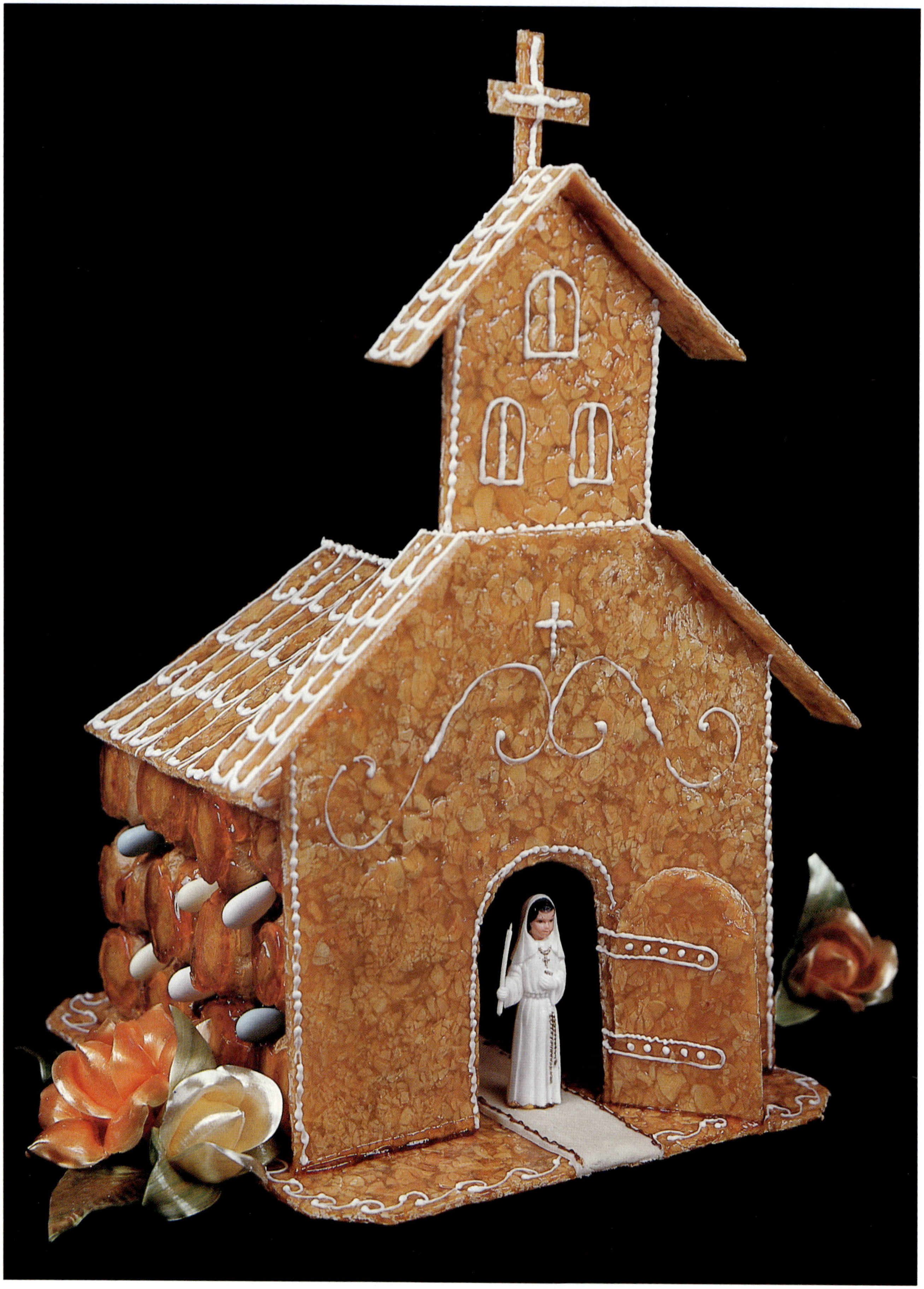

The Small Church
La Petite Eglise

This croquembouche is appropriate for most religious ceremonies. It is prepared in two steps.

Cardboard patterns are indispensable for cutting the nougatine efficiently and accurately. The pieces needed are a square or rectangular base, the facade with an opening for the door, the door, a steeple and cross, four strips for the two narrow roofs, and two panes for the larger roof.

Attach the facade to the base with caramel, being careful to keep it very straight. Immediately assemble 4–6 rows of choux on both sides behind the facade. The choux will give support to the facade. Attach the two roof panes and the steeple, then the narrow roof strips and the cross. Affix the door, open to one side.

Decorate with royal icing and dragées. Roll out a strip of marzipan to serve as the runner. A figurine can be placed at the doorway. Place pulled sugar flowers on either side of the church.

Variations

Following the same procedure as above, it is easy to make variations using personal creativity. For example, a church constructed with two steeples, or one large steeple flanked by two smaller ones. The church can also be assembled on a second nougatine disk with steps. Although the design presented here is constructed on a small scale, larger, more grandiose structures can be produced. In that case, it is assembled on a board to avoid the risk of the base breaking during transportation.

Houses, villas, or castles can also be constructed following the same procedure. For the first step, prepare cardboard models with the facade and roofing in chosen shapes. Use these to cut out the nougatine. The second step is to assemble the choux and nougatine. Decorate with royal icing and attach dragées and/or pulled or molded sugar flowers.

Facing Page: The Small Church

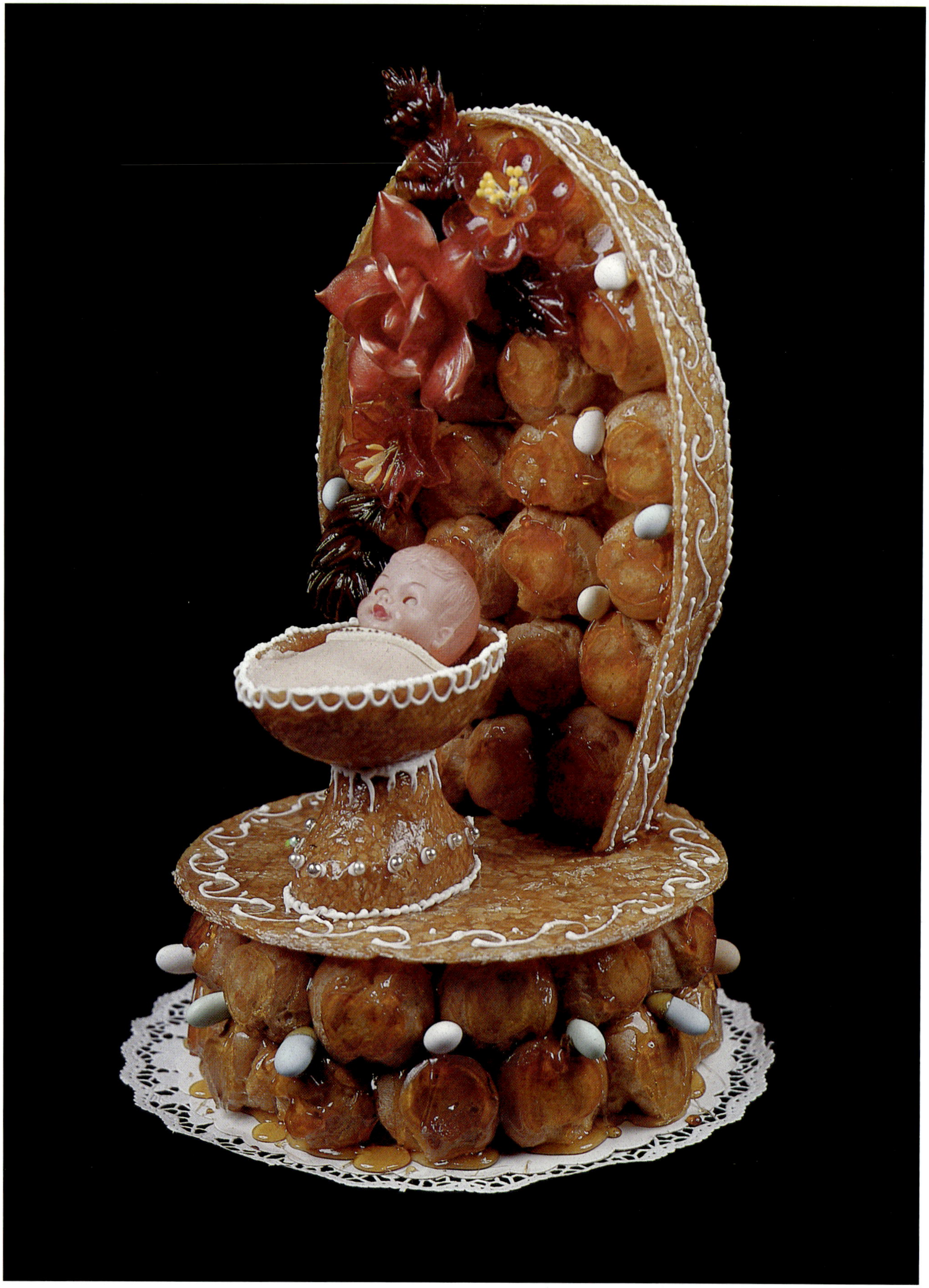

Podium

This croquembouche was designed for baptisms. However, it can be used for other occasions. The bassinet can be replaced with any other appropriate figure, such as two blown sugar doves for engagements.

In nougatine, cut out one round disk and one long oval disk with a flat end. Prepare the bassinet by lining nougatine in a half-egg mold or other half-round or oval form. Form its base in either half of an egg mold or the bottom of a cup. Cut a strip of nougatine 3/4 in/ 2 cm wide and long enough to wrap around the edge of the oval, stopping at the flat end.

Assemble the choux on a cardboard as for the drum (see page 185) in straight staggered rows. Attach the round disk on top. The choux can be assembled on a nougatine disk instead of a cardboard, but this would make the piece considerably more fragile if transported.

Soften the nougatine strip in the oven and wrap it around the edge of the oval plaque, leaving the flat end free. Cover the oval with choux. Use cooked sugar or caramel to attach the plaque upright to the nougatine base. Attach choux behind the base of the plaque to reinforce it.

Assemble the bassinet and make a baby blanket with marzipan. The baby's head can be made out of marzipan or a plastic figurine can be used. Decorate with dragées and pulled or molded sugar flowers and royal icing.

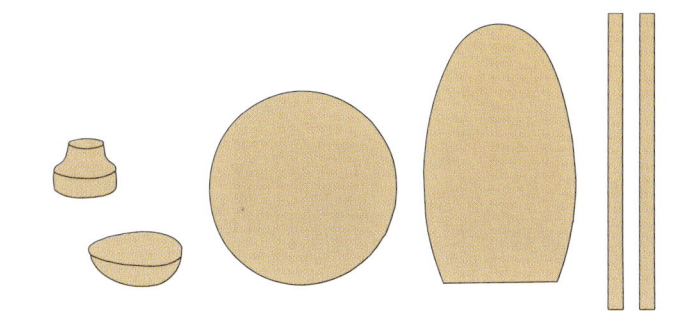

Chef's Note: *The podium can be used for other occasions by replacing the bassinet with another appropriate decoration. For example, bride and bridegroom figurines can be used for a wedding. The back of the oval plaque can be inscribed with royal icing and decorated with molded sugar flowers.*

This piece is fairly easy and practical to construct for large events. The bottom rows can be prepared with 25–40 choux as needed. The size of the oval plaque should correspond to the height and size of the base.

Facing Page: Podium

200   *Modern French Pastry*

Podium

Photo 1: Assemble the bottom section of the podium, attaching the choux in staggered rows on a rigid cardboard. Each row contains the same number of choux to create straight sides. For decoration, alternate rows can be made with choux coated with caramel and pearl sugar.

Photo 2: Attach a nougatine disk on top of the choux. This configuration can be used for large presentation pieces with 3–5 such sections made of 15–40 choux each.

Photo 3: Attach a strip of nougatine around the border of the oval nougatine disk. The disk will serve as the backboard. This piece can be made in other shapes, as long as the dimensions are proportional to the size of the base.

Photo 4: Attach the backboard to the nougatine disk with caramel and reinforce it by attaching small choux behind.

Photo 5: Attach one chou at the bottom, in front of the oval plaque, to assure its stability and alignment. Attach the small base, intended to support the decoration, to the disk.

Photo 6: Decorate with pulled or molded sugar flowers, any figurines used, and piped royal icing.

Croquembouches

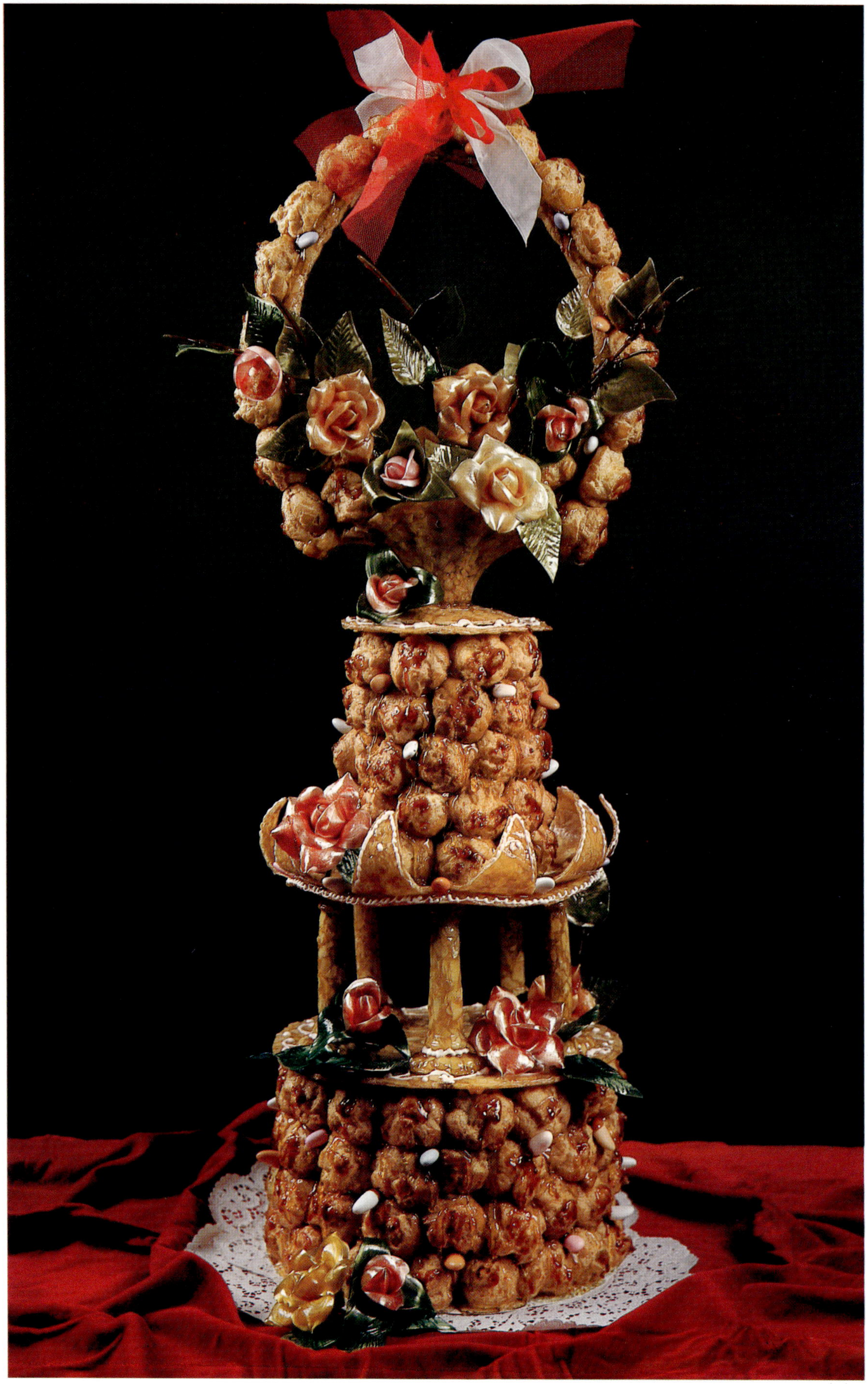

Pompadour

By changing the figurine in the center of the bouquet, this croquembouche can be used for any occasion. Cut out two disks of nougatine, the size of which is determined by the number of choux used. Prepare five nougatine columns and wolf's teeth. For the centerpiece on top, mold a nougatine basket and slightly convex base.

Make the basket handle by rolling out a thin cylinder of nougatine, and reinforce it with metal wire on the inside. Attach it to the interior of the basket and secure it inside with small choux.

Dip three dried tree branches in caramel and attach them inside the basket. They will be used to create a bouquet of sugar flowers. Attach small choux around the handle.

Assemble the choux in straight staggered rows the same diameter as the disks. Use caramel to attach the first disk on top of the choux. Affix the five columns, then the second disk with the wolf's teeth around the edge.

Assemble a second section of choux as for the first, but narrower; the height will vary according to the number of choux needed.

Decorate the nougatine with royal icing. Assemble the three sections on the table where the piece is to be presented.

Variation

This croquembouche can be finished in various ways. Eliminate the arched handle and simply place a bouquet of pulled sugar flowers and leaves on top. It is also possible to forego the basket and flowers and place a symbolic subject or figurine in the center of the croquembouche.

Facing Page: Pompadour

Special Nougatine

Several nougatine recipes offer equally excellent results. This volume includes a variety of recipes of traditional confectionary nougatine.

The criterion for a good nougatine is that it contain a high percentage of almonds. Nougatine prepared with few almonds will be difficult to bite into. In addition, a deep golden amber nougatine tastes the best. An overly dark nougatine is not as aesthetically pleasing and tends to soften quickly. Pale colored nougatine lacks luster but is more impervious to humidity. Therefore, light amber nougatine is most appropriate; attractive, and able to stand up to unpredictable conditions of high humidity and temperature. Caramelize the almonds thoroughly to bring out the most flavor.

Special Nougatine Recipe

This recipe is simple to prepare and stores well. It does not soften easily.

water	12.5 oz	350 g
calcium carbonate	1 oz	25 g
glucose	10.5 oz	300 g
sugar	35 oz	1,000 g
almonds,* sliced or chopped	24.5 oz	700 g

the quantity of almonds can vary according to taste

In a copper sugar pot (poêlon), combine the water, calcium carbonate, glucose, and sugar. Cook without stirring, to a deep golden amber caramel. Add the almonds and stir with a wooden spoon. Proceed, shaping and cutting as for any nougatine.

Chef's Note: *The calcium carbonate causes the sugar to recrystallize after cooking, which prevents the finished nougatine from softening. If it does soften, it will be rather insignificant.*

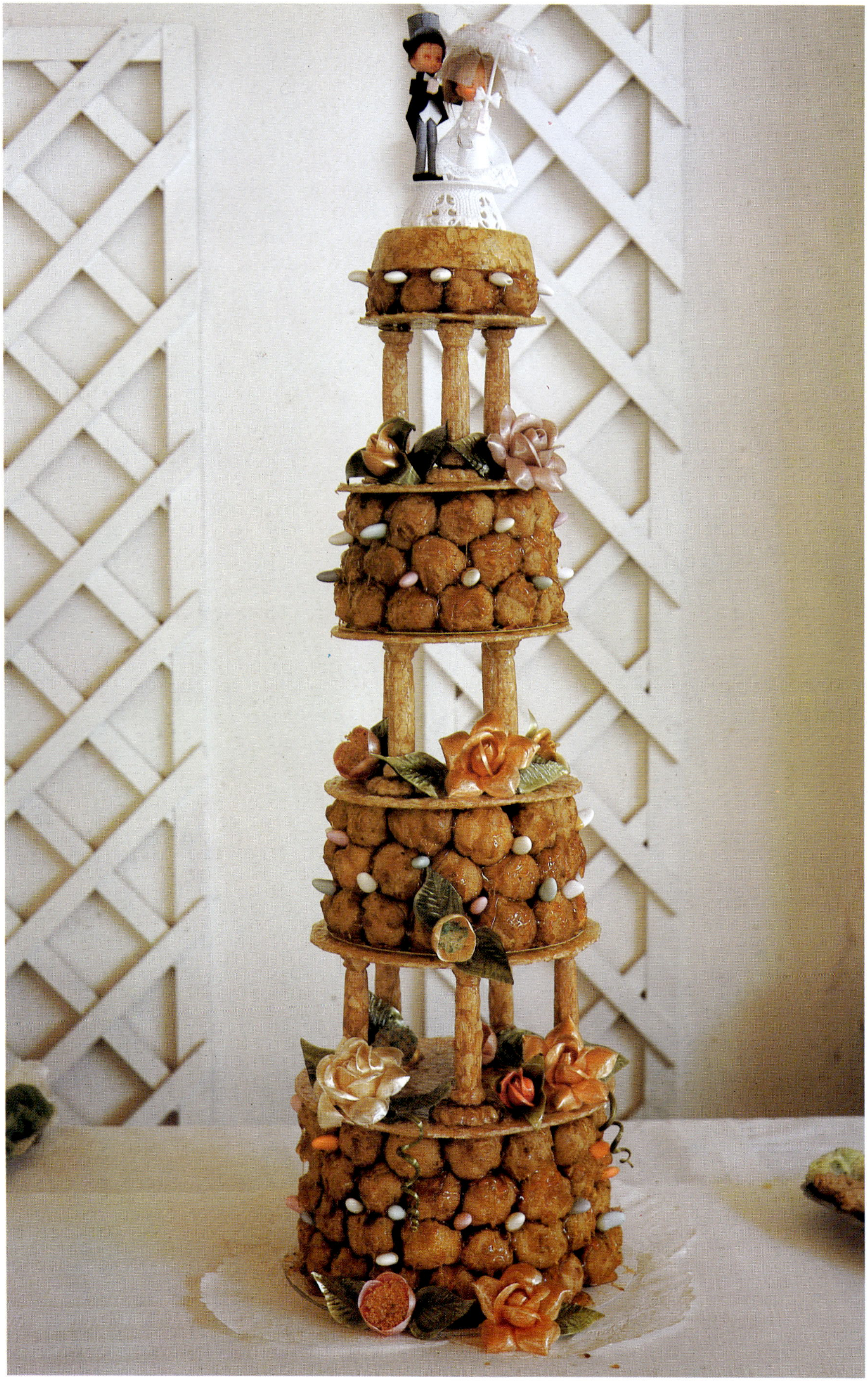

Prestige

This croquembouche works well for a large number of choux. The piece is divided into three sections, making it fairly easy to transport.

Assemble three separate tiers of choux built in staggered straight rows. Make each tier smaller, and narrower than the previous one. Prepare 12 nougatine columns and a small nougatine base molded in a génoise mold.

Attach a nougatine disk to the top of the largest section of choux to serve as the foundation. Affix the five columns (or more depending on the size of the piece) to the disk, evenly spaced apart. Attach a second disk of nougatine, the same size as the first, on top of the columns.

Repeat this construction—disk, columns, disk (use four columns on the second tier and three columns on the third)—on the other two tiers of choux. Check that each section is straight and balanced. If needed, align the tiers with additional pieces of nougatine.

Once the three tiers are completed, decorate each with pulled sugar or marzipan roses and leaves, and dragées. Assemble the three sections on the presentation table and place a figurine, if used, on top.

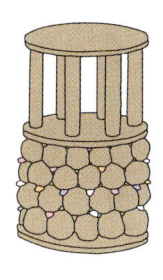

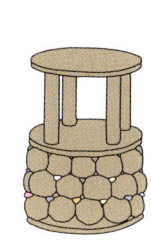

First Section
1 tier of choux
2 disks
5 columns

Second Section
1 tier of choux
2 disks
4 columns

Third Section
1 tier of choux
2 disks
3 columns
1 small nougatine base

Variation
This piece can also be prepared with two or four sections. The diameter of each section is determined by the number of choux used.

Facing Page: Prestige

206 *Modern French Pastry*

Phoenix
Phénix

This croquembouche is often used for weddings, although by simply changing the centerpiece decorations, it can be used for other occasions.

Prepare a large, thick nougatine base molded in a génoise mold. Assemble the center piece with rows of choux, increasing each row by one chou so the piece graduates outward. Cut out a nougatine disk the same size as the top row of choux. Make nougatine wolf's teeth.

Mold the vase out of nougatine using a mold intended for this purpose. Fill the vase with a bouquet of pulled sugar flowers and, if desired, one or more appropriate figurines.

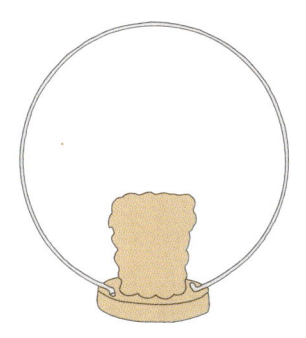

Diagram of how the wire is attached to the nougatine base

Make the arc by curving a twisted 1/16–1/4 in/4–6 mm thick wire, folding each end over to give greater stability. Cover the wire with a strip of nougatine. Attach alternating caramel-glazed and pearl sugar-coated choux to the outside of the strip.

The final assembly is made on the presentation table. First, place the base section, attach the vase and flowers, then the arc. Affix some small choux at junction points to give the arc more stability. Decorate with pulled sugar or marzipan flowers to conceal any visible joints.

Chef's Note: *Although the phoenix is a very elegant piece, it is also extremely delicate and must be assembled and finished on site, where it is to be served.*

Engagement Basket

This croquembouche is fairly easy to construct. The most important requirement is the mold for shaping the nougatine into a vase. The base is molded in a génoise mold and attached to a nougatine disk. Cut out the basket handle from a disk of nougatine, using a cake ring as a guide. An inscription or names can be written in royal icing on the front and back of the handle.

Use caramel to attach the base to the disk. Affix the bottom of the vase to the base, then attach the top half. Fill the vase with a dome of choux, making sure to incorporate the handle and reinforce it with small choux. Attach choux around the base.

Decorate by placing pulled sugar or marzipan roses or other flowers on the top and at the base. Finish with royal icing.

Facing Page: Phoenix

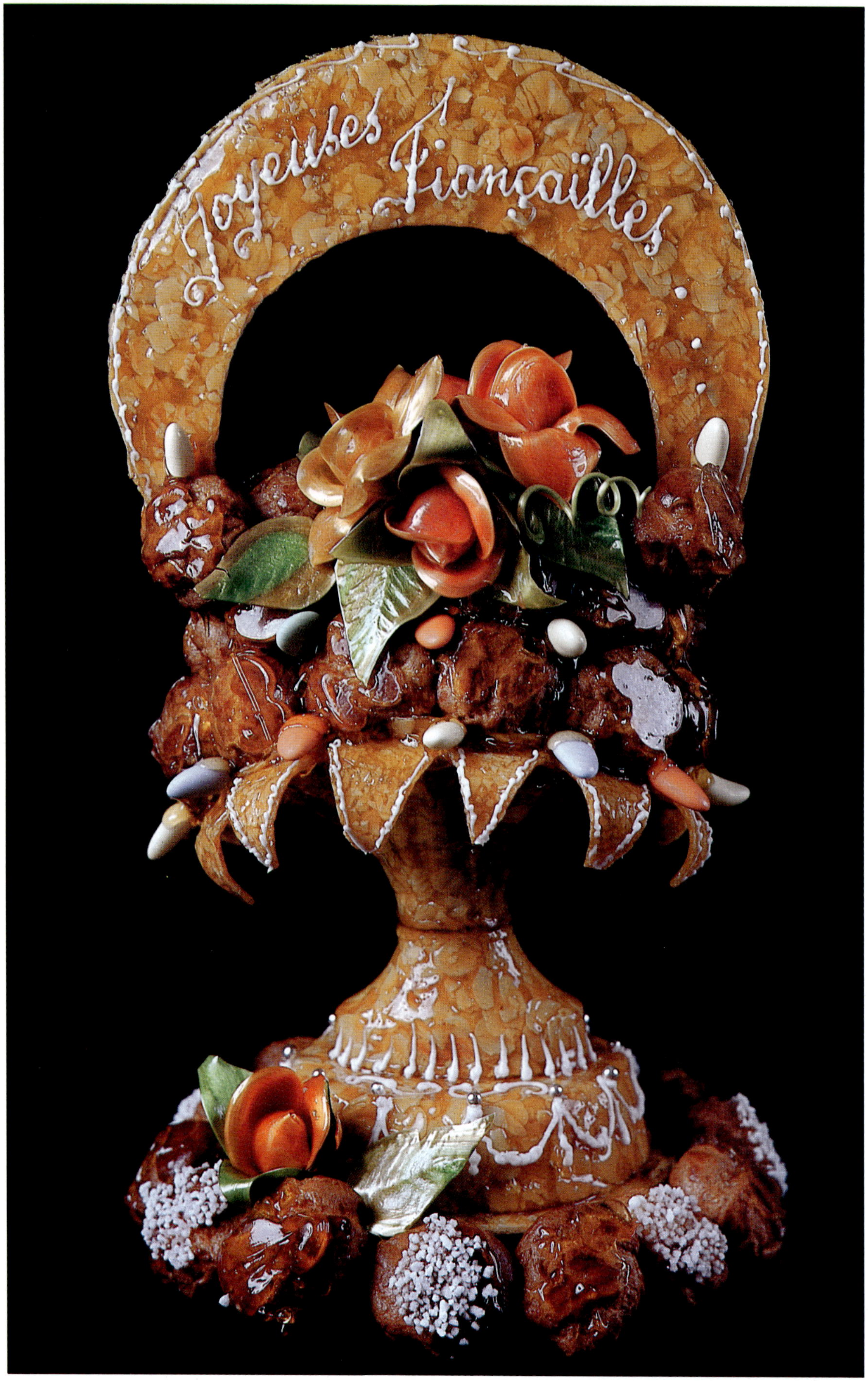
Joyeuses Fiançailles

Glazing the Choux with Caramel

Photo 1: Dip the top of a chou in caramel, drain off the excess.

Photo 2: Quickly place it, caramel side down, into pearl sugar. Wait until the caramel has completely cooled before turning the chou upright.

Photo 3: Dip the top of a chou in caramel, drain off the excess, and quickly place it, caramel side down, onto a non-stick surface. An oiled sheet pan, parchment paper, or plastic film can be used. Allow the caramel to cool completely before removing.

Facing Page: Wedding Basket

Croquembouches

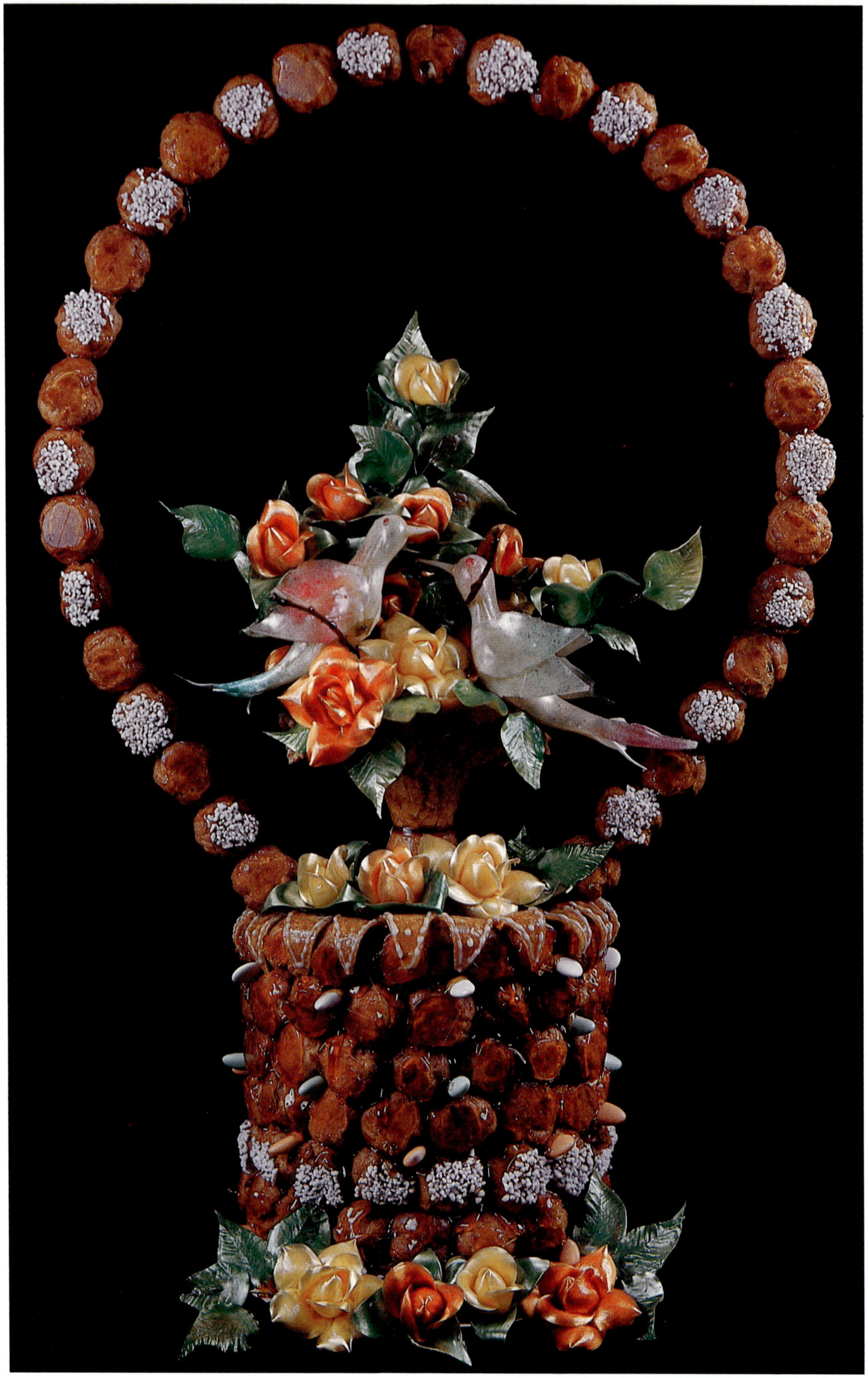

Cooked Sugar or Caramel

Water	12.5 oz	350 g
Glucose	7 oz	200 g
Sugar	35 oz	1,000 g

In a copper sugar pot (poêlon), cook all ingredients to 311°–320°F/155°–160°C. It is not necessary to reach the exact temperature for this caramel; it is more important to achieve the desired light golden caramel color. Remove the pot from the heat and place it in a cold water bath to stop the cooking process.

Precautions

Be sure the pot is perfectly clean and large enough for the amount of caramel prepared, so it will cook evenly. To prevent the sugar from cooling too quickly while assembling the croquembouche, place the pot on a wooden board or a flat bottomed cake pan that has been turned over, rather than directly on a cool marble or other refrigerated work surface. When necessary, return the pot of caramel to the heat.

Dawn Serenade
Aubade

This croquembouche is particularly suitable for weddings and engagements. Intended for large occasions, this piece is fairly easy to transport; the arc is attached on site.

This piece is made up of three sections: nougatine arc, nougatine basket and pulled sugar flowers, and the "drum" made of choux.

1. To give the arc support, curve a twisted wire 1/16–1/4 in/4–6 mm thick. Leave the two ends straight so it can be attached to the inside of the drum. Wrap a band of nougatine around the wire and attach choux to the outside of the nougatine.

Diagram of how the arc is affixed to the drum

2. Assemble the choux in the base in straight-sided, staggered rows. Each row should contain the same number of choux. A large number of choux can be used. The height can vary according to how many choux are needed. Decorate with nougatine wolf's teeth and dragées.

3. Form a basket out of nougatine in a mold intended for this purpose. Fashion a bouquet of pulled sugar flowers on 3–4 dried tree branches coated with caramel. Attach two blown sugar doves to opposite sides of the basket.

4. Set the choux base on the display table. Attach the arc, placing the unadorned ends of wire inside the choux base. Attach small choux to lend support. Place a support inside the choux base and set the nougatine basket and sugar flowers on top.

Facing Page: Dawn Seranade

Reverence

212   *Modern French Pastry*

Reverence

This croquembouche is used as a centerpiece for a buffet table. Constructed with 200–400 choux, it can be decorated to suit any occasion. It is an elaborate piece that, when placed on an elongated structure, fills out the table and catches the eye.

This piece is prepared and transported in three separate sections; it is assembled directly on the buffet table.

1. Prepare the nougatine, and pulled and blown sugar decorations. Twist a wire 1/16–1/4 in/4–6 mm thick to form the armatures for the central arch and two end pieces shaped like "S"s placed on their side. Wrap a band of nougatine around the wires.

Make a basket out of nougatine, using a mold for this purpose. Coat 3–4 dried tree branches with caramel and use them to construct a bouquet of pulled sugar flowers and leaves.

2. Attach caramel-glazed choux with and/or without pearl sugar on the bands of nougatine. Decorate with dragées.

3. Assemble a base made of straight-sided, staggered rows of choux to the size and height needed. In order to be sure the base is strong enough to support the weight of the bouquet, the base should be assembled on a wooden disk covered with a cake cardboard.

4. Place the disk directly on the buffet table, and place the choux base on top. Attach the center arch with caramel on the inside of the choux base as for the dawn serenade (see page 211). Attach the two end "s" pieces. Set the basket and flowers on top of a support in the center of the base. A pulled sugar ribbon and/or blown sugar birds can be attached on top of the arch.

Turtledoves' Cage
Cage aux Tourtereaux

This croquembouche is most appropriate for weddings or engagements. Relatively simple to construct with a large quantity of choux, it is set up in three separate sections.

1. Two reinforced nougatine arches.
2. A nougatine basket filled with a bouquet of pulled sugar flowers and two blown sugar doves.
3. A straight-sided base of choux, the size of which is determined by the number of choux to be used.

First assemble the base section in straight-sided, staggered rows, using the same number of choux in each row. For especially large pieces, assemble the choux

(Turtledoves' Cage recipe continued on page 215)

Floral Wheelbarrow

directly on a sturdy wood disk covered with cardboard. Choose a disk that will hold up to being transported.

Attach choux to the outside of the wire-reinforced nougatine arches.

Mold a nougatine basket, decorating it with a bouquet of pulled sugar flowers and leaves. Attach two blown sugar doves on top.

Place the choux base on the presentation table and attach the arches with caramel. Follow the diagram given for the dawn serenade (see page 211). Set the basket of sugar flowers on a support hidden inside the choux base. Decorate the finished piece with dragées and pulled sugar flowers. Place a cloth or sugar ribbon on the top where the arches meet.

Floral Wheelbarrow
Corso Fleuri

This croquembouche is especially fitting for birthdays, although it can be used for other occasions. Figurines can be placed in the center of the bouquet. It is recommended not to fill the wagon with more than 50 choux as it is one of the more fragile croquembouche. The most demanding and exacting part of this construction is cutting out the nougatine. Prepare cardboard patterns to facilitate this step.

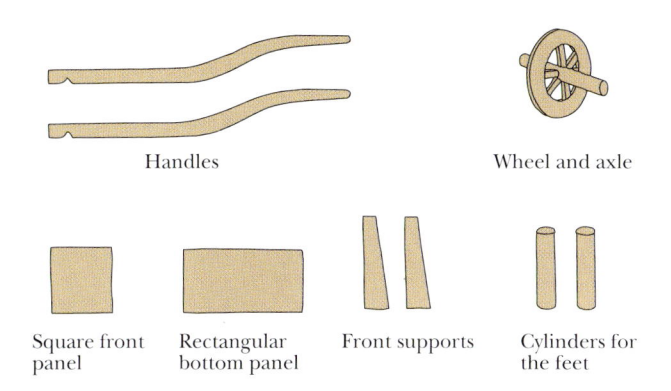

Handles — Wheel and axle

Square front panel — Rectangular bottom panel — Front supports — Cylinders for the feet

Cut two handles out of nougatine, making them thick enough to support part of the weight of the choux. Form spokes and circle for the wheel. Cut out two front supports, one square panel for the front, and one rectangular panel for the bottom. Make two thick nougatine cylinders for the back feet. Reinforce the wheel and axle with wire as this will be the most fragile point supporting the bulk of the wagon's weight.

Attach the two front supports to the handles, then attach the front and bottom panels. Assemble the choux on the sides, placing the greatest number of choux at the center and attaching the nougatine wolf's teeth to the top and down the side.

Decorate with royal icing and dragées. Place a bouquet of pulled sugar or marzipan flowers and leaves on top of the choux.

On the presentation table, attach the back feet and wheel to the wagon.

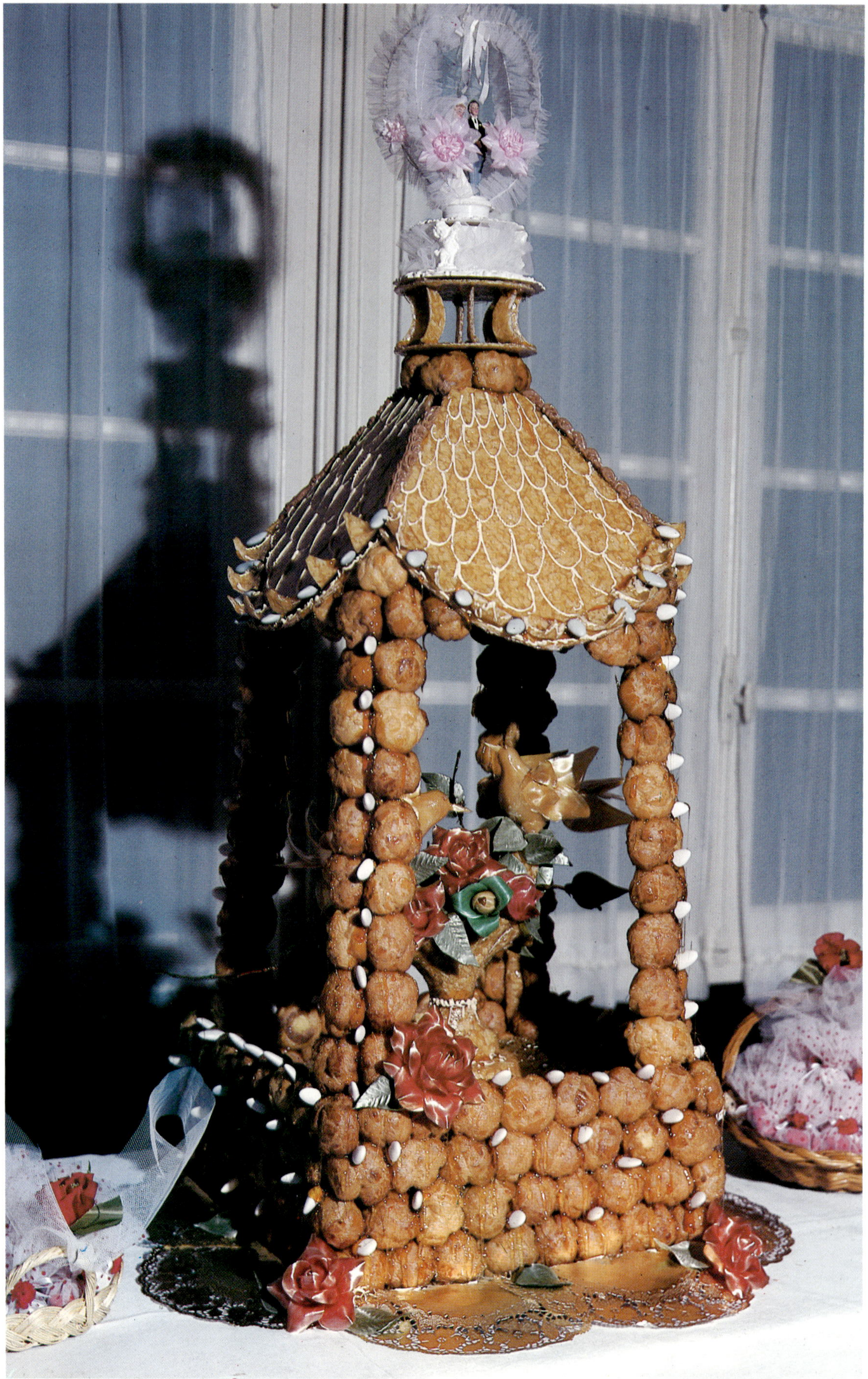

Dovecote
Columbier

This croquembouche is particularly appropriate for weddings or engagements. It is constructed in three separate sections:

1. Prepare and cut out the nougatine.
2. Make a bouquet of pulled sugar flowers and leaves, and two blown sugar doves.
3. Assemble the choux with caramel.

The ideal number of choux for a piece of this size is 200–300.

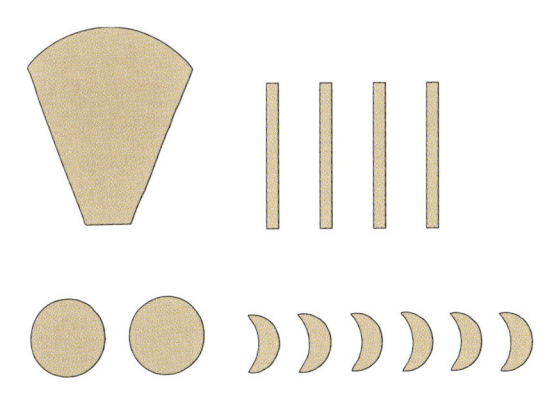

Top Decoration Piece
2 small nougatine disks
6 nougatine crescents
4 roof panels

This croquembouche is completely constructed in the pastry kitchen as the finishing touches are fairly complex, making it difficult to transport.

For the base, cover a wood square of the desired size with cardboard. Assemble the choux in straight staggered rows over the wood base. At each corner affix two arcs of nougatine reinforced with wire. Make them strong enough to eventually support the roof (see the diagram for dawn serenade, page 211). Attach two rows of choux, side-by-side on each arc. Attach the four panels to form the nougatine roof.

On the top of the roof, attach a ring of small choux and cover with a nougatine disk. Affix nougatine cut-outs such as the crescents shown here, and cover with another nougatine disk. Attach an appropriate figurine or decoration on top.

Decorate the piece with royal icing and dragées. Once the piece is set on the presentation table, place a nougatine basket filled with pulled sugar flowers (see below for procedure) and leaves seated on a support, in the middle of the dovecote. Camouflage the support with choux.

Basket of Flowers

The four pieces in the line drawing below represent what is needed to prepare a nougatine vase: disk, base, pedestal, and cup for the top of the basket.

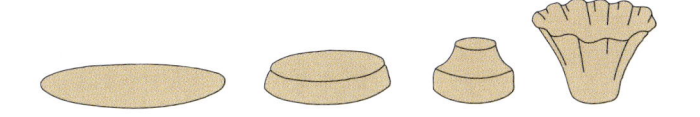

Prepare the stems by covering a few dried tree branches with caramel. This is done by either dipping them entirely in a saucepan of cooked sugar or caramel, which is the easiest procedure, although it requires a large quantity of sugar; or by holding a branch over the saucepan of caramel and ladling the caramel over the branches, allowing the excess to drip off back into the saucepan. Turn the branch around and continue to ladle the caramel until the entire branch is coated.

Attach the pulled or molded sugar flowers to the branches, followed by the leaves, finishing with the blown sugar birds.

Facing Page: Dovecote

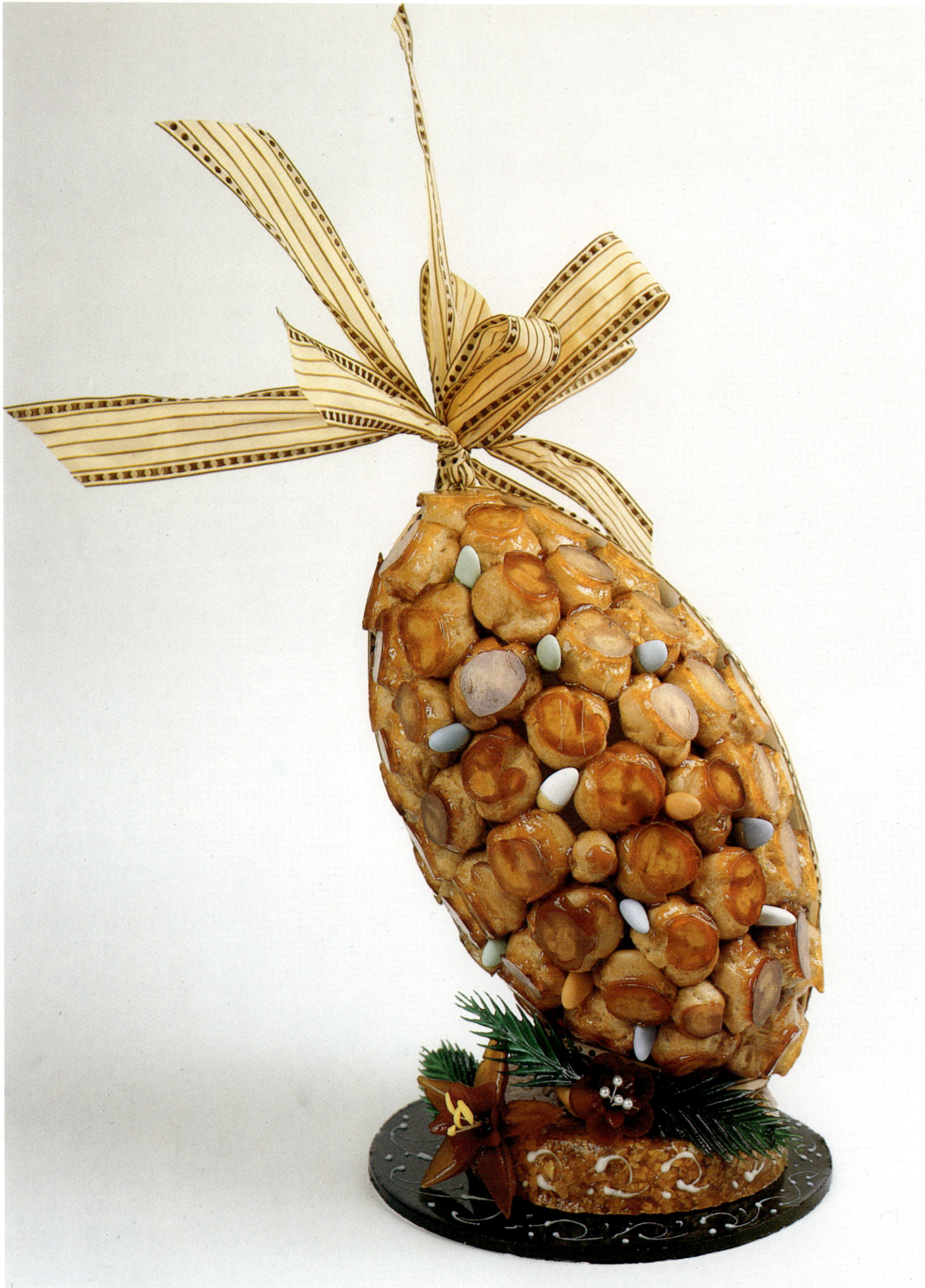

Victory Ball

This croquembouche is intended to celebrate a sports victory or event. The ball can be shaped as needed, oval or round, but the technique remains the same and is prepared in two sections.

1. Prepare the nougatine base in a génoise or cake mold. Cut out two round or oval disks of nougatine.

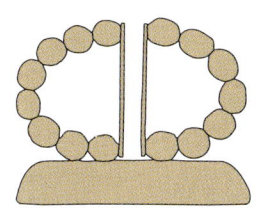

Diagram of how ball is assembled and attached to the nougatine base

2. Place choux around the edge of each disk, reducing the number of choux with each row, to form a half-sphere or ball according to the shape desired. Join the two disks back to back to obtain the whole ball.

Affix the ball to the nougatine base, being careful to attach it at the seam where the nougatine disks meet. This way, the stress of the weight of the ball is supported by the nougatine and not the choux.

Decorate with dragées and royal icing. Wrap a ribbon (with the colors of the team commemorated, if appropriate) to hide the seem where the disks meet.

Facing Page: Victory Ball

Mandolin
Mandoline

This croquembouche is very much appreciated for birthdays and engagements, and has room for an inscription. It is fairly easy to construct and it is intended for smaller gatherings, since no more than 60 choux should be used.

It is assembled in two sections:

1. Prepare and cut the nougatine pieces. The front of the mandolin is based on an oval with a hole cut out of the center. Cut out a strip for the neck and smaller pieces to support the strings. Mold a base out of nougatine using a génoise mold or bowl.

2. On the back of the oval nougatine disk, assemble the choux in a dome as if preparing a half-ball (see ball above). Affix this section to the nougatine base, supporting it at the back with two or more small choux. Attach the neck and other pieces.

Decorate with royal icing. The strings can be made out of pulled sugar or, more simply, nylon thread.

Croquembouches

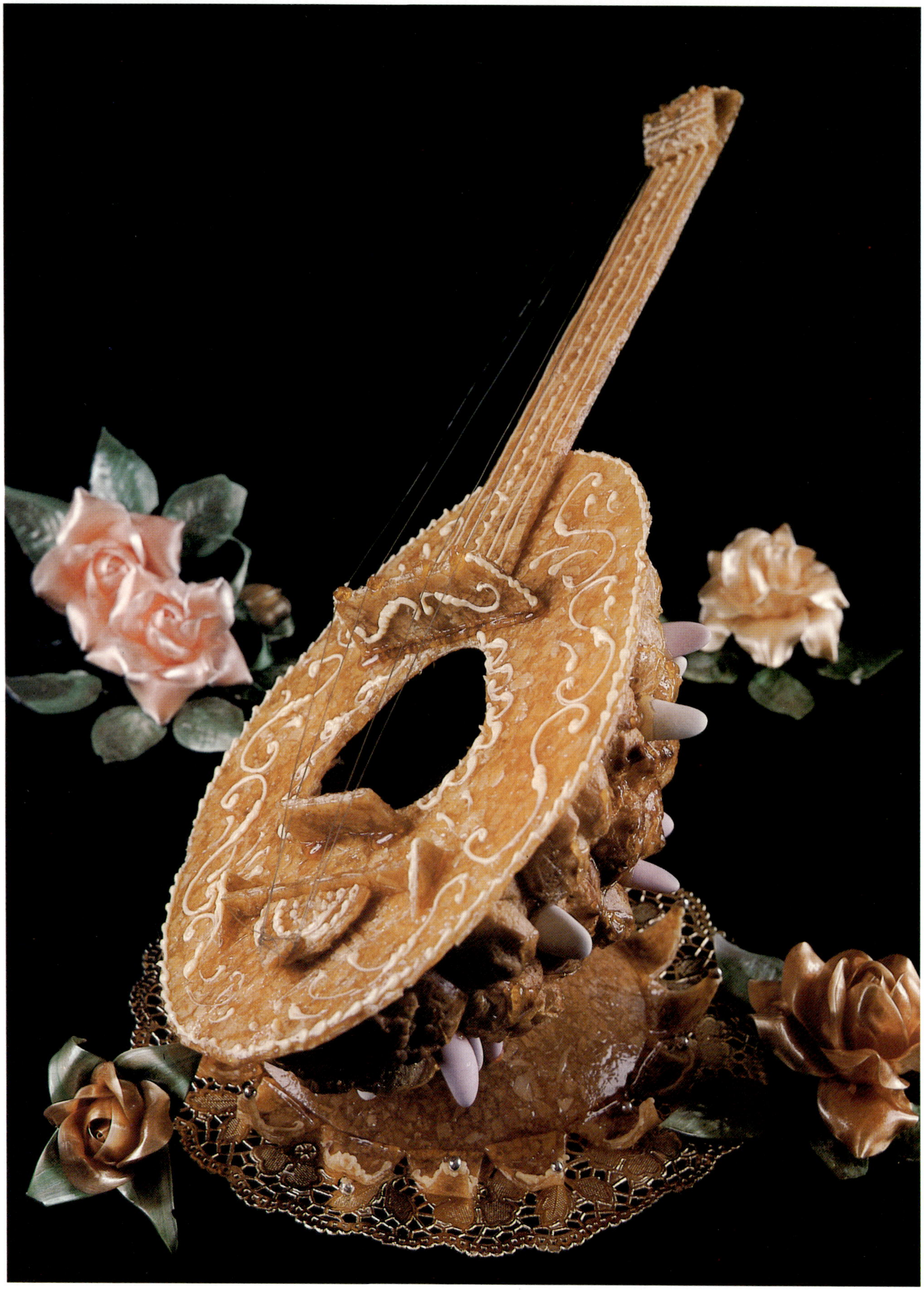

Piping Choux Paste

Photo 1: Pipe choux paste onto lightly buttered sheet pans using a pastry bag and 1/3–1/2 in/8–10 mm diameter tip.

Photo 2: Pipe the choux in staggered rows to allow for even baking. Leave space between the choux so they will have room to rise (they will triple in height), and dry out more quickly.

Photo 3: Brush the choux with egg wash. They can be scored lightly with a fork to produce an even rising. Bake in a moderate oven. It is best to bake the choux at least 24 hours before they are to be used.

Facing Page: Mandolin

Croquembouches

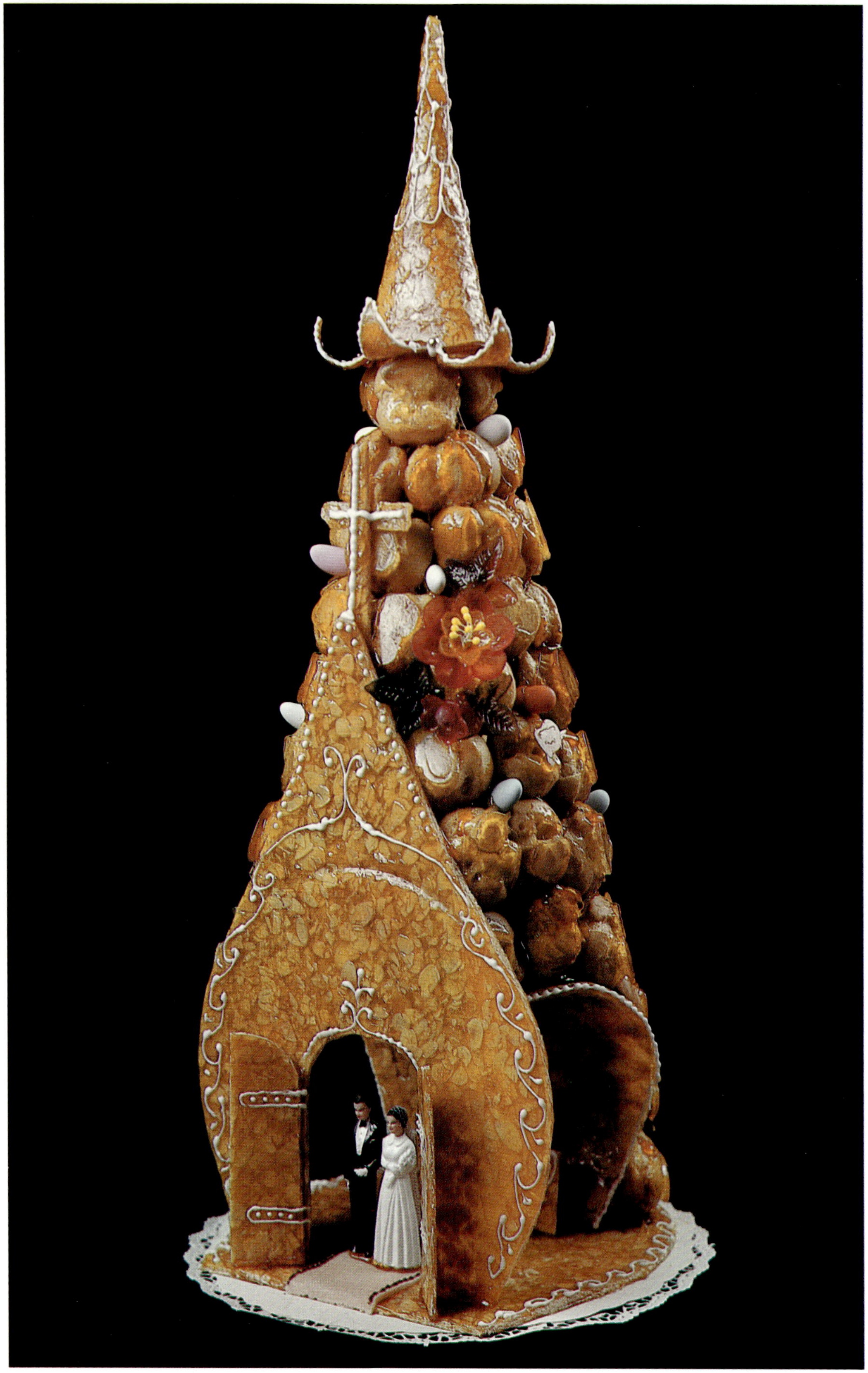

Modern Chapel

This croquembouche, original and easy to construct, is particularly suitable for communions, weddings, and baptisms. It is prepared in two steps: preparation of the nougatine pieces and assembly.

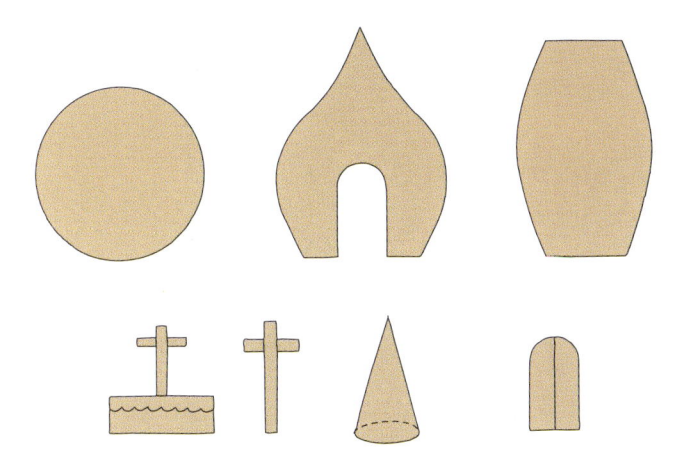

Prepare the nougatine and cut it to size using the line drawings shown here. Cut out a base, round or rectangular; the size will depend on the number of choux used. Cut out the facade, pointed at the top and flat on the bottom. Cut a rounded door out of the facade. Divide the door in half, from top to bottom.

Cut out a panel for the back of the chapel, and while warm, bend it to form an arch. This piece will help support the choux on the side. Cut out a small altar and 2 crosses. Form a cone and small wolf's teeth for the top of the chapel.

Attach the facade to the base with caramel. Immediately attach the arch to the base with one side affixed to the back of the facade as a support.

Assemble the choux, forming a cone above the arch. Reduce the number of choux with each row. Place the nougatine cone on top, and attach the wolf's teeth around the base of the small nougatine cone. Affix the altar inside, and attach the cross and doors to the facade. Place a marzipan runner and appropriate figurines in the doorway. Decorate with royal icing and pulled or molded sugar flowers and leaves.

Facing Page: Modern Chapel

Mousseline Cream
Crème Mousseline

Mousseline cream has a texture that is a cross between pastry cream and buttercream. It is undoubtedly the most suitable filling for croquembouche choux. It contains a high percentage of butter, which absorbs the humidity of the milk, preventing the choux from becoming soggy. The butter content also gives this cream a good shelf life. This cream is recommended for delicate pieces.

Mousseline Cream No. 1
Crème Mousseline

milk	34 fl oz	1 L
vanilla bean, split lengthwise	1	1
eggs	6	6
sugar	17.5 oz	500 g
cornstarch	3.5 oz	100 g
butter, softened	17.5 oz	500 g

Bring the milk and vanilla bean to a boil. Whisk the eggs and sugar until thick and pale, then stir in the cornstarch. Add the egg mixture to the hot milk and bring it back to a boil. Cook for a few seconds, whisking constantly. Remove from heat.

Whisk half the butter into the hot cream. Chill over an ice bath or by spreading it on a cold marble. When the cream has completely cooled, put it in the bowl of an electric mixer with the remaining softened butter. Whip with the whisk attachment until the cream is smooth and aerated.

Flavor to taste with rum, kirsch, Cointreau, Grand Marnier, coffee, praline paste, or other flavor of choice.

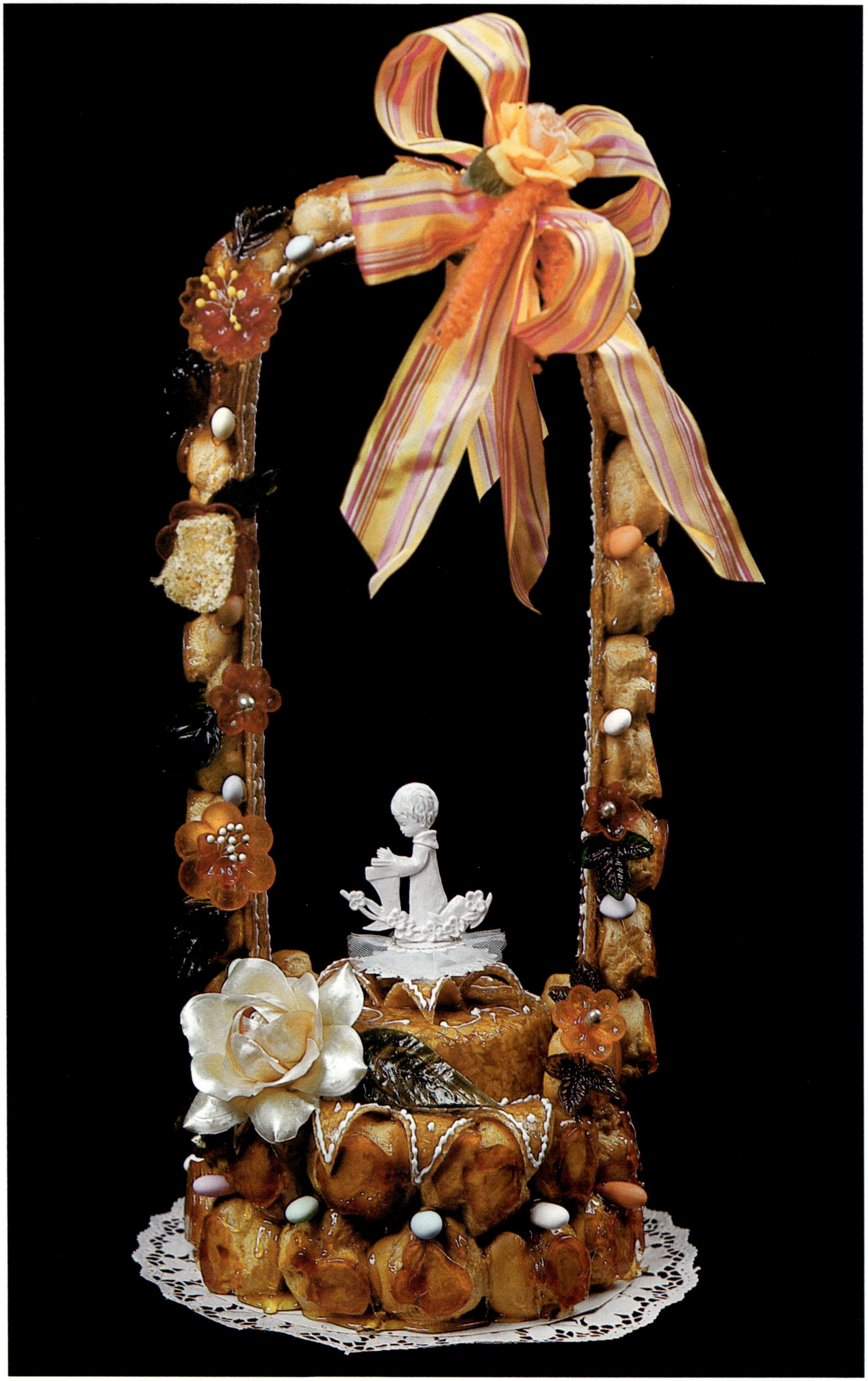

Mousseline Cream No. 2
Crème Mousseline

milk	34 fl oz	1 L
eggs	10	10
sugar	17.5 oz	500 g
flour	4 oz	120 g
butter	21 oz	600 g

Follow the procedure given for Recipe 1.

Variation
Whip 17.5 oz/500 g buttercream in the bowl of an electric mixer, using the whisk attachment, until smooth. Gradually add 17.5 oz/500 g pastry cream, whipping until well blended and aerated. Flavor to taste.

Marie-Antoinette

This croquembouche is appropriate for various festivities, especially for large groups, as a large amount of choux can be used to assemble this piece.

Cut a strip of nougatine 3/4 in/2 cm wide, and long enough for the size of the arch intended. While the nougatine is still warm, shape it as desired. Form a pedestal by lining a génoise or cake pan with nougatine.

Assemble the choux in staggered rows. The number of choux per row can vary as can the number of rows, according to how many choux are used. Place the arch on its side on an oiled marble and attach a row of choux to the outside. When the choux on the arch have cooled completely, affix the arch to the choux base. Place the nougatine pedestal in the center of the choux base and attach wolf's teeth around the bottom of the pedestal.

Place figurines on top of the pedestal and decorate with dragées and pulled or molded sugar flowers and leaves.

Chef's Note: *For large pieces it is important to support the arch with wire. Assemble the arch on the presentation table to facilitate transportation. To assemble the arch, follow the line drawing given for the dawn serenade (see page 211).*

Facing Page: Marie-Antoinette

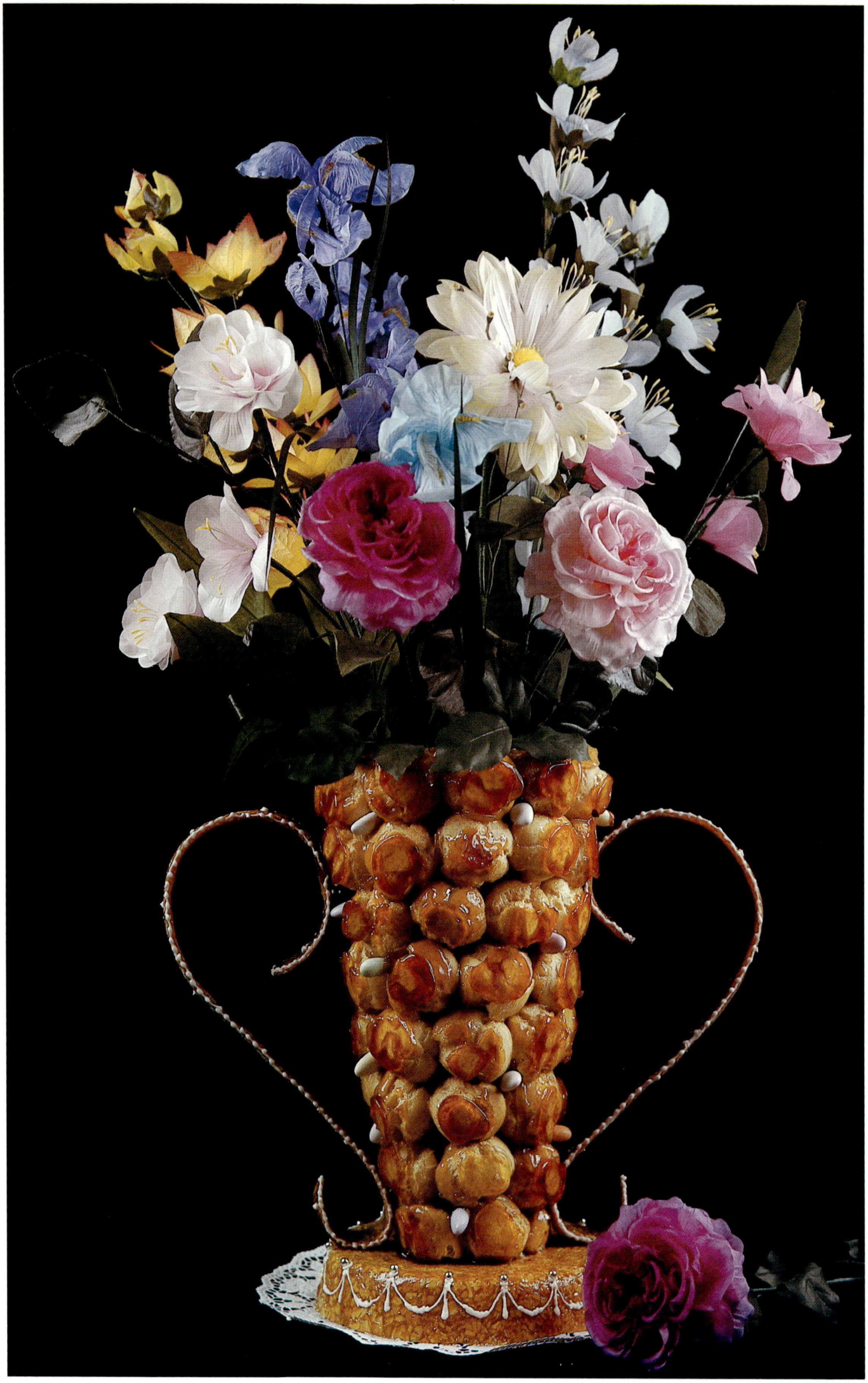

Flower Vase

This piece is popular, fairly simple to construct, and suitable for various occasions. The vase is made of choux and nougatine. It is filled with real or artificial flowers. It is also possible to use pulled sugar flowers, though real flowers are lighter. The number of choux used can vary according to need, although it is recommended not to use more than 100 as it makes the piece heavy looking and difficult to transport.

Line a génoise mold with nougatine to form the base. Cut two strips of nougatine 1 in/3 cm wide and bend each into an "s" to form the handles for the vase.

On a lightly oiled or non-stick sheet pan, construct the vase upside down. Assemble the choux in rows, reducing the number of choux by one for each row. The number of rows will determine the height of the vase. When the vase is completed, cooled and set, turn it upright. Dip the bottom, the narrow end, into caramel and place it on the nougatine base. With caramel, affix the two handles on opposite sides and dragées among the choux. Decorate with royal icing. Just before presenting, place the bouquet inside.

Chef's Note: *To secure the stability of this croquembouche, it is important to thoroughly dry the choux during baking, fill them with mousseline cream, and glaze them with special fondant caramel.*

Trammel
Crémaillèrie

Similar to the Marie-Antoinette and Wishing Well croquembouches, another variation on this style is the trammel, an adjustable hook for a caldron heated over a fire. This piece uses a large number of choux, 20 to 40 choux for the bottom alone, constructed in straight-sided, staggered rows.

Facing Page: Flower Vase

To the base, affix a pointed arch made of strips of nougatine and reinforced with twisted wire. Attach choux to the outside of the strips. Refer to the line drawing of the dawn serenade (see page 211).

Mold a caldron, chain, and hook out of nougatine. Roll a few thin cylinders of nougatine to imitate firewood. Attach the chain to the top of the arch with a cloth ribbon. Decorate with pulled or molded sugar flowers and leaves and dragées.

Royal Icing
Glace Royale

flour	1.5 oz	50 g
confectioners' sugar	17.5 oz	500 g
egg whites	4 oz	120 g

Sift together the flour and confectioners' sugar. In the bowl of an electric mixer, use the paddle attachment to beat in the egg whites until the icing is white and holds a peak.

(Royal Icing recipe continued on page 229)

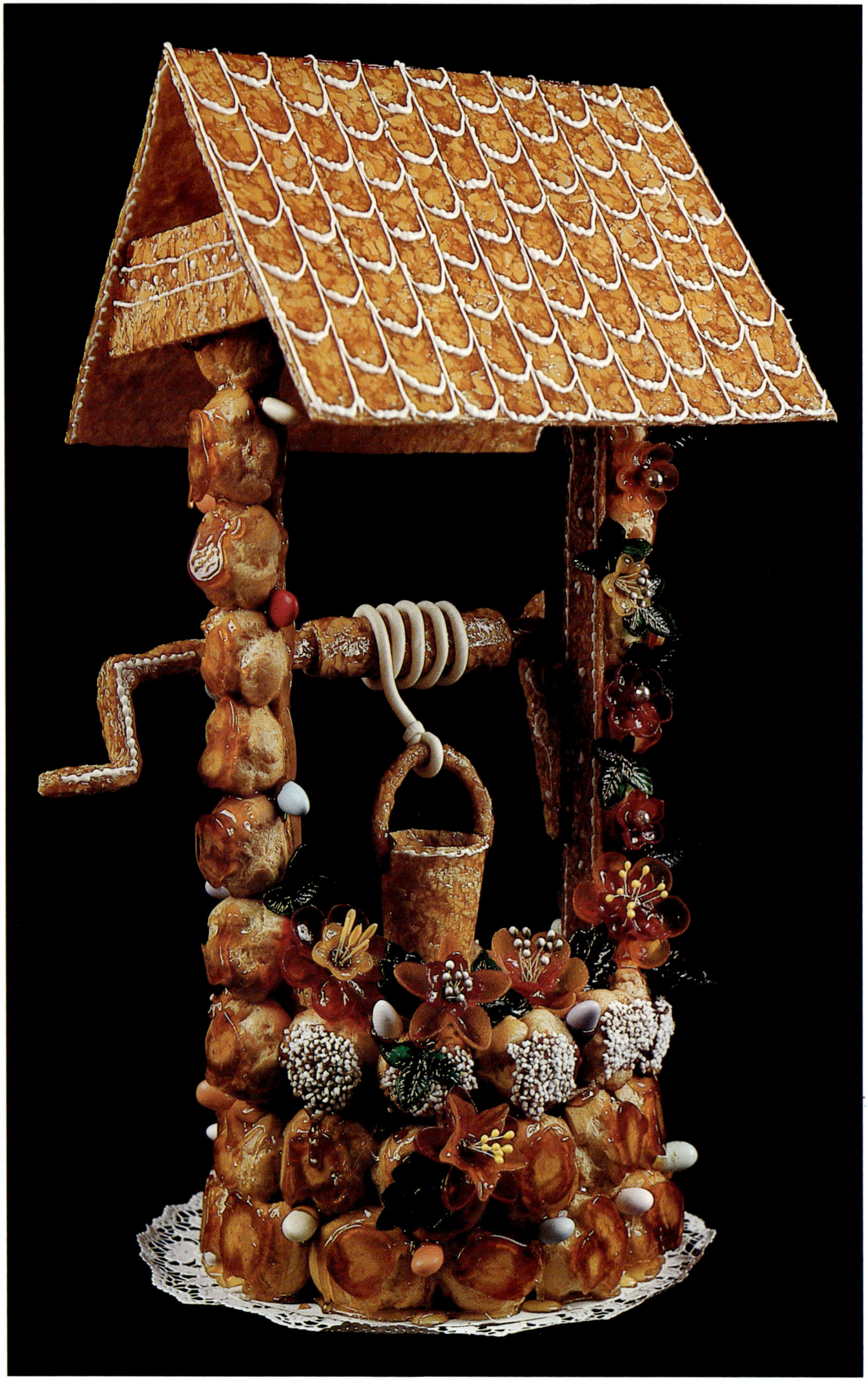

Variation

In a bowl, place 1–4 egg whites. Sift confectioners' sugar and stir it into the egg whites using a wooden spoon, or use an electric mixer with the paddle attachment. Add enough confectioners' sugar so that the icing is not runny or dry, but smooth and holds a small peak. Several drops of lemon juice can be added to whiten the royal icing.

Store the royal icing in an airtight plastic container.

Wishing Well
Puits

This croquembouche is suitable for various occasions and can be made for a large number of guests. For large pieces, the nougatine should be reinforced with wire.

From a sheet of nougatine, cut out two rectangular panels to form the roof, two posts 1/3–1 in/2–3 cm wide, and two triangles to hold the roof in place. Using nougatine, form a crank, bucket, and disk of the same diameter as the interior of the well.

To form the well, assemble choux in straight-sided, staggered rows. Extra choux can be placed on the inside.

Attach choux to the outside of the posts, leaving one end of each post free where they can be affixed to the inside of the well. Place the nougatine disk inside the well on the top row of the choux. Assemble the roof. Place the crank on two nougatine supports attached to the posts (one can be seen on the right side in the photo). Roll out a strip of marzipan to simulate the cord, tie it to the bucket handle, and run it around the crank.

Decorate with dragées, pulled or molded sugar flowers and leaves, and royal icing. An inscription or decoration in royal icing can be made on the roof panels.

Facing Page: Wishing Well

Victory

This croquembouche is for celebrating a victory in sports or business. It is fairly simple to construct, though it does require the use of a mold to form the cup. A mold can be made by using a model molded in plaster of paris.

This piece is built on two sections of choux; the one on the bottom is larger in diameter than the one above. Alternate the rows of choux, one glazed with caramel, the other with caramel and pearl sugar. Place a nougatine disk on top of each section. Attach wolf's teeth around the edge of the disks.

On the presentation table, superimpose the smaller section of choux over the larger one, and place the cup on top. Decorate with royal icing and pulled sugar or marzipan flowers and leaves.

Chef's Note: *This configuration can also be used for other occasions by interchanging the cup with an appropriate decoration or figure. The piece can be prepared for a large number of guests and transported in 2–4 sections (however many sections of choux are prepared), then assembled on site to prevent damage during transportation.*

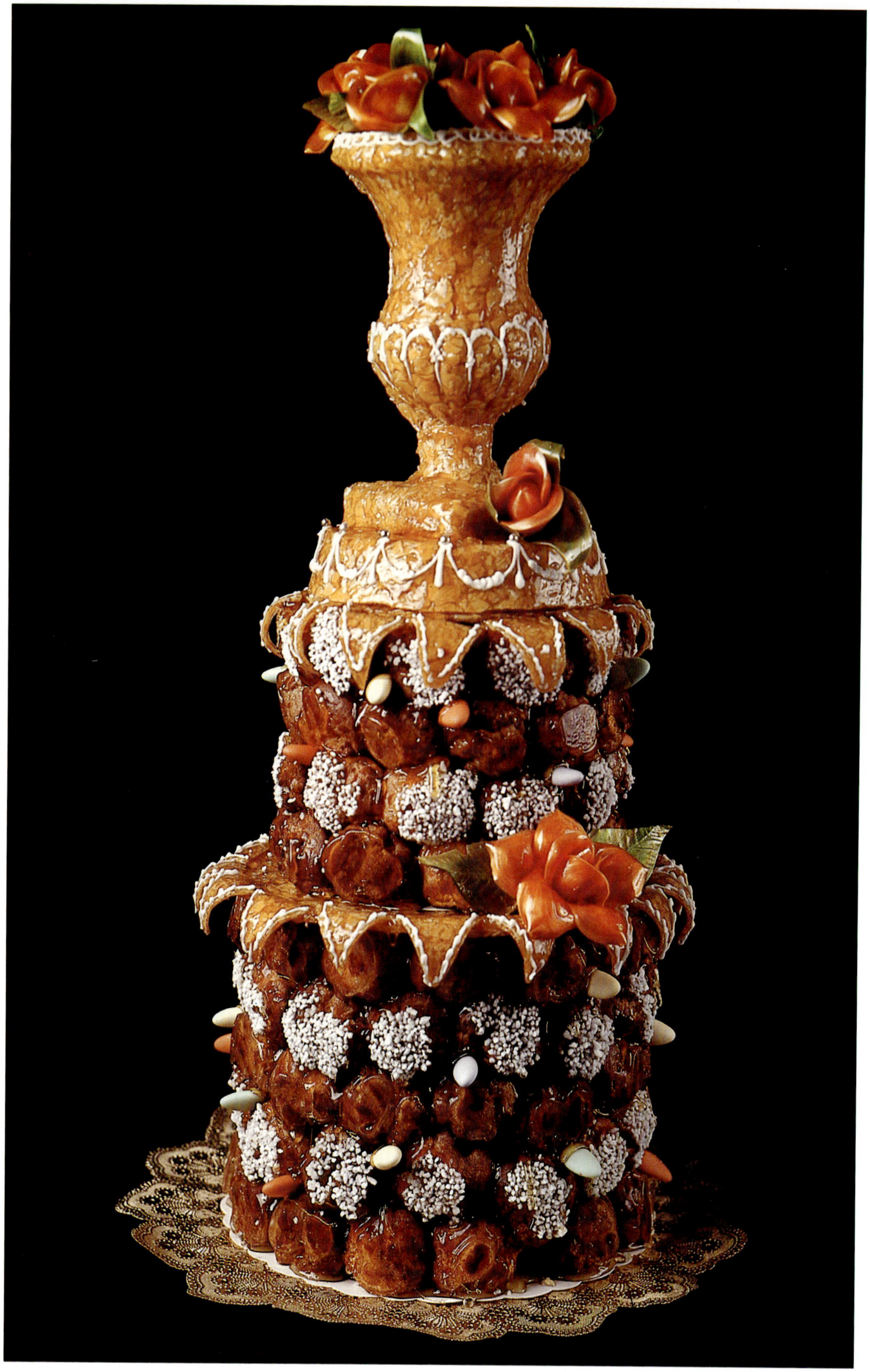

Assembling a Croquembouche

Photo 1: Assemble the croquembouche on a rigid cardboard, so the entire piece rests on a sturdy base. It can also be assembled directly on a nougatine disk or base.

Photo 2: The choux are arranged in rows; each progressive row is diminished by one chou.

Photo 3: The finished piece is decorated with dragées, pulled, molded, or caramel sugar flowers and leaves. Attach figurines with caramel. Place the croquembouche on a nougatine pedestal and decorate with royal icing.

Facing Page: Victory

Croquembouches 231

CHAPTER 5

Tiered Cakes and Presentation Pieces

Presentation Pieces

Presentation pieces prepared for celebrations and holidays offer the pastry chef the opportunity to display his or her talent, creativity, and knowledge.

There are few rules that govern the construction of a presentation piece. The pastry chef can use his or her imagination to reproduce and create pieces that represent the occasion celebrated and still respect the client's requests. Marzipan, chocolate, pastillage, nougatine, or sugar work in its varied forms—pulled, molded, blown, or poured—are used to obtain the desired effect.

Pastry chefs are often judged on the quality of their work on a presentation piece, as these are a true expression of their competence and experience. The chef's experience and personal taste will be deciding factors.

It is best to prepare a model before constructing the actual piece. A model allows the chef to work out the design and aids in the execution of the piece. It is equally important to decide which products and materials will be used for the decorations and where they will be placed.

Once this work is done, the piece is ready to be executed. As for all manual work, hands-on practice is the most effective way of learning, even more so than reading and studying. Especially because each pastry chef has a signature style.

Have all materials organized and ready when working. All the decorations are prepared in advance. By the day of the presentation, the piece is complete, with only the cake and assembly to be completed. Generally, the more elaborate pieces are assembled on site to facilitate transport and avoid breakage.

Certain pieces will have supports or columns to reinforce the structure, making it easier to assemble. The materials chosen will also play an important role in preparing the piece, as well as the types of molds, metal or plaster, used for different shapes.

The pastry chef must also devote considerable attention to the quality of the cake. Any cake base and filling may be used.

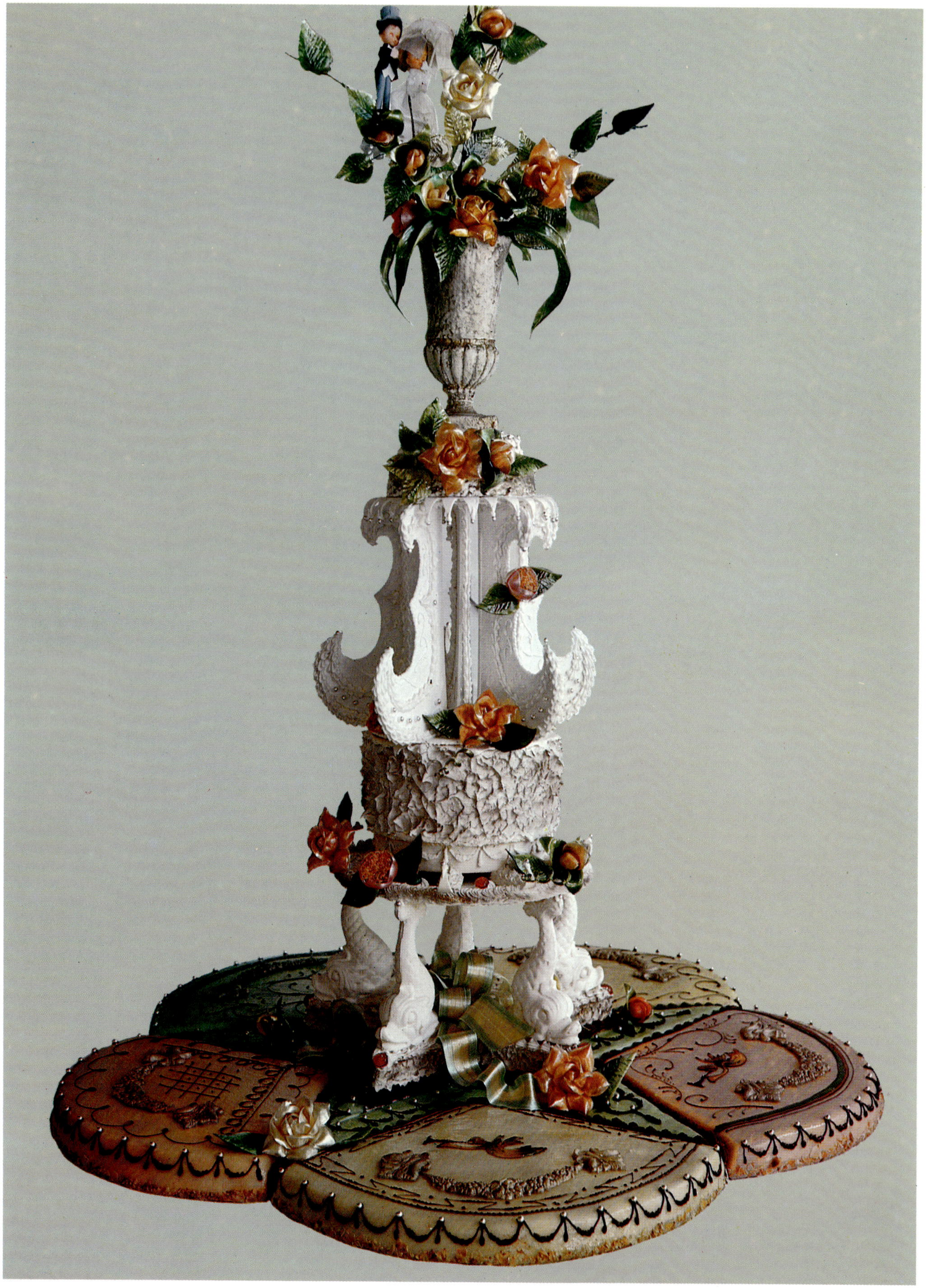

Presentation Piece

This piece measures 6.5 ft/2 m high, 5 ft/1.5 m wide, and is made in two sections.

1. The most important part of this piece is the presentation section. It is constructed on a base in the form of a star, glazed in fondant, or coated with colored marzipan. The star is made to look like a real cake. Molded pastillage in the form of a vase filled with a bouquet of pulled sugar flowers is placed on top.

2. The cake is set between the arms of the star.

A plywood base is needed in the shape of the cake. The outer part of the cake can be rounded to form a flower, or pointed to form a large star.

These cakes are made with layers of biscuit filled with mousseline or chiboust cream, generously garnished with poached or fresh fruit. The chiboust cream and simple syrup for moistening the biscuit are flavored to complement the fruits used in the cream.

Each cake is coated with a smooth layer of mousseline cream, then covered with a thin layer of marzipan, the color of which represents the flavor of the fruit used in the chiboust cream.

The cakes are chilled, then brushed with apricot glaze.

The decorations are made with chocolate icing piped with a paper cone. Some of the small designs can be filled in with different colored glazes. Molded marzipan can also be used for decorations.

Preparing the Presentation Piece

The base is given a star shape. It can be made out of plywood or styrofoam. First, coat with Italian meringue, then cover with marzipan. Decorate with chocolate icing, using a paper cone to imitate a real cake.

The pastillage centerpiece is composed of three parts:

1. Five dolphins attached to pastillage bases below and above.
2. Pastillage arabesques attached between pastillage bases and secured on both ends.
3. A pastillage vase.

The pastillage must be completely dried before assembly, making it necessary to prepare the pieces at least 8 days before. They are decorated with royal icing using a paper cone.

Place the star-shaped base flat on the presentation table. Assemble the pastillage pieces. Put a pulled sugar bouquet in the vase along with any figurines used. Affix several pulled sugar ribbons and/or flowers around the piece. Finish by placing the cakes around the base.

Chef's Note: *This piece can be easily transported unassembled.*

Facing Page: Presentation Piece

Tiered Cake Stands in Poured Sugar

Traditionally, tiered cakes were assembled on metal cake stands with several tiers (see French tiered cake, page 249). This is an expedient, although less creative, way of working. The pastry chef is limited to superimposing the cakes on the stand.

This technique confines the talent of the pastry chef, except when it comes to the final decoration. More personalized pieces can be made with poured sugar, which allows for greater originality.

The typical French cake stand is comprised of disks with a hole in the center for a post to pass through. Therefore, the cakes must fit each layer just right, with a hole cut out of the center. By contrast, poured sugar pieces can be assembled with cakes quickly prepared in cake rings. This is particularly helpful when there are time restrictions.

The poured sugar presentation stand can be prepared in advance, although the sections are usually assembled shortly before serving. This presentation can be particularly striking on a buffet table. This technique also works well with the style of the modern pastries.

The cakes are often filled with mousse, which is not always practical when working with the French cake stands. Poured sugar pieces are more delicate to transport, requiring greater care. The sections can be prepared and assembled in the pastry kitchen and transported separately. Place the sugar piece on the presentation table and set the cakes in place.

If proper precautions are taken, the poured sugar pieces are relatively sturdy, attractive, and can be made in infinite ways. They can be built with 4–7 tiers, for up to 100 people. For larger numbers of guests, it is best to prepare two separate pieces.

La Mistinguet Tiered Cake

Mistinguet was a celebrated French cabaret singer known for her descent down a long winding staircase when opening shows. This piece represents that effect. It is composed two principal sections:

1. A large poured sugar disk for the base.
2. A poured sugar piece which supports the cakes and imitates the winding staircase.

The height of each tier or level is equidistant, usually based on the height of the cake plus 1 in/3 cm For example, the cakes in the photo on page 240 are 2 1/3 in/6 cm tall with the additional 1 in/3 cm; the distance between the tiers is 3.5 in/9 cm.

Each step (tread) is made wider relative to the diameter of the poured sugar disks that support the cakes. The width of each step should always be wider (for example 3/4 in/2 cm) than the radius of the previous disk.

For presentation:

The first disk is 6.25 in/16 cm in diameter, with a 3 in/8 cm radius; the step is 4 in/10 cm long.

The second disk is 7 in/18 cm in diameter, with a 3.5 in/9 cm radius; the step is 4 1/3 in/11 cm long.

The third disk, with a 4 in/10 cm radius, will be set on a step 4.75 in/12 cm long.

The forth disk has a radius of 4 1/3 in/11 cm and will have a step 5 in/13 cm long. The last disk has a radius of 4.75 in/12 cm radius, with a step of 5.5 in/14 cm.

The poured sugar disks can have the same diameter as the cakes they are supporting, although generally they are made 3/4 in/2 cm larger so the cakes have a 1/2 in/1 cm border.

Preparation

To construct a poured sugar presentation piece, it is best to prepare a template after determining the number of cakes to be supported, the height and diameter of each, and distance between them. If available, use a flexible metal strip that can be easily shaped as seen on pages 330–333.

Pouring the Sugar

Place a sheet of aluminum foil or parchment paper on a flat work surface such as a pastry marble. Place the template on top. To secure the template, balance heavy objects on top to hold it flat against the paper or foil.

Pour the cooked sugar, made according to the recipe, inside the template. The thickness of the poured sugar will vary depending on the stability needed, usually between 2 1/3–4 in/6–10 cm. When the poured sugar begins to set, remove the template. To curve the poured sugar, slide it while still malleable on a cylinder, such as a large can, bucket, large pipe or tubing. Allow the poured sugar to set and remove the paper or foil.

For the base, pour a large disk. Before the base disk completely sets, place the poured sugar support on top so it rests evenly. This will help to ensure a solid adhesion between the base and the support.

Pour the poured sugar to the size needed for the disks that will support each cake. Make poured sugar triangles to help support the disks. Attach the disks, then the triangles, to the support piece.

(La Mistinguet Tiered Cake continued on next page)

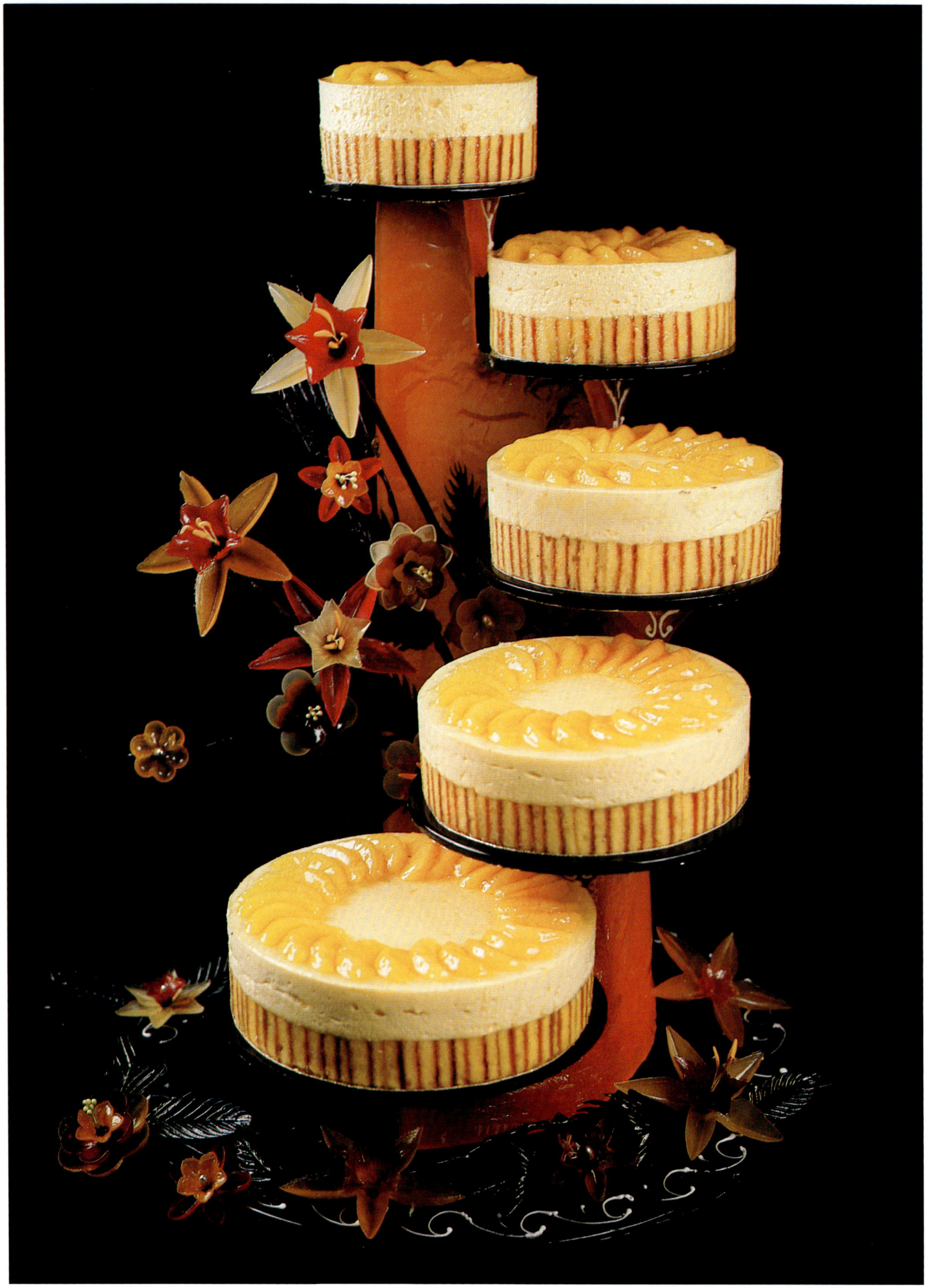

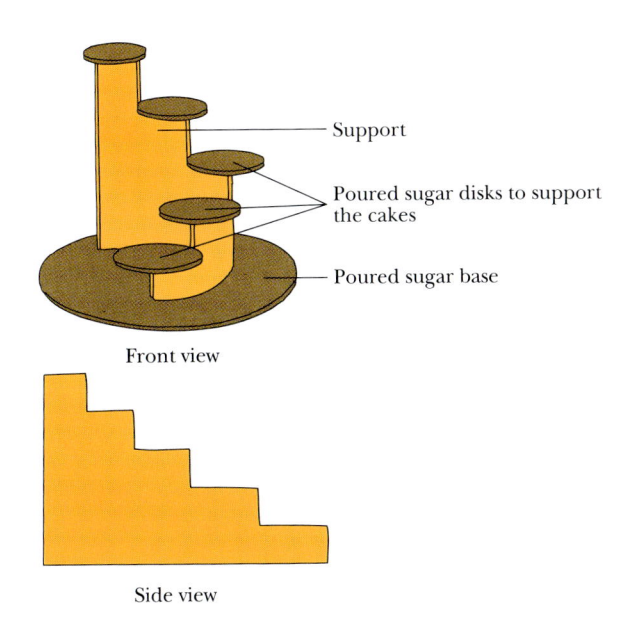

Front view

Side view

The accompanying diagram shows the poured sugar support before curving. The height of the tiers does not change; only the length of the tiers will vary depending on the size of the cakes used.

Presentation

Decorate the assembled piece with royal icing, using a paper cone. On the inside of the curve, position a bouquet of molded sugar flowers affixed to dried tree branches coated with cooked sugar. This decoration is independent of the cakes, making it easier to transport separately.

Place the piece on the presentation table and set the cakes on the support disks. It is recommended to place two cake cardboards under each cake. The two cardboards will prevent the cake from sticking to the poured sugar bases and make it easier to remove the cakes. This way the cakes can be easily lifted off the poured sugar base by sliding a metal spatula between the cardboards and removing the cake with the top cardboard. Remove the cake from the presentation piece before cutting to prevent the structure from breaking from the pressure of slicing.

Poured Sugar Disks and Triangles

Disks

Poured sugar pieces often use poured sugar disks as a base to support cakes. Lightly oiled tart or cake rings work well as a template in which the poured sugar is formed. The poured sugar disk should be slightly larger, approximately 3/4 in/2 cm, than the cake it is supporting. It should also be tinted darkly to show off the cake.

Triangles

Poured sugar triangles are used to brace a poured sugar piece and to provide balance. The sugar is poured onto aluminum foil between two lightly oiled parallel metal bars set 3–4 in/8–10 cm apart, or inside a lightly oiled rectangular metal tart frame. Before the sugar has completely set, remove the frame. With a large knife, cut the poured sugar into triangles of the size needed. The sugar should be hard but not brittle. Remove the aluminum foil.

Facing Page: La Mistinguet Tiered Cake

Open Book

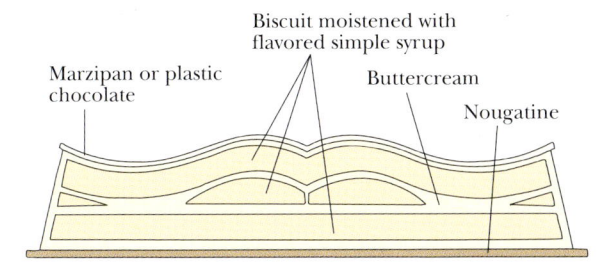

Marzipan or plastic chocolate
Biscuit moistened with flavored simple syrup
Buttercream
Nougatine

Open Book

This elegant presentation piece, made of layers of buttercream and biscuit, can be decorated to suit various occasions.

Roll out and cut a rectangular sheet of nougatine to serve as the book cover. Cut sheets of biscuit approximately 1 in/2.5 cm smaller than the nougatine. The cake is assembled directly on the sheet of nougatine or on a cake cardboard, which is considerably more practical.

The buttercream or mousseline cream filling is flavored to taste and can be garnished with either poached or candied fruit macerated in liqueur, or with crushed nougatine. The biscuit is moistened with simple syrup flavored to complement the filling.

To imitate an open book, place strips of biscuit between the layers of biscuit as needed to create the form desired.

Spread a smooth layer of buttercream over the entire cake. Refrigerate.

Draw horizontal lines on the side of the cake with a fine brush to give the appearance of pages. Tint the corners and center lightly with cocoa powder. Place the cake on top of the nougatine sheet if constructed on a cardboard.

Cover the top of each side of the cake with a sheet of rolled out marzipan or plastic chocolate, laying it flat on top. Cover with a second sheet of marzipan or plastic chocolate, this time lifting it at a few points to imitate pages in an open book.

Decorate with a paper cone, using chocolate, plain, and/or colored royal icing.

Chef's Note: *It is best to assemble very large books in two separate sections, constructing each half of the book separately. Place the two sections together on the presentation table.*

Closed Book or Agenda

This presentation is considerably simpler and faster to prepare than the open book. Several cakes can be prepared simultaneously for large gatherings on occasions such as New Year's.

Prepare two sheets of nougatine. One sheet is cut to serve as the top half of the book cover. The second sheet is cut for the bottom half, with extra width for the binding. The binding should be curved upward while still warm.

Assemble the cake on the bottom sheet of nougatine, the piece that has the binding. Place the top sheet of nougatine over the cake. Smooth the sides with buttercream. Pipe a decoration with buttercream or royal icing.

Modern French Pastry

Star

The large star can be used to celebrate a variety of occasions or to showcase a pastry shop window. This piece requires a star-shaped plywood board for the base. Cover the plywood with cardboard so the cake is not directly in contact with the wood. Cut sheets of biscuit to fit the shape needed, preparing three layers of biscuit. Use trimmings for the center of the star.

Buttercream, ganache, mousseline cream, mousse, or other fillings can be used between the biscuit layers.

After assembling the layers of biscuit and filling, coat the entire cake with a smooth layer of buttercream or Italian meringue. Cover with a thin layer of marzipan. Refrigerate.

Brush the top and sides with apricot glaze. Glaze the entire cake with a carefully prepared fondant.

Decorating with a Paper Cone

Delicate decorative work can be made with a paper cone, known in French as a "cornet." When applied with care, piping brings a very elegant look to a presentation piece, croquembouche, ceremonial piece, or centerpiece.

When piping is the principal decoration of a presentation, either for a private occasion or competition, it is important the work be performed with great care and attention. It is vital that the royal or chocolate icing have a perfect consistency. The piping cone should be tightly rolled. For a more distinguished decoration, the chocolate must be piped out as thin as possible. Any of several writing styles may be used. It is only through much practice and training that the skills needed for this work are acquired.

Facing Page: Star

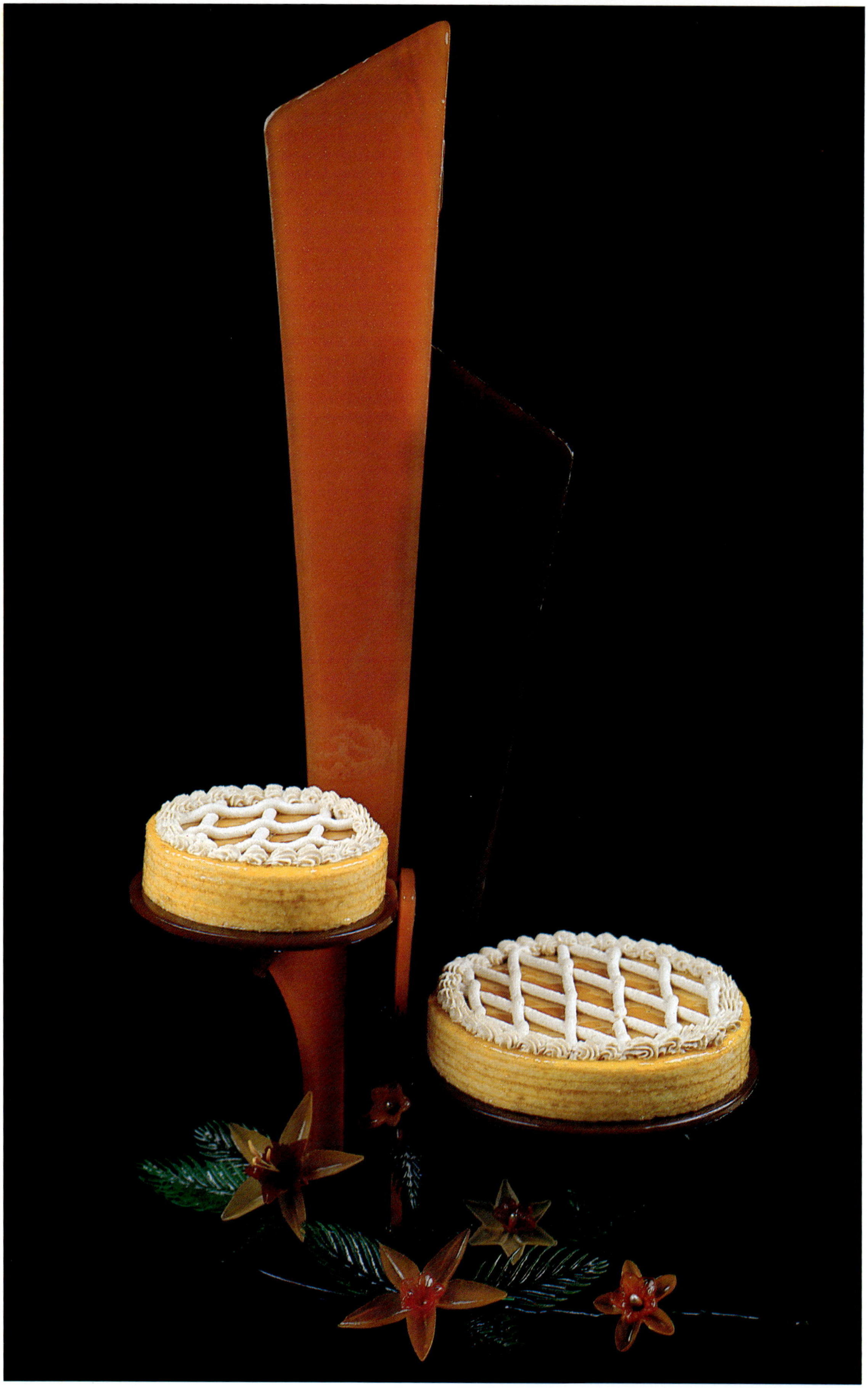

Cake Presentation

This poured sugar cake stand offers a simple, though attractive, way to present one to three cakes. The cakes can be the same or vary in size, serving up to 40 people. The largest cake is placed on the front pedestal.

It is prepared in three separate sections:

1. A poured sugar panel made up of two parts, each a different color.
2. A large poured sugar disk for the base.
3. Poured sugar supports and cake bases.

To prepare the back panel, bend a metal template into an elongated trapezoid; see the diagram below.

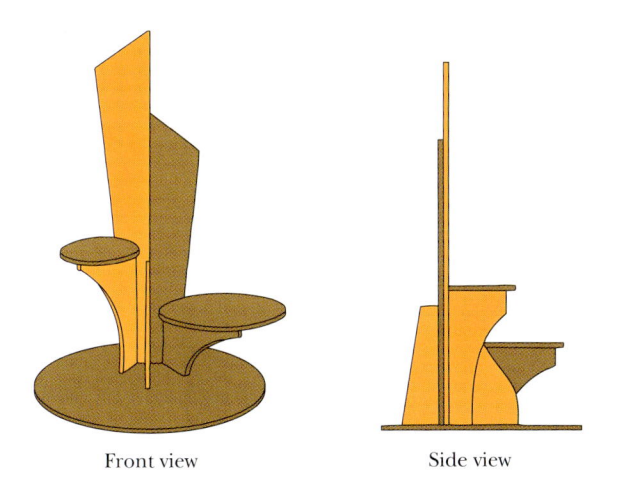

Front view   Side view

For the back panel, pour the lighter colored sugar into the template. After setting, unmold it. Turn the same template around so it faces the opposite direction and mold the darker poured sugar inside. Remove the template before the sugar has completely set; use a large knife to cut off approximately 6 in/15 cm from the bottom. Now there are two identically shaped panels, one shorter than the other. The cut-off section can be used as a back support.

For the base, mold a large disk of poured sugar. Pour three supports with the same template—one for the large cake (if more than one size is made), another for the smaller cake, and a third to support the large panels in front. Pour two disks for cake bases, each corresponding in size to the cakes.

Attach the two panels, superimposing the larger one in front of the smaller by approximately 1/2 in/1 cm. Dip the back of the bottom of the panels in cooked sugar and attach them to the base. Attach the front and back supports with caramel or cooked sugar so the panels stand erect.

Affix the support for the small cake base with cooked sugar, placing it on an angle approximately 45° to the larger panel. Affix the support for the larger cake also on a 45° angle to the panel, making sure the longer end is up for the disk to sit on. With poured sugar, attach the cake bases onto each support.

Place the piece on the table where it is to be presented. Position a few pulled or molded sugar flowers and leaves around the base of the piece. Set the cakes on their appropriate disks.

Facing Page: Cake Presentation

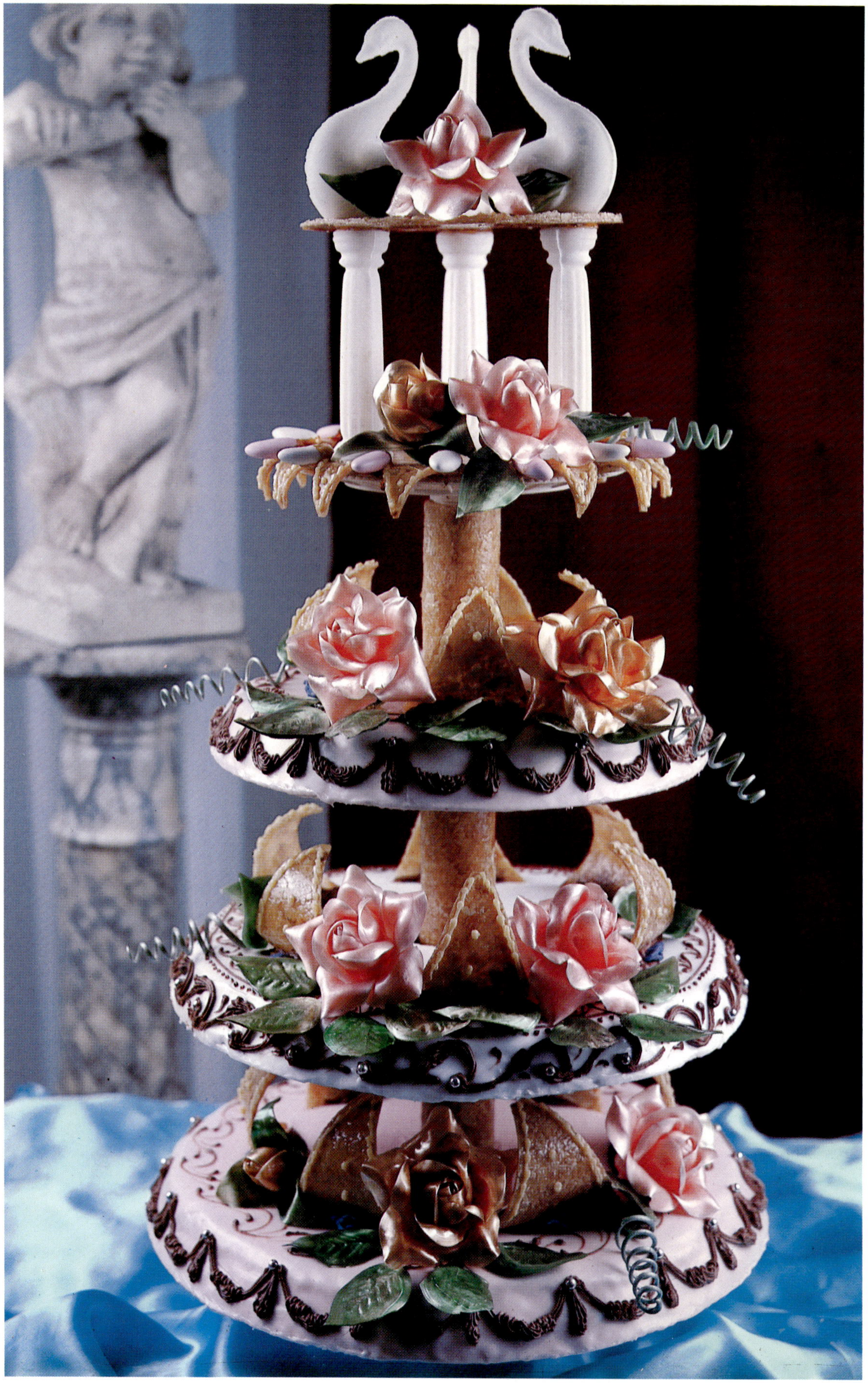

Classic French Tiered Cake

This is the most commonly used method in French pastry-making for presenting tiered cakes. A metal or plastic pedestal is used for the support.

The cakes are assembled and decorated separately on each tier. Biscuits or génoise are layered with buttercream, ganache, mousseline cream, or other filling of choice. The cakes can be flavored the same or differently from each other; the fondant coating should be colored to reflect the flavor of the cakes.

Each cake is coated with a smooth layer of buttercream, Italian meringue, or bombe batter. Refrigerate the cakes before glazing them. For a neat look, it is recommended to cover the top and sides of the cakes with a thin layer of marzipan before glazing. This will make it easier to evenly coat the cake with fondant and obtain a high sheen.

It is important that the marzipan and fondant layers be thin to maintain the elegance of the cakes.

Prepare rings of nougatine to wrap around the central post and nougatine wolf's teeth for decoration. For the top of the piece, cut out two disks of nougatine. Attach three sugar columns between them. Top with three sugar swans. Assemble the cakes on their appropriate tiers. Place a few pulled sugar flowers and leaves around the cakes to decorate.

Facing Page: Classic French Tiered Cake

Chocolate Icing No. 1

chocolate, ganache	17.5 oz	500 g
butter, softened	14 oz	400 g

Melt the chocolate in a proofing box or over a water bath system. Add the softened butter and whisk until smooth. Store this mixture at room temperature in an airtight container. It is ready to use for piping inscriptions and does not need to be heated.

Chocolate Icing No. 2

Pour very hot water over chopped chocolate, or chocolate pieces, without stirring. Set the mixture aside a few minutes, then pour out and discard the water that has not been absorbed. The chocolate will be soft but not fully melted. Add a bit of oil, stirring it in until the desired consistency is achieved.

Store this mixture at room temperature in an airtight container.

Chocolate Icing No. 3

Sift cocoa powder through a fine sieve. Stir in simple syrup, 30° baume, until the desired consistency is achieved. Although a fast procedure, this icing quickly forms a crust, making it necessary to freshly prepare it just before using.

Nougatine Jewelry Box

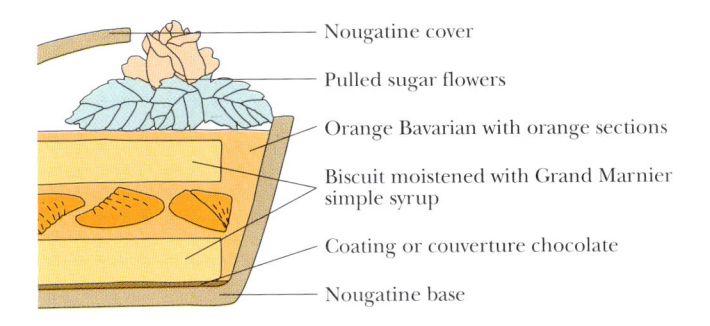

Nougatine cover
Pulled sugar flowers
Orange Bavarian with orange sections
Biscuit moistened with Grand Marnier simple syrup
Coating or couverture chocolate
Nougatine base

Nougatine Jewelry Box

This splendidly elegant cake may be served for any celebration.

It is best not to build the nougatine box larger then 13.5 in/35 cm in diameter, or it looses its delicate appearance. The piece is prepared in two separate sections:

1. The nougatine and pulled sugar work.
2. The biscuit and filling for the cake.

Line a génoise or cake mold with nougatine; the size can vary as needed. For the cover, cut a disk of nougatine slightly larger in diameter than the base. Place the still warm disk into a lightly oiled bowl, pressing down in the center of the nougatine until the desired curve is obtained. It is best to warm the bowl before molding to keep the nougatine malleable and prevent it from cracking.

Unmold the nougatine base. Wait for it to completely cool before assembling the cake inside. Layer biscuit, moistened with simple syrup flavored to taste, and buttercream, mousse, or other filling of choice.

With a paper cone, pipe royal icing or buttercream decorations on the nougatine. Place several pulled sugar flowers and leaves on the bottom half, and place the nougatine cover on top, set ajar to reveal the flowers. Attach pulled sugar flowers and leaves to the top of the cover.

Chef's Note: *The flowers can be prepared in pulled or molded sugar, or marzipan.*

Variation

Construct the nougatine bottom and cover pieces as above. With a pastry brush, lightly coat the inside of the nougatine bottom with coating chocolate or liquid couverture. Place a layer of biscuit or génoise, 1/2 in/1 cm thick, inside. Moisten with simple syrup flavored with Grand Marnier, Cointreau, Curaçao, or other orange liqueur. Spread a layer of orange Bavarian and scatter orange or mandarin sections on top. Cover with a second layer of génoise or biscuit, moistened with the simple syrup. Spread a layer of the Bavarian Cream. Refrigerate.

Finish decorating using the procedure above.

Orange Bavarian
Bavariose à l'Orange

orange juice	35 oz	1,000 g
dessert gelatin	5.5 oz	150 g
Grand Marnier extract	1 tbsp 2 tsp	200 g
heavy cream, whipped	53 oz	1,500 g

Orange Meringue

egg whites	8	8
sugar	17.5 oz	500 g
orange juice	14 oz	400 g
apricot glaze	1.5 oz	40 g

Warm half of the first orange juice, 17.5 oz/500 g, with the dessert gelatin to 104°F/40°C. Remove from heat and add the remaining orange juice and the extract.

Prepare an Italian meringue by cooking the orange juice, sugar, and apricot glaze to 250°F/121°C, while whipping the egg whites to soft peaks. Pour the cooked sugar in a fine stream, whipping it into the egg whites. Continue whipping until the meringue has completely cooled. Fold the meringue into the mixture. Whip the heavy cream to soft peaks and fold it into the batter. This Bavarian should be used shortly after it is prepared.

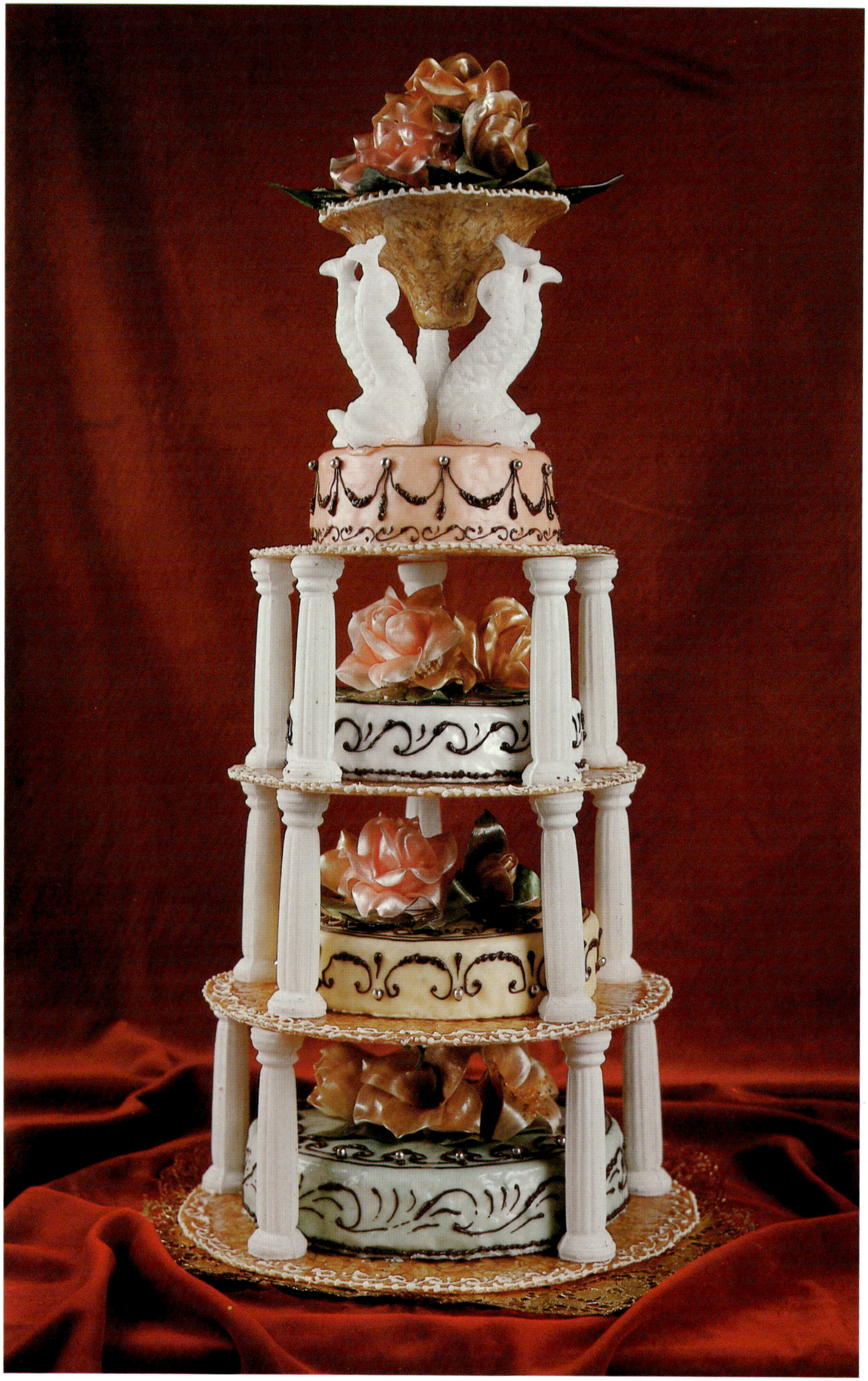

Spanish Tiered Cake

This is perhaps the oldest style of tiered cakes still made today. No metal or plastic structure is used as for the classic French presentation pieces. Instead, the cakes are prepared separately, progressively smaller or equal in size. Regardless of the size of the cakes, the procedure remains the same.

This piece is constructed in two sections:

1. The cakes are prepared, filled, and flavored according to taste. They are glazed with fondant, the color of which can be the same for all or colored to reflect the flavors used in the cakes. They are decorated using a paper cone with chocolate or royal icing.

2. Cut out nougatine disks, 2.5–3 in/7–8 cm larger in diameter than the cake it is meant for. Prepare five columns in blocked sugar for each tier. They must be exactly the same size and height so the piece will be level.

The decoration on the top tier is made from five blocked sugar dolphins that support a nougatine bowl filled with pulled sugar flowers.

Place the first and largest nougatine disk on the presentation table. Place the cake in the center. With cooked sugar, attach the five columns to the nougatine disk, spacing them evenly around the outside of the cake so they stand erect.

Place the second nougatine disk on top of the columns. It is not necessary to attach it with the cooked sugar, making it easier to disassemble the piece when cutting the cake. Repeat the same procedure as for the first tier, placing the cake in the center with the columns attached around it with cooked sugar. If the disks are progressively smaller, set the columns inward so the disk above will rest over the columns. Continue constructing the tiers, repeating the same steps for each.

This technique creates a solid structure as the weight of the cakes is supported by the columns and not the nougatine. However, it is obviously more fragile than pieces made with metal cake stands. Therefore, it is recommended not to build more than 4 or 5 tiers. The figurine on top can be modified to suit the occasion.

Chef's Note: *The nougatine disks can be replaced with poured sugar disks which provide greater strength.*

Facing Page: Spanish Tiered Cake

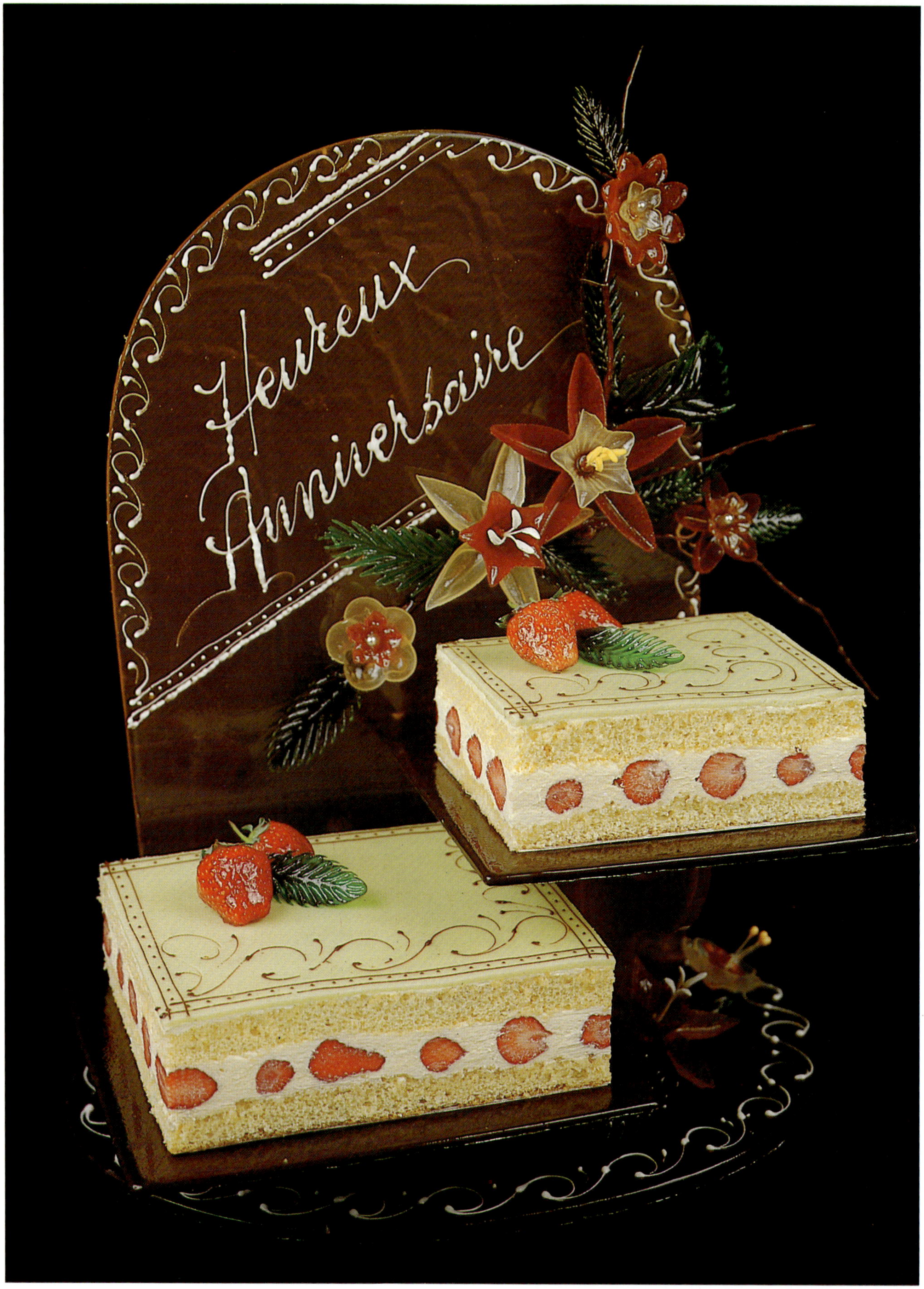
Heureux
Anniversaire

Cake Presentation

This cake stand is fairly easy to assemble. It is intended for two or three cakes. If more cakes are needed, place them around the base of the piece. Inscriptions for birthdays, anniversaries, or other events may be made on the back panel.

The same cakes are used for each tier. Although round cakes can be used, this better lends itself to square or rectangular cakes. The cake shown here is the fraisier (a strawberry/buttercream cake).

The piece is prepared in three sections:

1. The poured sugar back panel, oval as seen here, with a flat bottom to attach to the base. It may also be rectangular or square. Prepare a back support for the panel.

2. The poured sugar cake bases and supports. The cake bases should be given the same shape as the cakes.

3. The poured sugar base, round or square.

Prepare the metal templates, shaping them as needed (see pages 330–333). The back panel can be lightly or darkly colored, depending on the color of the cakes. The base and cake bases can be colored differently.

Use cooked sugar to attach the back panel to the base, then the back support to the panel and base. Attach the cake supports, with one end affixed to the cake bases, one to the back panel, and the third side to the presentation base.

Decorate the poured sugar with royal icing using a paper cone, and pulled or molded sugar flowers and leaves. Position the piece on the presentation table, then set the cakes in place.

Poured Sugar Columns

In the poured sugar section which begins on page 291, various techniques are shown for preparing and using poured sugar. For small pieces such as swans, columns, and dolphins, there exists a very simple procedure that offers excellent results.

Lightly oil tin or copper molds (such as those for chocolate). Two halves are needed for a solid two-sided piece. Fit the two halves together, securing them with clips.

Melt fondant in a saucepan, stirring constantly until very hot. Be careful to keep it opaque and prevent it from caramelizing. Pour the hot fondant into the mold. Wait several minutes for the fondant to firm. Remove the clips holding the two sides together, then unmold.

In the same pan, reheat remaining fondant. Add more fondant, if necessary, and fill another set of molds. Simply re-oil the mold each time before pouring in the fondant. Continue to mold as many figures as needed. This technique offers a fast way of preparing several of the same figures since the saucepan does not need to be cleaned between molding, and the fondant will reheat quickly once it has been cooked.

Facing Page: Cake Presentation

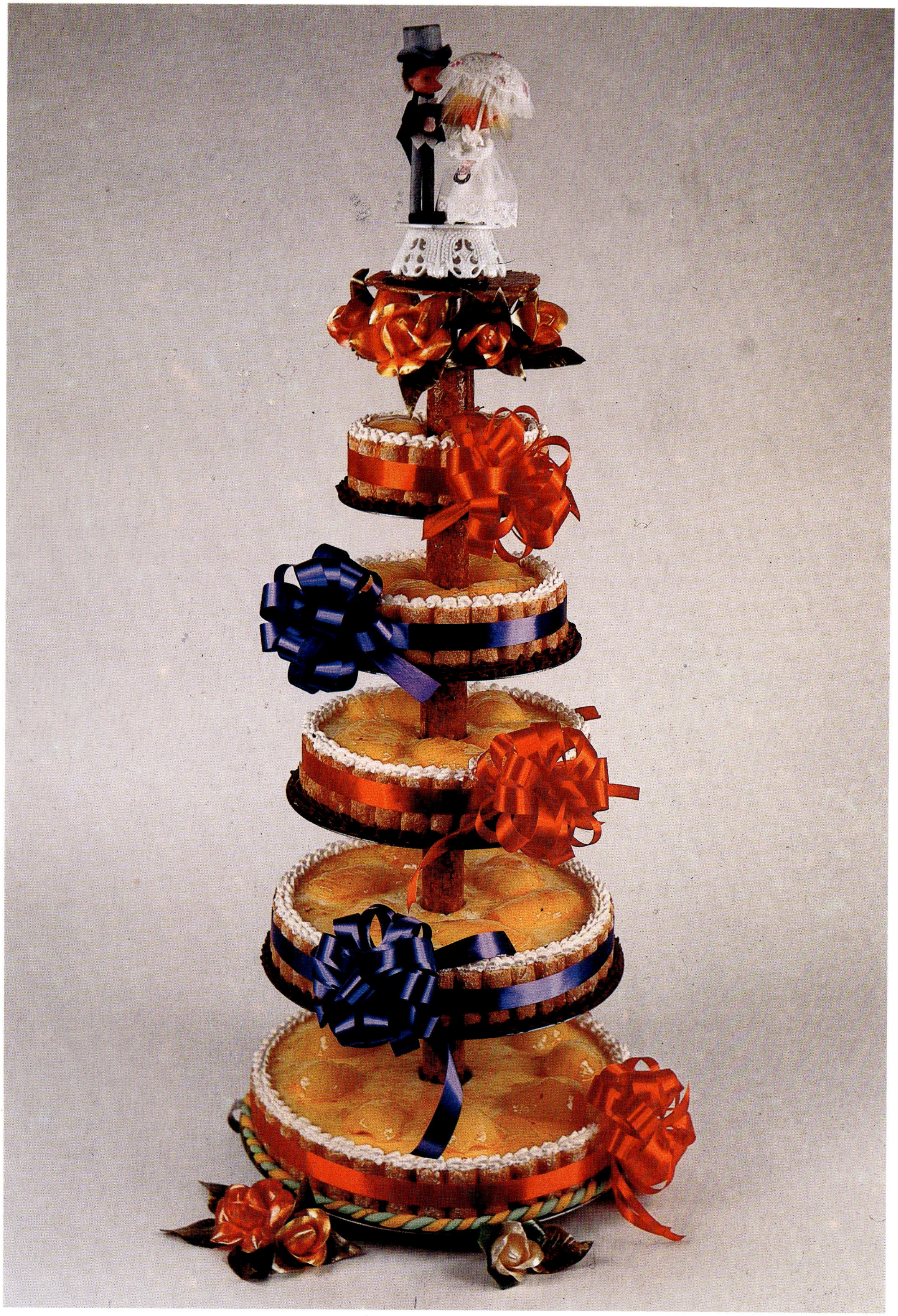

Tiered Charlottes

This is a modern, simple, and quick way of presenting tiered cakes. The cakes presented here are pear charlottes. Of course, any flavored charlotte and fruit can be used. It is also possible to use differently flavored cakes for each tier, such as lemon, blackcurrant, prune, orange, pineapple, strawberry, and pear. This offers the guests a choice and enhances the decoration with the assorted colors and textures of the fruit.

A tiered metal cake stand with round support disks is needed. As the disks are mounted, the next disk should be 1/2 in/1.5 cm smaller than the previous disk.

Place a cake cardboard over each disk, cutting a hole in the center for the central support post. Place a cake ring on each disk and line them with joined ladyfingers. Place a layer of biscuit or génoise inside the ring and spread a layer of filling. Repeat with a second layer of biscuit or génoise and finish with a layer of filling. Refrigerate.

Prepare nougatine to wrap around the central post when assembling the piece. For the top, prepare a nougatine base to support figurines or pulled sugar flowers.

Remove the cake rings and decorate the charlottes with fruit that correspond to the filling. Brush with apricot or jelly glaze. With a pastry bag and fluted tip, pipe a border of chantilly on the top edge of the cakes. Wrap a cloth ribbon around each cake.

To hide the metal support disks at the edge of the cakes, pipe a border of ganache, or twist two strips of differently colored marzipan around each other. With a dough cutter, cut a hole in the center of each cake for the center support.

Assemble the cake tiers on their respective disks, wrapping the nougatine around the central post. Finish by setting the decorative piece on top.

Chef's Note: *The number of tiers can vary according to the number of guests.*

Generally, a fruit coulis is served on the side.

Opera Presentation Piece

This poured sugar presentation piece is fairly easy to construct. For the best presentation, set up 3–5 cakes gradually decreasing in size. For this piece, modern style cakes are most appropriate. This cake typically serve 50–80; if more servings are needed, place additional cakes around the base of the piece.

The construction is based on three principal sections:

1. Four poured sugar supports, each taller than the previous one.
2. One large poured sugar disk for the base.
3. Four poured sugar cake disks.

(Opera Presentation Piece continued on page 259)

Facing Page: Tiered Charlottes

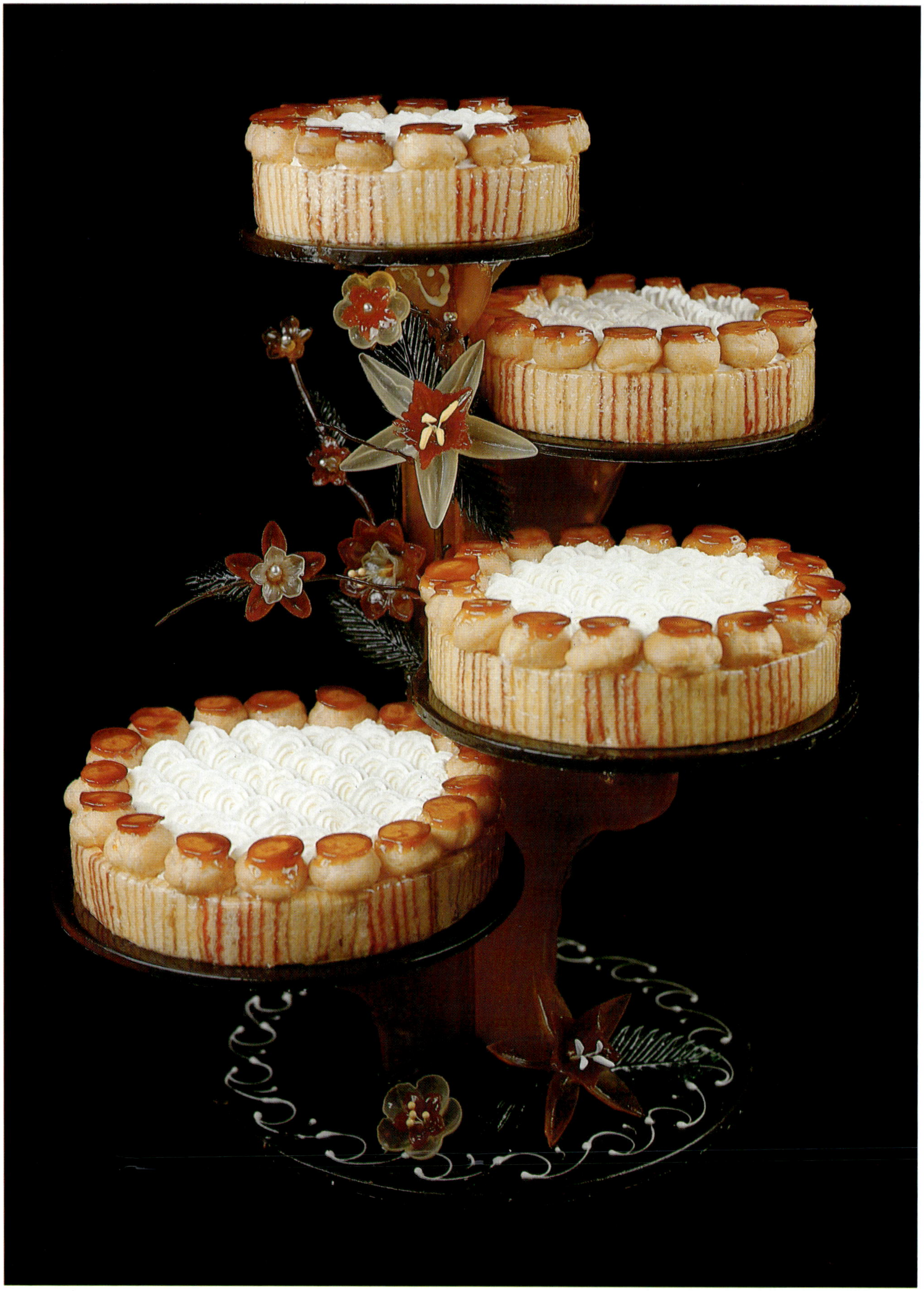

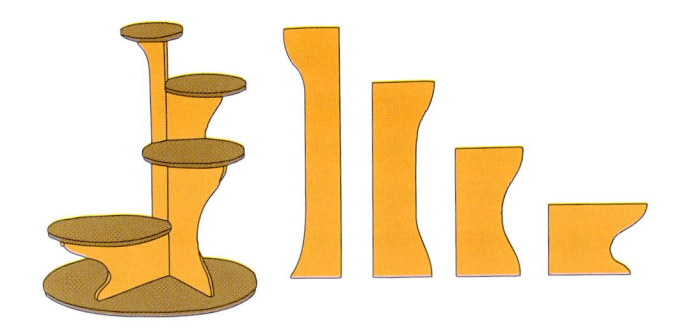

To prepare the cake supports, shape templates to the desired form (shown in the diagram above). Although the shape may vary, the technique remains the same. The different supports should be lightly colored and differ 4 in/10 cm in height from one to the next.

Prepare the poured sugar in a darker color for the base disk and the cake disks. Each cake disk should be 3/4 in/2 cm larger than the cake for which it is intended to support.

Use cooked sugar to attach the tallest support to the center of the base. Immediately afterwards, attach the second tallest support, affixing the long edge against the first support and the base to the bottom. Continue attaching the other two supports with this procedure. The four pieces affixed to each other assure stability.

Use cooked sugar to attach the cake bases; then attach poured sugar triangles. The triangles give greater stability to the bases.

Place the piece on the presentation table. Decorate with pulled sugar flowers and leaves. Set the cakes in place.

Chef's Note: *Each cake should be placed over two cake cardboards to prevent the cakes from sticking to the sugar disks. Slip a spatula between the cardboards, removing the cakes with the top cardboard. Then cut the cakes. They should not be cut directly on the piece, as it is too fragile.*

Tiered Wedding Cake

This is a modern wedding presentation with which any type of cake may be used. Fairly simple to assemble, it can be decorated to suit other occasions as well. The number and size of the cakes can vary as needed, between 3 and 7 tiers. For more than 100 servings, it is best to place additional cakes around the base of the piece to create an impressive display.

The preparation is composed of three sections:

1. Prepare a poured sugar descending form as for the Mistinguet (see page 239).
2. Large round or oval poured sugar base.
3. Poured sugar disks for the cakes and a small disk to support figurines.

Use a template cut to the size and shape needed for the staircase.

Follow the procedures and precautions given for the Mistinguet. The basic difference here is that the support piece is straight rather than curved. The rise of each step will be the same but the length of each step will depend on the size of the cakes used. Follow the calculations given for the Mistinguet.

Pour the sugar into templates on an even, flat pastry marble or work surface covered with aluminum foil. When the sugar has hardened, remove the template.

(Tiered Wedding Cake recipe continued on page 261)

Facing Page: Opera Presentation Piece

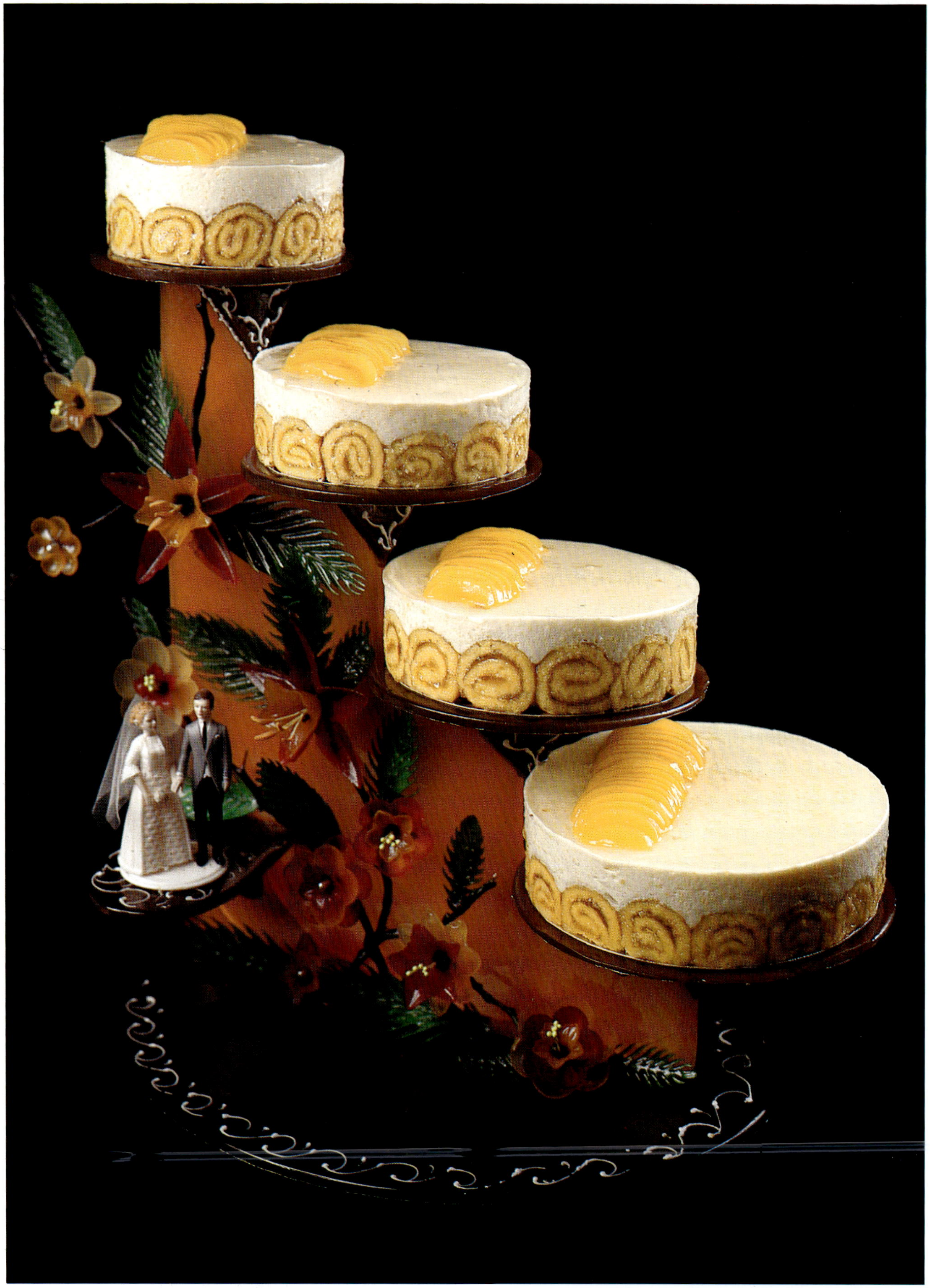

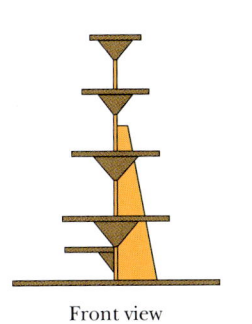

Front view 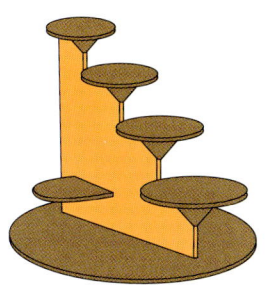   Side view

Follow this procedure for the large base disk. Before the base has completely set, attach the staircase. Attach a poured sugar triangle behind the piece for support. Affix the cake base disks to the staircase. Use caramel to attach poured sugar triangles under the disks for support. Attach the small poured sugar disk for the figurines to the side. Use a poured sugar triangle to give extra strength.

Decorate with pulled or molded sugar flowers, and royal icing piped with a paper cone. Set the figurine in place.

Place the piece on the presentation table. Set the cakes in place, each on two cake cardboards to facilitate removing and cutting. Place a metal spatula between the two cardboards and remove the cake, since the piece is too fragile to directly cut on.

Cooked Sugar or Caramel

When assembling poured sugar or croquembouches presentation pieces, directions will often indicate to attach two pieces together with cooked sugar or caramel. In both cases, the sugar is cooked to a minimum of 302°F/150°C (hard crack). Caramel is a sugar that has taken on color during the cooking process. Sugar cooked to a hard crack stage (150°C or more) and is uncolored is preferable for assembling sugar pieces. Caramel, whether golden or amber, works just as well, although the darker the caramel, the more likely it might soften after it has been applied.

Facing Page: Tiered Wedding Cake

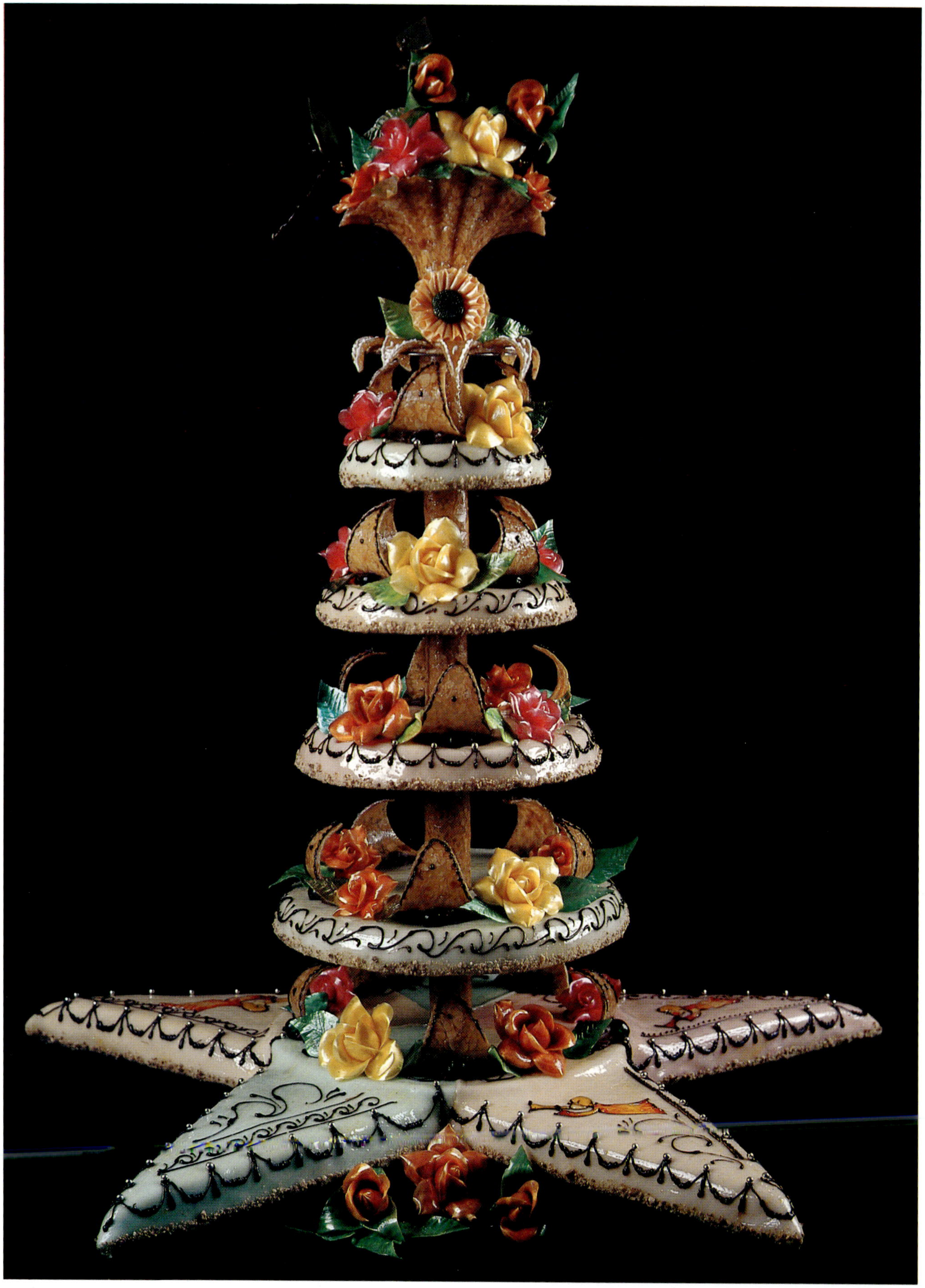

Classic French Tiered Cake

The tiered cake shown here is set over a star-shaped cake. It is necessary to have a wood or plywood star-shaped base on which to assemble the cake. The center of all the tiered cakes, as well as the base cake and the plywood base, will have a hole for the central post to pass through.

Assemble the cakes with layers of biscuit and mousseline cream generously scattered with fruit, such as poached pears or peaches, or fresh strawberries, or raspberries. Moisten the biscuit with simple syrup flavored to correspond to the fruit in the mousseline cream. This cake works well for this style of presentation.

Coat the top and sides of each cake with the mousseline cream. Cover each with a thin layer of marzipan, the color of which should correspond to the fruit used in the cakes. Refrigerate.

Coat the cakes with apricot glaze using a pastry brush. Decorate with chocolate icing using a paper cone. Press ground, toasted almonds around the bottom of the cakes. Note that these cakes are not glazed with fondant.

Prepare nougatine to conceal the central post and prepare nougatine wolf's teeth and a nougatine basket to hold the bouquet of flowers.

Place the star-shaped cake over the metal base of the cake pedestal. Assemble the rest of the pedestal with the cakes. Top with the nougatine vase filled with a bouquet of pulled sugar flowers. Place several pulled sugar flowers around the cakes.

Facing Page: Classic French Tiered Cake

Preparing Cakes to be Glazed with Fondant

To successfully glaze a cake with fondant, the cake must be carefully prepared. Assemble the cake on a cake cardboard or other sturdy tray. The top and sides should be as smooth as possible.

Several methods may be used for glazing:

1. Smooth the top and sides of the cake with buttercream and freeze. Glaze with fondant. This method requires some skill and is only suitable for small cakes.

2. Spread a thin layer of buttercream and cover with a thin layer of marzipan. Refrigerate. Brush with apricot glaze, then glaze with fondant. This method is particularly recommended for large cakes.

3. This is perhaps the most expedient method. Cover and smooth the top and sides of the cake with a firm Italian meringue. The meringue spreads on smoothly and is more resistant to melting under warm conditions than buttercream. Freeze. Glaze with fondant.

The meringue can be replaced with a bombe batter following the same procedure and offering identical results.

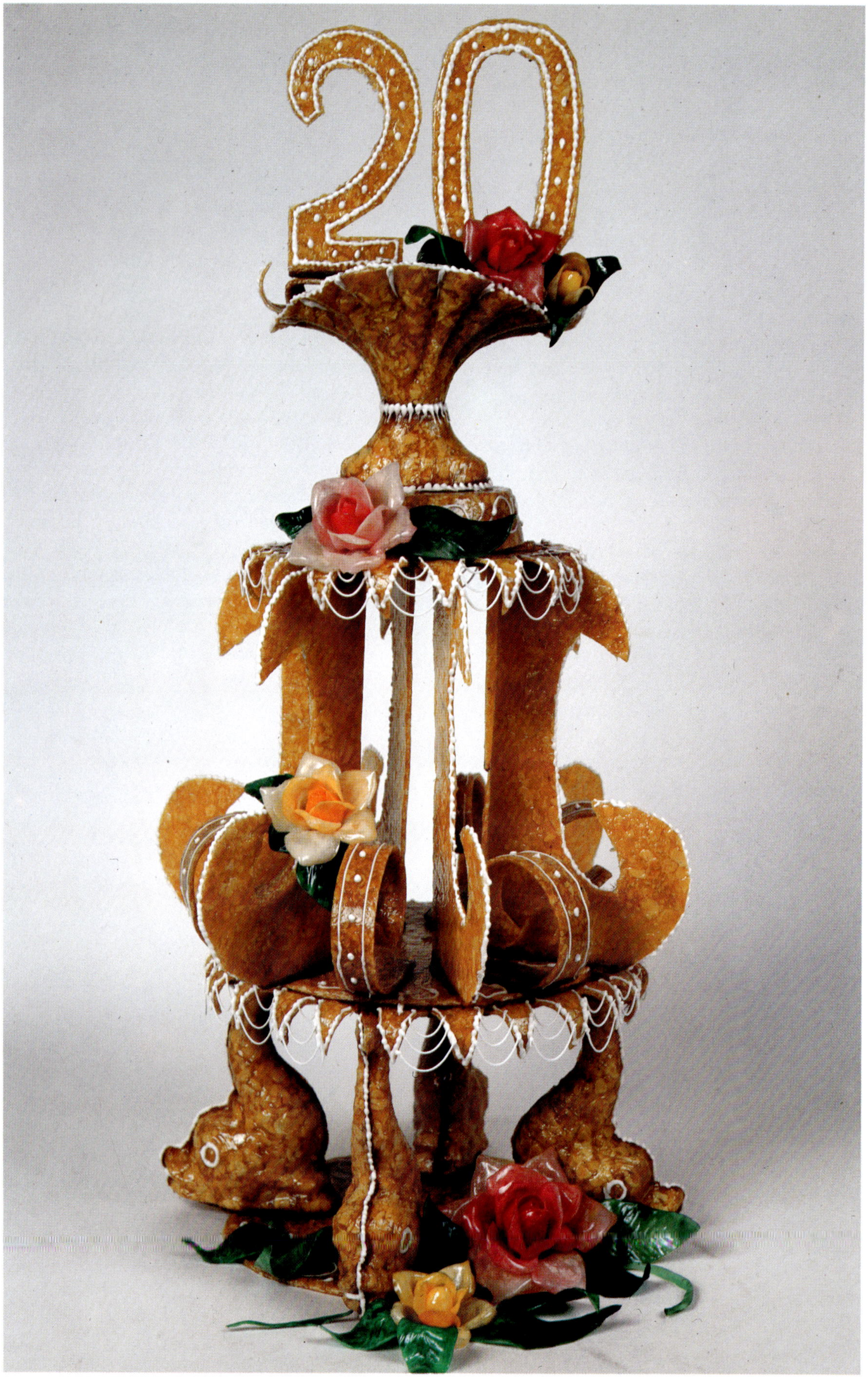
20

Nougatine Presentation Piece

This piece is intended for anniversaries or birthdays, although it can be decorated for other occasions. Constructed in three separate sections, it is transported in pieces and assembled on the presentation table.

1. Cut out two nougatine disks. Mold four or five dolphins in nougatine. Prepare the nougatine wolf's teeth. Assemble the bottom half with cooked sugar.

2. Cut out two nougatine disks. The top disk is smaller than the bottom disk. Cut out nougatine decorations. Assemble the middle section of the piece with cooked sugar.

To attach the wolf's teeth, turn the second section upside down on a lightly oiled pastry marble or other work surface. The top disk should lay flat on the marble. Attach the wolf's teeth, pointing upward, with cooked sugar. Turn the disk upright so the teeth are now pointing downward.

3. Form the basket in a mold for that purpose and the base in a génoise mold. For an anniversary or birthday, use a pattern to cut nougatine numbers to represent the years being celebrated. Assemble this third section with cooked sugar.

Decorate each separate section with royal icing. Assemble the piece on the presentation table. Decorate with pulled, turned, or molded sugar flowers.

Chef's Note: *This piece can also be assembled on a tiered cake stand. The assembly will be fairly simple and sturdier. Be sure to conceal all metal parts of the cake stand with nougatine.*

Facing Page: Turned Sugar Flowers and Leaves

Nougatine Roses

Nougatine roses can be used to decorate nougatine pieces. They can also be frozen then coated with chocolate using a spray gun for a velvet texture.

glucose	*14 oz*	*400 g*
confectioners' sugar	*17.5 oz*	*500 g*
cocoa butter, chopped	*1 oz*	*30 g*
almonds, sliced and lightly roasted	*10.5 oz*	*300 g*

In a saucepan, melt the glucose, add the confectioners' sugar, and cook to a golden caramel. Stir in the chopped cocoa butter. Remove from heat and add the slightly chopped almonds. Pour the mixture onto an oiled pastry marble or other work surface and work with a pastry triangle.

Roll the nougatine very thin. Cut out circles with a round cookie cutter. Set the nougatine circles on a non-stick pan or lightly oiled sheet pan. Place them in the oven for a few seconds until softened. With a rolling pin, flatten the edges and prepare a rose using the same technique as for marzipan. The nougatine is worked under a heat lamp or near an open oven.

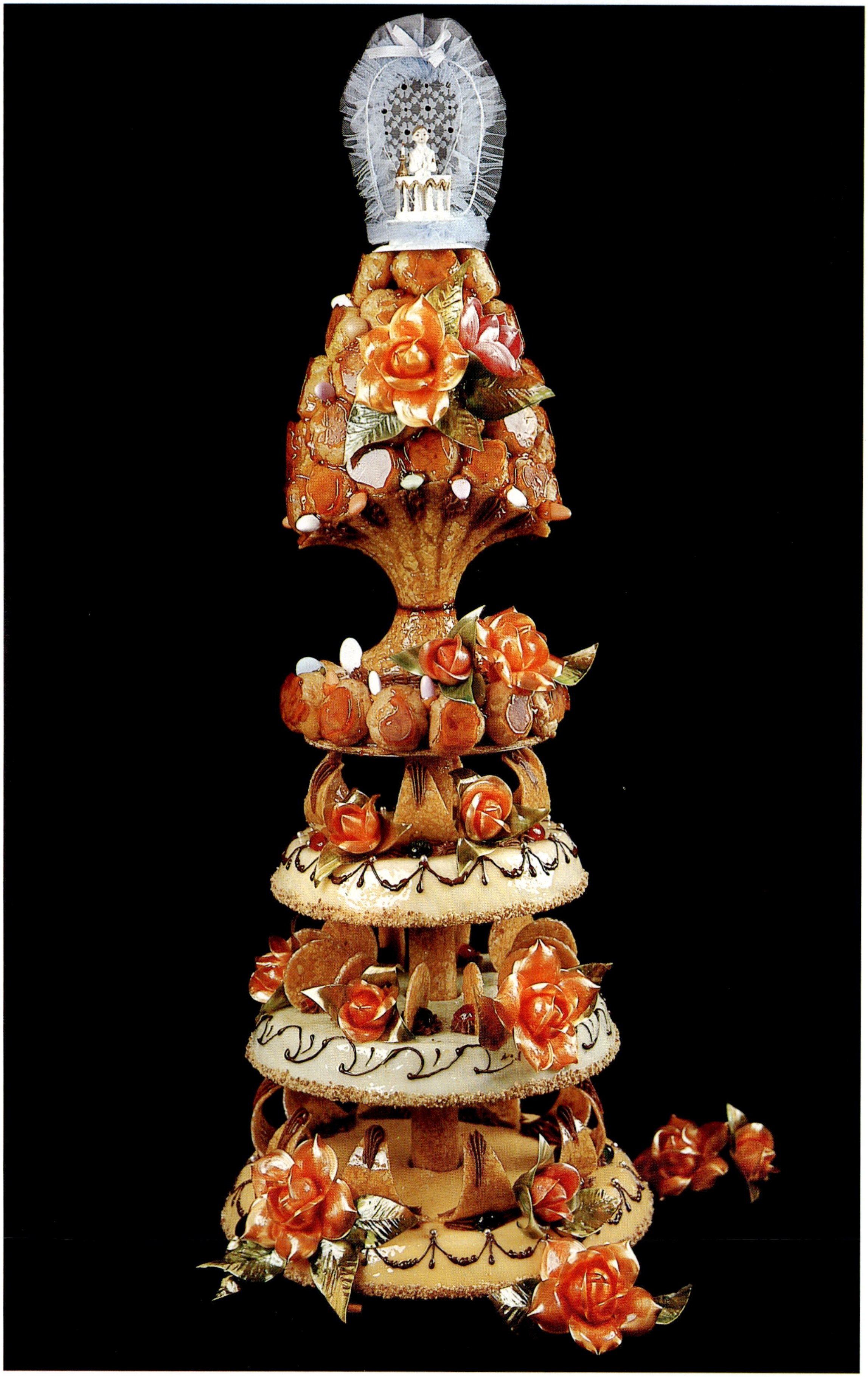

La Gaillacoise Tiered Cake

The name for this tiered cake comes from Gaillac, a city in the southwest of France. The presentation is particularly appropriate for family occasions like weddings, birthdays, and anniversaries.

It is constructed in two sections:

1. A traditional French tiered cake.
2. A classic or original croquembouche set on a vase, disk, or other nougatine base.

This piece is made with two to five tiers, according to the number of guests. It is important that the diameter of the top cake tier be slightly larger than the base of the croquembouche.

Assemble the cakes on cake cardboards placed directly on the metal disks of the cake stand. The cardboard will prevent the cakes from touching the metal of the stand. Biscuit or génoise is generally layered with mousseline cream generously filled with poached fruit such as apricots, cherries, prunes, pineapple, peaches, or fresh fruit such as strawberries or raspberries. Match the flavor of the mousseline with the fruit and simple syrup used to moisten the biscuit or génoise.

Smooth a layer of mousseline cream over the top and sides of the cake. Cover the cake with a thin layer of marzipan, the color of which should reflect the flavor used in the filling. Brush with apricot glaze. Decorate with chocolate icing using a paper cone. Place small nougatine circles and/or wolf's teeth on and around the cakes.

Chef's Note: *The cakes here are not coated with fondant, which would be too sweet.*

Constructing the Croquembouche

Although any croquembouche, including those given in Chapter 4 in this book, may be used for this section, a simple conical shape is shown here. The croquembouche is assembled on the top metal tier of the cake stand. It is important that the diameter of the base not be larger than that of the metal disk.

On the presentation table, assemble the cakes on the cake stand. Place the croquembouche on the top tier. Attach pulled sugar flowers with cooked sugar to the croquembouche and set them on and around the cakes. Top with an appropriate figurine.

Facing Page: La Gaillacoise Tiered Cake

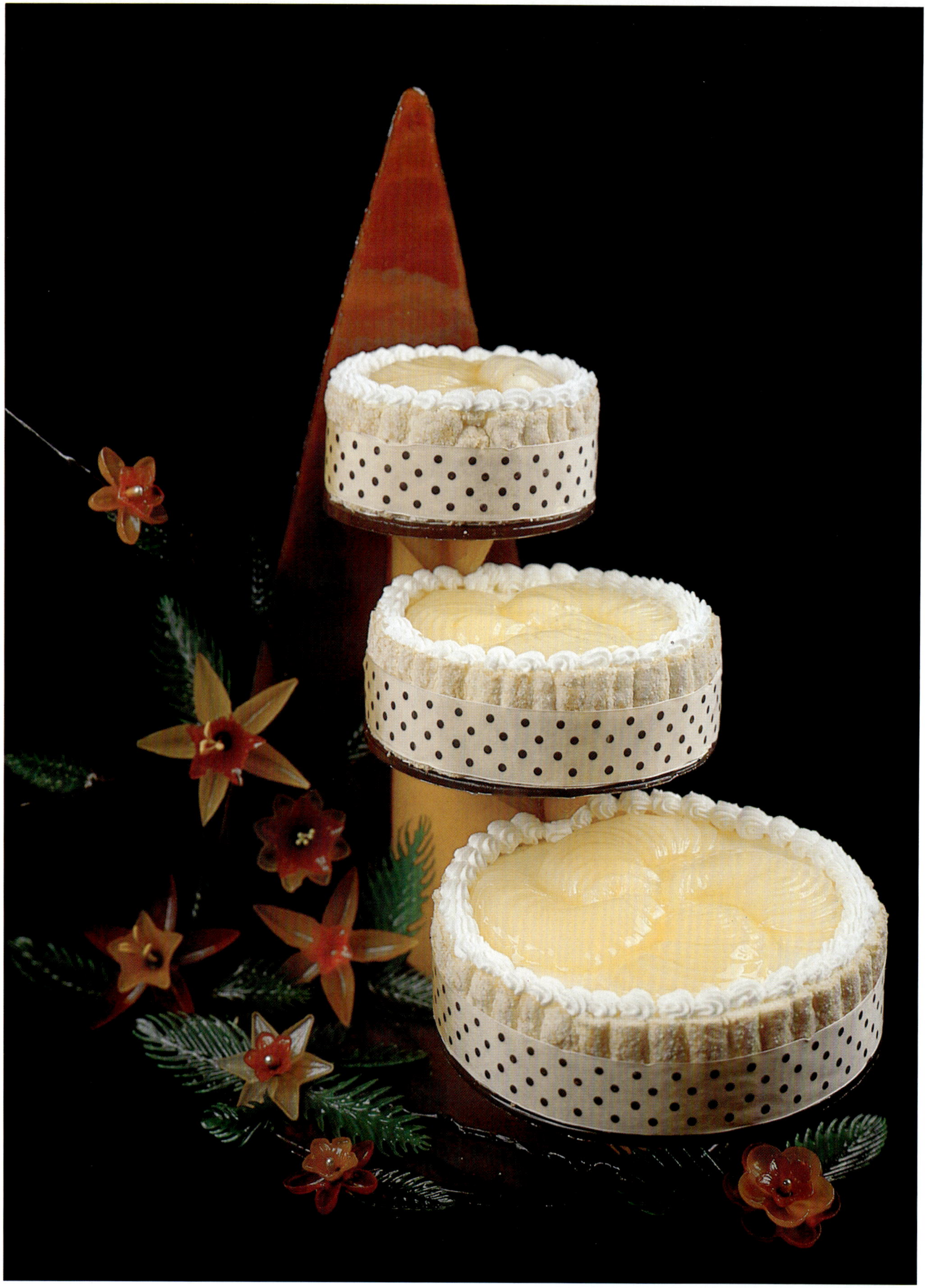

Poured Sugar Presentation Podium

This piece is assembled following the same procedure given for the wedding piece (see page 259), with a few alterations. Although fairly solid, the piece should not be made for more than 4–5 cakes. If more cakes are needed, place them around the base.

This piece is constructed in four separate sections:

1. A stair-shaped support with two to four tiers.
2. A triangle-shaped back support to strengthen the structure.
3. A round base upon which the structure is assembled.
4. Poured sugar disks, the sizes of which correspond to the sizes of the cakes.

Use a template to mold the poured sugar for the staircase and triangle. These two pieces should be colored differently. Pour out the base and cake base disks.

Use cooked sugar to attach the back triangle perpendicular to the staircase. Set both onto the base before it has completely set. Affix a small triangle with cooked sugar as an extension to each step to assure greater stability. Attach the cake bases over each stair and triangle.

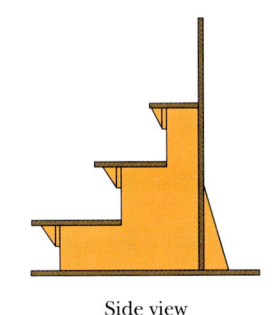

Front view   Side view

Facing Page: Poured Sugar Presentation Podium

On one side of the piece, attach a bouquet of molded sugar flowers mounted on dried tree branches or wire coated with cooked sugar.

Place the piece on the presentation table and set the cakes in place over two cake cardboards.

Various Poured Sugar Pieces

Poured sugar can be formed into an infinite number of designs. Here are a few more variations of pieces already shown.

Diagram 1—Poured Sugar Crescent Moon
Use cooked sugar to carefully attach the crescent to a round base disk. Support the crescent by affixing poured sugar triangles on both sides.

The bottom end of the crescent is cut flat to support a poured sugar disk on which the cake is placed.

Conceal the small triangle supports on either side of the crescent with poured or molded sugar flowers.

(Poured Sugar Presentation Podium continued on next page)

back and front panels supported by poured sugar triangles. Attach the largest cake base up front on a poured sugar panel. Attach a poured sugar triangle in front of and underneath the cake base for greater support. Affix the other disks, reinforcing them with poured sugar triangles.

Place several pulled or molded sugar flowers on the back support and on the base. The style and presentation of this piece may be varied according to taste and the number and sizes of the cakes.

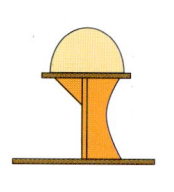

Diagram 2—Fish or Dolphin
Use a template to make the poured sugar fish or dolphin. Attach the bottom to a poured sugar oval. The tail is made or cut flat across to support a poured sugar disk on which to place the cake. Poured sugar fins stabilize the piece. Pulled or molded sugar flowers can be used to decorate and conceal any juncture points. Finish by decorating with royal icing using a paper cone.

Front view   Side view

Diagram 3—Various Level Supports
Prepare a back panel using a template and attach it to an oval base. Secure the back panel with poured sugar and poured sugar triangles. To assure the solidity of the platform holding the croquembouche, form a front panel out of poured sugar. The disk is set on the

Diagram 4—Horn of Plenty
Mold a horn of plenty and attach it to an oval poured sugar base. The front part of the horn (the large opening) supports a poured sugar disk with a cake or croquembouche. The smaller end supports a poured sugar disk for a smaller cake.

The piece is supported from behind by two poured sugar supports. The first is attached to the larger end of the horn and the base disk. The second is placed at the smaller end in the same way to support the smaller cake; see the side view shown in the diagram.

Conceal any junction points in front with pulled or molded sugar flowers. Decorate with royal icing using a paper cone.

Coloring and Tinting Poured Sugar

Poured sugar is always colored during cooking. Color with powdered food coloring diluted in a small amount of water or alcohol. Add the coloring about halfway through the cooking.

When using more than one color, always start with the lightest. Any leftover poured sugar can be added to the next batch without greatly affecting the color. This also makes it possible to prepare a presentation piece of several colors without having to clean the pot or being stuck with leftover sugar.

For example, following the basic poured sugar recipe, start with a white or uncolored sugar, then make yellow, then orange, red, and finish with a very dark color or even black. All these colors can be made in the same pot; simply add more sugar, water, and glucose, and color according to the recipe.

For poured sugar presentation pieces, the color is usually determined according to the type of piece or cakes to be presented. Of course, personal taste is the deciding factor. Generally, the bases are darkly colored to bring out the colors of the cakes.

It is a good idea to put calcium carbonate in the poured sugar recipe to make it opaque; otherwise, the sugar will be transparent and dull.

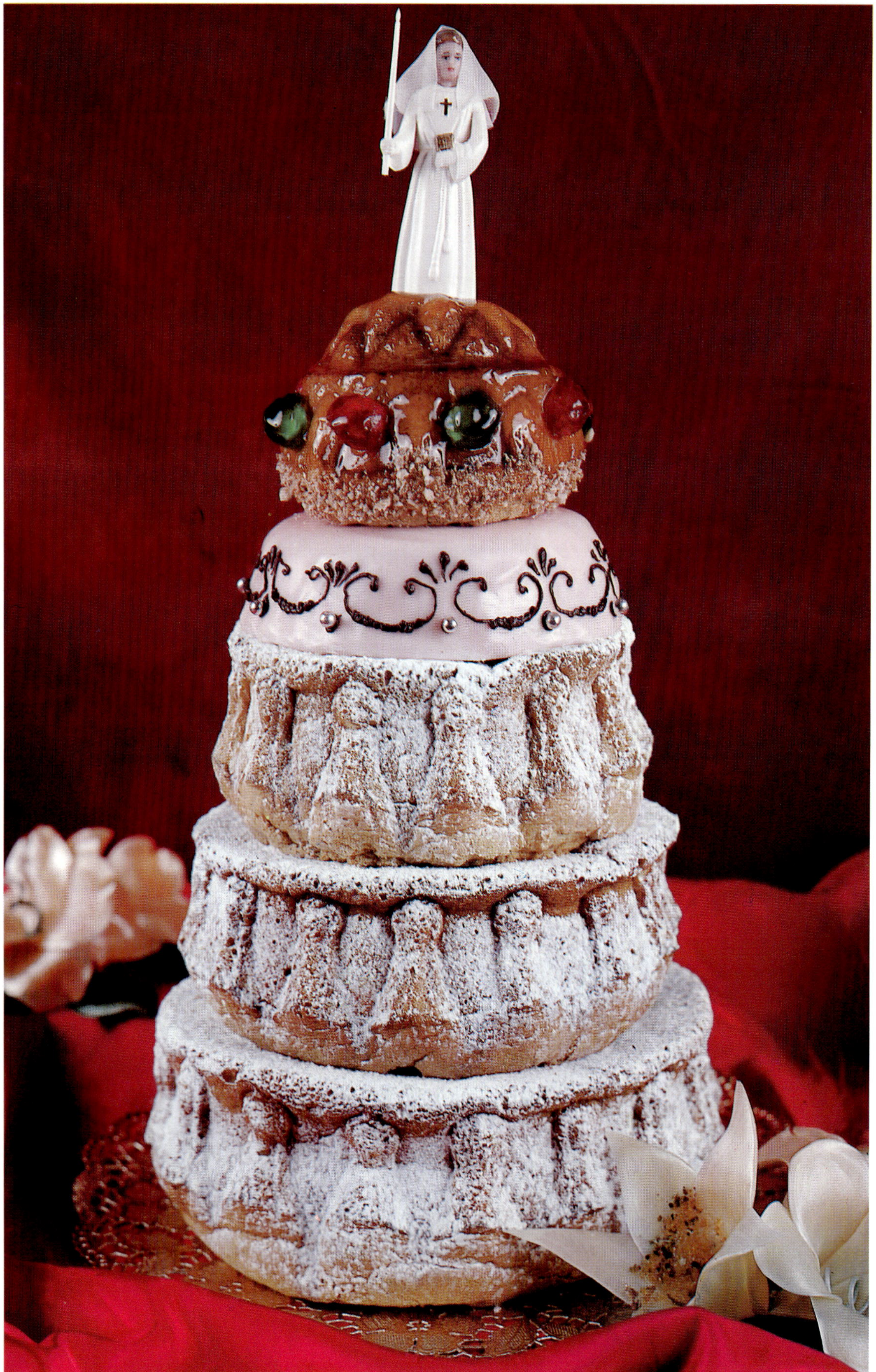

Breton Cake
Gâteau Breton

This is a traditional unfilled ceremonial cake prepared in Brittany. It is usually served with a sauce or cream such as a fruit coulis, sabayon, chocolate sauce, or crème anglaise.

The cakes are baked in special molds with a rounded or fluted border and a hole in the center. After cooling, they are stacked directly on top of one another in decreasing size, starting with the largest on the bottom and the smallest on top to form a pyramid.

Butter and flour the molds. Fill them two thirds full with almond biscuit or one of the the special almond génoise batters.

Bake in a moderately low oven, 320°–350°F/160°–180°C.

This cake may be presented in one of two ways:

1. After cooling, stack the cakes, starting with the largest and finishing with the smallest to form a pyramid. Glaze the entire cake with white fondant and decorate with chocolate or other colored icing using a paper cone.

2. After cooling, dust each layer with confectioners' sugar. Stack the cakes, starting with the largest and finishing with the smallest to form a pyramid. The top cake may be brushed with apricot glaze, as seen here, or glazed with fondant, then decorated with chocolate or other colored icing using a paper cone.

Facing Page: Breton Cake

Special Almond Génoise No. 1

eggs	12	12
egg yolks	4	4
sugar	17.5 oz	500 g
cake flour	17.5 oz	500 g
almond powder	3.5 oz	100 g
butter, melted	3.5 oz	100 g

This cake is prepared as for a regular génoise. In the bowl of an electric mixer, use a whisk attachment to whip the eggs, egg yolks, and sugar, warming them over a hot water bath or other heat source. Once the batter is warm, remove from heat and whip until completely cool.

Sift together the flour and almond powder; then gently fold into the batter with the melted butter. Quickly fill the molds and bake in a moderately low oven at 320°–350°F/160°–180°C.

Upon removing the cakes from the oven, unmold them onto a kitchen towel.

Special Almond Génoise No. 2

eggs	30	30
sugar	35 oz	1,000 g
almond powder	7 oz	200 g
cake flour	38.5 oz	1,100 g
butter, melted	5.5 oz	150 g

Whip the eggs and sugar over a warm water bath or other heat source until warm. Whip the mixture in the bowl of an electric mixer until completely cool. Sift together the flour and almond powder, then gently fold into the batter with the melted butter. Immediately fill the molds and bake in a moderately low oven, 320°–350°F/160°–180°C.

Upon removing the cakes from the oven, unmold them onto a kitchen towel.

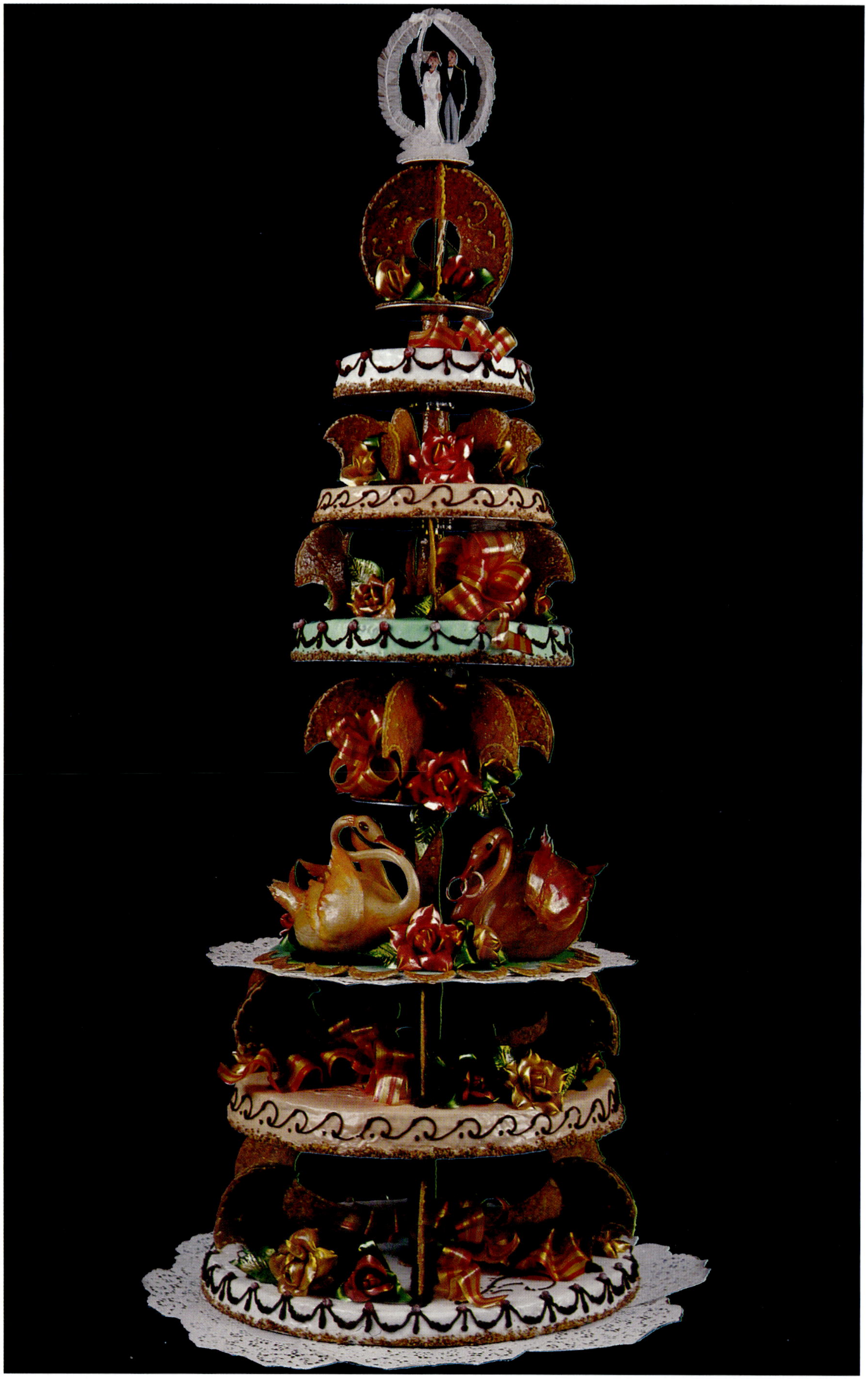

Classic French Tiered Cake

This piece is assembled using a metal cake stand as for all traditional French tiered cakes. The cakes, assembled on the metal disks, are usually made of biscuit layered with buttercream, mousseline, or other filling of choice. They are covered with a thin layer of marzipan and coated with fondant. The finished cakes are decorated with royal or chocolate icing using a paper cone or pastry bag and tip.

Generally, a figurine or decoration representative of the occasion is placed on top. If several decorations are used, they can be placed on one or more tiers in the center of the piece.

If prepared for a wedding, one variation is to place two blown sugar swans or doves, of which one is holding a set of rings in its beak.

Use patterns to cut out nougatine decorations. Place them on the cakes to decorate and fill in empty spots. The cutouts are given a flat bottom to stand erect and balanced on the cake. Small nougatine disks can be made with a cutter, 2 in/5 cm in diameter. They are attached to a nougatine base with cooked sugar to keep them stable.

With a pastry bag and fluted tip, pipe a border of ganache around each nougatine cutout for reinforcement. Wrap nougatine around the central metal posts.

It is necessary to cut a hole with a cutter in the center of each cake to allow for the central posts.

Place a nougatine decoration on the top tier and pulled or molded sugar flowers at various points on and around the cakes. Pulled sugar ribbons and the blown sugar birds decorate the center tiers.

Glazing Cakes with Fondant

Prepare and chill the cakes to be glazed with fondant as indicated in any of the ways above. Place the chilled cakes on a cooling rack set over a sheet pan or work surface. Cover with marzipan and coat the cake with apricot glaze, if used. Pour the warm, liquid fondant over the cake. Drain off the excess fondant by tapping the cooling rack by quickly and lightly lifting and dropping one corner. Repeat this motion until only a thin layer of fondant covers the cake.

For large cakes, it is necessary to use a long metal spatula or palette knife to spread the fondant over the surface of the cake, scraping off any excess until the desired thickness is obtained.

Lift the glazed cake by placing a metal spatula underneath the cake and scraping the bottom to remove any excess fondant that has pooled. Set the cake on a flat work surface.

If desired, press nuts or other garnish around the side of the cake before the fondant sets.

Allow the fondant to set and form a crust, being careful not to move the cake as the smallest disturbance will cause the entire surface to crack. After the fondant has completely set, finish decorating the cake using a paper cone filled with royal or chocolate icing.

Facing Page: Classic French Tiered Cake

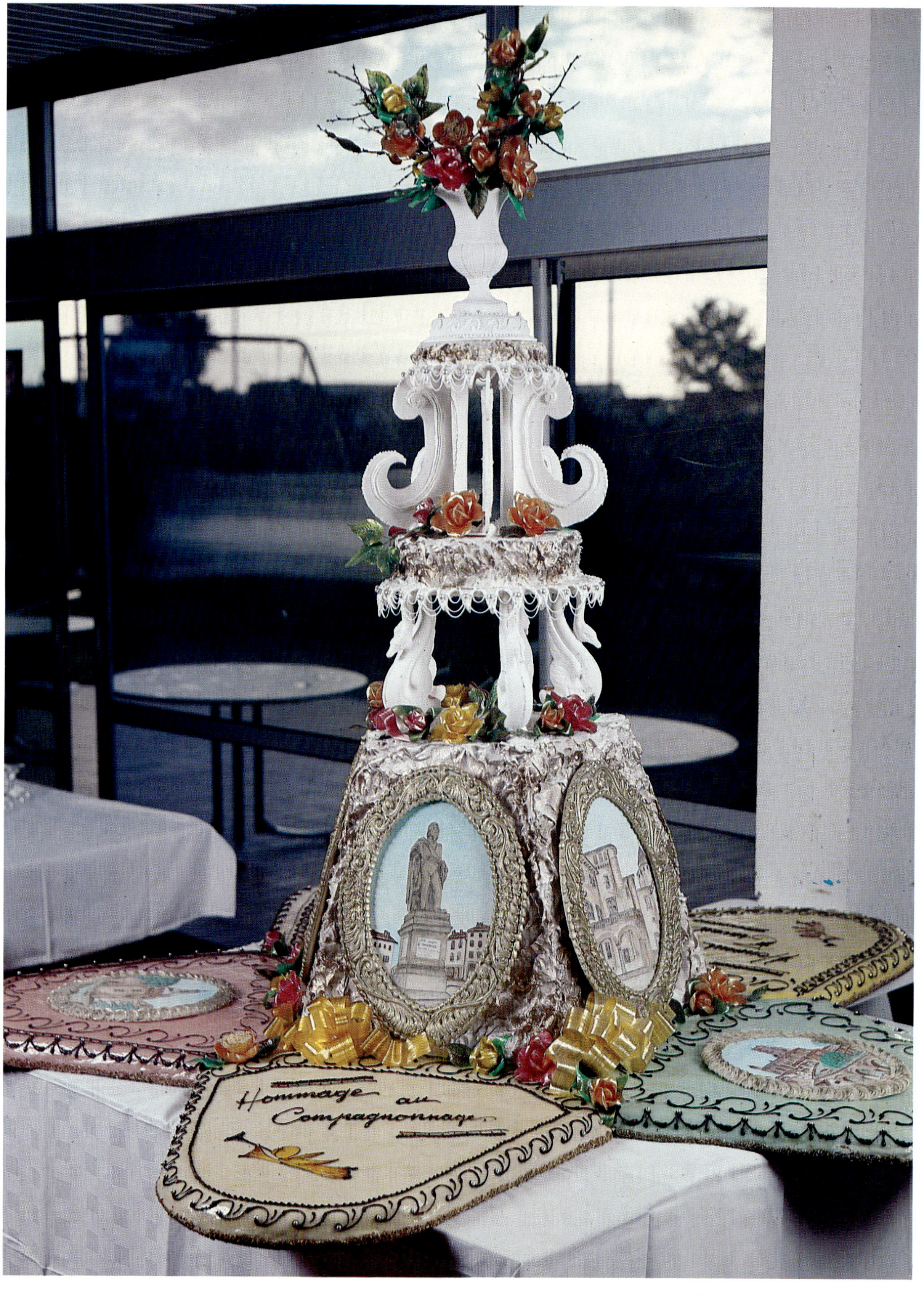
Hommage au
Compagnonnage

Presentation Piece

This piece is 8.25 ft/2.5 m high and 7.25 ft/2.25 m wide. It is constructed in two sections:
 1. The central section, which is purely decorative.
 2. The five cakes placed around the decoration piece.

The Presentation Section

The most dramatic part of this piece is the centerpiece constructed on an octagonal plywood base with five perforated plywood panels. Appliqué sugar (see page 279), is used to decorate and cover the wood. With a metal spatula or palette knife, pull up on the appliqué sugar to form peaks while spreading it. Spray with gold powder using an air brush. Allow the piece to dry for several days.

Prepare a selection of pastillage pieces, according to personal taste, such as dolphins or swans (shown here), using molds made for this purpose (usually from plaster or copper).

When the pastillage has completely dried, assemble the pieces on a pastillage disk and attach a second disk on top. Decorate with pastillage wolf's teeth.

Prepare a second level in pastillage, slightly smaller in diameter than the first. Again, mold pastillage forms or cut out shapes using a pattern. Cut out two pastillage disks, one for the base and one for the top. Allow all the pieces to dry completely. Assemble the pieces with royal icing or softened pastillage.

Place a pastillage vase on a pastillage base shaped in a génoise mold.

All pastillage pieces should be finished and decorated a minimum of 8 days before the piece is presented, so they will be fully dried. Decorate the panels by painting them with food coloring and cocoa powder.

Preparing the Cakes

Prepare the five plywood bases for the cakes, making sure that one end of each piece is cut straight across so it will fit flush against the bottom of the centerpiece. The outside end can be pointed or rounded as desired, depending on the shape of the cake and the presentation table.

The cakes are layered with sheets of biscuit cut to size, mousseline cream, chiboust cream, pastry cream or chantilly, and filled with poached or candied fruit or craquelin. The simple syrup used to moisten the biscuit should complement the flavor of the filling.

Coat the top and sides of the cake with mousseline cream or Italian meringue. Cover each cake with a thin layer of marzipan. Refrigerate. Cover the chilled cakes with a thin layer of apricot or clear glaze. Press candied almonds halfway up around the sides. Decorate with chocolate icing using a paper cone.

Transport the piece unassembled. On the presentation table, place the base of the centerpiece and assemble the top sections. Place the cakes around the centerpiece.

Affix the pastillage paintings to the centerpiece. Place pulled sugar ribbons and flowers on and around the centerpiece.

Chef's Note: *The centerpiece shown in the photograph was made for a special event for 500 guests of the "compagnons" or foremost craftsmen whose work is represented in the paintings.*

Facing Page: Presentation Piece

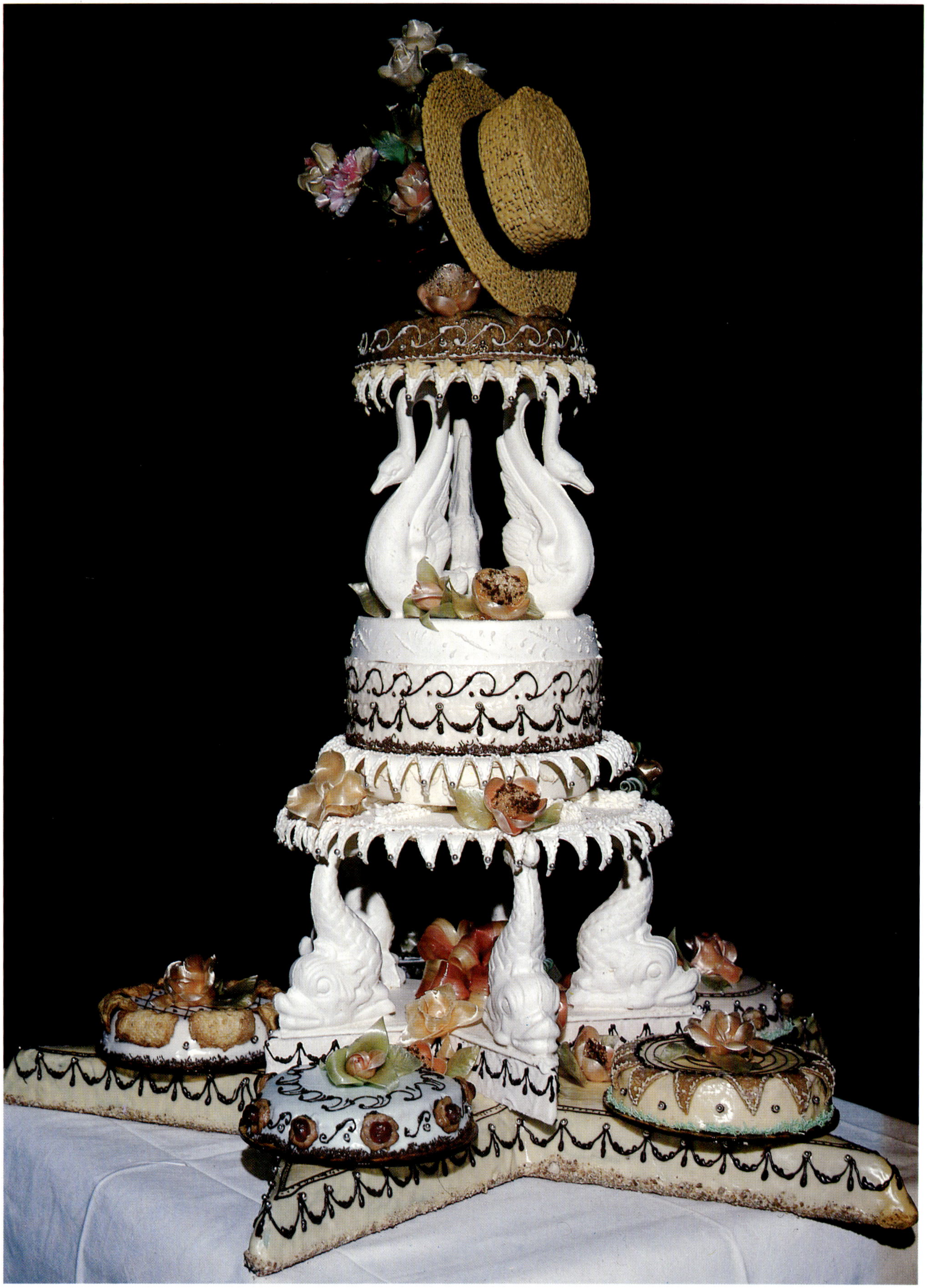

La Belle Epoque

This piece is 5.25 ft/1 m 60 cm high and 4 ft/1 m 20 cm wide. The Belle Epoque was made to celebrate the completion of the film by the same name. Because the greater portion of the piece is based on the presentation work, the only edible portions are the five cakes set on top of the star's points. This type of presentation is often prepared for competitions or important special gatherings. For these occasions the utmost care must be given to the presentation.

The bases or simulated cakes are decorated with marzipan or fondant. They can be constructed in various ways:

1. Biscuit that is completely dried out then covered with appliqué sugar which is dried then decorated.
2. A styrofoam or plywood base covered with appliqué sugar and dried for several days before decorating.

Simulated cakes are used for their solidity and long shelf life. This makes the second technique particularly practical.

Any of the prepared sugar techniques can be used to decorate the structure, such as pulled, molded, blown, or poured sugar or pastillage. In this case, pastillage is the most appropriate.

The sections are prepared separately, making them easy to transport, then assembled and decorated with royal icing on the presentation table.

Between the two tiers of pastillage, place a previously prepared simulated cake in pastillage, coated with appliqué sugar, glazed with fondant and decorated with chocolate icing using a paper cone.

The top section is composed of a nougatine base supporting a blown sugar vase filled with pulled sugar flowers and leaves. The straw hat is made of nougatine and the woven effect is made with colored royal icing.

Assemble the piece on the presentation table, setting the cakes in place. Place pulled sugar flowers and ribbons on and around the cakes and decoration pieces.

Facing Page: La Belle Epoque

Appliqué Sugar
Sucre Appliqué

Appliqué sugar offers a quick and simple way of coating and concealing joints and bases on artistic, competition, and presentation pieces.

gelatin sheets	8	8
sugar	35 oz	1,000 g
water	10.5 oz	300 g
egg whites	15	15

Cover the gelatin sheets with very cold water to soften.

Prepare an Italian meringue by cooking the sugar and water to 250°F/121°C, while whipping the egg whites to soft peaks. Pour the cooked sugar in a fine stream, whipping it into the egg whites.

While the meringue is still hot, squeeze out the excess water from the gelatin and whip them into the meringue. Continue whipping until the meringue is completely cool.

With a palette knife, smooth the mixture over the area to be covered. Allow the decorating sugar to form a crust, and dry in a cool, dry area or in a proofing oven for several days.

The piece can be left as is or glazed with fondant. The appliqué sugar can be piped out of a pastry bag with a fluted tip or coated with gold paint or powdered gold using an spray gun. Appliqué sugar is a fast and easy way to make spectacular pedestals for tiered cakes.

Confectioners' Sugar Nougatine

There are many recipes for preparing nougatine. Classic nougatine is made with granulated sugar. In the croquembouche chapter of this volume, the nougatine is made with fondant, which gives it good stability and shelf life. Here, the nougatine is prepared with confectioners' sugar.

glucose	*24.5 oz*	*700 g*
confectioners' sugar	*35 oz*	*1,000 g*
cocoa butter, chopped	*2 oz*	*50 g*
almonds, toasted, sliced, or chopped	*21–24.5 oz*	*600–700 g*

In a copper sugar pot (poêlon) or saucepan, bring the glucose to a boil. Stirring constantly with a wooden spoon, gradually add the confectioners' sugar until it turns to a light caramel. Add the chopped cocoa butter, and stir until melted.

Remove from heat, stir in the almonds. Stir until well blended and pour the mixture out onto a lightly oiled marble or other work surface. This will help to quickly stop the cooking. Work the nougatine with a pastry triangle to speed the cooling.

Place the nougatine in a mound on a lightly oiled sheet pan. Roll out and cut the nougatine as usual. It is best to work quickly with the nougatine while it is warm and soft. Using a sheet pan makes it easy to place the nougatine in the oven or under a heat lamp to rewarm as needed.

Always prepare all materials before making the nougatine. The most basic pieces, which should be clean and lightly oiled, are: metal rolling pin, pastry triangle, knife, cutters, any molds or patterns.

Store the nougatine in a cool, dry place. Trimmings can be softened by reheating, then reused.

Chef's Note: *This nougatine recipe holds up well, even uncovered, as the cocoa butter gives it an impermeable quality. For a better shelf life, it is also possible to add cocoa butter to other nougatine recipes, such as the one made with granulated sugar.*

CHAPTER 6

Sugar and Decoration Work

Artistic and Show Pieces

The most important aspect of certain pastries lies in the taste, texture, and flavor, all judged by the palate. The visual element, however, is based on the artistic expression of the pastry chef, affording an opportunity to reveal another side of his or her talent and abilities. All beginners, students, young professionals, and chefs should be encouraged to apply themselves in this area of pastry making.

Pastry chefs are not just "cake makers." It is not only the seasoned professional who is capable of intricate decorative work; those at any level can make good-tasting pastries that are also beautiful.

Many forms of decoration work exist, including pulled, blown, poured, and molded sugar, pastillage, marzipan, chocolate, and nougatine.

Pulled sugar offers the greatest potential and versatility, especially for preparing flowers. Blown sugar presentation pieces can be realized fairly quickly. Molded sugar is a newer form of sugar work where flowers, leaves, and other shapes may be formed easily and quickly. Poured sugar can be used decoratively, but is more commonly reserved to support artistic pieces. Rock sugar is also used as a decoration and support. Pastillage can be shaped in limitless ways, as a decorative structure or for ornaments.

Presentation pieces often require metal or plastic frames; metal wires are used to support flowers and other delicate pieces. These types of supports should be discreetly concealed so they do not detract from the finished work. Dried tree branches, coated with colored cooked sugar, are also used for bouquets and stems.

A showpiece or competition piece should incorporate a variety of techniques by combining pulled sugar flowers, pastillage, and blown sugar decorations, arranged tastefully. A piece in pastillage alone, no matter how beautiful, could be the work of a chef not skilled in all the techniques.

Presentation pieces may be enclosed in a hermetically sealed glass box with a desiccant: calcium chloride, carbon, or fresh lime to keep the sugar work free from humidity and conserve it for several months and, sometimes, even years.

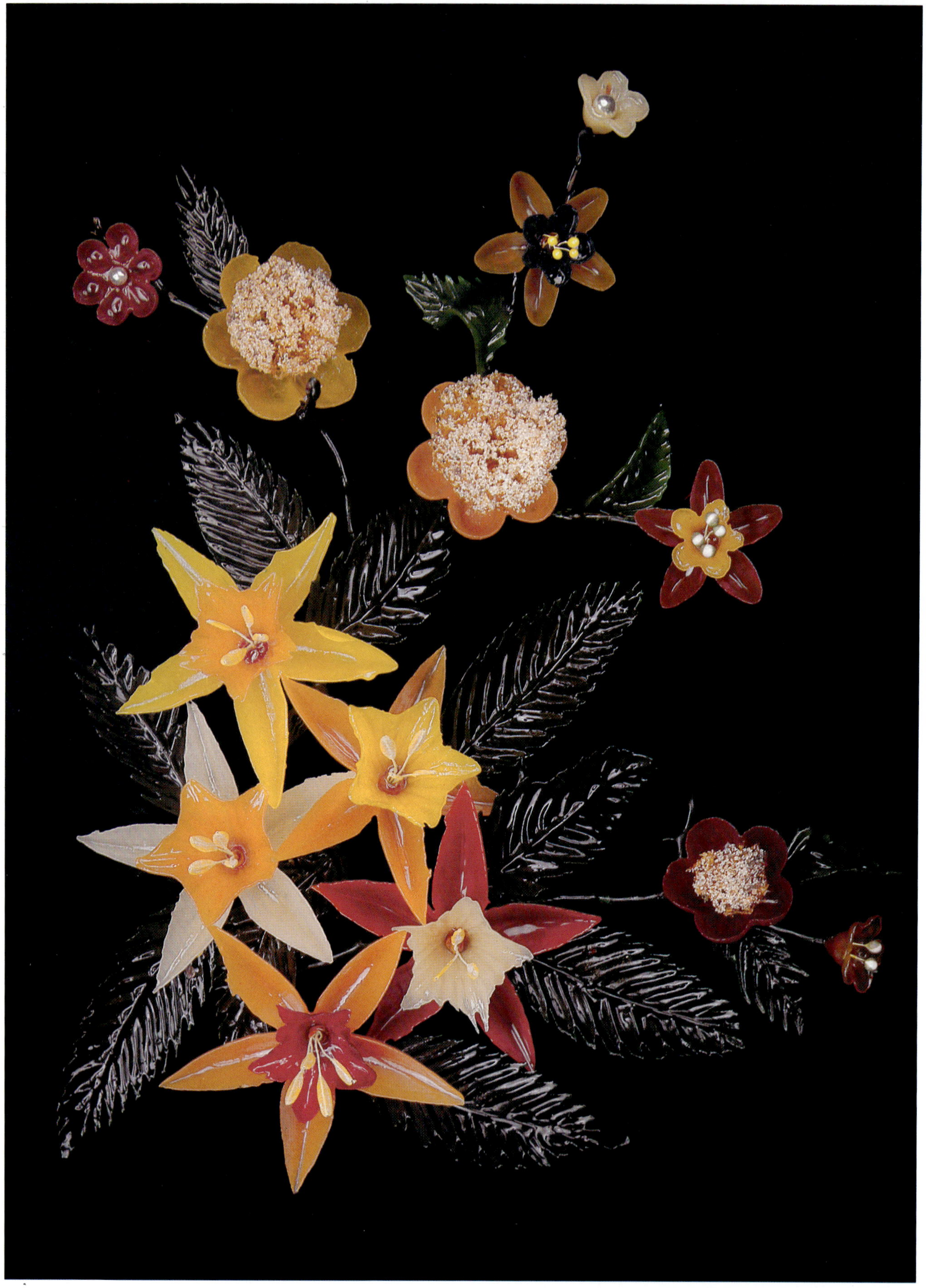

Molded Magyfleur Flowers

Pulled sugar flowers have been used for quite some time. They are discussed in a later section, with step-by-step photographs and explanations. However, this decoration form, although long respected, requires a great deal of practice, time, and artistic capability, and is often reserved for decorating important ceremonial or competition pieces.

I describe the Magyfleur method as "molded sugar" because the sugar flowers, and those in chocolate, are shaped on bronze molds. The bronze molds are shaped as flowers and leaves. They are chilled, taken directly from the freezer, then dipped 2/3–3/4 of the way into hot cooked sugar. The molds are quickly removed from the sugar which instantly detaches itself from the cold metal forms.

This simple procedure enables even those with a limited background in decorative work to prepare sugar flowers. The flowers are not meant to look realistic, they have a modern look appropriate for decorating cakes, frozen desserts, and presentation pieces.

It is irrelevant to compare molded sugar with pulled sugar flowers, as the two techniques are so different. However, a presentation piece that is carefully decorated with finely molded sugar flowers is far more attractive than one decorated with mediocre pulled sugar flowers. Molded sugar flowers can also be more attractively presented than marzipan flowers.

Magyfleur flowers allow those who do not have the time or the ability to pull sugar to quickly and efficiently prepare elaborate presentation pieces. Other advantages of molded flowers are the low production cost as compared to marzipan, how quickly they can be made with minimal skill, and the modern style of the flowers. Molded sugar flowers store considerably longer in open air than pulled sugar, which requires a desiccant.

Molded sugar flowers are presented according to personal taste. They may be colored to match and contrast the cakes being decorated. Molded flowers can also be made with caramel, which is a good way to make use of any extra caramel prepared for a croquembouche. This was not possible before.

In the same way that pulled sugar work requires special equipment, such as an infrared lamp, *Magyfleur* molds are essential for molded sugar. *Magyfleur* molds are made from bronze and intended to last a lifetime. Simply keep them clean and in their box, which will protect them from humidity while in the freezer.

Facing Page: Molded Magyfleur Flowers

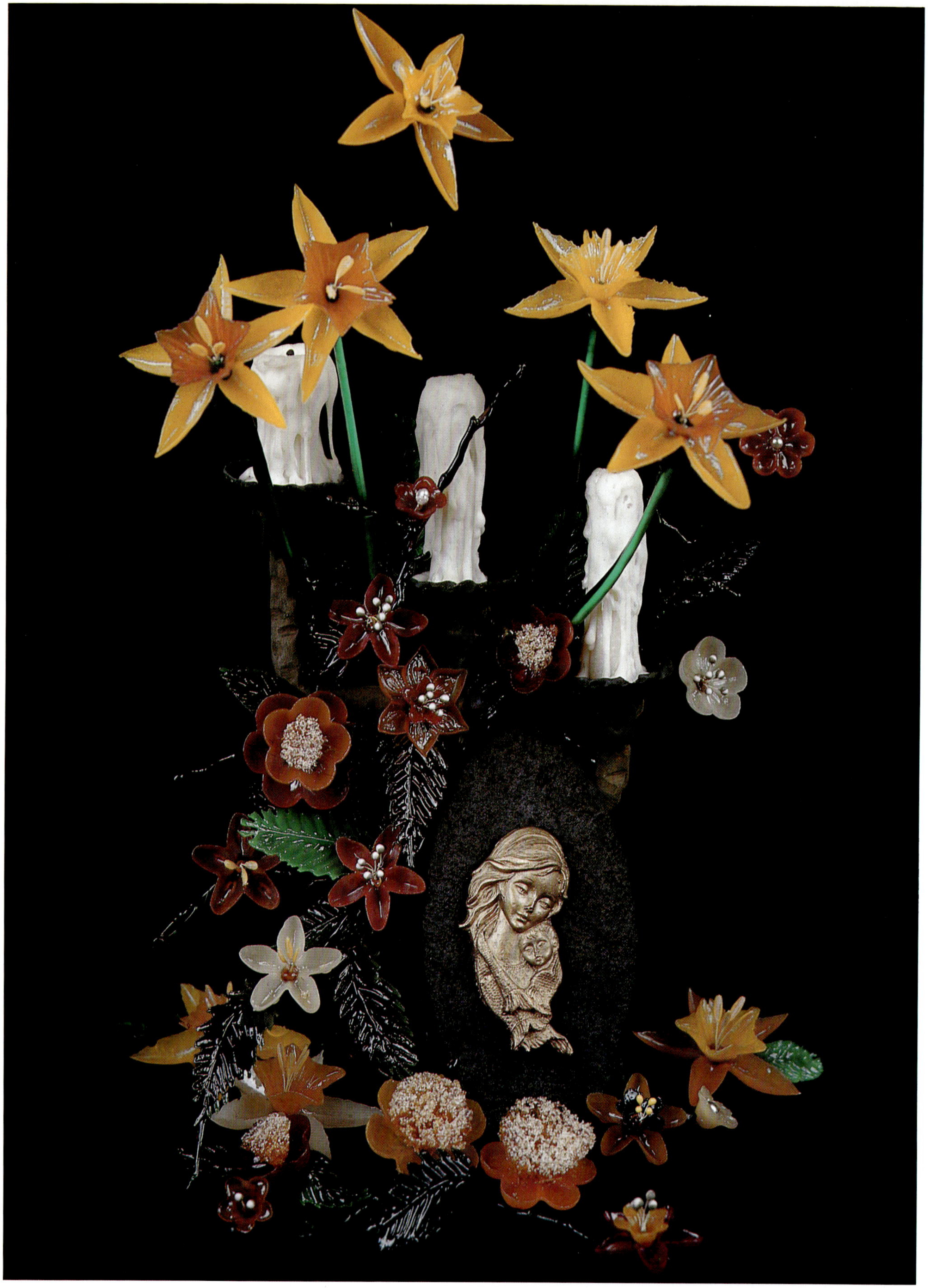

Molded Sugar
Sucre Moulé

water	12.5 oz	350 g
glucose	7 oz	200 g
sugar	35 oz	1,000 g
calcium carbonate, (optional)	1 tsp	4 g

Cook all ingredients in a copper sugar pot (poêlon) to 302°–311°F/150°–155°C. This sugar does not require an exact tempetature as for pulled sugar. The most important aspect is to reach 302°F/150°C, hard crack stage, or more. The sugar can be cooked up to 338°–347°F/170°–175°C, when it will caramelize. If color is desired, add it at the halfway mark, approximately 248°F/120°C.

To obtain an opaque effect, add a teaspoon of calcium carbonate, first diluting it in a little water. The diluted mixture is added before or halfway through the cooking. This step is optional although recommended; otherwise, the flowers will be transparent. In addition, the calcium carbonate causes the sugar to crystallize from the interior outward, helping to prevent the finished molded flowers from softening and extending their shelf life. The more calcium carbonate used, the more opaque the result, though too much causes the sugar to harden into a solid crystallized mass during cooking. If this should happen, add water, stir it in, and cook again until the desired temperature is reached. Calcium carbonate may be purchased in specialty stores or pharmacies.

The Magyfleur bronze molds are stored in the freezer inside their box. Take the molds directly from the freezer and dip them into the hot cooked sugar 2/3–3/4 of the way up the mold. The sugar will instantly adhere itself to the mold. Quickly remove the mold from the sugar. Unmold the sugar form onto a cooling rack, pastry marble, or foam surface, using the tip of a paring knife if necessary. Repeat these steps with all of the very cold molds. It is not necessary to oil the molds, but they must be well chilled and perfectly clean. Return the molds to the freezer after each one is used. Having more than one set helps molding go more quickly. As one set is being used, the other is chilling, which is particularly helpful when large quantities of flowers are needed. In this way even a novice can prepare several hundred flowers and leaves in a few hours.

Store the finished molded sugar flowers and leaves in an airtight container, preferably with desiccant (calcium chloride or limestone) on the bottom. They can be stored in this way up to several years.

Molded sugar flowers are assembled just before being presented. The flowers can be made in assorted colors and shapes.

Facing Page: Molded Sugar Presentation Piece

288   *Modern French Pastry*

Flower Pistils

Pistils are attached to the center of the flower with caramel. They can greatly affect the character of the flower.

The pistils are made of:

Spun sugar, the most commonly used (see pages 378–379).

Artificial pistils sold by florists, craft stores, or confectionery specialty stores.

Small balls of marzipan, dipped halfway in melted chocolate, then placed in chocolate or colored sprinkles until set.

Silver candied pearls or colored dragées.

Molded Sugar Leaves

Leaves are prepared according to the same technique as the flowers. To give the leaves more character and a natural shape, bend them after molding, but before they set.

To obtain leaves with more than one color, add two or three colors to the cooked sugar, stir lightly so the colors are swirled together but not enough for them to blend into one. Then dip as usual.

Coloring the Sugar

The sugar may be colored during or after cooking. Differently colored flowers may be created with one pot of cooked sugar:

1. Cook the sugar as usual with calcium carbonate; do not add coloring and use for white flowers.
2. Add yellow food coloring, reheat the sugar, and make yellow flowers.
3. Add a little red coloring, reheat the sugar, and make orange flowers.
4. Add more red coloring, reheat the sugar, and make red flowers.

By continuing to add colors in this way, many differently colored flowers can be prepared.

Caramel Flowers

Using Magyfleur molds is the only way that flowers can be made with (light or dark) caramel. Simply dip the chilled molds in the caramel and use the caramel to assemble the flowers according to the procedure given for cooked sugar flowers.

Keep in mind that the darker the caramel, the more quickly the finished flowers will soften. The golden color of caramel molded flowers and leaves offers an elegant touch to presentation pieces and cakes.

Facing Page: Chocolate Flowers Molded with Magyfleur

290 Modern French Pastry

Molded Sugar

sugar	35 oz	1,000 g
water	12.5 oz	350 g
glucose	7 oz	200 g

Photo 1: Cook the sugar, water, and glucose. The bronze Magyfleur molds should be kept in their case in the freezer.

Photo 2: The sugar is cooked to 302°–311°F/150°–155°C or higher. Color can be added at the beginning of cooking. For an opaque quality, dilute a little calcium carbonate in a small amount of water, adding it to the sugar either at the beginning or in the middle of cooking.

Photo 3: Color may be added after cooking, when the sugar has been removed from the heat and the bubbles disappear. Dip the well-chilled molds in the hot sugar 2/3–3/4 of the way up the molds.

Photo 4: The bronze molds are able to withstand very high temperatures. It is sufficient to quickly dip the mold in the sugar and immediately remove it. The cooked sugar will instantly adhere to the cold mold. The hardened cooked sugar will usually slip right off the mold; if not, the tip of a paring knife can be used.

Photo 5: Unmold the hardened cooked sugar onto a cooling rack, marble, or foam pad. Any of the bronze forms may be used to mold cooked sugar or caramel, but they must be very cold.

Photo 6: To change the color, reheat and stir in a darker color. Always start dipping with the lightest color, using it as needed before adding the next deeper color. Continue adding colors, finishing with the darkest. With this procedure several colors can be molded, such as white, yellow, orange, pink, and red.

(Molded Sugar recipe continued on page 293)

292

Modern French Pastry

Photo 7: After achieving the desired color, lightly reheat the sugar, and continue to dip with well-chilled molds. Work with only a few molds at a time, keeping any unused molds in the freezer.

Photo 8: Partially dip the cold bronze mold in the hot sugar, then immediately unmold it onto a cooling rack or foam pad. For caramel flowers, see page 177. Use the tip of a paring knife to help unmold the flowers, if needed. Wait several seconds for the sugar to set before unmolding or the flower may lose its shape. If unmolded too late, the flower may stick to the mold. By the third flower, it will be obvious how much time is needed before unmolding.

Photo 9: When enough flower bases have been prepared, the flowers are ready to be assembled. Any combination of colors and shapes can be used to create a large variety of styles.

Attach the pieces with cooked sugar. Attach the pistils with cooked sugar. For spun sugar pistils, see page 378. Silk or other artificial pistils can also be used, as well as silver candied pears, dragées, or small marzipan balls.

Photo 10: The finished flowers are arranged in a bouquet as a presentation piece or used to decorate cakes or other work. Use a few dried tree branches or metal wires dipped and coated in cooked sugar as stems. Attach molded sugar leaves of different color and size.

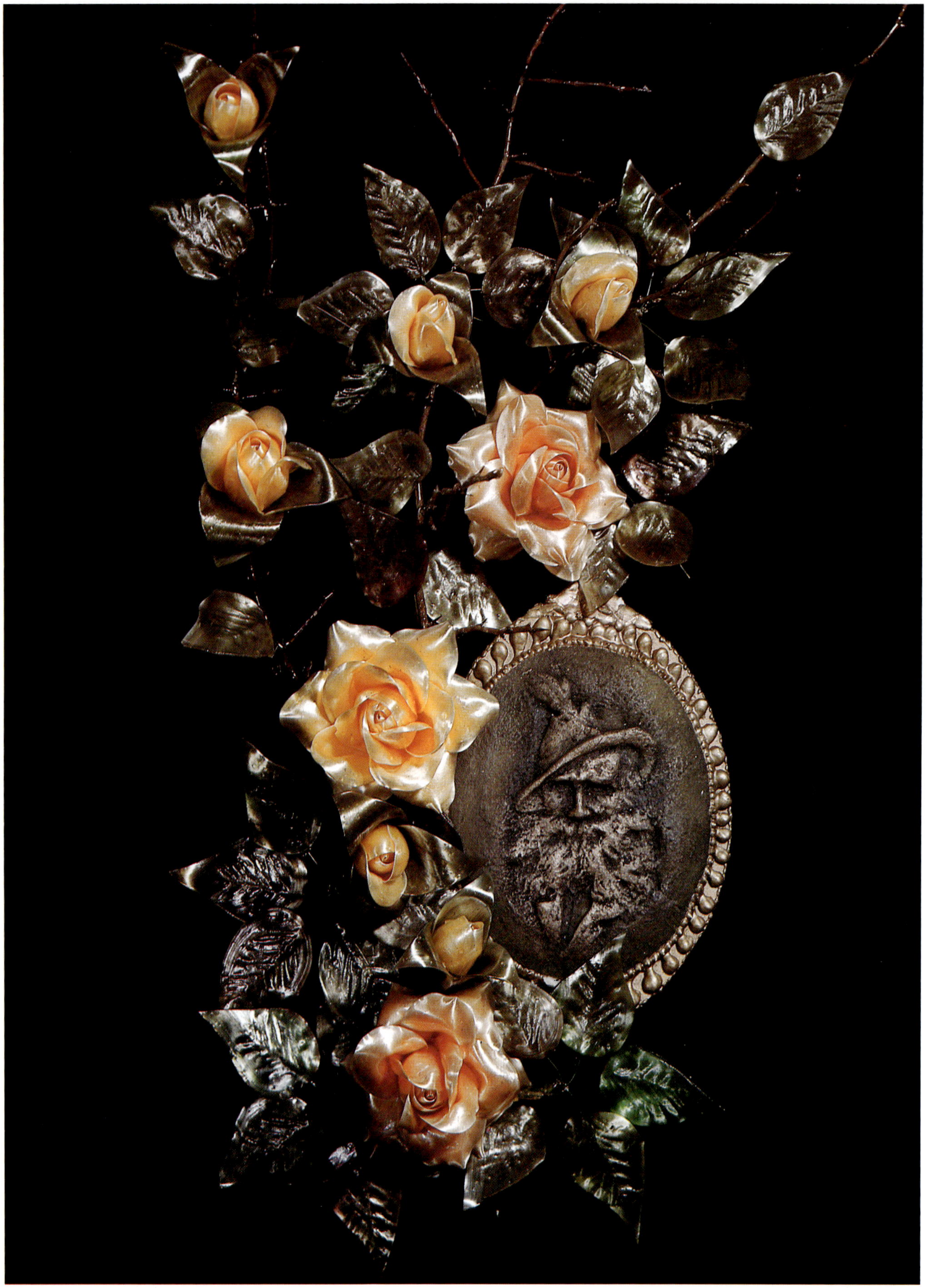

Pulled Sugar
Sucre Tiré

Pulled sugar work is the most commonly used decoration medium in French pastry making. One of the most highly respected pastry chefs in France, known for his work in pulled sugar, is Etienne Tholoniat, who has shared his considerable experience for over 50 years.

Sugar that is pulled in shimmering, mother-of-pearl colors can be shaped into any flower or leaf. However, this work requires a great deal of time and practice. Pulled sugar is essentially reserved for decorating ceremonial and presentation pieces.

The work presented here, including recipes, procedures, and step-by-step photographs, should make it possible to understand this exacting craft. Among the many recipes that I've had the opportunity to work with, the following are what I believe to be the best three. The results may vary slightly between different recipes, but the preparation and procedures remain the same.

Facing Page: Pulled Sugar Presentation Piece

Pulled Sugar No. 1
Sucre Tiré

This recipe is recommended for beginners as it offers good results and the sugar is relatively easy to work with because it does not get as hot as recipes made with glucose. This pulled sugar recipe is particularly appropriate for cakes served shortly after being decorated. It tends not to last as long or store as well as glucose-based pulled sugar and is, therefore, not recommended for decorations requiring a long lifespan.

sugar, granulated		
or cubed	*35 oz*	*1,000 g*
water	*14 oz*	*400 g*
cream of tartar	*1/2 tsp*	*2 g*

Cook all ingredients to 320°–323.5°F/160°–162°C.

Pulled Sugar No. 2
Sucre Tiré

This recipe offers results relatively similar to the first recipe. The sugar has a pearly sheen but it stores better than Recipe 1. It is recommended for pieces that will be stored or displayed for a period of time. However, the glucose makes the sugar retain the heat longer, making it more difficult to work with.

sugar, granulated		
or cubed	*35 oz*	*1,000 g*
water	*12.5 oz*	*350 g*
glucose	*9 oz*	*250 g*
cream of tartar	*1/4 tsp*	*1.5 g*

Cook all ingredients to 311°–314.5°F/155°–157°F.

(Pulled Sugar No. 2 recipe continued on next page)

Variation

It is possible to prepare pulled sugar with lemon juice. Add a few drops of lemon juice and use 10.5 oz/300 g glucose for every 35 oz/1,000 g sugar.

Cook all ingredients to 298.5°–302°F/148°–150°C.

This recipe is difficult to work with as the sugar is hot and breaks easily.

Pulled Sugar No. 3
Sucre Tiré

Pulled sugar with glucose has the longest lifespan and a beautiful pearl-like sheen. It is also very difficult to work with because the high glucose content makes it extremely hot and causes it to crack easily. Therefore, this recipe is not recommended for beginners or those with heat-sensitive hands. The low cooking temperature produces the whitest of the pulled sugar recipes.

sugar, granulated or cubed	35 oz	1,000 g
water	14 oz	400 g
glucose	14 oz	400 g

Cook all ingredients to 298.5°–302°F/148°–150°C.

Procedure for Pulled Sugar

Regardless of the recipe, the procedure remains the same.

Combine the sugar and water in a copper sugar pot (poêlon). Heat over a low temperature, stirring occasionally with a wooden spoon. When the sugar melts, add the glucose and cream of tartar. Increase the heat and bring the mixture to a boil. Frequently wash down the sides of the pot with a pastry brush moistened with water to prevent crystallization.

Finish cooking on a high heat. The flame should be under the pot and not lapping around the outside. This prevents the sugar from caramelizing around the inner walls of the pot.

Cooking Pulled Sugar

Temperature and cooking are important steps in preparing pulled sugar. The temperature can vary between 41°–50°F/5°–10°C depending on the recipe used, glucose or cream of tartar.

Some experienced pastry chefs will dip two fingers in ice water then into the sugar to pick up a bit, plunging it into the ice water to determine hardness by feeling the cooled sample. This technique requires practice, which is why the thermometer is recommended here.

Coloring the Sugar

Either liquid or powdered food coloring diluted in alcohol are added to the sugar during the cooking. For certain preparations, such as pulled sugar ribbons when more than one color is needed, the coloring is added to the sugar on the work surface after cooking, but before it is pulled.

Preparing a Syrup for Pulled Sugar

A practical way of preparing pulled sugar is to partially cook a large quantity of the recipe and use the amount needed when required. For example, if using Recipe 2, prepare five times the recipe:

sugar	11 lbs	5,000 g
glucose	2 lbs 12 oz	1,250 g
water	3 lbs 13.5 oz	1,750 g
cream of tartar	1 1/4 tsp	7.5 g

Bring all ingredients to a boil. Store the syrup in an airtight container.

Use as much as needed at a time. Pour the desired amount of syrup into a small copper sugar pot (poêlon), add coloring, and heat quickly over a high flame to the appropriate temperature. For the above recipe cook to 311°–314.5°F/155°–157°C.

The best pulled sugar is achieved with high temperatures, though it is more difficult to work with. Preparing a large batch of syrup allows beginners to determine the most suitable temperature after only one or two trials. It is harder to achieve regularity with several smaller recipes from scratch, as opposed to cooking from one large batch of syrup.

Even small amounts of cream of tarter can affect the cooking time.

Preparing a syrup will reduce or even eliminate certain problems such as the tiny grains that appear when pulling sugar, a result of impurities.

When the desired temperature has been reached, remove the pot from the heat and immediately dip the bottom into a bowl or other container of cold water to stop the cooking. After a few seconds, remove the pot so the cooked sugar does not chill too quickly. Set the pot aside so the sugar can rest for a few minutes, and to allow any bubbles to subside.

Pour the cooked sugar onto lightly oiled, unrefrigerated, pastry marble. Add coloring, if required. As the sugar spreads out on the marble, use a metal pastry triangle to fold the edges that have formed a skin underneath into the center. Do not touch still liquid sugar (that which has not formed a skin) with the triangle as it will stick. Continue to fold the edges over until a ball is formed. Repeat the procedure as the sugar spreads out again. This helps the sugar to cool evenly. Move quickly, turning the sugar over into the middle before it has time to form a skin on the sides.

When the sugar has cooled enough to be handled, it is ready to be pulled. Do not pull sugar that is too hot. Form a sausage shape and pull the two ends until it is double in length. Fold it in half and repeat this step, pulling and folding until the sugar takes on a high satin sheen. It is best to pull the sugar until it is fairly cool to obtain the best sheen. If the sugar is not pulled enough, it will be transparent and dull. If pulled too much it will be opaque, matte and deform quickly.

When the sugar has been properly pulled, shape it into a ball, place it on the marble or on a drum sieve under a heat source such as a heat lamp (infrared), electric heater, or open oven. The heat should keep the sugar warm but not so hot as to cause it to soften or melt. I have found the best heat source to be a portable electric heater with a sliding base so the distance can be adjusted as needed.

298 Modern French Pastry

Pulled Sugar

Photo 1: Prepare and cook the sugar according to the recipe (see pages 295–296). Regardless of the recipe, the procedure and preparation are the same. The sugar is colored during or after cooking with powdered coloring diluted in alcohol. Cook the sugar to the desired temperature. Stop the cooking by dipping the bottom of the pot in cold water for a few seconds. Set the pot aside for the sugar to rest a few minutes.

Photo 2: Pour the sugar onto a lightly oiled pastry marble. The marble should not be refrigerated but at room temperature or warm. The sugar may be colored at this point if it has not been before; add just a few drops of coloring directly onto the sugar. It is best to cook the sugar one or two degrees higher if coloring is to be added after the cooking as it thins the sugar a bit.

Photo 3: The sugar will spread itself out on the marble. With a lightly oiled metal triangle, scrape the edges from the bottom into the center, forming a ball. The sugar will spread out naturally; scrape the edges up into the center again, and again let it spread out. Repeat this step several times until the sugar has cooled evenly and taken on body. It is important that the sugar be worked so it does not develop a hard skin.

Photo 4: When the sugar is cool enough to handle, it is ready to be pulled. It is important not to pull the sugar when it is very hot. Shape the sugar into a cylinder and pull on the two ends until it is double in length. Fold it in half and pull again. Repeat this step until the sugar takes on a brilliant satiny sheen. The sugar should be pulled when it is as cool as possible to obtain the best sheen.

It is virtually impossible to write in a few pages the various manipulations necessary to produce all the possible pulled sugar flowers. Photographs are considerably more helpful for understanding the hands-on techniques.

Almost any flower can be reproduced in pulled sugar. It is helpful to use a real or artificial flower as a model. Certain flowers are built up from petals alone, such as roses. Other flowers are assembled in steps, such as dahlias, chrysanthemums, and violets, for which the petals are prepared separately and later attached.

It is recommended that beginners gradually adapt to the heat of the sugar. It is better to start by working one hour at three different times than three hours straight. There is no question that pulling sugar is a difficult procedure and the common blisters and burns acquired along the way are hopefully compensated for by the results. A great deal of patience is required for pulling sugar; it is important not to become discouraged in the beginning. Both patience and practice are necessary to obtain satisfying results.

300   *Modern French Pastry*

Pulled Sugar Roses

Photo 5: When the sugar is sufficiently pulled, it will offer resistance, sometimes make a popping sound as it is worked, and will have a glossy sheen. If it is not ready, it will be matte and transparent. If worked too much, it will be opaque and lose its sheen and shape as it sets. For all the different flowers, the preparation of the sugar remains the same.

Photo 6: Form a ball from the pulled sugar. Place it on a drum sieve and under a heat source. Pull with both hands in opposite directions to create a thin edge. With the sugar between the thumb and the index finger, pull off a petal. The sugar must be warm enough to remain malleable, yet not melt.

Photo 7: Fold a petal around itself to form the heart or bud of the flower. There are many ways of preparing a pulled sugar rose; each professional develops an individual style. Attach the petals as they are pulled, overlapping them in a spiral around the bud.

Photo 8: Wrap the petals around the bud so it appears to be blossoming. A decorative rose will have 10–12 petals. A more natural rose will have 20–25 petals.

Rosebud: The procedure for preparing a rosebud is the same as for a blooming rose, but only the heart of the flower is made. Three green sepals are attached around the bottom of the bud.

Storing Pulled Sugar Flowers

Pulled sugar does not hold up well in open air. The humidity in the air causes the sugar to lose its sheen and shape. Pulled sugar must be stored in an airtight container with a sachet of desiccant or loose calcium chloride, limestone, carbide, or other drying agent.

It is advantageous to have differently colored pulled sugars on hand. This way, by simply warming up the sugar under a heat source it can be shaped as needed.

Although the choice is not always available, it is best to prepare pulled sugar flowers when the weather is dry and carefully store them until needed.

As soon as each pulled sugar flower is completed, immediately place it in an airtight container with desiccant, keeping it closed until the flower is used.

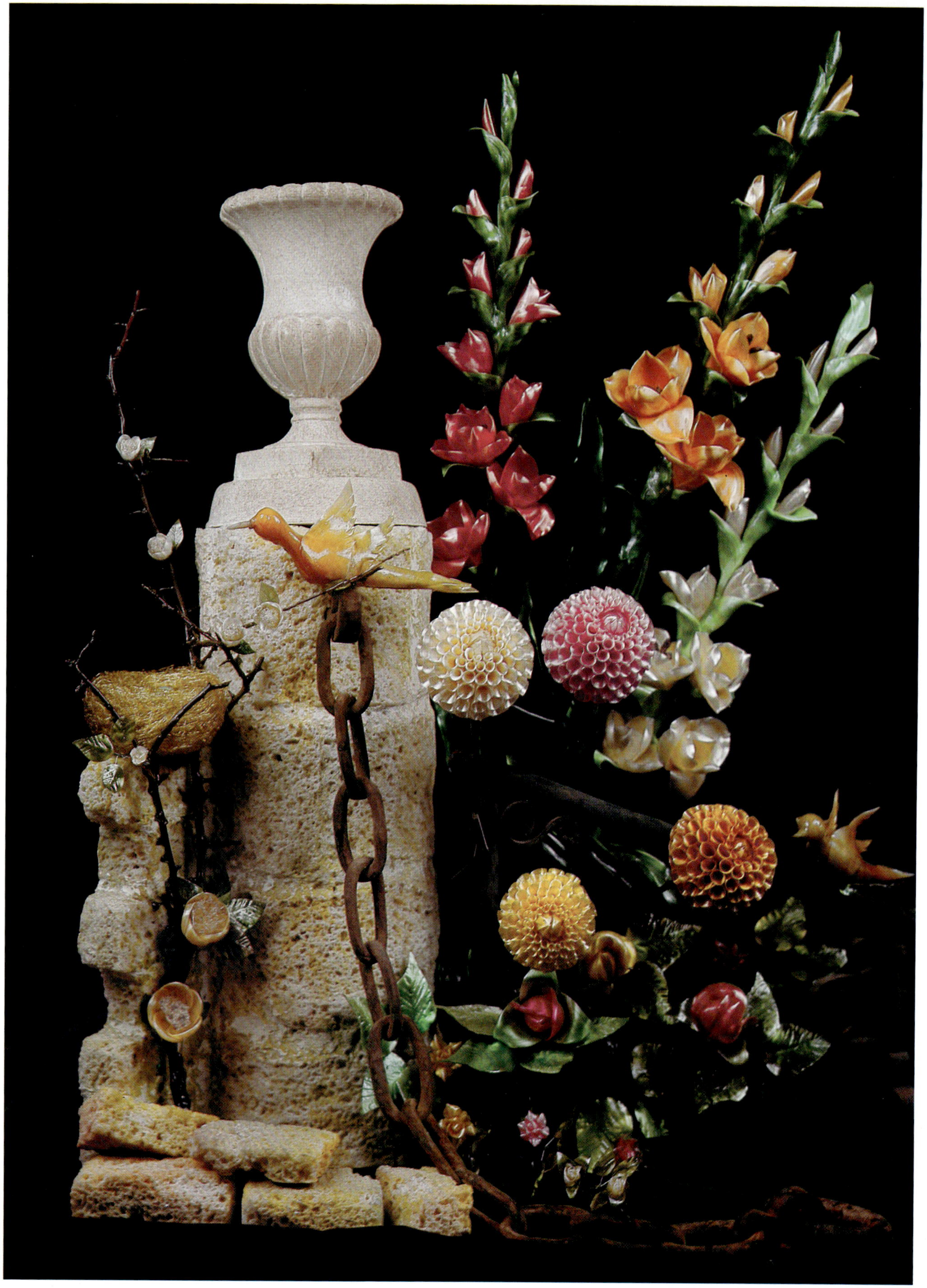

When All Hope Is Revived

This presentation piece represents a scene in the country with a stone column on which a vase rests. It is given an aged look to portray a passage of time where much activity has once occurred. A rusty chain is suspended from the column to give the impression that it was used by knights as a hitching post. Pulled sugar roses, dahlias, gladiolus, and birds brighten up the abandoned ruins. Meant to represent a lost corner in south-central France which actually exists, not far from my birthplace, a path leads out of the village to this spot. The last villagers of the area have long departed, the old have passed on, and the young have moved to the cities. I used to run by here as a boy and continue to cherish fond memories of that time.

Assembling an Artistic Piece

Before attempting to assemble an artistic piece, all the separate sections must be completed. The success of the finished piece often depends on the speed of assembly. A cool, dry area is required. If possible, it is best to work in an area other than the kitchen where the steam and heat of the ovens and burners can be troublesome. It is also best if the weather is dry so the pulled sugar will store better.

The construction is made on an unrefrigerated pastry marble or other flat, dry work surface. The materials needed are: a gas burner to heat the caramel or cooked sugar, an alcohol Bunsen burner, and a small propane torch.

If pastillage is used, the pieces must be thoroughly dried out. Dried tree branches or wires coated with sugar should be ready. Pulled sugar pieces should be stored in airtight containers with desiccant and removed just before using.

The finished pieces may be displayed in a glass or other see-through presentation box that was previously prepared. If this is used, make a double or false bottom so desiccant can be placed between two layers of wood or other material used. The top layer should have small holes for the desiccant to be effective. Once everything is prepared, the assembly will go quickly.

Fix the pastillage and sugar pieces to the base. Attach the cooked sugar coated branches and flowers. Set the birds and other elements in place. Put the desiccant in place and cover the piece with the transparent case.

Facing Page: When All Hope Is Revived

304   *Modern French Pastry*

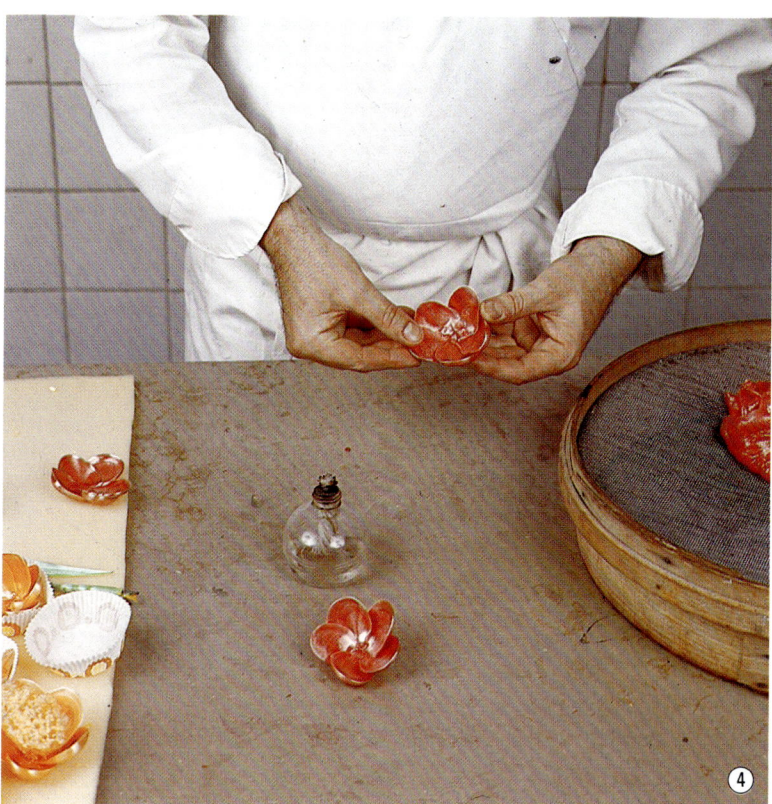

Christmas Roses

Photo 1: Cook and prepare the pulled sugar (see pages 295–296). Make a ball, place it on a drum sieve under a heat source. With the thumb and index of both hands pulling in opposite directions, spread out a thin edge of sugar.

Photo 2: With one hand, pinch the thin edge of sugar between the thumb and index finger, pulling off a piece quickly and sharply to form a petal. Prepare four more petals this way, five per flower.

Photo 3: When enough petals are made, the flowers are ready to be assembled. Heat the base or pointed part of each petal with an alcohol burner and attach the petals together at the ends.

Photo 4: The size of the petals will determine the size of the finished flowers. The flowers can also be shaped to appear more or less open by placing them closer or further apart.

Photo 5: Prepare pistils with spun sugar (see pages 377-378). Trim them to size. Heat the bottom end with a flame.

Photo 6: Immediately press the heated pistil into the center of the flower so it adheres. Store the finished flower in an airtight container with desiccant.

Sugar and Decoration Work

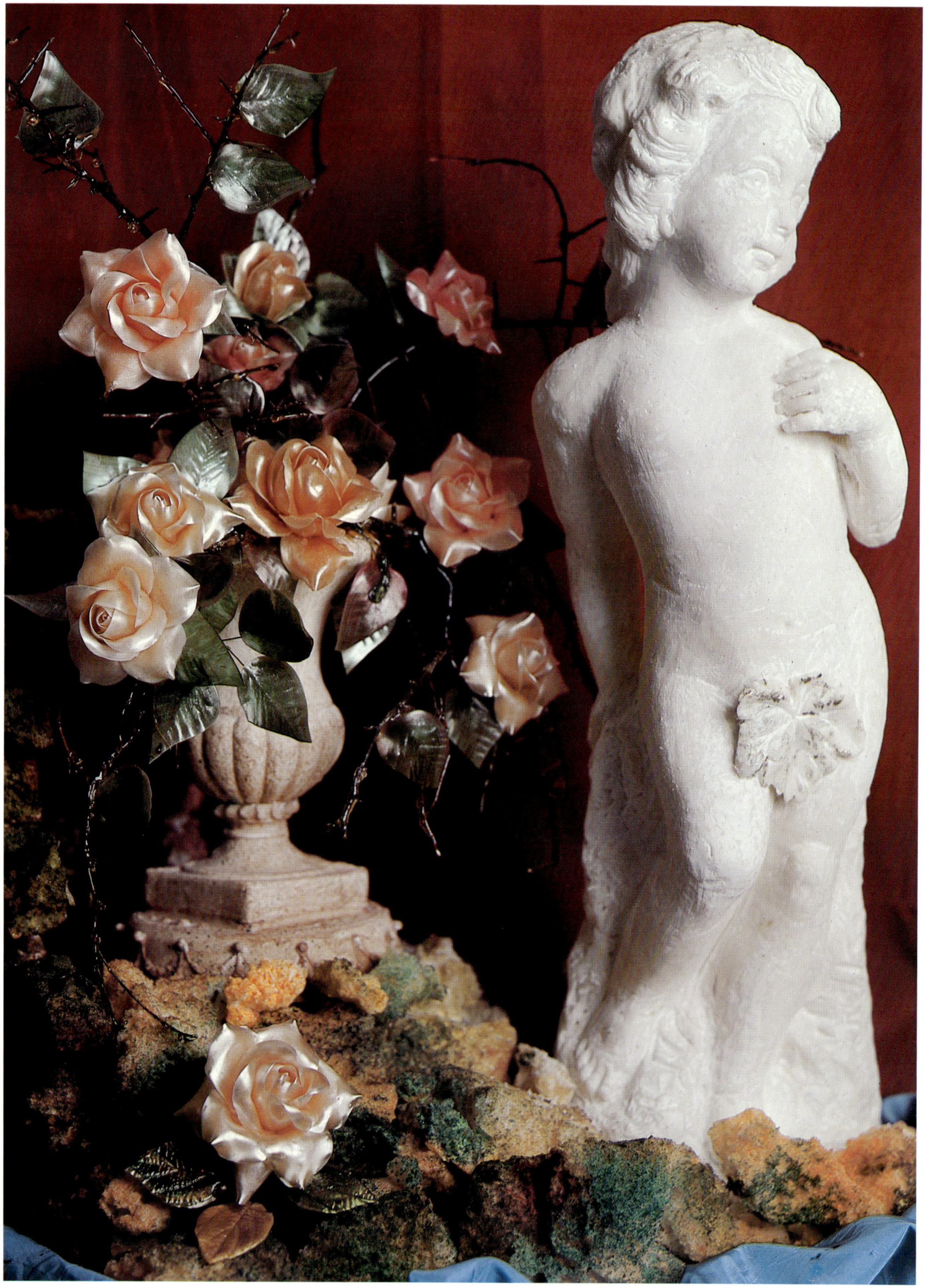

Park Corner

A cupid sculpted in white chocolate is the focal point for this presentation piece set beside a vase filled with pulled sugar roses. Rock sugar is used to create the impression of old tumbled stone.

Rock Sugar
Sucre Rocher

Rock sugar is generally only used for artistic pieces. It does not require a great deal of work or practice and is fairly easy and quick to prepare. It is rarely used on its own, but rather with other types of sugar work. It is used to enhance blown, pulled, or molded sugar, or chocolate carvings. It is meant to imitate old stone work or loose rocks.

Unlike pulled sugar, rock sugar stores well uncovered and is not affected by heat or humidity.

sugar	35 oz	1,000 g
water	14 oz	400 g
royal icing	1 tbsp	1 tbsp

Chef's Note: *Rock sugar does not contain glucose, cream of tartar, or other acid to prevent it from crystallizing.*

It is important to use an extra large saucepan to accommodate the sugar when it rises.

Cook the sugar and water to 275°–284°F/135°–140°C. Quickly stir in the royal icing, being careful not to overmix. The sugar will rise and fall, then rise again. When the sugar rises for the second time, quickly pour it into an aluminum foil-lined carton. If necessary, additional layers may be poured over the first layer, such as for columns. Set the rock sugar aside for 12–24 hours until it sets.

Unmold the set rock sugar and cut to the size and shape needed. Cut the rock sugar with small wood saws and files. To give extra strength to fragile pieces or those meant to support a weight, set a metal wire inside the sugar when it is being poured.

After giving the rock sugar the desired shape, it may be shaded or tinted with color using a brush or spray gun. The rock sugar can also be colored during cooking as for molded sugar. To imitate old stone, it is best to color with a spray gun.

To attach two rock sugar blocks together, or prepare a wall, use royal icing as an adhesive and set aside to dry for several days. A considerably faster method is to use cooked sugar to attach the pieces together. It will be ready when the cooked sugar sets, but the results are not as solid as royal icing.

To give a coarse-grained effect, such as for bread, place the cooked rock sugar in a moderate oven immediately after pouring it out of the pot. The heat of the oven keeps the sugar from falling. This step is not necessary for creating old or worn stone.

When it is necessary to stack more than one layer of rock sugar, the crust that forms at the surface should be scraped smooth to enable the two pieces join more easily.

Carefully wash the copper sugar pot (poêlon) before cooking a new batch of sugar. If the rock sugar is too crumbly or sandy, it was probably overstirred when the royal icing was added; this step should be done quickly and briefly.

Facing Page: Park Corner

308 Modern French Pastry

Rock Sugar

Photo 1: Prepare and cook the recipe for rock sugar on page 307 to 275°–285°F/135°–140°C. Remove the pot from the heat.

Photo 2: Stir a spoonful of royal icing into the cooked sugar with a wooden spoon or whisk. It is important that this step be done quickly.

Photo 3: As soon as the royal icing is well blended, the sugar will rise in the pot. Do not stir during this time; allow it to rise. It is important to have a pot large enough to accommodate the sugar when it rises.

Photo 4: After the sugar has risen, it will fall, then rise a second time.

Photo 5: After rising for the second time, immediately empty the sugar into a mold or container lined with aluminum foil.

Photo 6: The sugar will again rise slightly in the mold or container. It is recommended to place the sugar in an oven for a few minutes to prevent it from falling excessively. Allow the sugar to harden and set for 12–24 hours.

Chef's Note: *The quantity of royal icing does not have to be absolutely precise; although, if too little is used, the rock sugar will be heavy; if too much is used, the rock sugar will be too crumbly. It is important to stop stirring when the sugar begins to rise, soon after incorporating the royal icing, or the rock sugar will break down and crumble.*

Sugar and Decoration Work

310 Modern French Pastry

Working with Rock Sugar

Photo 7: After the rock sugar has completely cooled, it is ready to be unmolded.

Photo 8: Remove the aluminum foil. The rock sugar is ready to be cut and shaped. Regardless of the mold used, the procedure remains the same.

Photo 9: The rock sugar cuts easily and cleanly with a wood saw.

Photo 10: Cut the rock sugar into the shapes and sizes needed.

Photo 11: The rock sugar can be filed with a wood file, or sculpted as for carved stone.

Photo 12: The pieces are assembled with royal icing or softened pastillage.

Coloring

Rock sugar can be colored during cooking to create a uniform color. To imitate a wall or loose stones, a more natural effect can be obtained by coloring with a spray gun. More than one color can be sprayed on to create tints and sheen for a more realistic touch.

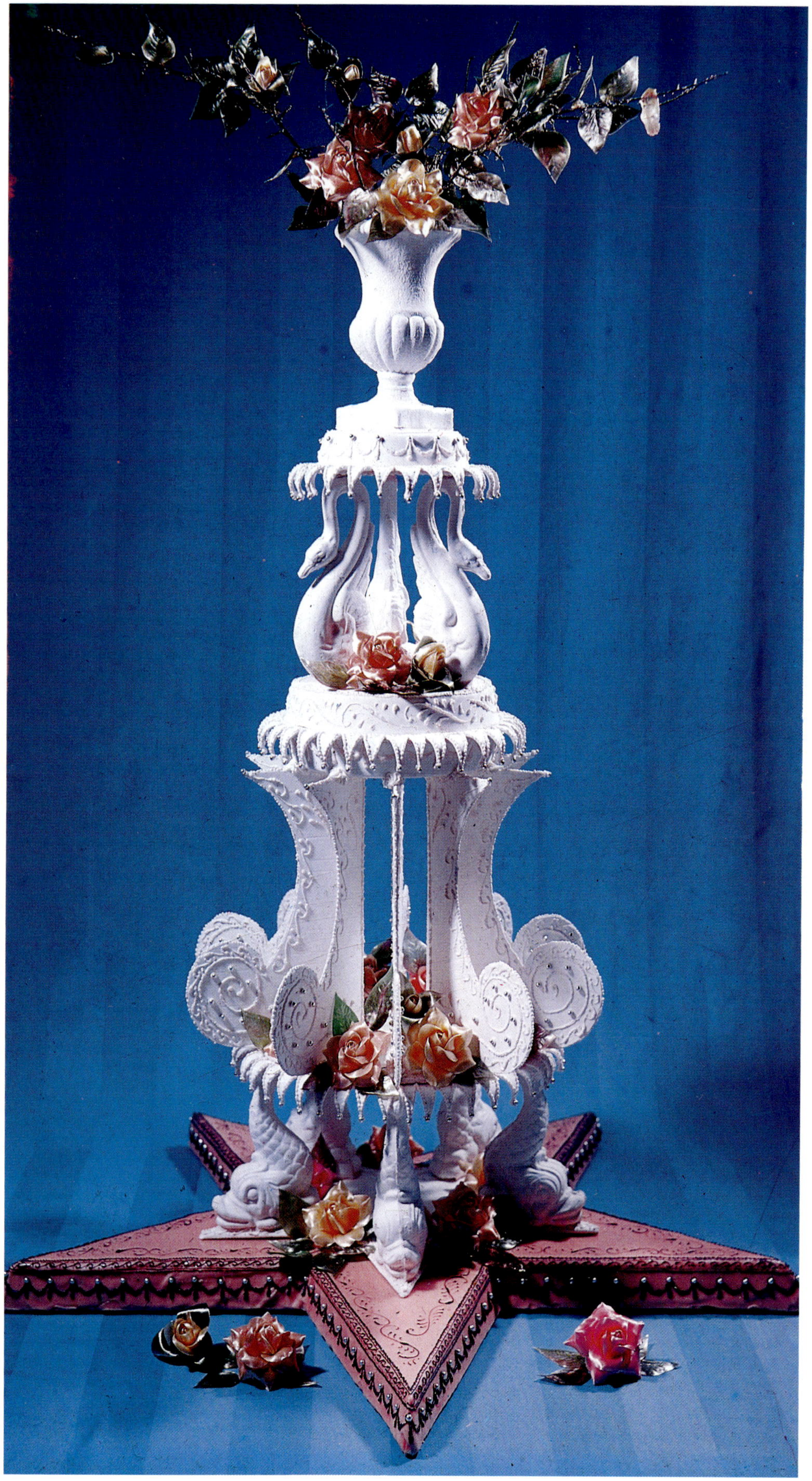

Galacté

This piece is made for a buffet or other presentation. Receptions and buffets often serve a modest presentation of petits fours or small tea cakes. This presentation piece can formally decorate a table. It is not an edible piece; rather, it is intended to create an elegant ambiance for surrounding cakes.

Buffet decoration pieces are often made in pastillage. With slight alterations, they can be used for several events. This type of work is indispensable for hotels, restaurants, or other facilities that offer buffets.

The pulled sugar flowers have a short shelf life, making it necessary to prepare new ones for each presentation. This particular piece is composed of five separate pastillage sections. Depending on the importance of the event, the presentation can be assembled with fewer sections. This offers a variety of different presentations.

The sections are:

1. A star-shaped dummy cake covered with fondant and decorated with chocolate icing using a paper cone.

2. Pastillage molded dolphins held in place by two pastillage bases.

3. Pastillage arabesques, also attached to a flat base placed on the bottom and another base on top.

4. Pastillage molded swans, attached to a base molded in a génoise pan, and covered with a pastillage disk decorated with wolf's teeth.

5. A pastillage vase set on a podium molded in a génoise pan.

6. A bouquet of pulled sugar flowers in the vase, and pulled sugar flowers placed on and around the piece.

Facing Page: Galacté

Pastillage

Of all the different types of sugar work discussed in this book, pastillage requires a very different treatment. Pastillage must be stored in the open, uncovered, to dry and thereby assure its solidity.

Pastillage is made in the following steps:

1. Kneading

Although usually prepared by hand, pastillage can also be made with an electric mixer, using a dough hook or paddle attachment.

2. Cutting and Molding

Pastillage is cut and molded similarly to nougatine, except that pastillage is worked cold, not warm, as for nougatine.

3. Drying

Pastillage pieces must be air dried before being assembled; the necessary amount of time depends on the thickness and size of the piece. It is important that the pastillage be completely dried; the drier the pastillage, the stronger it will be.

4. Assembling

After the pastillage sections are thoroughly dried, they are ready to be assembled. Use royal icing or fresh pastillage softened with egg white or water. For very large pieces, sections should be allowed to dry from time to time and assembled in stages. After attaching all the sections, allow some time for the pastillage and the joints to dry completely.

5. Coloring

Pastillage can be colored while it is being prepared, during the kneading, which will result in a uniform coloring. It can also be colored after being assembled with a paint brush or air brush.

(Pastillage recipe continued on next page)

The high white of natural pastillage is very elegant looking, making it preferable to leave it uncolored when it is used to decorate a cake.

Numerous recipes can be used to prepare pastillage. The only restriction is that the mixture be based primarily on confectioners' sugar with a small percentage of starch. The dry ingredients are brought together with water and a gelatin such as powdered gelatin, Arabic gum, tragacanth, or other of the same family.

Pastillage No. 1

confectioners' sugar	35 oz	1,000 g
starch	7 oz	200 g
tragacanth	2 oz	50 g
water, warm	7 oz	200 g

Combine the confectioners' sugar, starch, and tragacanth. Make a well in the center and gradually add the warm water. The pastillage should feel firm, but malleable, so it can be cut, shaped, and molded without crumbling or feeling sticky.

The mixture can also be prepared with an electric mixer, using the dough hook.

Pastillage No. 2

gelatin, powdered	1 oz	30 g
water, warm	5.5 oz	150 g
confectioners' sugar	35 oz	1,000 g
cornstarch or potato starch	3.5 oz	100 g
citric acid or lemon juice (optional)		

Several hours before preparing the batter, dissolve the gelatin or tragacanth in the warm water.

Combine the confectioners' sugar and starch. Make a well, add the water/gelatin mixture and citric acid or lemon juice, if used. Knead by hand or in the bowl of an electric mixer, using the dough hook. If necessary, add more confectioners' sugar to firm the mixture, or a few drops of water to soften.

On a pastry marble or other work surface lightly dusted with cornstarch, roll out the pastillage to the desired thickness with a rolling pin. Using a cardboard pattern, cut the pastillage with a knife to the shape and size needed.

Allow the pastillage pieces to dry half-way on a cooling rack, then turn them over to finish drying.

For molded subjects such as dolphins and swans, dust molds lightly with cornstarch and line them with rolled out pastillage. Trim off the edges. Fill the molds with starch or flour. Place a cardboard on top of the mold and turn it over (see photos, pages 317–319). The pieces will dry more rapidly once they are unmolded.

Several days later, lift the pastillage pieces and remove the excess starch that has been supporting them. Continue to dry the pieces, placing them on a cooling rack. When fully dry, attach the two halves with royal icing or softened pastillage.

Compared to other types of decorative sugar work, pastillage does not require a great deal of experience, the most exacting part of the work being the molding and shaping. However, although it is the easiest of the decorative sugars to prepare, it also takes the most time, from start to finish, due to the required drying time. It is sometimes necessary to allow several weeks until the pieces are completed, shaped and fully dried.

Pastillage

Photo 1: Follow one of the recipes on page 314 to form a pastillage swan as shown here. Prepare confectioners' sugar, starch, warm water, and gelatin or tragacanth.

Photo 2: Combine the confectioners' sugar and a starch, such as cornstarch. Make a well with the ingredients on a pastry marble or other work surface. Gradually stir in the warm water and dissolved powdered gelatin or tragacanth.

Photo 3: The mixture can be kneaded by hand or with an electric mixer, using the dough hook. Add just enough of the water to form a dough, which will be soft at first, taking on more body as it is kneaded.

(Pastillage continued on page 317)

316   *Modern French Pastry*

Photo 4: Add more water or confectioners' sugar, if necessary. The dough should be firm and well blended. If the dough is too soft, add a bit of confectioners' sugar; if it is too firm, add a bit of water to soften.

Photo 5: Cut off the amount of pastillage needed for each mold. Roll it out with a rolling pin on the pastry marble or other work surface lightly dusted with starch or confectioners' sugar. The thickness can vary between 1/16–1/6 in/2–4 mm depending on the mold.

Photo 6: Dust the mold (a plaster of Paris mold is used here) with starch and line it with a layer of pastillage.

Chef's Note: At this point the pastillage can be lined in a plaster of Paris or copper mold, or it can be trimmed with a knife using a cardboard pattern to form a motif, base, arabesque, wolf's teeth, etc. Regardless of the shape, the procedure remains the same.

Photo 7: Carefully press the pastillage against the inside of the mold. If the pastillage is too firm, it will crack during this step; if too soft, it will stick to the mold or lose its shape upon unmolding.

Photo 8: After lining the mold, check that the pastillage is pressed into all the details. With a serrated knife, trim the excess pastillage.

Photo 9: Fill the pastillage-lined mold with flour or starch, pressing it into the mold and smoothing it to the rim.

Pastillage is generally molded in two halves. The second half of the swan is made following the same procedure as for the first half.

Filling the lined mold with the flour or starch makes it possible to unmold the undried pastillage while maintaining its shape. The procedure for molding pastillage is the same for all molds.

(Pastillage continued on page 319)

318 Modern French Pastry

Photo 10: To unmold the pastillage, place a cardboard on top of the mold filled with flour or cornstarch. Turn the mold over, right side up.

Photo 11: Lift the mold, exposing the first swan half. The mold can immediately be reused, lined with pastillage, filled with flour or starch and unmolded as many times as needed. Allow the unmolded pastillage forms to dry for several days.

Photo 12: After drying, remove the flour or starch from beneath the pastillage form and place it on a cooling rack for the interior to dry.

Photo 13: When the molded pastillage has completely dried, use a pastry brush to remove any excess flour or starch. With a paper cone, pipe out royal icing or softened pastillage around the border of the figures.

Photo 14: Gently press the two molded halves together (the assembled swan is shown here). Again allow the pastillage and royal icing to dry.

Photo 15: The swan is finished after the seams have fully dried. The seams should be lightly filed or smoothed with sandpaper. The figure can be attached to a dried pastillage base with royal icing, after which it must again be allowed to dry.

Sugar and Decoration Work

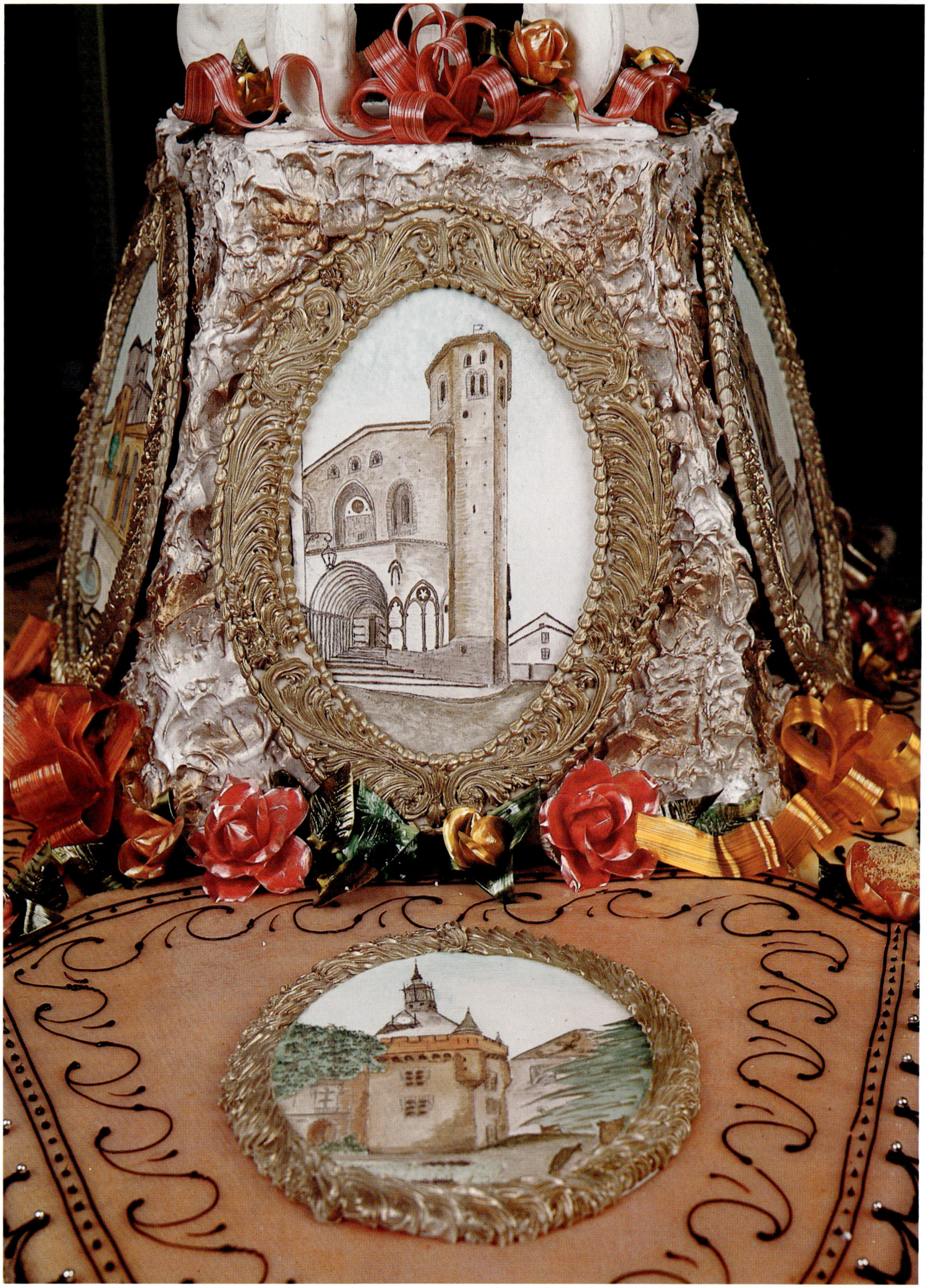

Painting on Pastillage

The same technique used for painting with water colors is applied to painting on pastillage. In France, one of the chefs most respected for his ability in this area of pastry decoration is Jean Deblieux.

Preparation
Prepare even, flat, well-dried sheets of pastillage. If necessary, the surface can be smoothed by lightly sanding with sandpaper.

Equipment
The tools required include a ruler, pencil, and large selection of paintbrushes. Use only food coloring, either liquid or powdered diluted in alcohol. Although it is possible to purchase almost any color needed, assorted colors can be obtained by mixing primary colors, such as yellow and blue to make green. To paint with chocolate, dilute cocoa powder in alcohol and simple syrup, 30° baume.

Procedure
Place the dried sheet of pastillage on a flat surface, preferably over a thin layer of foam rubber or a cloth. Carefully draw or trace the intended design in pencil on the pastillage sheet. This step will greatly affect the end result. Paint on the pastillage, keeping in mind that it is always possible to deepen a color but very difficult to lighten a dark color. Colors can be lightened with alcohol as needed before applying them. Very concentrated colors are often too dark and unappealing.

The Frame
The frame, also made in pastillage, is prepared separately. It can be decorated with royal icing using a pastry bag and fluted tip. After drying, brush on gold-colored powder or gold dust. Once the frame is completely dried, it is attached to the painting with royal icing, making it stronger. Check the stability.

Painting on Pastillage with Cocoa Powder
Pastillage can also be painted with cocoa powder alone, diluted in alcohol. It is recommended to first practice on a white cardboard surface, copying a black and white photograph.

The same procedure is applied as for painting with color; first trace or draw the design in pencil. It is easier to work with a good assortment of paintbrushes. Gradations of tinting can be acquired by dipping the brush in alcohol.

Facing Page: Painting on Pastillage

Pulled Sugar Ribbon

Pulled Sugar Ribbons

Refer to the recipe for pulled sugar on pages 295–296. As for pulled sugar flowers, the first recipe with cream of tarter is the easiest to work with and the third, made with glucose, is the most difficult. For ribbons, the sugar is prepared and cooked much like the sugar for pulled flowers, with a few additional precautionary measures:

1. The final cooking temperature should be a bit higher than for pulled sugar flowers. If the sugar is not sufficiently cooked, the ribbon will quickly lose its shape and sheen. If the sugar is slightly overcooked, it will easily crack when pulled, making it difficult to work with, though it will better maintain its sheen and form.

2. Impurities in both the sugar and water can sometimes result in a grainy texture when the sugar is pulled. To avoid this problem, choose highly refined sugar cubes, and clean (distilled) water. While the sugar is cooking, use a pastry brush dipped in water to wash down any sugar crystals that form around the sides of the pot.

If the sugar was not first cooked to a syrup and set aside to rest, it is best to cook the sugar in two stages. First cook the sugar to 284°F/140°C. Cool, then cook again, starting gently until the syrup melts, then cooking to the desired temperature, turning the heat up high.

Cooking in two steps prevents or considerably diminishes the chances of a grainy texture, which is more obvious on pulled sugar ribbons than flowers. After reaching the final temperature, dip the bottom of the pot into a bowl of cold water for a few seconds to stop the cooking. Set the cooked sugar aside in the pot to rest until the bubbles dissipate.

Color and Sheen

Pour the cooked sugar into two or three separate mounds, based on the number of intended colors, onto a lightly oiled marble. Color each batch with powdered food coloring diluted in alcohol.

Use a pastry triangle to bring the edges of each mound toward the center by lifting underneath. The triangle can be oiled to prevent sticking. Repeat this step until each mound of cooked sugar has sufficiently cooled.

Form each batch of cooled sugar into a sausage shape and pull them separately under a heat source such as an infrared lamp, near an oven door, or portable radiator. When each batch of sugar has obtained a satin sheen, stretch each sugar out and fold in half.

Shaping

Join the strips of sugar at the sides and press down to flatten. This can be done on a non-refrigerated marble or drum sieve. Stretch the pulled sugar to twice its length and fold it in half, joining two sides together in the middle (see Photo 5, page 325). Repeat this step one to three more times depending on the desired width. The more the sugar is pulled, the greater number of alternating colored stripes of color will be obtained. Pull the sugar near a heat source, being careful not to let it get too warm or the sugar will lose shape.

When working with a large quantity of sugar or when pulling very large ribbons, it is easier to work with a second person, each taking an end. The pulled ribbon is placed on a marble or two sheet pans turned upside down, touching side by side.

Assembling the Ribbon

Heat a knife in a flame using a gas burner or propane torch, and cut the ribbon into 6–8 in/15–20 cm long sections. Place each section under a heat lamp just long enough to be able to bend it in half to form loops for the bow. Press the ends together but keep the loop open, forming a teardrop shape. Repeat this step with all the cut pieces of pulled sugar except those intended for the ends of the bow, which are not bent but lightly rippled. Attach the loops to form the bow by heating the ends with an alcohol burner. Assemble the bow starting on the outside and finishing in the center. Attach the ends under the bow. The novice should begin with a solid color ribbon before attempting two or three colors.

As soon as the ribbon is finished, store it in an airtight container with desiccant until needed.

324 *Modern French Pastry*

Preparing a Pulled Sugar Ribbon

Photo 1: Prepare and cook the sugar using recipes on pages 295–296. For a ribbon containing two colors, pour two separate pools of sugar onto an oiled marble. Add the desired coloring to each batch of sugar.

Photo 2: Using a pastry triangle, cool the sugar and blend in the coloring by folding it over onto itself from underneath the edges into the center.

Photo 3: As soon as the sugar is cool enough to handle, shape each color into a sausage shape and place it under a heat source. Pull each section evenly. Fold it in half, repeat the pulling and folding until the sugar has acquired the proper sheen.

Photo 4: On a lightly oiled marble or drum sieve, press the sections together on the sides and flatten them. Pull the strip of sugar evenly.

Photo 5: Fold the strip in half, joining it on the sides in the middle. The sugar is now thinner and wider. At this point, the ribbon could be folded again. This would produce a much wider and shorter ribbon.

Photo 6: The ribbon shown here is now striped green, yellow, green. If it is pulled and folded a second time it will be striped green, yellow, green, yellow, green. This step can be repeated depending on the pattern desired.

The sugar is always worked near or under a heat source, such as an infrared lamp or portable electric heater.

(Preparing a Pulled Sugar Ribbon continued on page 327)

Sugar and Decoration Work

326 *Modern French Pastry*

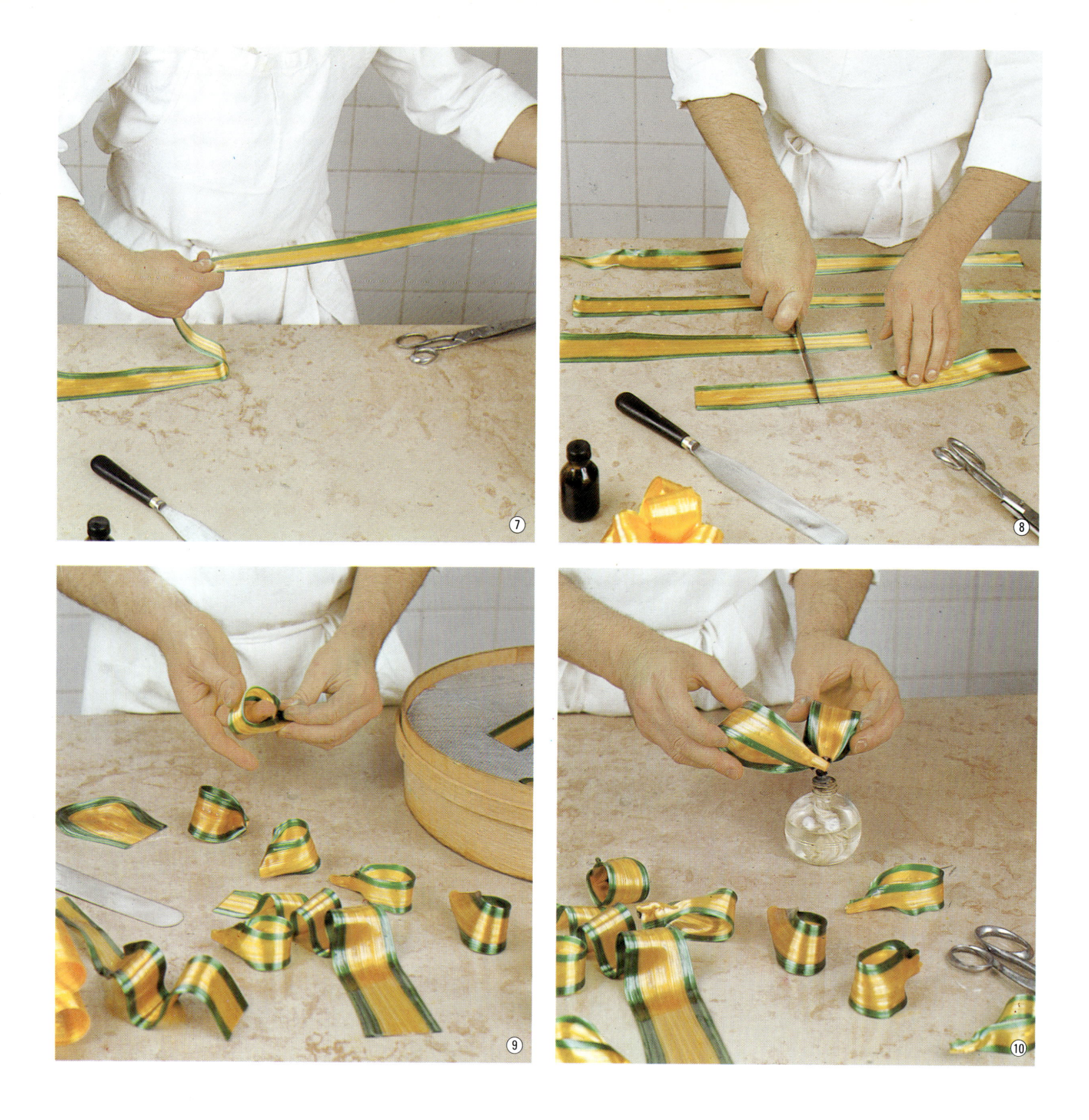

Photo 7: Pull the ribbon evenly and place it on lightly oiled marble. For very long and/or wide ribbons, it is best to work with a second person.

Photo 8: Heat a knife in a flame and use it to cut the strip into 6–8 in/15–20 cm long sections.

Photo 9: Place the shorter strips of pulled sugar on a drum sieve under a heat source only long enough for them to soften slightly. Round them in half to form a loop and pinch the ends together. Use the longer sections to make the ends of the bow. Warm the strips until malleable and ripple them.

Photo 10: Heat the ends of the loops or bowed pieces using an alcohol burner.

Photo 11: Begin by attaching the heated ends, one at a time, starting around the sides and finishing in the center of the bow.

Photo 12: Attach the rippled ends to the bow.

Chef's Note: Follow the same procedure if using three colors; simply pour the cooked sugar into three separate mounds onto the marble and color as desired (see Photo 1). Join the three sections after pulling by pressing them together on the sides (see Photo 4). It is recommended that beginners start with one color.

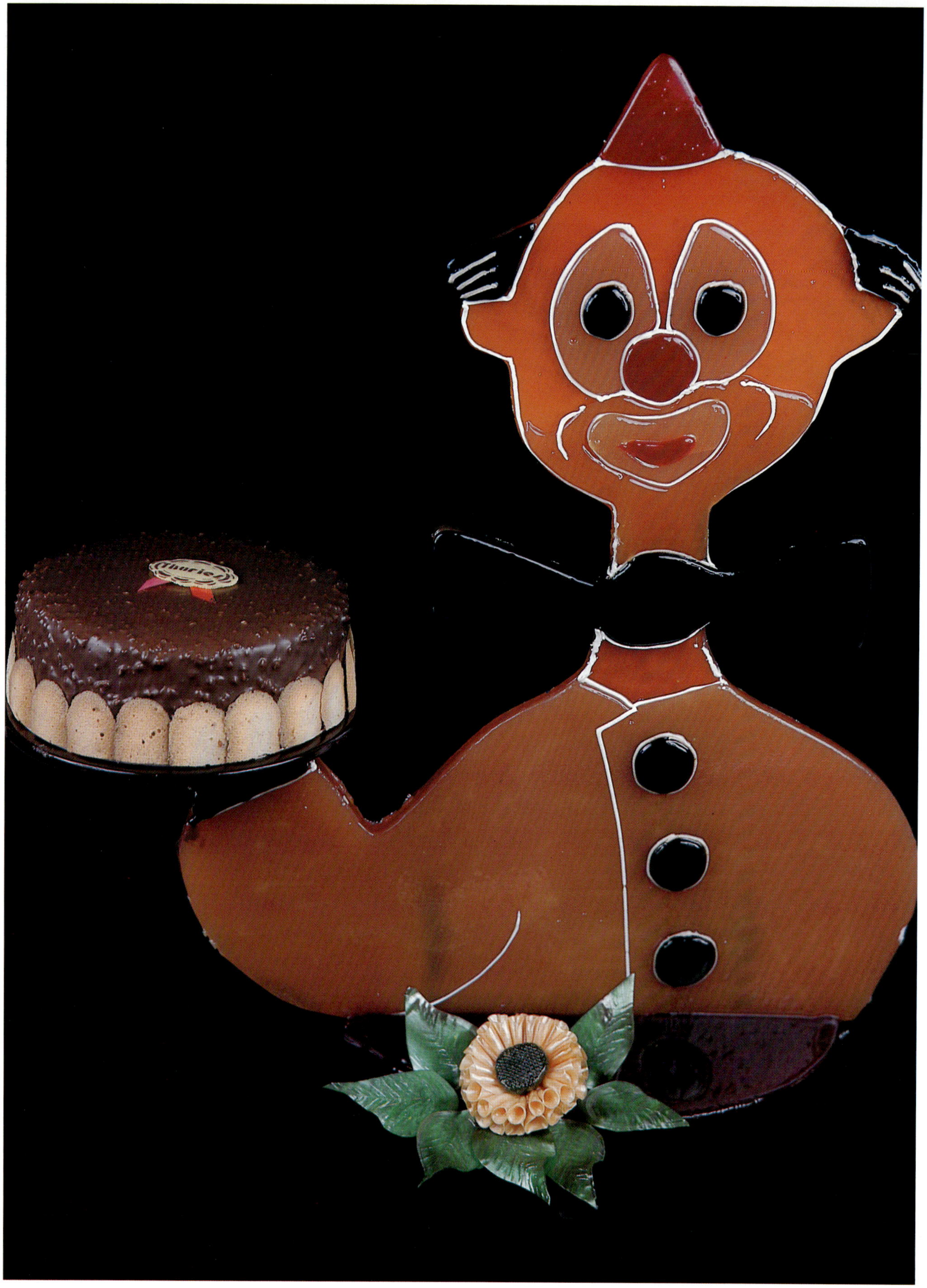

Clown

Follow the photos on pages 330–333 to prepare the poured sugar clown.

Assembly

Use cooked sugar to attach the clown to a large poured sugar base, with two poured sugar triangles in the back for support. Prop the piece, securing it until the supports are set in place.

To support cakes and pastries on the presentation piece, attach a poured sugar disk, braced by two small poured sugar triangles on either side. This piece can be used to present cakes or other pastries. Other figures and shapes can be prepared using the same technique, such as a poured sugar crescent. Pulled or molded sugar flowers can be used to decorate the pieces.

Poured Sugar

Poured sugar is a good medium to use for presenting cakes and pastries. It is the easiest of all the decorative sugars as it requires no manipulation or special preparation before being poured and shaped.

sugar cubes	*35 oz*	*1,000 g*
water	*12.5 oz*	*350 g*
glucose	*9 oz*	*250 g*

Facing Page: Clown Presentation Piece

Combine all ingredients and cook to 302°F/150°C for small pieces and 311°C/155°C or more for large pieces. The coloring is added before the cooking is finished, at approximately 275°F/135°C, using a powdered food coloring diluted in alcohol. To give an opaque appearance, dilute 1 tsp calcium carbonate in water, and add to the sugar either before or halfway through cooking. Color as indicated for non-opaque pieces.

The most challenging aspect of poured sugar work is preparing the border for molding. For a round base, use a lightly oiled tart or cake ring of the desired size placed over aluminum foil. For more elaborate shapes, the border can be made in different ways:

1. A lightly oiled metal band that bends easily.
2. Modeling clay, being careful to lightly oil the contours and hard-to-reach places.
3. A special fondant piped with a pastry bag and plain tip.

Pour the sugar, preferably using a pan with a pouring spout, into the prepared form set over aluminum foil or parchment paper. Be careful to pour the sugar around the borders evenly, as it cannot be corrected once the sugar has set. After the sugar has completely cooled and hardened, the pieces can be unmolded and assembled. Use cooked sugar to attach the sections.

Certain poured sugar subjects require more than one color. In this case, pour one base color into the mold. When the sugar has set, pipe out the special fondant or royal icing. Pour the desired color of poured sugar into the borders. It is also possible to pour different colors side by side.

Precautions for Making Poured Sugar Pieces

When the sugar has reached the proper temperature, immediately dip the bottom of the pot into cold water for a few seconds to stop the cooking. Set the sugar in the pot aside to rest until all bubbles have dissipated.

The form is placed over aluminum foil or parchment paper lying completely flat on a marble or other work surface. To obtain a perfectly smooth surface, begin pouring the sugar from one side of the mold to the other. Do not pour more sugar over an area that has already been poured.

Special Fondant for Creating Borders for Poured Sugar

With a wooden spoon, stir two thirds cold fondant with one third royal icing until well blended. Pipe the mixture using a pastry bag and tip, 1/3 in/8 mm in diameter. Pipe the contours of the subject on aluminum foil or parchment paper. Allow 12–24 hours for the special fondant to fully set. Pour the cooked sugar inside the special fondant borders.

Poured Sugar

Photo 1: Prepare and cook the sugar according to the recipe on page 329. Make a frame with flat, flexible metal as shown here, modeling clay, or special fondant, shaping as desired. Place the frame over aluminum foil or parchment paper set on a flat work surface.

Photo 2: Pour the cooked sugar into the frame. It is important to pour from one side to the other. Do not pour more sugar over an area that has already been poured or the surface will not be even. The thickness is determined by the strength required; usually 1/4–1/2 in/7–10 mm is sufficient. Check the thickness of the border carefully, because it should not be retouched once set.

Photo 3: Trace designs with royal icing or special fondant over the poured sugar using a paper cone.

Photo 4: A thin layer of a differently colored poured sugar can be poured inside the piping. Keep the sugar inside the piped border. Use a pot with a spout for greater control.

Sugar and Decoration Work 331

332   *Modern French Pastry*

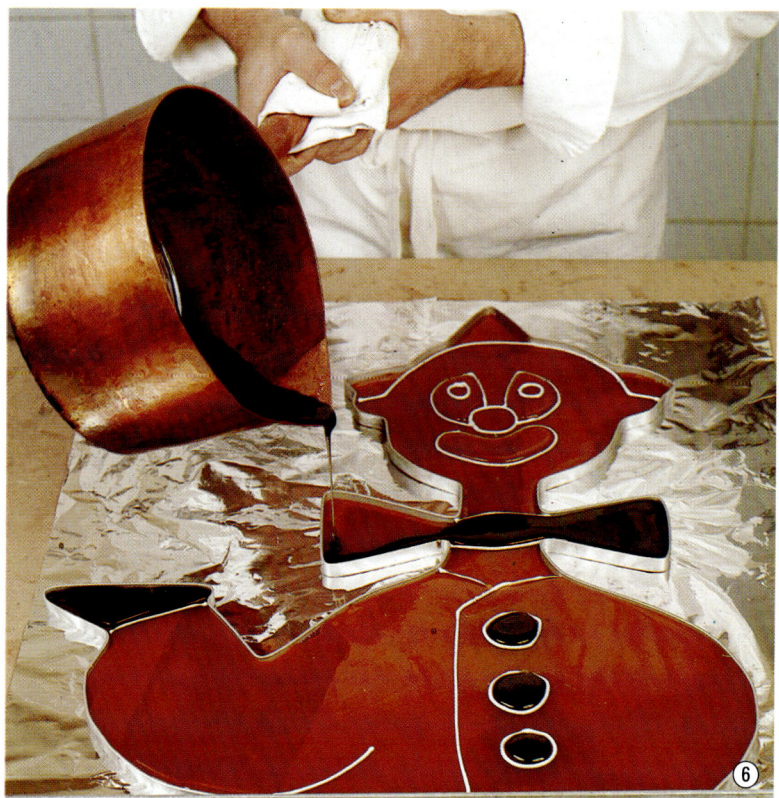

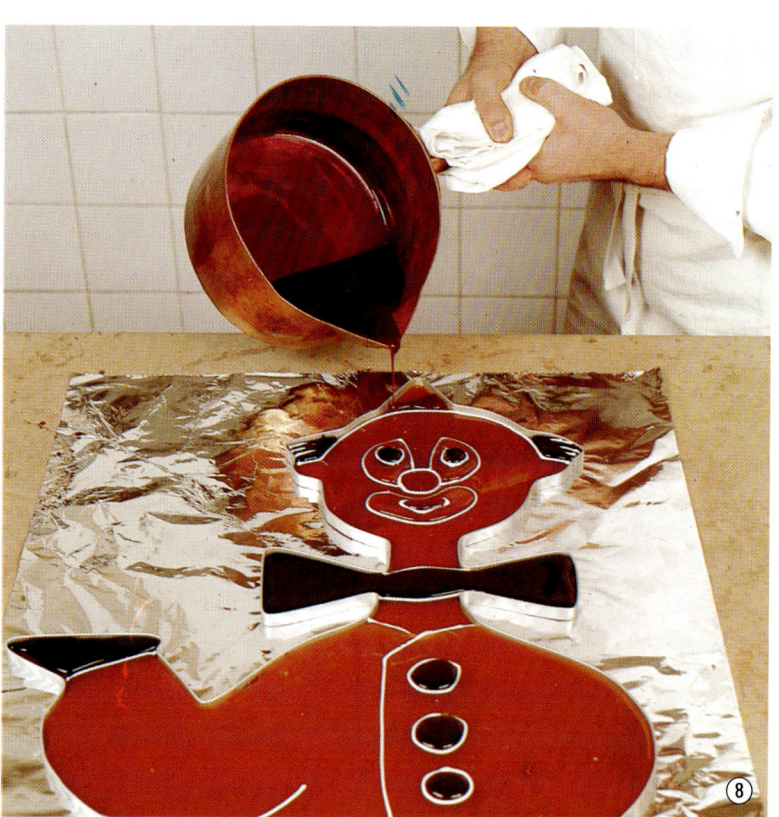

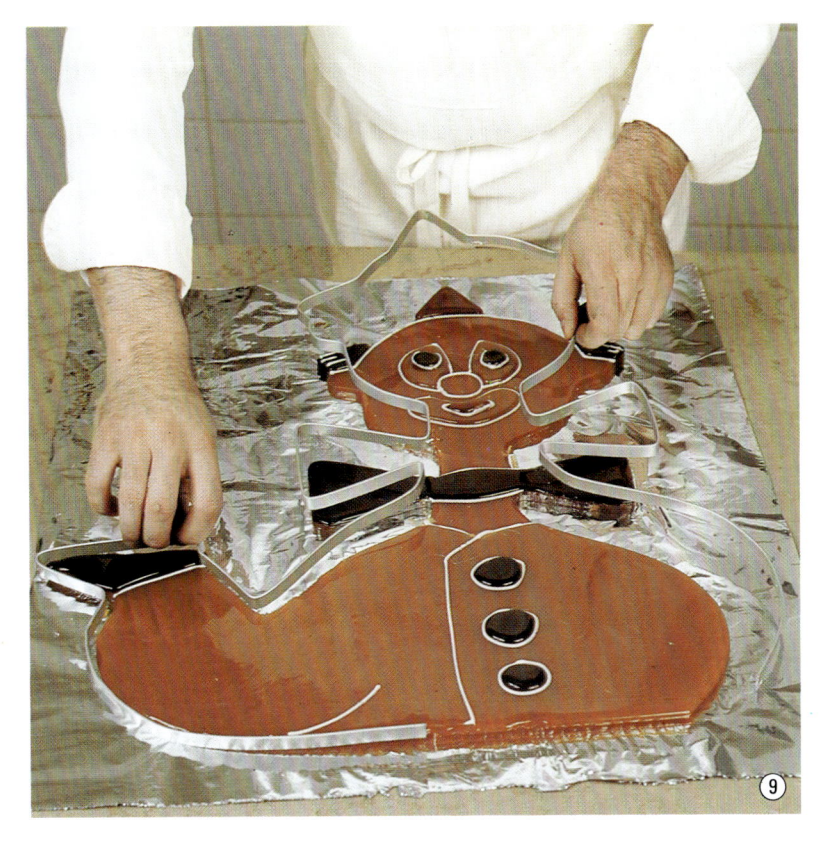

Photo 5: To pour a third color of poured sugar, use a paper cone filled with royal icing or special fondant to trace the design for the eyes, buttons, and bow tie.

Photo 6: Pour the desired color in the border of the frame and bow tie. The border is formed by the mold and the piping.

Photo 7: Use the same colored sugar for the hair, buttons, eyes, and hand.

Photo 8: Use the paper cone filled with royal icing or fondant to trace the mouth and the hat and fill them with red poured sugar.

Photo 9: After the sugar has completely cooled and set, remove the frame.

Photo 10: Remove the aluminum foil or parchment paper. The clown is now ready to be attached to the base with cooked sugar and supported in the back with a poured sugar triangle.

Use cooked sugar to attach a poured sugar cake base, supporting it with two triangles.

Chef's Note: *Follow this procedure for all the poured sugar pieces in this volume. Only the frame and coloring change. Poured sugar is fairly easy work with and allows for much creativity.*

Sugar and Decoration Work

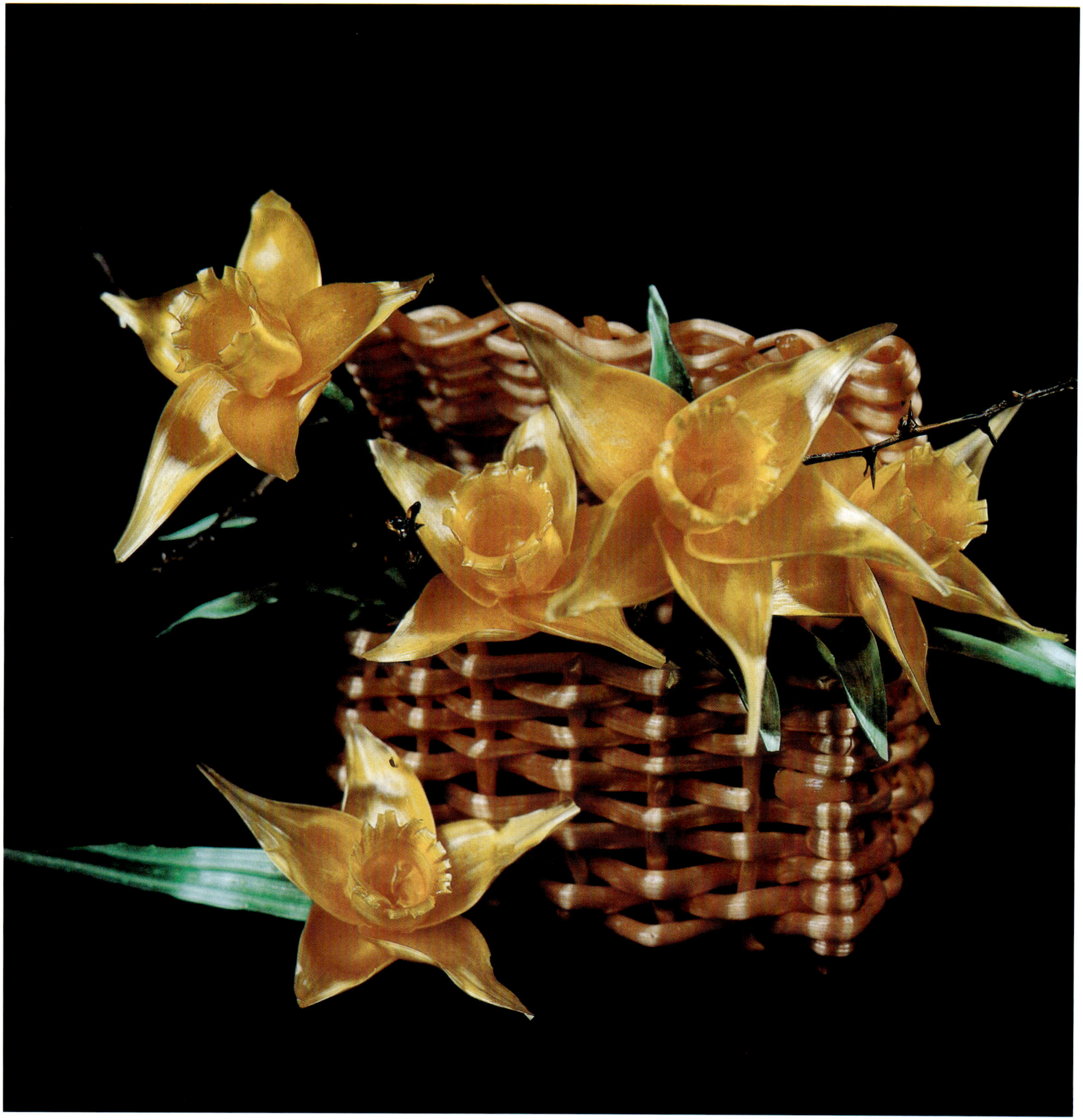

Parcel from Nice
Envoi de Nice

This piece, made in woven sugar, is fairly simple to prepare and less fragile than many pulled sugar pieces. Any of the pulled sugar flowers can be used to decorate the basket. Here, a few pulled sugar daffodils are positioned to hold the cover ajar. Follow the photographs on pages 336–337 for the procedure.

Woven Sugar

The pulled sugar weaving shown here can be applied to any type or shape of woven basket. The pulled sugar recipe is the same for all pulled sugar flowers, see pages 295–296. Only the way they are formed differs.

Preparation

This type of sugar work requires a weaving board. The board can be purchased from a pastry supply store or can be handmade. The base, usually made of wood, has perforations to support metal stakes. The sugar is woven around the stakes. The holes in the base can be vertical or slightly angled. In order to make baskets that flare out, the holes need to be at an angle. The procedure remains the same, regardless of the shape made—round, square, oval, or rectangular. The form is determined by the type of weaving board.

The base can be easily made by drilling evenly spaced holes into a block of wood. Be sure to make an uneven number of holes for each row.

Shaping

An uneven number of metal spikes are positioned in the base. The pulled sugar should be pulled, colored, and shaped into a ball. Pull a strip from the ball of sugar—the thickness can vary according to taste—keeping it attached to the ball. Work under or near a heat source to keep the sugar malleable enough to pull, but not so warm that it loses shape.

Begin to pull the strip from the ball of sugar, weaving around the stakes, alternating from the front of one and going around the back of the next. Keep the strip of pulled sugar taut. Continue to weave around the stakes in this fashion until reaching the desired height. Cut the end off of the ball of sugar.

Pull a strip from the ball of sugar to make strands thin enough to fit inside the weaving to replace the metal stakes. They should be cut to the height of the weaving. Remove a metal stake and immediately replace it with a sugar stake. Repeat until all the metal stakes have been replaced with sugar stakes. Twist two strands of sugar around each other and attach the strands to the top of the basket. Carefully remove the basket from the wood base and place it on a lightly oiled marble or sheet of aluminum foil.

Make a border around the base of the basket in special fondant, modeling clay, or a flexible metal strip (as used for poured sugar). Pour a thin layer of poured sugar inside the basket to affix the pieces together for greater strength.

A handle can be made out of woven sugar and supported with a metal wire. Attach it to the top of the basket with poured sugar. A cover in the same shape as the basket can also be made. Set it ajar on top of the basket to reveal pulled sugar flowers or other decoration.

For baskets that are given a more fanciful shape, curved or widening on top, pulled sugar stakes cannot be used. Prepare the basket following the same procedure as above, using cooked sugar coated wires to replace the metal stakes in the wooden base. Weave the pulled sugar around the coated stakes as above. These supports become part of the basket and are not replaced.

Facing Page: Parecel from Nice

336   *Modern French Pastry*

Woven Sugar Basket

Photo 1: To prepare the cover of the basket, place metal stakes in the wood base. Prepare pulled sugar as given on pages 295–296, pulling and coloring it. Shape the pulled sugar into a ball. Pull out a strand, keeping it attached to the ball. Weave the strand around the metal stakes alternating from the front of one to the back of the next. Continue until the desired height is reached.

Photos 2 and 3: Remove the metal stakes used to support the weaving and replace them with pulled sugar stakes of the same thickness. Cut them to the height of the weaving.

Photo 4: Place metal stakes into the perforations in the base forming the shape desired, shown here as a square. The procedure is the same, regardless of the form. Special bases allow for a greater variety of shapes.

Photo 5: The weaving should be done under a heat source to keep it malleable enough to pull without losing shape. Pull a strand of desired thickness, weaving around the metal spikes. Keep the strand slightly taut to maintain an even thickness.

Photo 6: Continue to weave the pulled sugar until the desired height is reached. Remove the metal spikes and immediately replace them with pulled sugar strands of the same thickness and height of the weaving.

Twist two strands of pulled sugar around each other and attach them to the top edge of the basket.

Make a border around the base of the basket in special fondant (as used for poured sugar), modeling clay, or a malleable metal. Pour a thin layer of poured sugar inside the basket for greater strength. Decorate the basket with pulled sugar flowers; the basket shown here can be seen finished on page 334.

Blown Sugar

Although not as artistic as pulled sugar, blown sugar is a fairly popular form of pastry decoration. A wide variety of shapes and subjects can be made from blown sugar, such as vases, fruit, and animals, in a reasonable amount of time. Blown sugar work is somewhat easier than pulled sugar. The sugar doesn't have to be worked to produce a sheen in the way pulled sugar does. It is helpful to have a pump for blowing the sugar; these are available from companies who specialize in pastry supplies.

Some experienced professionals use recipes for pulled sugar to make blown sugar pieces, though this is after considerable practice. Blown sugar is made with sugar, water, and glucose. The cooking temperature is lower than that of pulled sugar.

Blown Sugar No. 1

sugar, refined,		
granulated or cubed	*35 oz*	*1,000 g*
water	*14 oz*	*400 g*
glucose	*7 oz*	*200 g*

Cook all ingredients as indicated below, to 295°–298.5°F/146°–148°C for small pieces, and 298.5°–302°F/148°–150°C for large pieces.

Blown Sugar No. 2

Sugar, refined,		
granulated or cubed	*35 oz*	*1,000 g*
Water	*14 oz*	*400 g*
Glucose	*14 oz*	*400 g*

Cook all ingredients as indicated below, to 305.5°–309°F/152°–154°C.

Procedure 1

Bring the sugar and water to a boil, then add the glucose. Use a pastry brush and water to frequently wash down any sugar crystals that form around the inside of the copper sugar pot (poêlon). Add coloring when the temperature has reached 248°–266°F/120°–130°C. Cook the sugar to the recommended temperature, according to the recipe and size of piece being made. Immediately dip the bottom of the pot in cold water for a few seconds to stop the cooking. Do not rest the sugar as for pulled sugar; instead, promptly pour the sugar out onto a lightly oiled marble. Use a pastry triangle to cool the sugar by folding it from underneath over into the center, as for pulled sugar. The sugar does not have to be pulled; or, if desired, only a little. Shape it into a ball. The sugar is ready to be blown.

Procedure 2

This procedure is used primarily for shaping fruit and small pieces. Pour the cooked sugar onto lightly oiled marble, inside a frame of four 1/2 in/1 cm high metal bars (made specifically for candy and sugar work). Before the sugar has completely set, cut it into squares of the size needed.

Soften the squares under a heat source such as an open oven, infrared lamp, or small electric radiator. When a section of cooked sugar has softened sufficiently, round it.

Shaping Blown Sugar

One of the most important aspects of blowing sugar is the temperature of the sugar at the time it is blown. The sugar should be cool, yet soft enough to be shaped. If the sugar is too warm or not cooked enough, the piece will not hold its shape. Form a cavity inside the ball of sugar, and place the tube of the pump inside. Tightly enclose the sugar around the tube. Begin to pump air with one hand while holding the sugar with the other. Check the sugar frequently to make sure it is well sealed around the tube and no air escapes from the sides when pumping.

The air should be pumped slowly and carefully so the sugar expands evenly. It is not uncommon for thin sections to appear in the sugar. If this should occur, place the palm of the hand over the thin section, holding it in place so it does not expand while pumping air. Continue to pump air until the rest of the piece reaches the same thickness.

For large pieces, it is best to work with a second person. One person pumps the air while the other shapes the piece with both hands.

Work near a heat source so the sugar maintains the proper temperature. It must be malleable enough to expand and be shaped. After shaping, use a fan to quickly cool the sugar so it does not lose shape. While cooling, continue to gently pump a small quantity of air into the sugar to maintain the shape. To facilitate cooling, dip the piece into 90° rubbing alcohol or daub on the alcohol with a brush. The alcohol will evaporate upon contact with the hot sugar.

Heat a knife in a flame and cut off the sugar around the tube. Touch ups can be made by reheating an area with an alcohol burner or propane torch. The piece can be colored using an airbrush with food coloring, either liquid or powdered diluted in alcohol.

Blown sugar requires much patience and practice. It is best to begin with simple subjects such as fruit and vases before attempting animals and figures.

Chef's Note: *When preparing elongated shapes, it is important to hold the sugar below the tube of the pump so the weight of the piece pulls itself, as for a banana. For round pieces, it is the opposite—the sugar should be held above the tube, as for an apple. Cool the piece quickly with a fan or alcohol before it loses its shape.*

Blown sugar is not adversely affected by humidity to the extent that pulled sugar is, and by liberally dusting blown sugar pieces with confectioners' sugar, the shelf life can be extended for several years if properly stored.

After rubbing with confectioners' sugar, the pieces can be colored using a paintbrush or, more commonly, an airbrush or spray gun. Spraying a color results in a more realistic effect. Always start with the lightest shades, finishing with the darkest. For example: first yellow, then pink, red, green, and last, black.

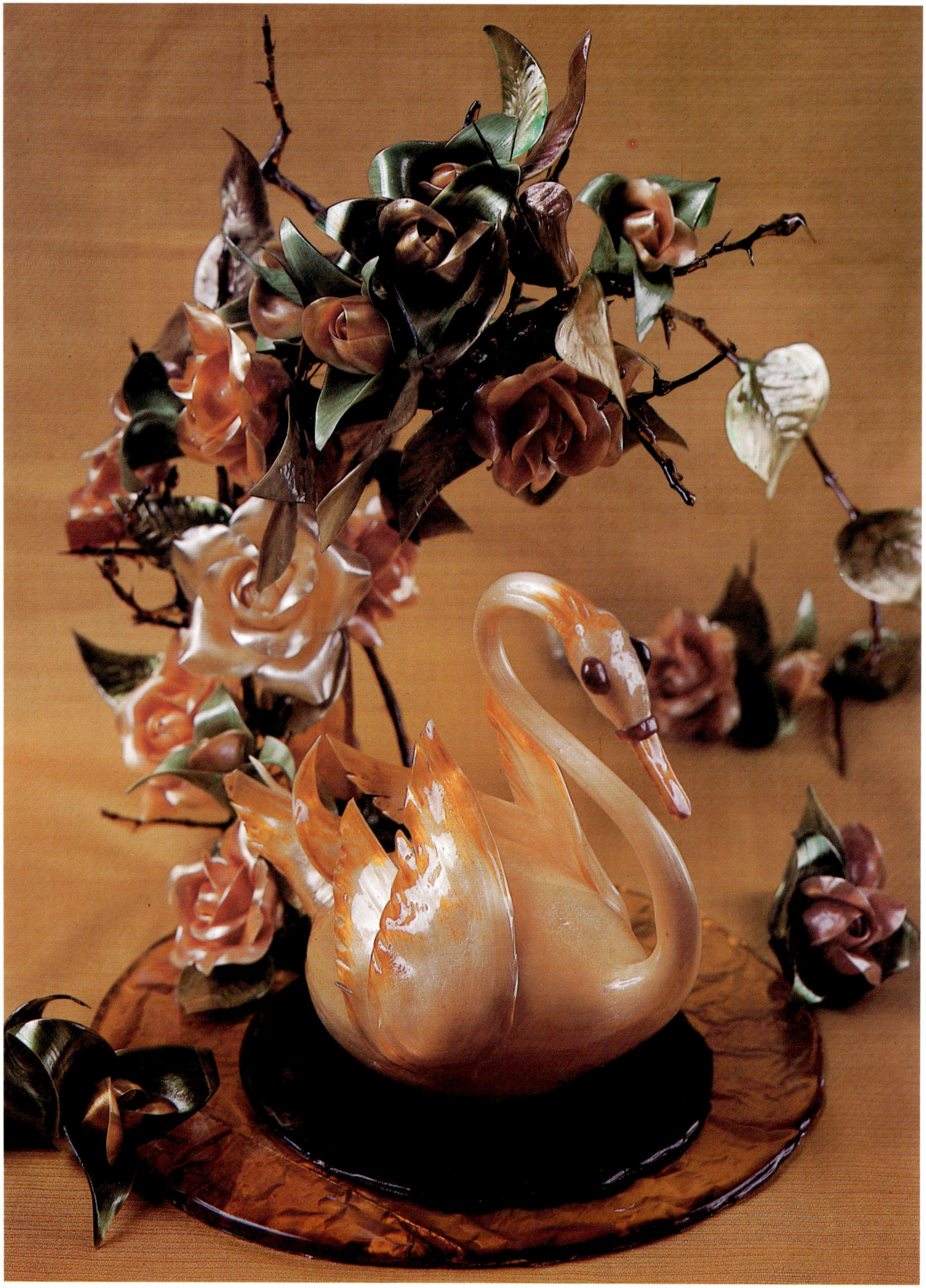

Blown Sugar Swan

The blown sugar swan is supported on a poured sugar base and decorated with pulled sugar flowers and leaves.

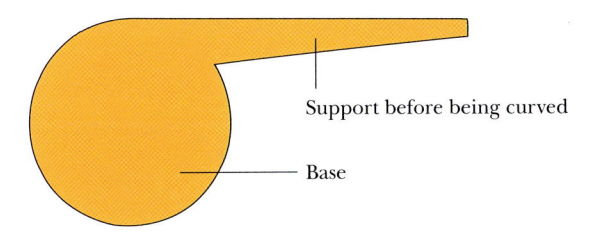

Support before being curved

Base

Poured Sugar Base

The base is shaped with one rounded section and the other elongated as shown in the diagram. The elongated section will be curved before setting to serve as a base for the pulled sugar flowers.

The base is poured inside a metal frame. The elongated section that is later curved can be reinforced with metal wire. This will make it considerably stronger.

Floral Decoration

Use cooked sugar to attach dried tree branches coated with cooked sugar to the narrow curved section of the piece. Attach pulled sugar roses and leaves to the branches.

Procedure 1

Prepare the recipe for blown sugar. Use the photographs on the following pages as a guide to prepare the swan. First form the swan's body, pull the neck, and cut the sugar off the tube just below the swan's head. Cool the piece quickly with an electric fan.

From the same batch of sugar, pull the wings and the tail. Shape the head and bill under a heat source and attach them to the neck. Heat the tail and wings over an alcohol burner and attach to the swan. Shape the eyes with a differently colored pulled sugar. Use an airbrush or paintbrush for shading.

Attach the swan to a poured sugar base and place on the first base under the pulled sugar flowers.

Procedure 2

This procedure results in a more stylized swan. The swan is prepared in one step, blowing the body, neck, and head from the same piece of sugar. Place the tube of the pump into the cavity of the prepared ball of cooked sugar. Lightly pump air into the sugar, forming a rounded head. Pull on the neck, giving it the desired shape. Continue pumping air into the sugar to make the body, including the tail. Cut the sugar off of the tube at the tail. Make the bill and wings out of pulled sugar, attaching them as in the first procedure.

Facing Page: Blown Sugar Swan

342   Modern French Pastry

Blown Sugar

Photo 1: Prepare the sugar as indicated in the recipe on page 338. It can be left as is or lightly pulled. Place the cooked sugar on a drum sieve under a heat source. Cut off the amount needed and form a ball.

Photo 2: The sugar should be warm enough to be malleable. Form a cavity in the center of the ball of cooked sugar so the sides have the same thickness all around, allowing the piece to expand evenly.

Photo 3: Wrap the sugar firmly around the tip of the pump, making sure the sugar is well sealed around the tube and no air escapes from the sides when pumping.

Photo 4: Slowly pump air into the ball of sugar. Turn it under the heat source to keep it warm while pumping air, shaping as needed.

Photo 5: Hold the sugar in one hand and the pump in the other. It is not uncommon for thin sections to appear. If this should occur, place the palm of a hand over the thin section to prevent it from expanding while continuing to pump air until the rest of the piece acquires the same thickness.

Photo 6: After forming the body, pull the sugar to form the neck, shaping it as desired. When finished, remove the piece from the heat source so it can cool as quickly as possible and maintain shape. Large pieces should be cooled with a fan or daubed with 90° rubbing alcohol.

344   *Modern French Pastry*

Assembling the Swan

Photo 7: Cut the sugar cleanly off the tube.

Photo 8: Shape the bill from the same sugar. Pull a strip of sugar and use it to attach the bill to the neck. Shape it to form the head at the same time. This step is fairly simple, but can only be applied to birds with long necks and small heads.

Photo 9: Use scissors to cut two to four large wings from the same batch of sugar.

Photo 10: Warm the rounded part of a wing over an alcohol burner and immediately attach it to the swan's body. Repeat this step for all the wings.

Photo 11: Shape the wings as they are attached, one or two per side. For a more elaborate presentation, the wings can be covered with feathers pulled from the same batch of sugar.

Photo 12: Use an airbrush to tint or color the swan. Mark the eyes with a different colored melted sugar.

Blown Sugar Bird

The procedure is relatively the same as for the swan. First pump air to form the head, pull the sugar to make the neck to the desired length, pump more air to make the body. Finish by pulling the sugar to form the tail.

Sugar and Decoration Work

Blown Sugar Dog, Elephant

Blown Sugar Animals

All animals can be made out of blown sugar. Some are formed from one piece of sugar, others require attaching several separate sections together. Marzipan animals can be used for ideas on making these animals.

Blown Sugar Dog

This dog is prepared in five sections: body and front paws, tail, head, ears, and nose.

Body
Blow a ball of sugar in the form of a large pear shape, elongating it slightly and bending it in half. Cut the sugar off the tube with a scissors. Use the scissors to cut and separate the front paws.

Tail
Blow a sphere of sugar to form an elongated pear and curve it.

Head
Blow a sphere of sugar and make two indentations for the eyes.

Ears
Blow a sphere of sugar, elongate it, making it thinner in the middle and wider at the ends, and curve it to fit over the head.

Nose
Blow a small sphere of sugar, flatten it on one side. Dip the rounded side in simple syrup, 30° density, then immediately roll it in sugar.

The tongue is the only piece made out of pulled sugar. The base is made from poured sugar.

Use cooked sugar to attach the body to the poured sugar base. Appropriately attach the head, tail, ears, nose, and tongue to the body. Two flat disks of white paper are colored for the eyes and set in place with the cooked sugar.

Blown Sugar Elephant

This piece is blown in three separate sections: the body, head and trunk, and four legs.

Body
Blow a large ball of sugar, elongating one end to a point.

Head
Blow a smaller ball of sugar, shaping the head and elongating a section to form the trunk.

Legs
Blow a ball of sugar, elongating it to a point and curving slightly. Make four.

Pull the ears from the same batch of sugar used for blowing.

Make a base of desired size from poured sugar.

Use cooked sugar to attach the body to the poured sugar base. Attach the head, legs, and ears. Two flat disks of white paper are colored for the eyes and set in place.

348   *Modern French Pastry*

Blown Sugar Carp

This presentation piece is set on a base and supported by poured sugar sections. The flowers and leaves are made from pulled sugar. The fish and bird are made from blown sugar.

The support is made like the one used for the swan (see diagram, page 341). Attach dried branches coated with cooked sugar to the base. Use cooked sugar to attach pulled sugar roses and leaves to the branches. Set the blown sugar bird in the branches.

Blown Sugar Fish

Following the recipe given for blown sugar, prepare the sugar and color it deep blue or green, though lighter tones, even red, can be used. After cooking the sugar, shape it into a ball. Hollow out the cavity and wrap it around the tube of the pump. Gradually pump air, pausing occasionally to shape the head of the fish.

Continue to pump air and lengthen the body, finishing by pulling out the tail. Use a scissors to cut the sugar off the tube. Immediately cool the fish with a fan or by daubing with 90° rubbing alcohol.

Pull and cut sugar to form the fins and tail, and attach them with cooked sugar. Heat a knife in a flame and cut a V-shaped opening for the mouth. The eyes can be made either with circles of rigid paper or small flat disks of pulled sugar. Use an airbrush for shading in different colors. Attach the fish to the poured sugar base, beneath the floral display.

Blown Sugar Squirrel

The squirrel is formed from one piece of blown sugar. The head is formed first, then the tail. Use a scissors to cut the two front feet apart. Form the body and back feet. Color the squirrel using an airbrush to create highlights. Two colored circles of rigid paper can be used for the eyes. Attach the finished squirrel to a poured sugar base.

Chef's Note: *To make a fuller, more elaborate tail, form it separately for greater control. In this case, blow the body and front feet separately from the head and attach all three pieces with cooked sugar.*

Blown Sugar Dog

This piece is prepared in three separate sections: body, tail, and head. Form the body by blowing a long pear shape and curve it slightly underneath for the back legs; the front is tapered to a point, stopping at the neck.

Curve the tail, making it fairly thick at one end and elongated at the other.

For the head, begin with a pear shape, flattening the sides for the jowls. The muzzle is made by wrapping a strip of sugar pulled from the same sugar used for blowing. Use the same sugar to make the ears, pulling and cutting them to shape. Attach them to the head while the sugar is still hot enough to adhere, and curve them on top. The nose is made with a different color of pulled sugar, shaped into a ball.

Coloring

An airbrush can be used to create highlights, coloring to taste. Use circles of rigid paper for the eyes.

Facing Page: Blown Sugar Carp

Blown Sugar Dog, Squirrel, Rabbit

A few possible shapes for blown sugar vases

Blown Sugar Vases

Blown sugar vases are fairly easy to make. It is important to pay attention to the final cooking temperature of the sugar. The larger the vase, the higher the temperature. When attaching the ball of sugar to the tube of the pump, the walls of the cavity should be even in thickness so the vase expands uniformly.

When forming the large vases, it is sometimes necessary to keep the sugar warm by constantly turning it under a heat source, so it is evenly heated. After the vase is shaped, quickly cool it by placing it in front of a fan or by daubing it with 90° rubbing alcohol. Cut the vase off the tube using a knife heated in a flame. Warm the top of the vase and finish shaping the neck.

It is sometimes necessary to prepare a ring of pulled sugar to attach to the bottom of the vase so it stands upright. The vase can be colored either while the sugar is cooking or after the vase has been formed, using an airbrush.

Blown Sugar Rabbit

The rabbit is blown in three sections: head and ears, body and front feet, and the tail.

Body
Blow the prepared sugar into a pear shape, curving it underneath and pulling to elongate. With a scissors cut the elongated section underneath to form the front feet.

Head
Blow the head, beginning with the mouth. Narrow the upper section to allow for the eyes, and finish shaping it flat on top. Cut the sugar off the pump and warm the thin flat section of the head. Cut it in half for the ears, curving them upward.

Tail
Blow a small ball for the tail.

Use cooked sugar to attach the body to a poured sugar base. Attach the head and tail. The rabbit can be colored and highlighted using an airbrush. Set two rigid paper circles in place for the eyes.

Blown Sugar Still Life

Blown Sugar Still Life

This piece is appropriate for a competition or display. It consists of a woven sugar basket, blown sugar fruit, and pulled sugar flowers and leaves.

Woven Basket

Using the sugar weaving base as explained on page 335, place cooked sugar coated metal wires in the holes to form a basket shaped as desired. The sugar coated wires will serve as the armature for the basket and are not replaced. This technique allows for more imaginative shapes with greater finesse, as the coated wires are considerably thinner than the pulled sugar strands. Prepare the sugar and weave the basket.

Pour a poured sugar base the same size as the basket. While the base is still hot, place the basket on top so it will adhere. This base gives stability to the basket. Attach a twist or braid of pulled sugar on the bottom and top of the basket.

Blown Sugar Grapes

The grapes are blown individually, forming small balls one at a time. Although this work is not difficult, it is somewhat tedious. Grapes can also be prepared by forming the ball and elongating the cavity over a finger. Remove the sugar from the finger and round the tip to form a grape. Repeat this step until enough grapes are prepared. The cluster of grapes is ready to be assembled. This can be done by attaching the grapes to a dried tree branch coated with cooked sugar or a grape vine dipped in caramel. Finish the cluster using an airbrush to color and/or highlight.

Blown Sugar Banana

Shape sugar prepared for blowing into a ball with a cavity, wrapping it around the tube of an air pump. Pump air into the sugar, shaping as needed. For long pieces such as the banana, hold the sugar below the tube so it can pull on itself.

Use an airbrush to color the entire piece yellow. When dry, use a small paintbrush to mark the edges of the fruit with a brown cocoa coloring.

Blown Sugar Pear and Apple

Shape sugar prepared for blowing into a ball with a cavity, wrapping it around the tube of an air pump. Begin blowing the sugar and make the fruit, shaping as desired. For round fruit such as apples and prunes, the sugar should be held above the tube so the fruit develops roundly. Heat a knife in a flame and cut the piece off the tube. Attach a small strip of sugar for the stem where appropriate.

Color the fruit, giving it a yellow base. Use an airbrush to create highlights of green and red. Paint the stem brown using a paintbrush.

Blown Sugar Peach

Shape the peach, beginning as for the apple mentioned above. It is helpful to have the real fruit on hand as a guide.

When the peach is formed, roll it in confectioners' sugar. Color the fruit, giving it a yellow base, and create red highlights using an airbrush. Dust the peach with cornstarch to imitate the texture of a real peach.

Turned Sugar

Turned sugar has many advantages over pulled sugar. It can be used to prepare all kinds of flowers; it is worked when cold or nearly cold; it can be left uncovered and is not adversely affected by humidity. After forming the desired shapes, the sugar pieces are set aside for a few days. Turned sugar takes on an attractive, slightly opaque quality, giving it a more realistic look than when first shaped.

Turned sugar is not as widely used as pulled sugar. Although it is easier to work with, it does not offer the same elegance or artistic choices as does pulled sugar.

Turned sugar is prepared very differently than pulled sugar. The following step-by-step photographs for preparing a turned sugar rose should help make the process easier to understand. To form other flowers, the technique remains the same, only the shaping changes. The individual segments are attached with cooked sugar.

sugar	*35 oz*	*1,000 g*
water	*14 oz*	*400 g*
glucose	*2–3.5 oz*	*50–100 g*

Put the sugar and water in a copper sugar pot (poêlon) over a high flame; when melted, add the glucose and continue to cook. Frequently wash down the sides of the pot with a pastry brush dipped in water to prevent sugar crystals from forming. Cook to 284°–293°F/140°–145°C. If undercooked, the sugar will not maintain shape; if overcooked, the sugar will be difficult to work with and crack easily. If the sugar has too much glucose it will have trouble "turning" (becoming opaque), not take on the proper consistency or hold shape. Without glucose, it will turn too quickly, not allowing any time to shape the petals, and crack easily, making it difficult to shape.

After reaching the proper temperature, pour the sugar onto lightly oiled pastry marble between four metal bars. When the sugar begins to set, remove the bars and cut the sugar into small squares using a large, sharp knife. The sugar can be prepared up to this point and stored in a cool, dry area until needed.

Place the squares of sugar on a lightly oiled sheet pan. Set the sheet pan near a heat source, such as an oven door. Start warming the sugar squares at one end of the sheet pan, gradually rotating it so the squares do not soften at the same time. Use a low heat source; the sugar should soften but not melt.

Use both hands to work a square of sugar thin, keeping it near the heat source, and form a petal by rubbing with the fingertips. The sugar will turn opaque as it is rubbed. Once this occurs, the petals are shaped as for pulled sugar. If the sugar turns too opaque it will not adhere to the other pieces. In this case, reheat the piece and attach it immediately. Use a scissors to trim off any excess sugar.

The sugar can be colored during the cooking, but is generally colored while being shaped. Combine a powdered food coloring with a small amount of cornstarch or confectioners' sugar. Lightly dip the fingertips in the powdered colored mixture and incorporate it into the sugar during shaping. This procedure makes it easy to control the amount and placement of color, and obtain highlights and nuances. Flowers of many different colors can be made with the same sugar by simply changing the coloring.

To shape turned sugar leaves, use a green powdered food coloring mixed with a small amount of cornstarch or confectioners' sugar following the same technique, shaping and coloring at the same time. Cut the leaf to a point with a scissors and immediately press it against a leaf imprint (purchased at pastry supply stores).

Cooking Sugar

There are several ways to measure sugar when cooked to a syrup or other stage. Syrups are usually measured in degrees baume, which evaluates the density. Cooked sugar is usually measured with a thermometer in degrees of Fahrenheit or Celsius.

To check the accuracy of a thermometer, place it in a pot of boiling water; the thermometer should read 212°F/100°C. If the temperature does not register exactly, note the difference and make the appropriate adjustment when using this thermometer for cooking sugar.

Temperatures for Cooking Sugar

Degrees Baume	Degrees Fahrenheit	Degrees Celsius	Texture
32–33	112	100	
32–33	221	105	Small pearl
33–35	225.5	107.5	Large pearl or thread
37	232.5	111.5	Soft soufflé
39	234.5	112.5	Hard soufflé
39–40	239	115	Soft ball
	242.5	117.5	Medium ball
	250	121	Hard ball
	269.5	132	Soft crack
	291	144	Hard crack

356 *Modern French Pastry*

Turned Sugar

Photo 1: Prepare and cook the sugar according to the recipe and procedure given on page 354. Frequently wash down the sides of the pot using a pastry brush and water to prevent crystals from forming.

Photo 2: Place four metal bars on lightly oiled marble. Allow the sugar to rest a moment in the pot before pouring it between the bars

Photo 3: When the sugar begins to set, remove the bars. The sugar should be transparent; if not, either not enough glucose was added or the pot may not have been properly cleaned. If the sugar appears crystallized or cloudy, it cannot be corrected and should be discarded.

Photo 4: Before the sugar has completely set, cut it into small squares with a large knife. The sugar can be prepared up to this step and stored in a cool, dry area until needed.

Photo 5: Place the sugar squares on a lightly oiled sheet pan near a heat source such as a small electric heater on an oven door. Begin warming one side of the pan, turning it slowly, so the sugar squares do not soften at the same time. The sugar should be soft and malleable but not melted.

Photo 6: Using both hands, thin a square of sugar and shape a petal while working near a heat source. The rose is assembled following the same procedure as for pulled sugar: first form the center bud and attach petals around it. A scissors can be used to trim any excess sugar.

(Turned Sugar recipe continued on page 359)

Sugar and Decoration Work 357

358 Modern French Pastry

Photo 7: The sugar should turn opaque and crystallize while being shaped. Simply rub the squares with the fingertips to form the petals. Assemble the petals around the center bud, attaching them as they are formed or warming them if they have cooled.

Photo 8: The sugar can be colored during the cooking, but is generally colored afterward, when shaped. To color while shaping, lightly dip the fingertips in a mixture of powdered food coloring and cornstarch or confectioners' sugar. This technique makes is easy to create highlighting.

Photo 9: The flower is assembled as for pulled sugar flowers. If a petal has been overworked, it will not adhere to the flower. In this case, warm the petal using a heat source such as an alcohol burner and immediately attach it to the flower. Turned sugar made with too much glucose will not crystallize easily making it difficult to shape. If made with too little glucose, it will crystallize too quickly, cracking before it can be shaped.

Photo 10: Turned sugar flowers can be stored uncovered. After several days, the sugar will fully crystallize, giving the flowers a more realistic quality. They are not greatly affected by humidity or heat.

Guidelines for Cooking Sugar

The following guidelines explain how the sugar will look and feel throughout the various stages, making it possible to forego using a thermometer.

Dip the fingertips of one hand in iced water, then immediately, without drying them, dip the tips of the thumb and index finger into the cooking sugar to remove a pinch of sugar. Immediately plunge the fingers and sugar sample in the ice water. Lift the fingers out of the ice water, still holding onto the pinch of sugar. Spread the thumb and index finger apart and look at the sugar to determine the stage.

221°F/105°C—Small pearl
When the fingers are spread apart, a small pearl of sugar will appear.

225.5°F/107.5°C—Thread or large pearl
When the fingers are spread apart, a thread of sugar will pull away between them.

232.7°F/111.5°C—Soft soufflé
When the fingers are pulled apart, the sugar will be viscous but will not form a ball.

239°F/115°C—Soft ball
Though not easily, a small, very soft ball can be formed by rubbing the fingers together.

242.5°F/117°C—Medium ball
A malleable ball can be more easily formed between the fingers.

250°F/121°C—Hard ball
The firmer ball with resistance can be easily formed between the fingers.

269.5°F/132°C—Soft crack
The sugar breaks when bent but will stick to the teeth if bitten.

291°F/144°C—Hard crack
The sugar will break easily but sometimes needs a bit more cooking up to 302°F/150°C, so it does not stick to the teeth. This is important for candy making.

Caramel
The sugar takes on color ranging from lightly golden to deep, dark amber.

Burnt sugar
The caramel is very dark brown or black and smokes. Burnt sugar is not used alone, in pastry making, due to its bitterness, although it can be combined with other products for preparations such as coffee extract or used as a coloring agent.

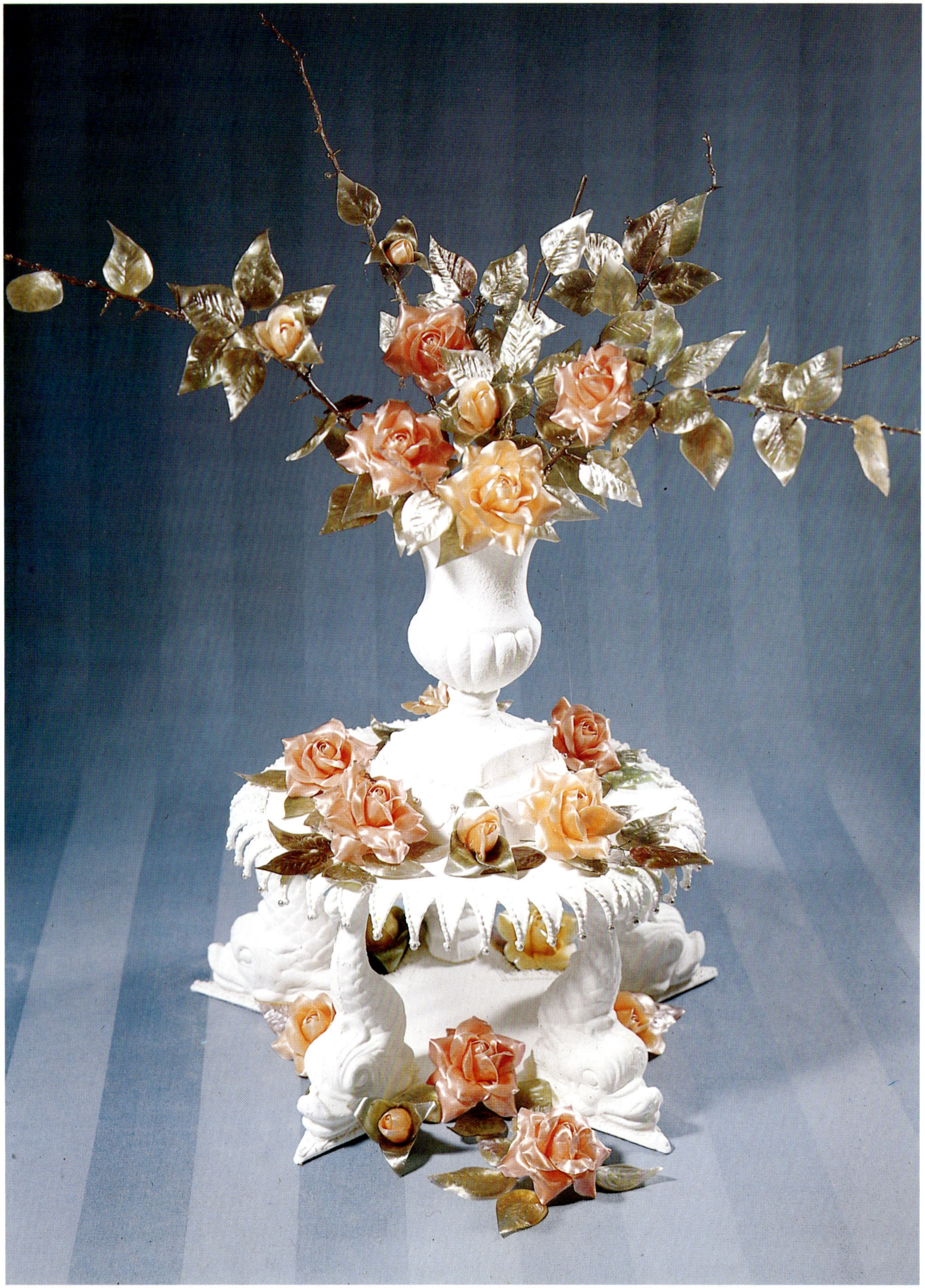

Vase Filled with a Bouquet of Flowers

This presentation piece, appropriate for a buffet or as a showpiece, is prepared in two sections: the pastillage vase, and pulled sugar flowers and leaves.

Pastillage

Follow the recipe given for pastillage on page 314. A good number of molds, in different shapes and sizes, is essential for this presentation. It is also possible to mold pastillage in metal molds sold in speciality shops. However, I feel it is preferable to make plaster molds from these metal molds. Refer to the section on making plaster of paris molds on page 373.

After rolling out the pastillage to the desired thickness, line it in a mold that has been dried in a proofing oven and dusted with starch to facilitate unmolding. Prepare the various pastillage decorations and set them aside to dry.

The pastillage vase shown here is prepared in two sections:

1. A pastillage star-shaped base on which five pastillage molded dolphins are attached with royal icing. A pastillage disk bordered with wolf's teeth is attached on top.

2. The vase is made by molding two halves and attaching them after drying. Affix the assembled halves to a dried pastillage base that was molded in a cake pan. After it is dry, the vase is placed on the first section.

Assembling a Pulled Sugar Bouquet

Coat dried branches with a deeply colored cooked sugar. Attach them inside the bottom of the vase with poured sugar. Affix pulled sugar roses and leaves, being careful not to put too much weight on the tips of the branches. Place the larger roses on the center of the branches and the lighter rosebuds and leaves near the tips. Attach groups of 3 to 5 pulled sugar leaves on the branches, securing and supporting them with thin metal wires.

Chef's Note: *A sugar bouquet or other pulled sugar presentation piece should be quickly assembled so the sugar does not have time to absorb humidity, which would cause them lose their shape and sheen. When the piece is finished, place it in an enclosed presentation case with a transparent (plastic or glass) cover and place desiccant on the bottom. These cases usually have false bottoms to conceal the desiccant.*

Attaching Pulled Sugar Leaves

When assembling a pulled sugar bouquet, pulled sugar leaves can be directly attached to the branches with caramel. Although this is a fairly quick and easy method, the result is somewhat rough as the caramel is often visible. For a more polished look, the leaves are grouped together on a thin wire in sets of 3, 4, or 5. This makes it easier to attach the leaves so the juncture points are not apparent. Cut thin metal wires 2 1/3–3 in/6–8 cm long. These can be purchased from a florist or pastry supplier. Attach a wire to the back of one leaf with caramel, and attach the remaining leaves so they hide the wire. Then attach the group of leaves to a branch from behind.

Facing Page: Vase Filled with a Bouquet of Flowers

Pulled Sugar Leaves

Photo 1: Cook the sugar and color it green according to the recipe for pulled sugar on pages 295–296. Shape the pulled sugar into a ball and place it on a drum sieve under a heat source. With the thumb and first two fingers of both hands, pull the sugar to create a thin edge. With one hand, pull the sugar between the thumb and index finger and use the other hand to cut off the leaf at an angle with scissors.

Photo 2: Immediately, while the leaf is still malleable, place it on a metal or plastic leaf imprint covered with plastic film to prevent sticking.

Photo 3: Press the leaf with the palm of the hand so it takes on the veins of the imprint.

Chef's Note: *For autumn-colored leaves, prepare three differently colored batches of pulled sugar: green, red, and yellow. Roughly combine them when pulling the leaves so the colors are distinct in some parts and blended in others.*

362 *Modern French Pastry*

Pulled Sugar Stems

Photo 1: Cook, color, and prepare a batch of pulled sugar. Shape it into a ball and place it on a drum sieve under a heat source. Cut a metal wire to the length needed. The wire should be lightly warmed so the sugar will adhere to it. Press the wire against the pulled sugar.

Photo 2: Push the wire into the sugar and pull on it from the other side so it is coated evenly with the pulled sugar.

Photo 3: Continue to pull on the stem until it is completely covered with pulled sugar and cut the sugar at the end to release it.

364   *Modern French Pastry*

Aged Cask

Prepare the frame of the cask in pastillage. Assemble the parts after they have fully dried. Prepare a batch of light brown pulled sugar, pulling it just enough so it maintains different tints of brown, but not enough to become uniform in color. This will lend a more realistic quality to the finished piece. Pull strips of sugar slightly longer then the distance between the ends of the cask, imitating slats of wood. Cover the cask with these strips of pulled sugar, attaching them one-by-one. Heat the strips and, immediately, while still warm, curve them to take on the shape of the cask. Affix them with cooked sugar, overlapping them as they are attached. Trim the ends with a knife heated in a flame.

Pull three narrow bands of sugar and wrap them around the cask, one at either end and one in the middle, to imitate metal rings.

Chef's Note: *The cask can also be prepared entirely in pastillage. After assembling the piece, paint it with food coloring.*

Earthenware Pitcher

Fashion a pitcher in blown sugar and attach the spout and handle with cooked sugar. Liberally rub the piece with confectioners' sugar until it takes on a crystallized texture. Prepare coating sugar and use a spatula or paintbrush to coat the entire pitcher. Allow the piece to dry for several days.

Paint the pitcher yellow using an airbrush. Airbrush the top and bottom with a deeper color to replicate old pottery.

Chef's Note: *It is best to work with a model when preparing pieces intended to be realistic looking. Try to match the colors as closely as possible. This technique makes it possible to reproduce all types and shapes of earthenware.*

Pastillage Candlesticks

This candlestick requires an armature for support, which makes this otherwise simple piece more intricate. Twist a metal wire to form the frame of the candlestick, from the foot base up to the base of the candles. Cover the armature with pastillage, shaping the candlestick; it is sometimes difficult to hide.

When the pastillage has completely dried, cut or file small nicks and notches to imitate forging. Set pastillage bolts in place to simulate real ones.

Color the candlestick only after it has fully dried. Combine dark brown and blue food coloring to make black and paint the candlestick to imitate iron. Lightly rub cocoa powder on various spots to simulate rust.

Facing Page: Aged Cask, Eathenware Pitcher, Pastillage Candlesticks

Pulled Sugar Tulips

Photo 1: Make the petals in pulled sugar. The tulip shown here is a slightly elongated version of the pulled Christmas rose on page 305. Lightly pinch the petals at the ends. Assemble the flower, petal by petal, attaching them as they are made.

Photo 2: Use a real or artificial tulip as a model. Generally, three petals form the heart of the flower and three more petals are placed around them.

Photo 3: Coat a wire with pulled sugar for the stem. Attach a small ball of pulled sugar to the base of the tulip, then attach the stem. Pull the leaves and affix them to the bottom of the stem.

366   *Modern French Pastry*

Pulled Sugar Daffodils

Photo 1: Cook, color, and prepare a batch of pulled sugar following the recipe on pages 295–296. Place the pulled sugar on a drum sieve under a heat source. With both hands, thin an edge of sugar.

Photo 2: With one hand pull the sugar between the thumb and index finger, pinching it off with the other hand. The top of the petal (where it is pinched off) should be thin and long. Five petals are needed for one daffodil.

Chef's Note: *This work is done under a heat source, such as a small electric heater or infrared lamp. The heat must be strong enough for the sugar to be malleable, but not melt. If the sugar becomes too hot it will lose its sheen. Best results are achieved when the sugar is pulled as cold as possible; it will make the sugar more difficult to work with as it will crack more easily, but the finished flower will have a beautiful pearly sheen.*

(Pulled Sugar Daffodils recipe continued on page 369)

Sugar and Decoration Work

368 Modern French Pastry

Photo 3: To make the corolla (center), pull a thin band of sugar and make small incisions on the edge of one side using a scissors. Cut the strip to an appropriate length.

Photo 4: Roll the strip around a finger or dowel to form a ring. Pinch the bottom (uncut side) closed forming a bell shape, and lightly flare the fringed top.

Photo 5: After preparing enough corollas and petals, the flowers are ready to be assembled. This is done without the infrared lamp or other heat source to prevent misshaping, although a flame from an alcohol burner or propane torch is needed.

Photo 6: The bases (round sections) of the petals are heated in a flame and immediately attached to the base of the corolla.

Photo 7: Five petals are attached flat to the bottom of the corolla, overlapping. This technique is applied to any flower with a corolla, such as the narcissus. Only the shape of the petals and color are changed.

Photo 8: Heat the top of a stem made from wire coated with cooked sugar and attach it to the base of the flower.

Sugar and Decoration Work

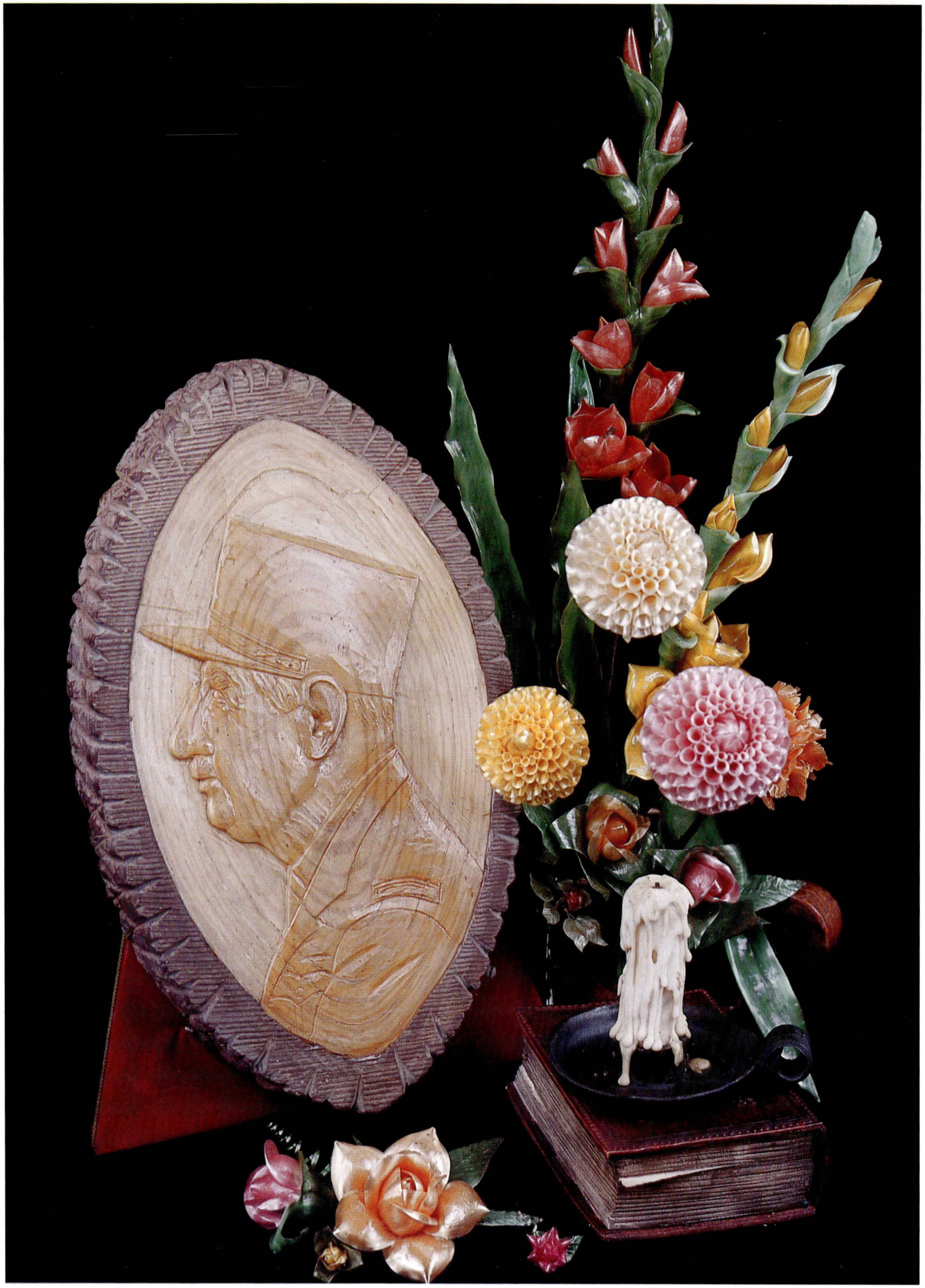

Memoires of War

This presentation piece was requested in honor of the release of *Memoires of War* by General Charles De Gaulle. The portrait of De Gaulle was made in white and dark chocolate, designed to imitate a section of a tree trunk. A dark chocolate varnish is used to bring out the profile. The bas relief is presented on a pastillage easel.

Behind the portrait is a pastillage vase with a bouquet of pulled sugar flowers. In front is a closed book also made from pastillage, to represent the newly finished edition. A candlestick in pastillage supports a poured crystallized sugar candle.

Fabrication of the Tree Trunk Section

Place an oval cake ring or shape a round one into an oval, 1.5–2 in/4–5 cm high, and set it over a sheet of aluminum foil placed on a sheet pan.

The white chocolate interior is prepared first to make the rings of the trunk. Temper white couverture. With a paintbrush, paint a ring of white tempered chocolate on the foil just inside the cake ring. Allow the chocolate to set. Temper more white chocolate, this time tinting it lightly with a bit of dark couverture chocolate. Paint a ring of the tinted white chocolate just inside the ring of plain white chocolate. Allow it to set. Continue to paint rings, alternating between the white and tinted white chocolate until reaching the center.

Remove the cake ring and replace it with a larger ring. Pour a layer of tempered dark chocolate over the surface, making the bark. This layer should be rather thick as it will support the entire piece. After the chocolate has completely set, the ring is removed and the piece is finished by sculpting the bust and the edge to imitate bark.

Chef's Note: *It is recommended that beginners try to sculpt a landscape or still life before attempting a portrait, which requires considerably more skill.*

Facing Page: Memoires of War

Sugar Candles

Sugar candles are fairly simple to prepare and offer impressive results. Prepare pastillage and shape a cylinder to the length needed for the candle. Allow the pastillage to dry. Faster alternatives are to mold poured sugar in a column mold, or shape a cylinder out of pulled sugar.

Heat fondant in a copper sugar pot (poêlon) with a spout, and stir often so the fondant does not overheat or it will become transparent, making it inappropriate for a candle. Place the cylinder, regardless of the medium chosen, standing upright on a marble. Pour the fondant over it, completely coating it. Immediately place the candle in the candlestick. Pour more cooked fondant from the top over the candle until it appears as though it was once lit and wax has dripped down over the sides. If the fondant starts to set before the procedure is finished, warm it lightly and continue pouring.

Make a hole with a fingertip on the top of the candle while it is still soft and place a thin strand of pastillage or marzipan inside sticking up to represent the wick.

Poured Crystallized Sugar

Poured crystallized sugar is molded in special plaster or copper molds meant for this work. It can be used for molding numerous figures such as animals, vases, columns, and figurines. The molds can be purchased from pastry suppliers specializing in decorative work. This procedure is rather simple when the required mold is on hand.

Poured Crystallized Sugar No. 1

sugar	35 oz	1,000 g
water	14 oz	400 g

In a clean copper sugar pot (poêlon), melt the sugar and water over moderately high heat. Occasionally brush down the sides of the pot with water to prevent crystals from forming. Take the sugar off the heat when it has reached 244.5°F/118°C.

After removing the sugar from the heat, use a wooden spoon to stir the sugar around the side of the pot until it begins to whiten, which indicates the sugar is crystallizing. Combine this border of crystallized sugar with the unstirred sugar in the middle of the pot, stirring until the whole batch is crystallized. Immediately pour the sugar into a mold that is lightly moistened with water. Allow the molded piece to set for several hours, depending on the thickness. It is important the sugar be completely cooled and crystallized before unmolding.

If a second batch of poured crystallized sugar is to be made, it is very important the pot be carefully cleaned or the sugar will not cook properly.

Most often, poured crystallized sugar is left white, as for pastillage. However, it is possible to add food coloring during cooking or after molding with an airbrush. Poured crystallized sugar has a long shelf life; even uncovered, it is not affected by heat and humidity. Poured crystallized sugar is a fast and easy way to embellish a pastry shop window or presentation piece.

Variation for Poured Crystallized Sugar

This variation is intended for hollow molds. The poured crystallized sugar is based on the recipe above, but the final temperature is slightly lower, 239°–244.5°F/115°–118°C.

The molds are soaked in water, not dried, and set on a flat work surface such as pastry marble. Prepare the sugar according to the recipe above, immediately pouring it into the molds after the sugar has crystallized. Always start with the largest mold. The sugar will quickly form a thin white crust around the side of the mold. At this moment, turn the mold over, pouring the sugar that has not adhered back into the pot. Turn the molds upside down and place them on a cooling rack or between two bars so they are above the work surface. This will enable them to dry evenly and not puddle in the middle.

As the crystallized sugar must be quickly poured into the molds, it is indispensable to use a pot with a spout to facilitate this step. The leftover crystallized sugar can be warmed and used again. To reinforce the molded piece, a second layer of crystallized sugar can be poured over the first layer. After pouring out the excess of each layer, it is important to scrape the sides of the molds to maintain a clean edge.

For lighter and smoother pieces, the sugar can be cooked to the higher end of the temperature range, or add 1 oz/30 g glucose to each recipe for 35 oz/1,000 g sugar. The syrup can be made ahead of time.

Bring the sugar, water, and glucose to a boil (syrup) and set aside for later use. If food coloring is used, also add a few drops of acetic acid to help fix the color.

Poured Crystallized Sugar
No. 2

Heat fondant, stirring constantly with a wooden spoon. When the mixture is hot but not yet fully melted, pour it into the prepared molds. If the fondant is overly soft, thicken it with sifted confectioners' sugar until the proper consistency is achieved.

Chef's Note: This procedure is particularly convenient for small figures such as columns and swans.

Preparing Plaster Molds

Plaster molds are usually prepared in two to four sections, depending on the subject. Soak the entire mold in cold water for at least one hour before using it. The sections are then assembled and the mold is ready to be filled.

If copper, tin, or lead molds are used, they do not require soaking but must be lightly coated with oil or petroleum jelly.

Making Plaster Molds

It is possible to purchase a wide selection of plaster molds, though they are fairly easy to make from scratch. To make a plaster mold, a model is required. Prepare the plaster according to the directions. Either hard plaster or plaster of Paris can be used. Fill a cardboard carton or wood box slightly larger than the model with the plaster. Lightly oil the model and push it half way into the plaster. Set aside for the plaster to set.

After setting, lightly brush the top half of the model and the top of the plaster with oil. The oil will prevent the plaster from sticking to the model and to the first half of the mold. Extend the sides of the box if necessary. Pour the second layer of plaster inside the box, smoothing it around the sides.

After the plaster has set, remove the box. Separate the two plaster halves and remove the model. For molding pastillage, leave the mold as is. For poured sugar, cut a hole at one end through which the sugar can be poured. The mold can be prepared in two or more pieces, depending on the subject. Be sure to brush oil on each section after it dries but before pouring the next section of plaster so they can be separated after setting.

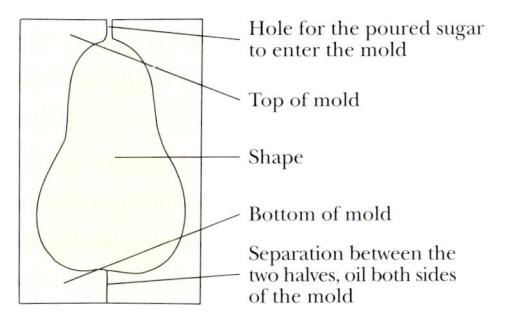

- Hole for the poured sugar to enter the mold
- Top of mold
- Shape
- Bottom of mold
- Separation between the two halves, oil both sides of the mold

Example: pear-shaped plaster mold.

Sugar and Decoration Work 373

374 Modern French Pastry

Pulled Sugar Gladiolus

Contrary to the way most pulled sugar flowers are constructed, the gladiolus is not assembled directly on the stem, but in two separate sections. First, the flowers are made; then, they are attached to a wire that serves as the stem.

When preparing a pulled sugar gladiolus, it is recommended to work with a real flower as a model. The smallest flowers are made by rolling strips of pulled sugar around pulled sugar buds. Make the flowers so the petals gradually open as they get larger. When all flowers are prepared, the buds are attached to the top of a wire stem with larger flowers toward the bottom.

Photo 1: Prepare the pulled sugar flowers. The smallest flowers are made by rolling a strip of pulled sugar around a pulled sugar bud. The first set of slightly open flowers are given two open petals, the next, three open petals, and finish with the largest flowers for the bottom, fully opened.

Photo 2: When all the flowers are finished, they are ready to be attached to a long wire sturdy enough to support the weight of the flowers. Begin at the top, attaching the smallest bud to the stem by wrapping a green pulled sugar leaf around the base of the bud and around the wire.

Photo 3: The flowers are all attached in this way, from top to bottom with green pulled sugar leaves.

Photo 4: Finish with the largest flowers on the bottom. Cut out a large leaf to wrap around the flower and stem.

Photo 5: The flowers are separated and attached by the pulled sugar leaves, which at the same time covers the wire to create the stem.

Photo 6: The bottom flowers are shaped in full bloom. Finish by wrapping the remaining wire with green pulled sugar.

Sugar and Decoration Work

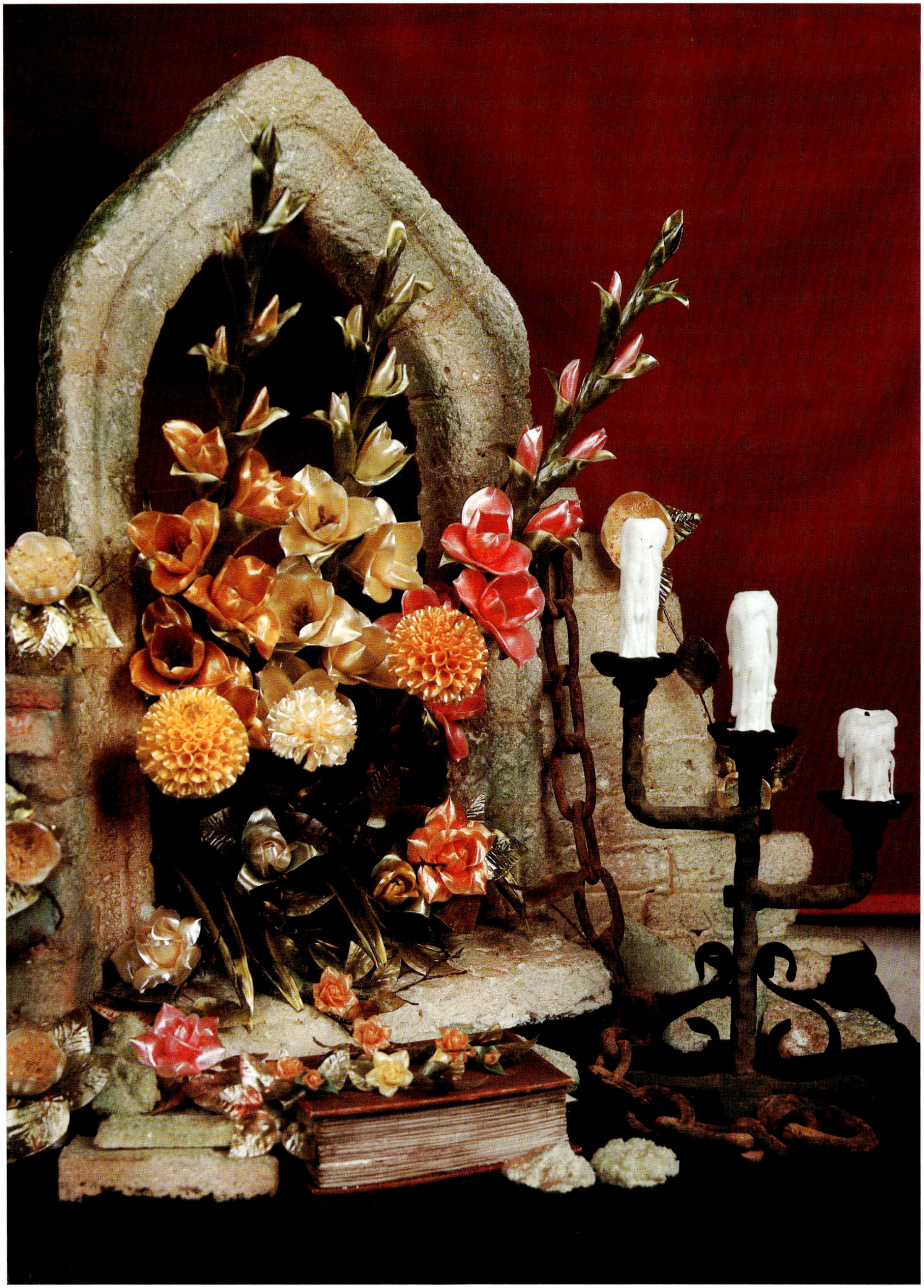

Remnants of Time Passed

This presentation piece represents a ruin. A stone arch is supported by the remains of the walls. The flowers are meant to appear as though they self-seeded. A book gives the impression it can be read by candlelight. A rusty chain is attached to the wall. This image is meant to arouse the imagination as to the origin of the different elements.

The stone arch and walls are made of rock sugar; the chain, book, and candlestick are made of pastillage; the candles of poured sugar; and the flowers and leaves of pulled sugar.

Spun Sugar

Spun sugar is used to decorate desserts such as croquembouches, frozen desserts, or ice creams. Cut into short segments, it is used as pistils for certain flowers.

Spun sugar is very sensitive to hot and humid conditions. It is best prepared as close to being served as possible. If stored, place it in a cool, dry area until needed. It can be frozen for several days.

sugar, cubes	35 oz	1,000 g
water	12.5 oz	350 g
glucose	9 oz	250 g

Combine all ingredients in a copper sugar pot (poëlon) and cook to 311°F/155°C. When the temperature is reached, dip the bottom of the pot in cold water for a few seconds to stop the cooking. Set the sugar aside in the pot for approximately 5 minutes to rest. After resting, the sugar should be fluid but slightly thickened. The thickness of the sugar when spun is the most important facet of the procedure. If too thin, the sugar will drip and not form threads; if too thick, it will stick and make overly thick strands.

Place a metal rolling pin or bar so it hangs 8–12 in/20–30 cm over the edge of a pastry marble. Place two sheet pans underneath the rolling pin to catch the sugar. Dip a fork or whisk (with the rounded end cut off to create long, straight rods) into the sugar. Quickly wave the fork or cut whisk back and forth over the metal bar or rolling pin. The sugar will pull on itself to create long threads. When enough sugar has been spun, lift it up and immediately wrap it around the subject to be decorated. It is best to handle the spun sugar as little as possible.

Chef's Note: *When a large quantity of spun sugar is required, a special appliance specifically made for spun sugar may be used. This appliance is essential for those chefs who use a lot of spun sugar decoration.*

Flower Pistils
Gather several strands of spun sugar to form a fairly compact cylinder. The thickness of the cylinder will determine the thickness of the pistils; the length is determined by how many pistils are needed. Pinch one end of the cylinder closed. Heat a knife in a flame cutting through the cylinder 1.5–2 in/4–5 cm from the pinched end. Immediately dip the cut ends in colored (red, yellow, or green) granulated sugar. Heat the pinched end in a flame and immediately attach it to a pulled sugar flower.

If the pistils are not immediately attached to a flower after being made, they can be stored in an airtight container with desiccant.

(Spun Sugar recipe continued on next page)

Facing Page: Remnants of Time Passed

The sugar can be colored brown, pink, yellow, green, or other color of choice. It is also possible to color the sugar during the cooking by bringing it to a caramel; any shade of caramel can be used. The only disadvantage to this technique is that the darker the caramel, the more limited the storage, as caramelized spun sugar softens more quickly and loses shape. Caramelized spun sugar is recommended when it is to be used soon after being made.

Spun Sugar Pistils

Photo 1: Cook the sugar and prepare the spun sugar according to the procedure on page 377. Gather several strands of spun sugar to form a fairly compact cylinder. The thickness of the cylinder will determine the thickness of the pistils; the length is determined by the number of pistils needed.

Photo 2: Pinch one end of the cylinder. Heat a knife in a flame and cut the cylinder 1.5–2 in/4–5 cm from the pinched end.

Photo 3: Immediately dip the cut ends in colored (red, yellow, or green) granulated sugar.

Photo 4: The colored sugar is meant to imitate the pollen on the tip of the pistils. Continue to prepare the pistils by pinching the end of the spun sugar cylinder and repeating the procedure, making as many as needed.

Chef's Note: *The finished pistils are heated at the pinched end and immediately attached to the inside center of pulled sugar flowers, such as the Christmas flower shown here. If not used immediately, the pistils can be stored in a cool, dry area inside an airtight container with desiccant.*

Sugar and Decoration Work

379

380   *Modern French Pastry*

Photo 2: Immediately after cutting the petal, roll it around the tip of the scissors to form a cone. This procedure should be done quickly and with a heat source such as an infrared lamp, small electric heater, or in front of an open oven. Prepare between 100 and 120 petals, calculating how many will be needed per row, making them larger for the bottom row and gradually smaller for the upper rows.

Photo 3: When enough petals have been prepared, the flower is ready to be assembled. With a scissors, cut a disk of pulled sugar approximately 1–2 in/3–5 cm in diameter. Place the disk flat on lightly oiled pastry marble. Heat the small closed end of a petal and immediately attach it to the edge of the sugar disk. Use the larger petals for the first row. Repeat this step, attaching one row of petals around the disk.

Photo 4: The next row is made, attaching the petals in the same way by heating the tips. The first petal is placed on top of the first row, between two petals and slightly inset, so the flower will be round when finished. Continue with the row of petals in this way. Each following row is made the same, setting the petals slightly inside between the previous row. Each will have one less petal. The petals should be slightly smaller for each consecutive row for a more realistic appearance.

Photo 5: The top of the dahlia can be finished in one of two ways; either entirely with petals, or to better imitate a real dahlia, a small bud can be placed on top in the center, with very small petals around it.

Place the flower upside down on a piece of foam and attach a row of larger petals to the bottom (which would otherwise be flat), slightly inset from the previous row. This will make for a very rounded flower.

Pompon Dahlias

Photo 1: Cook and prepare pulled sugar according to the recipe on pages 295–296. Place the pulled sugar on a drum sieve under a heat source. With both hands, use the fingertips to stretch a section of sugar, thinning an edge. With one hand, pull the edge of the sugar and, using scissors in the other hand, cut it off at an angle as for a small leaf.

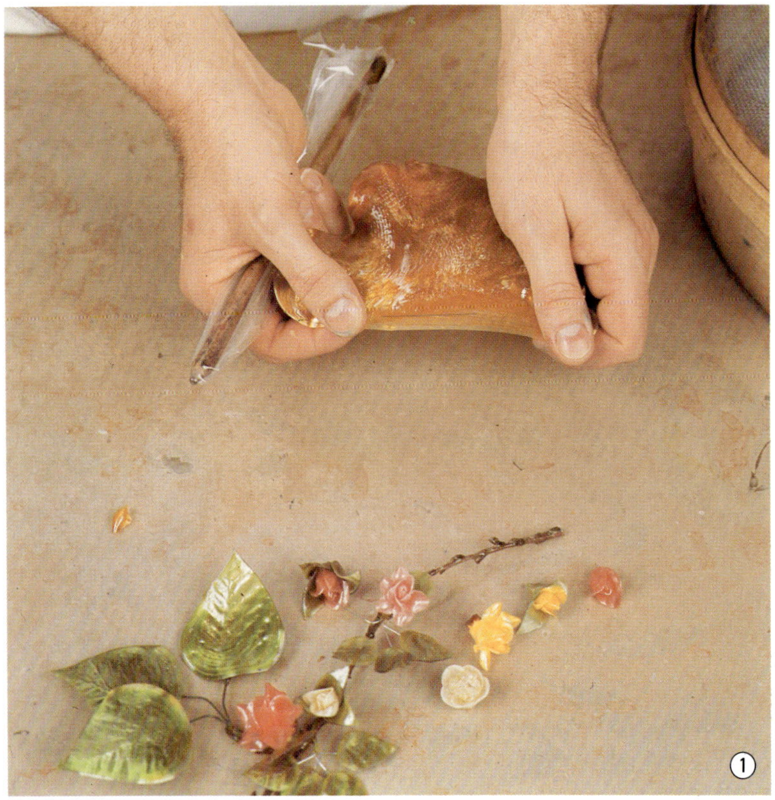
1

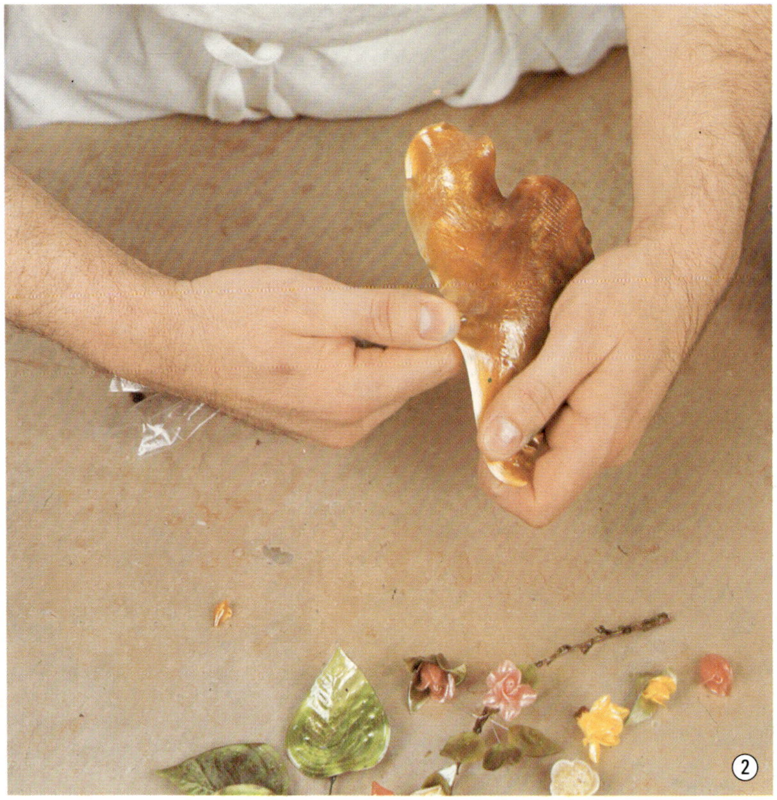
2

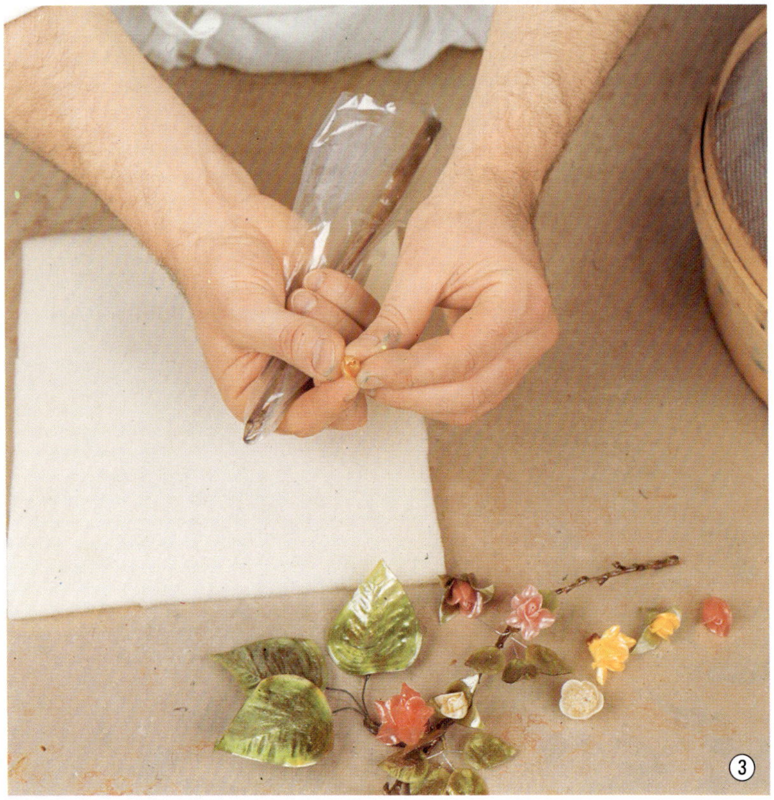
3

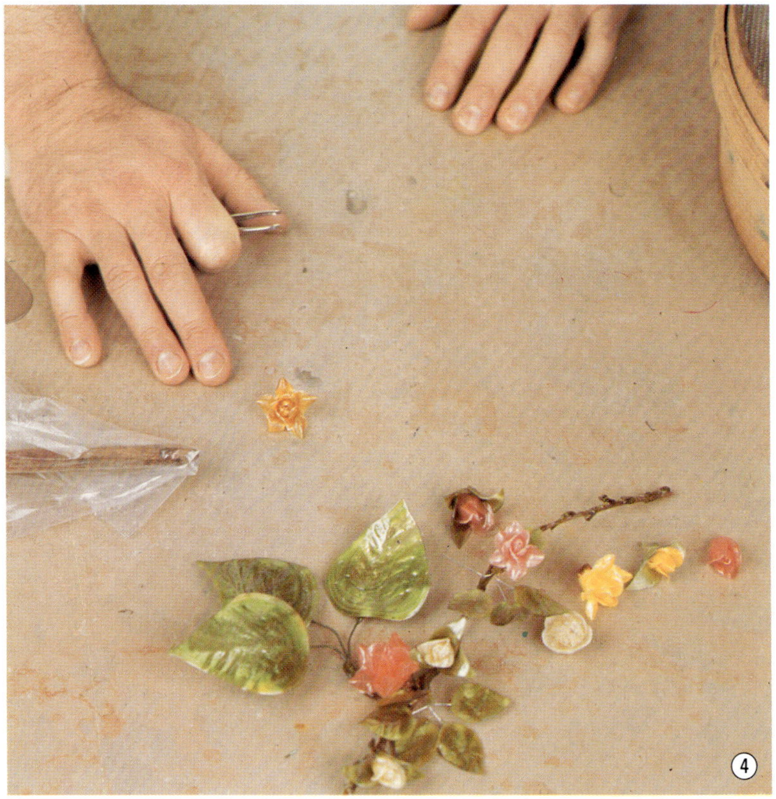
4

Pulled Sugar Miniature Rose

Photo 1: Cook and prepare pulled sugar according to the recipe on pages 295–296. Place the pulled sugar on a drum sieve under a heat source. With both hands, use the fingertips to stretch a section of sugar, thinning it.

Photo 2: Use a narrow cylinder (wood or metal) with a rounded end, such as a pen, wrapped in plastic film, to pull off a small petal. There are also special tools made for miniature flowers.

Photo 3: Assemble the miniature rose as for a full-size rose. The sugar should be pulled near a heat source to prevent it from cracking.

Photo 4: With the plastic film-covered cylinder, various miniature flowers can be prepared for artistic presentations or to decorate iced petits fours. Any miniature flowers can be made, such as the Christmas rose or lily of the valley. The procedure is the same as for the larger flowers only the thumb and index finger that are normally used to pull the petals are replaced by the cylinder to pull very small pieces.

Pulled Sugar Carnation

Photo 1: Cook and prepare pulled sugar according to the recipe on pages 295–296. Place the pulled sugar on a drum sieve under a heat source. With both hands, use the fingertips to stretch a section of sugar, creating a thin edge.

Photo 2: Using scissors, cut small incisions on the thinned edge. This will create a ruffled effect as is typical of a carnation.

(Pulled Sugar Carnation recipe continued on page 385)

Sugar and Decoration Work

Modern French Pastry

Photo 3: With one hand, pull on the ruffled section and use the other hand to cut off a petal with scissors. This must be done under a heat source so that the petal can be shaped.

Photo 4: Immediately after cutting the petal, fold it loosely, finishing with one long end. This will allow the petals to fit in place when assembled. Pinch the bottom (unruffled side) together. Approximately 30–50 petals are needed, depending on the size of the flower desired.

Photo 5: Assemble the carnation by heating the pinched ends in a flame and attaching them to each other, one-by-one, starting at the center of the flower.

Photo 6: Continue building around the petals that were joined in the center. Assemble the petals so they are not perfectly aligned, for a more realistic effect.

Photo 7: Finish the flower with the last row of petals underneath, giving the carnation a rounded shape.

Photo 8: Coat a metal wire with pulled sugar and attach a small ball of pulled sugar to one end. Heat the ball of sugar and attach the base of the flower to it. Three sepals in green pulled sugar can be attached to the bottom of the flower.

Chef's Note: The carnation can also be assembled directly on the ball of pulled sugar attached to the stem (coated pulled sugar wire). In this case the flower is assembled from the outside, and finished in the center. The two procedures offer the same results.

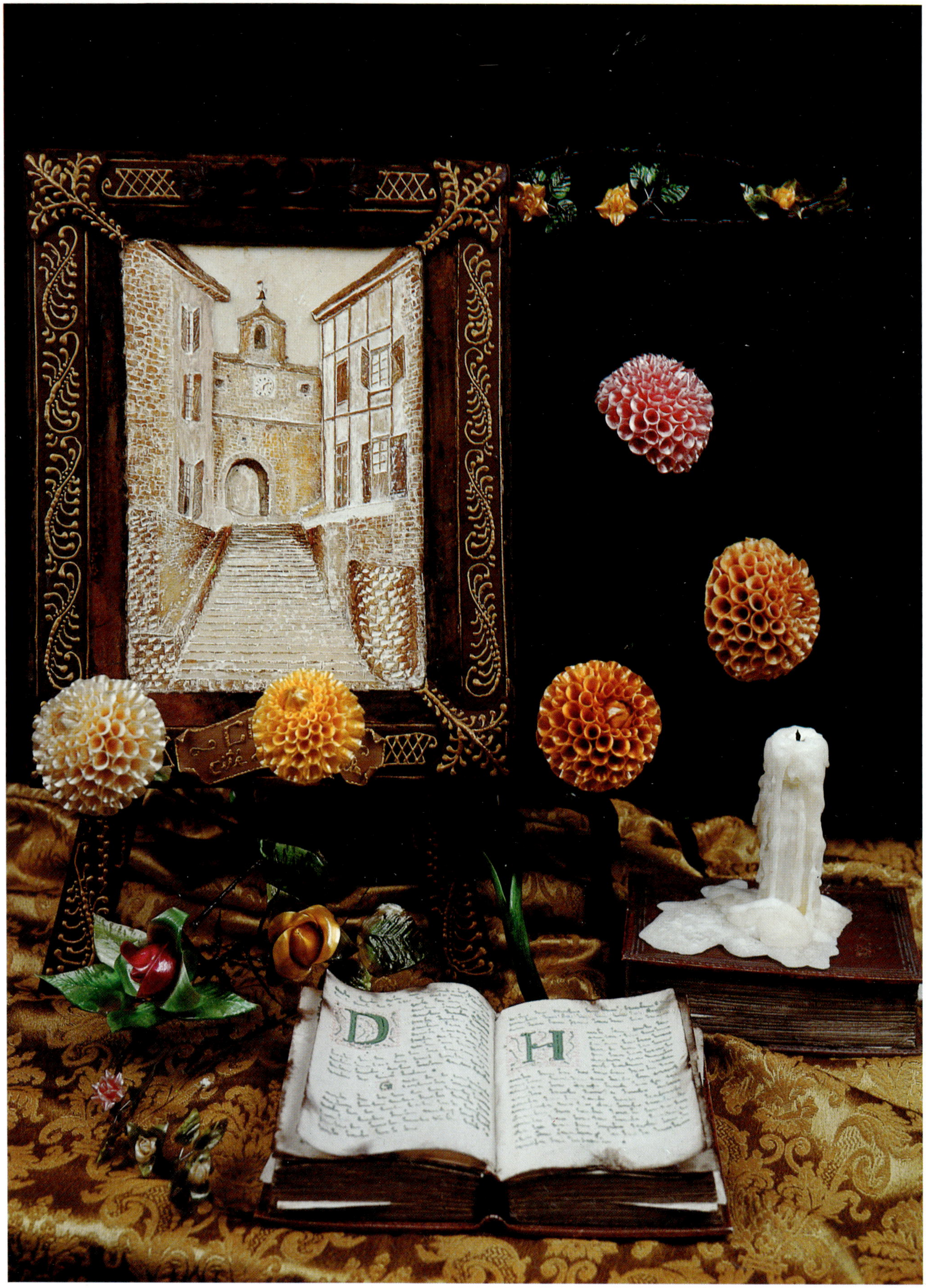

Pastillage Book

The open book made from pastillage is assembled in three sections:

1. The cover of the book is made from a sheet of pastillage which can be cut to any size. After drying, it is colored.

2. Two blocks of pastillage are prepared to represent the two sides of the book, and set aside to dry flat on a sheet pan. After several days, when the top has formed a crust, they are turned over. The bottom will still be tender. The center is then scraped hollow. This is an important step because if left solid, the pastillage will swell during the drying period, contract after drying, and crack.

3. The pages are made from very thin sheets of pastillage prepared, one-by-one; cut, shaped, and dried in the form desired.

The pages that stick out of the book are placed in the hollowed sides of the book while still soft. The top pages are given an aged look by shading sections along the edges with dark brown coloring or cocoa power. The writing is made with a paper cone filled with colored royal icing.

After several weeks, when all pastillage pieces are fully dried and decorated, the book is ready to be assembled. Place the two hollowed blocks, or sides of the book, over the cover. Carefully set the pastillage pages in place and pipe colored royal icing to imitate the seam and help hold the pages in place.

To prepare a closed book, the procedure is basically the same, except that it is made with only one hollowed block of pastillage. The cover is cut in two sections to fit over and under the block. The binding is prepared separately. After fully drying, the separate sections are assembled in a book.

Facing Page: If History Were Mine to Tell

Presentation Piece: If History Were Mine to Tell

This composition is presented on a gold-colored cloth. Pulled sugar pompon dahlias and roses are placed around an easel made in chocolate and decorated with plastic chocolate flowers and piping in gold-colored chocolate icing. A poured block sugar candle, set on a book made from pastillage, appears as though it was once lit and has partially melted down. A second pastillage book is left open. The easel supports a painting of Cordes-sur-Ciel, a city built in the twelfth century, with a view of the entrance to the city. The view is sculpted in white chocolate decorated with various tints of cocoa powder.

Sculpting in Chocolate

The basic technique for sculpting in chocolate is the same as for sculpting in wood. The materials needed are scissors, chisel, and various sized gouges. First trace the design, then prepare the subject. It is important to have a brush to wipe away the chocolate shavings as necessary.

Following Page: Pulled Sugar Presentation Piece

Modern French Pastry

Glossary

Aerate: To whip a batter so it increases in volume by whipping in air.

Almond paste: A mixture of ground almonds, sugar, and a liquid such as water, glucose and/or egg whites. It is made with varying percentages of almond. A higher percentage of almond will produce a more flavorful paste, but it will have a shorter shelf life. When more sugar is used the paste keeps longer, but is not as flavorful. Almond paste or raw almond paste generally refers to an uncooked mixture often used for fillings and batters. An almond paste made with cooked sugar is called marzipan. The recipes in this book usually call for a marzipan of 33% almond (also called confectioners' or fondant almond paste). Marzipan is used especially to cover cakes and form figures or flowers.

Baumé: Degrees by which the weight of a syrup is measured using a hydrometer. A syrup of 30° on the Baumé scale has a density of 1.2624.

Biscuit: A base used as the basis for many types of cakes. It has many different variations: chocolate, almond, *de Savoie* (sponge cake), *à la cuillère* (ladyfingers) to name a few. It differs from the génoise in that the yolks and sugar are beaten together without a heat source and the whites are beaten separately. The *biscuit* has a firmer texture and keeps longer than the génoise.

Blanche: To immerse fruit in boiling water in order to soften.

Blanched almonds: Almonds with their skin removed, named for the blanching process often used to skin them.

Blind baking: To bake a pastry shell without a filling. The shell can be partially cooked, as for custard tarts where the shell will be cooked further with a filling, or fully cooked, as for tarts filled after the shell has cooled. Always line the raw shell with parchment paper or other non-stick paper that will not burn in high heat. Pie weights, such as dried beans, rice, or metal weights specifically made for this procedure are added. The weights maintain the shape of the shell.

Caramelize: 1. To heat a cake or dessert sprinkled with sugar or meringue in a hot oven or broiler, or with a propane torch or hot iron until it takes on a caramel color. For meringue, usually only the ridges or peaks are colored. This emphasizes the texture of the meringue and covers the surface with a light protective skin. 2. To heat sugar to a hard crack stage until it takes on a color ranging from a light amber to a dark brown.

Chantilly: Sweetened whipped cream.

Chocolate paste: A paste made of cocoa and vegetable fat available from various suppliers. Can be substituted with unsweetened chocolate.

Chou (choux, *pl.*): A cream puff usually filled with pastry cream, mousseline cream, or chantilly.

Coulis: A thick sauce or pureé. In pastry, it is generally made from fruit.

Craquelin: Ground nougatine.

Cream: To whip butter until it is light and aerated.

Crème Anglaise: A custard sauce made from eggs, milk, and sugar, often vanilla flavored. The crème anglaise is cooked over low heat (to avoid curdling the eggs) until it coats the back of a spoon (*nappé* stage) or a temperature of 176–185°F/80–85° C.

Croquembouche: A traditional French dessert made from filled cream puffs (choux) attached with sugar cooked to a hard crack stage.

Deglaze: To add a liquid to a pot with caramel, caramelized pan juices (in pastry making), or a sauce to stop the cooking and render it more fluid for a sauce or other preparation.

Dessicant: A drying agent such as limestone. It is placed in an airtight container with pulled sugar work to protect it from humidity.

Dock: To pierce a dough before baking so that steam can escape.

Dragées: Candy-coated almonds.

Enrobe: To entirely coat with chocolate. Usually a small pastry or chocolate center is enrobed with chocolate.

Flambé: To ignite alcohol in a sauce or on a cake so it flames up and burns off the alcohol. This creates a dramatic effect for presentation.

Gelatin: In this book, gelatin is used in sheets unless otherwise stated. Before adding to a mixture, the sheets are softened by completely submerging them in very cold water for approximately 10 minutes. Once softened, remove the gelatin sheets from the water and squeeze them to extract any excess water. They are now ready to be melted. Never to allow the gelatin to boil. Even if melted in a liquid, it will lose its bonding properties.

Gelée: A jelly made from a high pectin fruit juice and sugar. It is used as a filling or to glaze cakes.

Glaze: *n.* A clear coating brushed onto cakes or pastries. In pastry, a glaze is typically made from apricots, though other flavors may be used. *v.* To spread or brush a layer of hot liquid onto a pastry. The coating is clear and shiny when set and protects the food from drying and oxidation.

Gouttière: A long, rounded, "gutter" shaped mold. Often used for making mousses in the shape of yule logs.

Hot water bath/Bain-marie: A method to gently cook, warm, melt, or poach in a double boiler. If used on top of the stove, the item melted (such as chocolate) or cooked (such as a custard) is placed in a pot or bowl over a larger pot of hot water. If melting chocolate, the bowl should not come directly in contact with the water. If the bain-marie is used in the oven, as for cooking crème caramel, the product to be poached is placed in a serving dish (ramekin or ovenproof dish). The dish is then set in a larger pan filled with enough water to come approximately halfway up the side of the dish.

Infuse: To add flavor by soaking vanilla beans, tea, coffee, herbs, or other flavorings in a hot or boiling liquid for a few minutes. For example, heating milk with a vanilla bean when preparing a crème anglaise.

Macerate: To soak fruit—dried, candied, poached, or fresh—for several hours or days in a flavored liquid containing alcohol.

Marzipan: See almond paste.

Modeling Chocolate: A special chocolate used for shaping flowers or figures.

Nougatine: A type of almond brittle. It is generally cut into shapes or formed in molds and used to decorate cakes or to assemble croquembouches.

Plastic Chocolate: See modeling chocolate.

Poach: To simmer gently at approximately 194°–203°F/ 90°–95°C, never boiling.

Poêlon/Copper sugar pot: A pot with a spout. When used for sugar it should be made of solid copper and unlined.

Raw almond paste: See almond paste.

Reduce: To cook a sauce or liquid slowly until it thickens to the desired consistency.

Ribbon stage: A stage of cooking or whisking when a batter is thick enough to fold over onto itself as it falls from a spoon or spatula. Also, whipping egg yolks and sugar until the mixture is homogeneous, thick, pale, and can fold over onto itself.

Satinage: The process of pulling and folding sugar to produce a satiny sheen before forming flowers in pulled sugar work.

Simple syrup: A syrup used for moistening cakes such as biscuit or génoise. Boil 34 fl oz/1 liter water and 47.5 oz/1350 g of sugar to a density of 1.2624 or 30° baumé. The syrup is then flavored to taste.

Skim: To remove the foam and impurities that rise to the surface of a liquid while simmering.

Spatula: A scraping, stirring, or spreading tool available in wood, plastic, rubber, or metal. A wooden spatula is a practical tool used for stirring; it is more effective than a spoon. Though most commonly made out of wood, they are also made in a strong heat-resistant plastic. A rubber spatula is not recommended as a substitute for a wooden spatula as it easily melts even at low heat and is too flexible for stirring. A rubber spatula is primarily used for scraping.

A metal spatula is long and narrow and used to spread icings and fillings. They come in many sizes and varieties, such as the angled spatula or pallet knife. Choose the size and shape according to the work being done and personal comfort.

Steep: To moisten a baba, savarin, biscuit, or other cake by totally immersing it in syrup.

Sterilize: To heat a liquid to a minimum of 212°F/100°C to destroy bacteria.

Tant pour tant (TPT): Equal weights of a ground nuts and sugar (powdered or granulated). Almonds are generally used, but other nuts, such as hazelnuts, can be used as well.

Tragacanth: A vegetable gum used as a thickener (also called gum tragacanth).

Tuile: An almond cookie that is shaped in a mold or over a rolling pin while warm to give it a curved shape.

Wolf's teeth/Dents de loup: Curved triangles usually made from nougatine or pastillage used to decorate pedestals and presentation pieces.

Index

Italicized page numbers refer to recipes in *Classic and Contemporary Recipes of Yves Thuriès: French Pastry*

A

Alhambra cake, *347–348*
Almond biscuit, 114, 160–161
  chocolate, 39, 162, *367*
  coffee, 161
  mousseline, 121
Almond buttercream, 29
Almond cake
  cherry, 29–31
  coffee, 25
  cognac, 13
Almond cream, 33
Almond cream filling, 138
Almond glaze, 149
Almond génoise, 122, 273, *365*
Almond meringue, 13
Almond paste, *9, 79, 116, 215,* 32, 95
Almond paste filling, 149
Almonds, caramelized, 12
Angels' cake, 27
Animal decorations, 341–351
  bird, 341–345
  dog, 347, 349
  elephant, 347
  fish, 349
  rabbit, 351
  squirrel, 349
  swan, 341–346

Apple, blown sugar, 353
Apple-cherry mousse cake, 70–71
Apricot mousse, 73
Apricot simple syrup, maraschino, 73

B

Baba, *4–5*
Banana cake
  chocolate, 35
  rum, 119
Banana cream filling, 119
Banana mousse, 56, 61
Bananas, blown sugar, 353
Banana Willy, 61
Banania cake, 69
Basket decoration, blown sugar, 353
Batter, cigarette, 38
Bavarian cream, 117, *360*
  coffee, 123
  coffee-caramel, 115–117
  vanilla, 99
Bavarian cream filling, 142
Bird decorations, blown sugar, 341–345
Biscuit, *366–369*
  almond, 160–161
  almond chocolate, 39, 162, *367*
  almond mousseline, 121
  as a cake and pastry base, 160–165
  cherry, 162–163
  chocolate, 6, 161, *367–368*
  coffee, 161

  coffee almond, 161
  dacquoise, 31
  dobos, 163
  hazelnut, 164
  honey almond, 114
  joconde, *367*
  lining a cake ring with, 109
  lining a mold with, 91, 109
  majestic, 46
  nougat, 163–164
  orange, 162, 165
  pistachio, 163
  sacher, 165
  walnut, 164
Blackcurrant cake
  Charlotte, 111
  Saint Ange, 79
  supreme, 49
Blackcurrant Charlotte cream, 113
Blackcurrant gelée, 79–80, 113
Blackcurrant mousse, 50, 59, 79
Blackcurrant mousse filling, 136, 145–146
Blackcurrant simple syrup, 50, 79, 113
Blackcurrant Willy, 59
Blown sugar decorations, 338–353. *See also* Decorations
  apple, 353
  banana, 353
  basket, 353
  bird, 341–345
  dog, 347, 349
  elephant, 347

  fish, 349
  grapes, 353
  peach, 353
  pear, 353
  pitcher, 365
  rabbit, 351
  shaping, 339
  squirrel, 349
  swan, 341–346
  vase, 351
Bouquets, pulled sugar, 361–363. *See also* Flower decorations
Brandy mousse, pear, 77
Brazilian cake, 5
Burnt sugar stage, 359
Buttercream, 15, *315, 353–356*
  almond, 29
  as filling, 141
  special, 83
Buttercream cake, coffee, 19–20
Butter ganache, 7
Butter génoise, 159

C

Cake. *See also* Charlotte cake; Cheese cake; Chocolate cake; Croquembouches; Meringue cake; Mousse cake; Tiered cake
  angel's hell, 32
  angels', 27
  biscuit bases for, 160–165
  blackcurrant, 49, 79, 111

  black rose, 29
  borsalino, 50–51
  Brazilian, 5
  brillat savarin, 125
  caprice, 75, 77
  Charlemagne, 41
  Charleston, 6
  checkerboard, 15
  cherub, 38–39
  coating with couverture, 150–151
  colisée, 63–65
  Creole soufflé, 56
  Cupid, 73
  diablotin, 21
  délice, 114
  dome, 31
  Duchess Anne, 121
  Easter nest, 151
  ganache, 7
  Gascony Prince, 117
  gemini, 43
  Gentleman's whiskey, 88
  glazing with fondant, 263, 275
  gratin, 33
  imperial, 129–131
  indulgent, 61, 63
  ingot, 21
  Little Duke, 71
  majestic, 46
  Mandarin, 53
  marigny, 115
  mazarin, 9
  Milanese gratin (macaroni), 33
  mirror, 98, 103
  misérable, 17

393

mogador, 147–149
Cake. *(continued)*
  moistening with simple syrup, 150
  opera, *275*
  Peteroff, 84
  presentation pedestal for, 75
  Prince Albert, 122
  princess, 81–83
  Saint Ange, 79, 80, 81
  Saint Christopher, 89
  Saint Hubert, 37
  Seville, 128
  soufflé, 56
  sovereign, 27
  spiral, 11
  spraying with chocolate, 35
  sublime, 93
  sully, 83
  Sultan, 69
  Valencia, 55, 56, 95
  vatel, 127
  white rose, 17
  Willy, 57–61
Cake bases. *See also* Presentation pieces
  biscuit, 159–165
  croquembouche, 175
  nougatine, 173
  for tiered cakes, 238
Cake cream. *See also* Cream; Filling
  diablotin, 23
  spiral, 9
Cake fillings, 135–155
Cake mold, lining, 118
Cake ring, lining with biscuit or génoise spiral, 109
Cake rings, using, 20
Cake stands, tiered, 238. *See also* Tiered cake
Candles, sugar, 371
Caramel
  cooking, 211, 261
  for croquembouches, 195
  glazing choux with, 209
Caramel cream, 115
Caramel cream filling, 138
  Charlotte, 143
Caramel délice cake, 114
Caramel flowers, 289
  molded, 177
Caramelized almonds, 12
Caramel mousse, 6
Caramel sauce, 110
Caramel simple syrup, 114
Caramel sugar stage, 359
Carnations, pulled sugar, 383–385

Chantilly, *303, 352–353*
  chocolate, 98
Chantilly cream filling, 146–147
Charleston cake, 6
Charlotte cake
  belle Hélène, 99
  blackcurrant, 111
  Brazilian, 123
  caramel, 143
  chestnut, 105
  lemon, 101
  passion fruit, 89
  peach, 87
  pear, 85, 92
  pineapple, 104
  presenting, 110
  raspberry, 103
  sauces for, 110
  strawberry, 97
  tiered, 257
Charlotte cream, *261*
  blackcurrant, 113
  chestnut, 107
  chocolate, 111
  coffee, 110
  lemon, 101
  passion fruit, 92
  peach, 87
  pear, 85–87, 92–93
  pineapple, 104–105
  praline, 111
  raspberry, 101
  strawberry, 97
  vanilla, 111
Charlotte cream filling, 144
Cheese cake, fromage blanc, 67
Cherry biscuit, 162–163
Cherry cake
  almond, 29–31
  apple, 70–71
  strawberry, 70
Chestnut cake, Charlotte, 105
Chestnut Charlotte cream, 107
Chestnut Charlotte cream filling, 143
Chestnut gelée, 105
Chestnut mousse, 84
Chestnut mousse filling, 136
Chestnut paste, 85
Chocodream cake, 45
Chocolate
  sculpting in, 387
  sprayed, 35
Chocolate biscuit, 161, *367–368*
  hazelnut, 164
Chocolate cake

banana, 35
biscuit, 6
coating for, 5, 9, 41
cream, 23
ganache, 7
Mazarin, 9
Chocolate chantilly, 98
Chocolate Charlotte cream, 111
Chocolate Charlotte cream filling, 144
Chocolate cigarettes, 155
Chocolate craquelin mousse filling, 136
Chocolate filling
  mousse, 135, 145
  Suzanne cream, 146
Chocolate génoise, 159, *365*
Chocolate icing, 249
Chocolate mousse, 29, 45, 69, 127, *241, 285, 362–363*
Chocolate sauce, 110
Chocolate shavings, 43
Chocolate strips, 155
Choux
  glazing, 187–189
  glazing with caramel, 209
Choux paste, 179–181
  piping, 221
Clown, poured sugar, 329
Coconut génoise, 159–160
Coffee, flavoring with, 149
Coffee almond biscuit, 161
Coffee Bavarian cream, 123
Coffee biscuit, 161
Coffee cake
  almond, 25
  buttercream, 19–20
  indulgent, 63
  rum, 37
Coffee-caramel Bavarian cream, 115–117
Coffee Charlotte cream, 110
Coffee cream filling, Charlotte, 143
Coffee extract, 149, *375*
Coffee gelée, 123
Coffee mousse, 25, 43, *281, 363*
  Brazilian, 5
  chestnut, 84
  indulgent, 63
  Saint Hubert, 38
Coffee simple syrup, 123, 149, *374*
Coffee yule log, 142
Cognac cake, almond, 13
Cognac cream, 39

Cognac simple syrup, 46, 107
Colisée, 63–65
Cones, paper, 245
Coulis
  pear, 85
  strawberry, 110
Couverture, coating with, 150–151
Craquelin mousse filling, 136
Cream. *See also* Bavarian cream; Cake cream; Charlotte cream; Filling; Ganache; Pastry cream
  almond, 33
  caramel, 115
  classification of, 3
  cognac, 39
  fromage blanc, 67
  mousseline, 223–225
  praline mousseline, 12
  rum mousseline, 35
  sovereign, 27
  whipped, 147
Cream cake, chocolate, 23
Croquembouches, 169–231
  assembling, 231
  baby's bassinet, 191
  baby buggy, 195
  caramel for, 195
  chapel-shaped, 175
  choux paste for, 179–181
  conical, 171
  dawn serenade, 211
  decorating and presenting, 173
  dovecote, 217
  drum, 185
  engagement basket, 207
  floral wheelbarrow, 215
  flower basket, 179, 217
  flower vase, 227
  glazing choux for, 187–189
  grandmother's basket, 181
  grand prize, 187
  jewelry box, 181–185
  lovers' windmill, 189
  mandolin, 219
  Marie-Antoinette, 225
  modern chapel, 223
  nougatine for, 189–191
  pastry cream for, 185–187
  phoenix, 207
  podium, 199–201
  pompadour, 203
  presentation bases for, 175
  prestige, 205
  reverence, 213

small church, 197
temple of love, 191
trammel, 227
turtledoves' cage, 213–215
victory, 229
victory ball, 219
wishing well, 229

D

Dacquoise, 11, 12, *373*
Daffodils, pulled sugar, 367–369
Dahlias, pulled sugar, 381
Decorations
  animal, 341–351
  basket, 353
  bird, 341–345
  blown sugar, 338–353
  candles, 371
  clown, 329
  croquembouche, 173
  dog, 347, 349
  elephant, 347
  fish, 349
  fruit, 353
  molded sugar, 287–293
  paper cone, 245
  pastillage, 313–321
  pitcher, 365
  poured sugar, 329–333
  pulled sugar, 295–301
  pulled sugar ribbons, 323–327
  rabbit, 351
  rock sugar, 307–311
  spun sugar, 377–378
  squirrel, 349
  swan, 341–346
  turned sugar, 354–359
  woven sugar, 335–337
Dog decoration, blown sugar, 347, 349

E

Elephant decoration, blown sugar, 347

F

Filling. *See also* Cream; Ganache; Mousse
  almond paste, 149
  banana cream, 119
  blackcurrant mousse, 136
  buttercream, 141
  cake and pastry, 135–155
  caramel cream, 138
  Chantilly cream, 146–147

Charlotte caramel cream, 143
Charlotte coffee cream, 143
Charlotte cream, 144
chestnut Charlotte cream, 143
chestnut mousse, 136
chocolate Charlotte cream, 144
chocolate mousse, 135, 145
chocolate Suzanne cream, 146
coffee mousse, 135–136
craquelin mousse, 136
fruit mousse, 145–146
hazelnut mousse, 146
Italian meringue, 144
lemon cream, 139
lemon mousse, 147
liquor mousse, 144–145
Mandarin orange mousse, 144
nougatine cream, 139
nougatine mousse, 141
orange buttercream, 138–139
orange mousse, 137–138, 147
pistachio mousse, 137
vanilla milk cream, 138
walnut mousse, 137
wine Bavarian cream, 142
Fish decorations, blown sugar, 349
Flower decorations
bouquets, 361–363
caramel, 177, 287
carnations, 383–385
daffodils, 367–369
dahlias, 381
gladiolus, 375
magyfleur, 285
molded sugar, 285
nougatine roses, 265
pulled sugar, 301, 366–369, 375, 381–385
roses, 265, 301, 383
spun sugar pistils for, 377–378
tulips, 366
Fondant
as a border for poured sugar, 330–333
glazing with, 263, 275
pulled sugar, 383–385
Fromage blanc cheese cake, 67
Fromage blanc cream, 67
Fruit caprice cake, 77

Fruit decorations, 353
Fruit mousse filling, 145–146

G

Ganache, 151–153, *335*, *351*
butter, 7
Ganache cake, chocolate, 7
Gelatin, for reinforcing meringue, 125
Gelée
blackcurrant, 79–80, 113
chestnut, 105
coffee, 123
raspberry, 81, 121–122
Valencia cake, 56
Gladiolus, pulled sugar, 375
Glaze
almond, 149
fondant, 263, 275
Génoise, 35, 159–160, *172*, *229*, *354*, *365*
almond, 122, 273, *365*
chocolate, *365*
mousseline, 88
Génoise spiral, lining a cake ring with, 109
Grapefruit mousse, 57
Grapefruit syrup, 56
Grapes, blown sugar, 353

H

Hard ball sugar stage, 359
Hard crack sugar stage, 359
Hazelnut biscuit, 164
Hazelnut cake, progrès, 41
Hazelnut génoise, 160
Hazelnut mousse filling, 146
Hazelnut progrès, *287*
Honey almond biscuit, 114

I

Icing
chocolate, 249
royal, 227–229, 309, *364*

J

Joconde biscuit, *367*

K

Kirsch mousse, 71, 77

L

Large pearl sugar stage, 359
Leaves, sugar, 361–362

Lemon cake
Charlotte, 101
mousse, 65
supreme, 47
Lemon Charlotte cream, 101
Lemon cream filling, 139
Lemon mousse, 49, 67, 129, *319*, *320*
Lemon mousse filling, 147
Lemon simple syrup, 49
Lemon syrup, 129
Liqueur mousse, 63, 131
Liquor mousse filling, 144–145

M

Magyfleur, 177
Magyfleur flowers, 285
Maraschino/apricot simple syrup, 73
Maraschino mousse, 70
Medium ball sugar stage, 359
Melon mousse, 61
Meringue, *253*, *311*, *361*, *362*, 371–373
almond, 13
Italian, 49, 125, *253*, *361*
orange, 251
princess, 83
Meringue cake, princess, 81–83
Meringue filling, Italian, 144
Molded pastillage, 313
Molded sugar decorations, 287–293
caramel, 177
flowers, 285
Molds. *See also* Presentation pieces
assembling croquembouches in, 171
lining with biscuits, 91, 109
nougatine, 173
plaster, 373
Mousse, 3. *See also* Chantilly; Cream; Filling
apricot, 73
banana, 56, 61
blackcurrant, 50, 59, 79
Brazilian coffee, 5
caramel, 6
chestnut, 84
chocolate, 29, 45, 69, 127, *241*, *285*, *362–363*
coffee, 25, 43, 63, *281*, *363*
grapefruit, 57
kirsch, 71, 77
lemon, 49, 67, 129, *319*, *320*

liqueur, 63
mandarine, 95–97
mandarin orange, 53–55
maraschino, 70
melon, 61
orange, 53, 55, 95–97
passion fruit, 47
peach, 125
pear brandy, 77
pineapple, 59, 128
praline, 7, 13, 32
prune, 117
raspberry, 59, 80, 89, 95, 103–104, *321*
rum, 61–63
Saint Hubert coffee, 38
strawberry, 59, 65, 81, 95, 98
strawberry liqueur, 131
whiskey, 88
white wine, 51, 84
Mousse cake
apple-cherry, 70–71
lemon, 65
orange, 51
strawberry-cherry, 70
Mousseline cream, 223–225, *295*, *356–357*
Mousseline génoise, 88
Mousse yule log, 142

N

Nougat biscuit, 163–164
Nougatine, *373*
as a croquembouche base, 173
confectioners' sugar, 280
for croquembouches, 189–191
cutting, 183
molding, 193
special, 203
Nougatine cream filling, 139
Nougatine molds, 173
Nougatine mousse filling, 141
Nougatine roses, 265
Nougatine tiered cake, 251
Nouvelle pastry, 3

O

Orange Bavarian, 251
Orange biscuit, 162, 165
Orange buttercream filling, 138–139
Orange mousse, 53, 95–97
mandarin, 53–55
special, 55
Orange mousse cake, 51

Orange mousse filling, 137–138, 144, 147
Orange simple syrup, 55

P

Paper cones, decorating with, 245
Passion fruit cake
Charlotte, 89
supreme, 47
Passion fruit Charlotte cream, 92
Passion fruit mousse, 47
Passion fruit simple syrup, 47
Paste. *See also* Choux paste
almond, 9, *79*, *116*, *215*, 95
chestnut, 85
Pastillage, 313–321. *See also* Presentation pieces
book made of, 387
candlesticks of, 365
painting on, 321
Pastry
bases for, 159–165
coating with couverture, 150–151
nouvelle, 3
Pastry cream, 32. *See also* Cream
for croquembouches, 185–187
Pastry fillings, 135–155. *See also* Filling
Peach cake
brillat savarin, 125
Charlotte, 87
Peach Charlotte cream, 87
Peaches, blown sugar, 353
Peach mousse, 125
Pear brandy mousse, 77
Pear cake
caprice, 75
Charlotte, 85, 92
Pear Charlotte cream, 85–87, 92–93
Pear coulis, 85
Pears
blown sugar, 353
poached, 85
Pear simple syrup, 87
Pineapple cake, 128
Charlotte, 104
Willy, 57
Pineapple Charlotte cream, 104–105
Pineapple mousse, 59, 128
Pistachio biscuit, 163
Pistachio ganache, 153
Pistachio mousse filling, 137

Plaster molds, 373
Poured sugar decorations. *See also* Poured sugar presentation pieces
Poured sugar decorations. *(continued)*
  clown, 329
  coloring, 271
  columns, 255
  crystallized, 372–373
  disks, 241
  fondant borders for, 330–333
  triangles, 241
Poured sugar presentation pieces, 247, 269–271, 329
Praline cake
  dome, 31
  Mazarin, 9
Praline Charlotte cream, 111
Praline ganache, 151
Praline mousse, 7, 13, 32
Praline mousseline cream, 12
Presentation bases. *See also* Cake bases
  for cakes, 75
  for croquembouches, 175
Presentation pieces, 235–237. *See also* Decorations
  aged cask, 365
  artistic, 283
  assembling, 303
  closed book (agenda), 243
  flower-filled vase, 361
  galacté, 313
  If History Were Mine to Tell, 387
  la belle epoque, 279
  memoires of war, 371
  nougatine, 265
  open book, 243
  opera, 257–259
  parcel from Nice, 335–337
  park corner, 307
  pastillage, 277
  poured sugar, 247, 269–271, 329
  remnants of time passed, 377
  for several cakes, 255
  star, 245
  When All Hope Is Revived, 303–305
Progrès, *372*
  hazelnut, 41, *287*
Prune mousse, 117
Pulled sugar decorations, 295–301
  bouquets of, 361–363
  carnations, 383–385
  daffodils, 367–369
  dahlias, 381
  flowers of, 301, 366–369, 375, 381–385
  fondant, 383–385
  gladiolus, 375
  ribbons, 323–327
  roses, 301, 383
  tulips of, 366

R

Rabbit decoration, blown sugar, 351
Raspberry cake
  Saint Ange, 80
  Saint Christopher, 89
  Charlotte, 103
  mirror, 103
Raspberry Charlotte cream, 101
Raspberry gelée, 81, 121–122
Raspberry mousse, 59, 80, 89, 95, 103–104, *321*
Raspberry mousse filling, 145–146
Raspberry Saint Hubert, 38
Raspberry simple syrup, 80, 101
Raspberry syrup, 121
Raspberry Willy, 59
Rock sugar decorations, 307–311
  coloring, 311
Roses
  Christmas, 305
  nougatine, 265
  pulled sugar, 301, 383
Rum banana cream filling, 119
Rum cake
  banana, 119
  coffee, 37
  indulgent, 61
Rum mousse, 61–63
Rum mousseline cream, 35
Rum simple syrup, 107

S

Sauces
  Anglaise, 110
  for Charlotte cakes, 110
Simple syrup, *374*
  blackcurrant, 50, 79, 113
  caramel, 114
  coffee, 123, 149, *374*
  cognac, 46, 107
  lemon, 49
  maraschino/apricot, 73
  moistening cake with, 150
  orange, 55
  passion fruit, 47
  pear, 87
  raspberry, 80, 101
  rum, 107
  strawberry, 81, 98, 131
  whiskey, 89
Small pearl sugar stage, 359
Soft ball sugar stage, 359
Soft crack sugar stage, 359
Soft soufflé sugar stage, 359
Spun sugar, 377–378
Spun sugar pistils, 377–378
Squirrel decorations, blown sugar, 349
Strawberry cake
  Charlotte, 97
  cherry mousse, 70
  colisée, 63–65
  diablotin, 21
  mirror, 98
  Saint Ange, 81
  sublime, 93
Strawberry Charlotte cream, 97
Strawberry coulis, 110
Strawberry liqueur mousse, 131
Strawberry mousse, 59, 65, 81, 95, 98
Strawberry mousse filling, 145–146
Strawberry Saint Hubert, 38
Strawberry simple syrup, 81, 98, 131
Strawberry Willy, 59
Succès, *371*
Sugar
  appliqué, 279
  coloring, 289, 296
  cooking, 211, 261, 355, 359
  molded, 287–293
  poured, 269–271
  poured crystallized, 372–373
  pulled, 295–301
  woven, 335–337
Sugar bouquets, 361–363
Sugar candles, 371
Sugar clown, poured, 329
Sugar columns, poured, 255
Sugar decorations. *See also* Decorations
  blown, 338–353
  molded, 287–293
  poured, 329–333
  pulled, 295–301, 323–327
  rock, 307–311
  spun, 377–378
  turned, 354–359
  woven, 335–337
Sugar disks, poured, 241
Sugar flowers, 285, 301, 361–363, 367–369, 375, 381, 383–385
Sugar leaves, 361–362
Sugar ribbons, pulled, 323–327
Sugar stems, 363
Swan decorations, blown sugar, 341–346
Syrup. *See also* Simple syrup
  grapefruit, 56
  lemon, 129
  for pulled sugar, 296
  raspberry, 121

T

Tant pour tant (TPT), *370*
Tarts, lemon cream filling for, 139
Thread sugar stage, 359
Tiered cake. *See also* Presentation pieces
  Breton, 273
  Charlottes, 257
  classic French, 249, 263, 275
  la Gaillacoise, 267
  la mistinguet, 239–241
  nougatine jewelry box, 251
  Spanish, 253
  stands for, 238
  wedding, 259–261
TPT (tant pour tant), 12
Triangles, poured sugar, 241
Tulips, pulled sugar, 366
Turned sugar decorations, 354–359

V

Vanilla cream, 99
  bavarian, 99
  Charlotte, 111
Vanilla milk cream filling, 138
Vases, blown sugar, 351

W

Walnut biscuit, 164
Walnut mousse filling, 137
Wedding cake, 259–261
Whipped cream, 147
Whiskey cake, 88
Whiskey mousse, 88
Whiskey mousse yule log, 142
Whiskey simple syrup, 89
Wine mousse, 51, 84
Wine mousse yule log, 142
Woven sugar, 335–337
Woven sugar basket, 337

Y

Yule logs, 141–142, *273–275*

DATE